ANSWERS

James Creed. Jr.

ANSWERS

Volume 1

James Creed, Jr.

Library of Congress Number: 2003090266
ISBN : Hardcover 1-4010-9270-5
Softcover 1-4010-9269-1

This book was printed in the United States of America.

To order additional copies of this book, contact:
Xlibris Corporation
1-888-795-4274
www.Xlibris.com
Orders@Xlibris.com
17792

CONTENTS

Jesus said, I am come that they might have life, and that they might have it more abundantly. John 10:10.

The wages of sin is death; but the gift of God is ETERNAL LIFE through Jesus Christ our Lord.

Guilt associated with sin disrupts the proper functioning of the mental system and causes the immune system to become weakened. Any amount of drugs or therapy cannot permanently correct this problem.

John 7:38 Jesus said, He that believeth on me—Out of his belly shall flow rivers of living water. (39) This spake he of the Spirit, which they that believe on him should receive.

Is eternal life dependent upon proper foods?

Jesus called the multitude, and said unto them, Hear, and understand:

Matthew 15:11 (It is) not that which goeth into the mouth defileth a man; but that which cometh out of the mouth, this defileth a man.

Matthew 15:17 (Peter) do not ye yet understand, that whatsoever entereth in at the mouth goeth into the belly, and is cast out into the draught? (18) But those things which proceed out of the mouth come forth from the heart; and they defile the man. (19) For out of the heart proceed evil thoughts, murders, adulteries, fornications, thefts, false witness, blasphemies: (20) These are the things which defile a man:

Doesn't food play a part in the health of the body?

Yes! God gave the instructions regarding the intake of proper foods for the strength of the natural body.

Gen. 1:29 And God said, Behold, I have given you every herb bearing seed, which is upon the face of all the earth, and every tree, in the which is the fruit of a tree yielding seed; TO YOU IT SHALL BE FOR MEAT.

Should we worry about which foods we should eat at any particular time?

Jesus said,(Matthew 6:25) Take no thought for your life, what ye shall eat, or what ye shall drink; nor yet for your body, what ye shall put on. Is not the life more than meat (food), and the body than raiment?

Matthew 6:26 Behold the fouls of the air: for they sow not, neither do they reap, nor gather into barns; yet your heavenly Father feedeth them. Are ye not much better than they? (28) Consider the lillies of the field, how they grow; they toil not neither do they spin: (30)—If God so clothe the grass of the field, which today is, and tomorrow is cast into the oven, shall he not much more clothe you?

With man and woman, this is all directed by the spirit after the Holy Ghost is received.

God speaks first, then the human mind takes over. The thoughts of men have always led other weaker minds to their way of thinking: to their imaginary heavens. But heaven will never be enjoyed by the human race until they draw near God through the mediator he placed in the world for the benefit of all mankind. That mediator is His only begotten Son, Jesus. This is the name that must be called upon to reach His Father God.

Matthew 1:21 And she (Mary) shall bring forth a son, and thou shalt call his NAME JESUS: for he shall save his people from their sins.

Joel 2:32 It shall come to pass, that WHOSOEVER shall CALL on the NAME of the LORD shall be delivered—.

Zeph. 3:9 Then will I turn to the people a pure language, that they may ALL CALL upon the NAME of the LORD, to serve him with one consent.

Acts 2:21 And it shall come to pass, that WHOSOEVER shall CALL on the NAME of the Lord shall be saved.

Romans 10:13 For WHOSOEVER shall CALL upon the NAME of the Lord shall be saved.

****

Angels

What happened to all those angels?

Who has even seen an angel?

Although Jim had been raised in religion as far back as he could remember, he could never really believe there was a real God or angels. He considered the story of God in the same line of thinking as Santa Clause.

But Jim's life was coming to an end at the age of about thirty one—.

St Louis, Missouri—1960

"You may go to bed now children," Jim said, as he arose from the bed, and made his way toward the kitchen window. He felt the cold wind coming in the cracks around the window, and from underneath the door. The weather was turning cold. The next day was not a school day, but it was becoming late.

"It's too cold in here," complained Charlene.

"I know, it's too far from the stove. I'll light the burners before I go to bed." Jim said. The four children's bedroom was just off to the right of the living room. That made it the fourth room from the kitchen stove which was used for heat. They hadn't purchased a heating stove yet.

Jim stood by the window. Everything became quiet. The children had all crawled under the warm quilts, and had forgotten about the cold. Ruby, exhausted from the evening had already fallen asleep. He stood gazing into the cold dark night; into a world of hate and fear; into a world of violence which he had helped to produce. He, who never believed in violence had helped to produce it in the minds of people by playing the part in Tombstone, Arizona, hanging upon the pole before their eyes.

JIM SLOWLY TWISTED THE FOUR KNOBS.

Why did his life have to turn out that way? Jim had always used the open gas flame to heat the house, but that night the weather was colder. He didn't have the strength to cope with living anymore. Despite the air coming in around the windows and doors, maybe it would do the job for him at least.

THE GAS IGNITED, EACH IN TURN BY THE PILOT LIGHT.

Standing to watch the blue flame with its orange trim, he continued to think. He had become misplaced, to do a different work after twelve years in the banks. It was too much. He didn't have the ambition for it. It's all right. The poison from the open burning flame won't hurt them. They are too far away. It may affect Jim, but it doesn't matter. Someone will care for them. He couldn't continue that way. It's better in death. A tune came to his mind. He began to hum.

Jim thought, "I will walk into the night where calm is, and there I will be delivered from this hell. The hell that is in my mind that I cannot rid myself of."

Slowly he walked to the bed, pulled back the covers, and crawled in. He was ready. It's complete. The living know that they shall die; but the dead know not anything, neither have they any more a reward, for the memory of them is forgotten. Also their love, and their hatred, and their envy, is now perished;

neither have they any more a portion forever in anything that is down under the sun. There is no work nor knowledge of either good or evil in the grave where he's going. With his face toward the wall he hummed softly, but with a higher tone.

Yes, he will go away, but his last word was going to be Jesus, for not a heart beat had passed without saying Jesus with his inner voice ever since he had determined it.

As he lay there silently calling upon God, by His name Jesus, three groups of mist began to filter through the wall. The fog was dense enough to form three distinct individuals. They did not come all the way through the wall; but just head and shoulders. They looked in Jim's direction. He watched them. Not a word was exchanged. A line of an old song drifted into Jim's memory.

"A BAND OF ANGELS COM'N AFTER ME, COM'N FOR TO CARRY ME HOME."

Jim fought for his breath as they disappeared through the wall, into the cold darkness of the night. Jim wondered if it was cold, and dark for them too. Sleep, sleep, a heavy sleep came upon him without even a dream.

****

Note: It was never anticipated that the carbon monoxide from the open flame would do any harm to anyone since this type heating was used for years while living in St. Louis. This was only written to show how Jim felt inside himself and his feeling of despair.

****

OH GOD,—RENEW A RIGHT SPIRIT WITHIN ME.

Psalms 51:10

A tingling, like electricity, brushed across Jim's right leg, just above the ankle. Looking quickly, there was no one. The same sensation awakened Ruby by a touch on her left side. She looked at Jim. "What is it?" They checked the clock. It was 2:40 a.m., Saturday morning. Without more thought Jim arose from the bed and went to the bathroom. Ruby waited at the door until he came out. Without a word she went in while Jim stepped to the kitchen window. There was nothing out there except the large flakes as they fell evenly, piling themselves lightly one upon the other.

Without thinking, Ruby emerged from the bathroom at ten minutes before three. They both stepped quickly to their respective sides of the bed, as if they were being led by unseen persons. Without hesitation, and in one motion they lay upon the bed, flat upon their backs. Jim's left hand was placed behind Ruby's neck. Contact was made with an uncontrollable power when Jim's left foot touched her right one. It took approximately ten minutes for the entire operation. All that time the feeling of electrical current was passing from each to the other. It was impossible for them to separate. Just before their release, Jim's head was raised from the bed about a foot, and a husky voice came from him which said, "I don't know whether I can undergo this."

It didn't sound like Jim's voice. It sounded exactly like his father's, who was still in Tombstone.—It was completed. They were released. No one was there. They arose from the bed, glanced around the room. There was not a sound. Who was it? What was it? Jim walked to the kitchen window. There was nothing unusual to be seen. Everything was the same out there. The snow had let up a little.

Jim walked back to the bedroom. "Ruby, did you feel that tremendous power that clamped us together?"

"Yes, what do you think it was?"

"I don't know. Do you think something could be wrong with Pop at Tombstone?"

"Maybe, but it's too early to call them now. If we don't hear anything from them, we will call sometime this evening. We shouldn't bother anybody in Tombstone this early in the morning. We should go back to bed for a few hours before the kids arise."

While lying there, Jim said to himself, "Why did I come back? What about the angels that came through the wall? Now this? Did the angels have anything to do with it? What are all these things about? What will be next?" He continued to question, as he drifted back into the slumber world, still calling upon Jesus.

****

Khills asked this question

Does God exist?

(1) Have real or actual being.

(2) Live.

James gave this response.

Psalm 14:1 The fool hath said in his heart,

'THERE IS NO GOD.'

I was a fool!

In defending the idea that there is a God, the idea of the construction of flowers, birds, and the intricate development of the many cells in the human body to produce the eyes, nose, hands, feet, heart, etc., had been impressed upon my mind for years, but still I could not fathom such an intelligent being. The idea of such a being was categorized with that of Santa Claus.

Church was a part of my younger years, so I had heard of the Name of the Son of God, and that he came in His Father's Name (John 5:43). The words were also impressed upon the mind that we should praise that Name from the rising of the sun until the going down of the same (Psalm 113:3), and that we should remember his name in the night (Psalm 119:55). But the greatest of all those sayings was the idea of Calling upon the Name of the Lord as advocated in Joel 2:32, Romans10:13, and Acts 2:21. And it shall come to pass, that WHOSOEVER shall call on the NAME OF THE LORD, shall be saved. I needed to be saved from the hurt that was in my mind and the general confusion with so many doctrines in the world.

My trouble was 'believing'. Even though I did not believe, I said (Mark 9:24), Lord, I believe, help thou mine unbelief.

The words came back to the mind that had been spoken by the preacher's mouth: (Hebrews 11:6)—Without faith it is impossible to please him (God): for he that cometh to God MUST BELIEVE THAT HE IS, and that he is a rewarder of them that DILIGENTLY SEEK HIM.

With all this in mind I decided to call upon the Name of the Lord, Jesus, with every heart beat and with every breath. The prayer was, 'God, give me strength to say Jesus just one more time, forever.' Ten days after determining this and doing it, a vision occurred.

GOD IS HERE

In vision, Jim saw the form of a man dressed in a blue suit descending through the ceiling, and came even with the floor, just in front of him. His head and hands were not visible. Jim turned toward the north, and as the form of God stepped back into Jim's body He began to speak,

> ***"THIS IS WHAT I TOLD ADAM TO DO IN THE BEGINNING.***
>
> ***ALL THE WAY DOWN THROUGH THE AGES, I HAVE TRIED TO HELP MAN, BUT EVERY TIME I TURN MY BACK, MAN FORGETS. THREE ANGELS SAW THESE WORDS COMING UP SO THEY CAME DOWN TO SEE WHO WAS CAUSING THEM. AFTER THEY SAW WHAT WAS HAPPENING, THEY CAME BACK UP AND TOLD ALL THE OTHER ANGELS, 'THERE'S A MAN DOWN THERE THAT HAS FOUND THE FORMULA.' ALL THE ANGELS ARE JUST SO TICKLED; IT HAS NEVER HAPPENED BEFORE. WE WENT TO THE BOOKS, AND FOUND THAT HIS NAME WAS JIM, AND THAT HE HAD BEEN MARRIED TWICE. IT WAS RECORDED THAT JIM WAS NOT A GOOD MAN, SO WE KILLED HIM. YOU SHOULD GO BY THE NAME OF JAMES. I WILL BLESS ALL FIVE OF YOUR CHILDREN," He said, as he moved to the end of the line; stooping to speak with Maxine and Terrence, "SAY JESUS ALL THE TIME, AND TELL ALL THE OTHER CHILDREN TO SAY JESUS. WE NEED EVERYONE. I WILL GIVE EACH ONE OF YOU A PLANET TO PLAY WITH."***

Then placing His hand with James' on the top of their heads; first Maxine, then Terrence, Zenaide, then Charlene. The last was the abdomen of Ruby. (She was not pregnant yet).

"YES, I MADE EVE THE WAY IT WAS DESCRIBED, BUT SHE WASN'T AS OBESE AS YOU ARE. THEY NAMED YOU WRONG. YOUR NAME SHOULD HAVE BEEN RUTH."

"WELL, YES, THE BIBLE IS TRUE." (It happened the way it was written).

"NO, THEY WILL NOT REACH THE OTHER PLANETS THE WAY THEY ARE TRYING TO DO IT. THEY WILL NOT LAST THAT LONG." (Not satellite) (Space machines must use a different fuel, and travel faster in order for the astronauts to survive the length of time necessary to complete the trip to other planets).

"YES, I UNDERSTAND ALL LANGUAGES. YES, I HAVE A SOUL. IT IS A LITTLE DIFFERENT THAN YOURS, BUT I HAVE ONE. I AM A SCIENTIST. I AM NOT LIKE THEY HAVE IMAGINED ME TO BE."

"YOU MAY HAVE A GLASS OF WATER IF YOU WANT IT."

They walked together to the kitchen, picked up a glass, filled it with water, and drank it together. As God and James stood drinking the water, James wondered why God, that had created everything, should spend so much time with him. Why?

Upon sitting the glass down in the sink they returned to the bedroom where everyone still waited in a perfect line.

"THEY CAN'T EVEN COME TO YOU IF I DON'T WANT TO HELP THEM. YOU WILL THINK YOU ARE DOING THINGS IN YOUR OWN SELF, BUT YOU WON'T BE, I WILL BE WORKING THROUGH YOU. ALTHOUGH YOU HAVE BEEN MARRIED TWICE, WE WILL DO ALL WE CAN FOR YOU

ANYWAY, BECAUSE YOU HAVE FOUND THE FORMULA. JIM DID MUCH READING, BUT HE DIDN'T UNDERSTAND. YOU WILL BECOME DISCOURAGED, BUT WE WILL HELP YOU ANYWAY, BECAUSE OF THE FORMULA."

Sitting down within James on the side of the bed, He looked at each one as He asked, "ARE THERE ANY QUESTIONS?"

Everyone stood calmly, and without a word. He sat there for a few moments, then went upward to—James wished he had asked Him where.

****

If it is decided to Call upon the Name of the Lord, expect spiritual advancement, but do not become too discouraged when results are not as emphatic as this experience. This was given so that it could be written for the benefit of those that will believe, and to show the way to God and to receive the ultimate power within.

John 3:18. He that believeth on him is not condemned: but he that believeth not is condemned already, because he hath not believed in the NAME of the only begotten SON of GOD.

****

Rain, Latter

Jdg asked this question. What is meant by the LATTER RAIN?

James gave this response.

THE LATTER RAIN

The desert shall rejoice, and blossom as the rose.

Zechariah 10:1 ASK ye of the Lord RAIN IN THE TIME of the latter rain; so the Lord shall make bright clouds, and give them showers of rain, to every one grass in the field.

IT'S DIFFERENT THIS TIME, I PROMISE YOU.

The spiritual war is on the horizon, and along with it is coming the LATTER RAIN (the rain that comes in the spring time). When the rains begin, they will not continue forty days, but FORTY YEARS. (during fall and spring, and then with no time limit for those that continue in His Name).

We must bare in mind that the term 'Latter Rain', in this case, is a spiritual one. Those spiritual rains will never come to an individual unless he/she asks and looks for them. The power of God (Christ) is returning to the earth to THEM THAT LOOK FOR HIM. Hebrews 9:29—unto them that look for him shall he appear the second time—.

For those that will call upon God's Name, it will be like a GENTLE WHIRLWIND TO TAKE AWAY THE SIN OF THE WORLD.

Is it necessary to go somewhere else to find Christ, and the Latter Rain?

NO! Stay where you are.

Romans 10:6—Who shall ascend into heaven? (that is, to bring Christ down from above):

Romans 10:7 Or, Who shall descend into the deep? (that is, to bring up Christ again from the dead).

Romans 10:8 But what saith it? The word is nigh thee, EVEN IN THY MOUTH, and in thy heart: that is, the word of faith—.

TOWER—ARK

The Name of the Lord is a strong tower. Call upon that Name!

Come into the Ark and be saved from the destruction that is already in the world. The destructive element is a part of the earth, that is the reason for the offsetting (providing an opposite or equaling effect) power by faith in the Name of God.

WAIT—THE RAIN IS COMING.

(REMAIN IN READINESS OR EXPECTATION).

James 5:7 Be patient therefore, brethren, unto the coming of the Lord, Behold, the husbandman waiteth for the precious fruit of the earth, and hath long patience for it, until he receive the EARLY and LATTER RAIN.

James 5:8 Be ye also patient; stablish your hearts: for the coming of the Lord draweth nigh.

Note: This was written approximately two millenniums ago, but it is good for all times. When men, women, boys and girls begin seriously calling upon the Name of the Lord, the rains will come, in their seasons. (Early Rain—Fall, Latter Rain—Spring). There is no reason to have long periods of spiritual draught (as in the dark ages), as long as people continue calling upon God by His Name. Faith in that Name will make the human race whole.

****

Rain: Spiritual

Ruth asked this question.

When will the spiritual rain come?

James gave this response.

The New American Bible-Collins World.

Psalms 72:3 The mountains shall yield peace for the people, and the hills justice.

Psalms 72:4 He (Christ) shall defend the afflicted among the people, save the children of the poor, and crush the oppressor.

Psalms 72:5 May he (Christ) endure as long as the sun, and like the moon through all generations.

COMING OF THE LORD—LIKE RAIN

King James version

James 5:7 Be patient therefore, brethren, unto the coming of the Lord. Behold, the husbandman waiteth for the precious fruit of the earth, and hath long patience for it, until he receive the early and the latter rain.

James 5:8 Be ye also patient; stablish your hearts: for the coming of the Lord draweth nigh.

ASK IN SEASON

Eccl. 3:1 To everything there is a season, and a time to every purpose under the heaven:

Zech. 10:1 Ask ye of the Lord rain in the TIME of the latter rain; so the Lord shall make bright clouds, and give them showers of rain, to every one grass in the field.

2 Peter 3:9 The Lord is not slack concerning his promise, as some men count slackness; but is longsuffering to us-ward, NOT WILLING THAT ANY SHOULD PERISH, BUT THAT ALL SHOULD COME TO REPENTANCE.

2 Peter 3:8 But, beloved, be not ignorant of this one thing,

THAT ONE DAY IS WITH THE LORD AS A THOUSAND YEARS, and a thousand years as one day.

If man and woman had eaten of the Tree of Life (Christ—the anointing of God through His Name) they would have always maintained the waters of life flowing freely throughout their system.

When people learn to draw near God by calling upon His Name fervently, then (John 7:38) out of his/her belly shall flow rivers of living water. This water comes from within and is not dependent upon the outward showers of spiritual rain. But this drawing near God will cause the eventual rains to come to all in this world.

It should be remembered that there is a time for every purpose but the formula has always been the same from the beginning. When men and women, boys and girls draw nigh God, He will draw nigh to them. (James 4:8)

****

Automatic Writing and Telekinetic Energy.

Please explain Automatic Writing and Telekinetic Energy.

AUTOMATIC WRITING

Is it possible to throw yourself into a trance and write without conscious thought?

Yes, If you can throw yourself out of a conscious state. But what you write will only be based on what you have already learned.

God gave man a brain. He wants him to have dominion over the world and everything in it, including himself.

If the brain is working properly, we will not want to throw ourselves into a trance and risk damaging other parts of the body.

The conscious mind can reason and extract logical answers. The subconscious mind uses only what has been placed there by conscious thought and effort.

When we see a demonstration of 'Automatic Writing,' we must examine what is written, and enquire as to the type and quantity of reading and education the demonstrator has received during their lifetime. We will find it all ties in unless there is an element of trickery.

Refer to the Autobiography by James Creed, Jr.,

> Copyright 1994.
> TX4-212-041
> ST LOUIS

The apartment returned. James sat at the table in the kitchen. He was still calling upon Jesus. He read the Bible and wrote on the wall paper. It was the Book of James, but it must be written by a power greater than himself. James needed to summon that power. Jim Creed read before his death (spiritual), where some people threw themselves into a trance and began writing without any control over what was written and because of that, it was all truth. It all came by the direction of outside spirit and had nothing to do with that which was recorded in their own brain.

James forced relaxation and with eyes closed he tried to let his mind go blank. "Come spirit," he said. "Take my mind. Write with my hands. His arms went limp. His body was completely relaxed. He waited but nothing happened. "Come on God or angels, write through my hand." He used only enough strength to hold the pencil. Something was being written on the wall paper. James waited for a while, then slowly opened his eyes. The vision, with effort, focused upon the scroll.

THERE WAS NOTHING BUT MUCH SCRIBBLE.

When James didn't use intelligent force, nothing intelligent was being written; just scribbling. If there was anything to the things Jim Creed had been writing on the wallpaper, it was produced by previous knowledge stored in his brain. Likewise, he determined, people that engage in such activities, were having mental problems, they did it for monetary gain, or their brain was filled with misguided information.

TELEKINETIC ENERGY

Throughout all supposed spirits, spooks, devils or angels, nothing physical was moved. If a person thinks material things move without reason, it is a trick of the mind or they do not understand the reason for the movement. Physical things cannot be moved except through some physical force. Spirit deals with the mind, the body does the work. Subconscious actions of the body are not necessarily produced by the power of God.

Wind will carry a seed. Water will move earth and change the form of rocks. A broom can be moved by the hands of a person or some other physical object, even magnetic force can do many things, but not by spirit. God works through physical things to control or change physical things. God can talk to the mind of men to perform special tasks, but very seldom does. After all, God gave the formula for eternal life. He expects men to use that formula. Nothing more is needed. Every time God has talked with men, it has been publicized world wide. Words that come to men and women, for the most part, are the products of their own thoughts.

****

Bible passages selected Randomly

Can we randomly open the Bible, place our finger on a scripture, and be assured it is a message from God?

James looked at the Bible lying on the table. "Ruth," James said, "It is not necessary to read the Bible or memorize scriptures. Take for example, if I wanted to talk about eyes, I just open the book."

Quickly opening the Bible, James put his finger upon a scripture. It was located in Exodus 24:17, 'And the sight of the Lord was like devouring fire on the top of the mount in the eyes of the children of Israel.'

"Now to prove this to you, so that you cannot doubt, I will turn to another place where it speaks of eyes." It couldn't be, but there it was, the book was opened to Matthew 6:22. It startled James when he looked at the page. "Ruth, it is unbelievable, but it is true. Read it so you will know it is the truth. Some may not believe me. It will have to be confirmed by you. Two witnesses are all that is necessary to establish proof of anything. But to be thoroughly convinced, and blot out the shadow of any doubt I will open the book again." James' finger went directly to Revelation 1:14. 'His eyes were as a flame of fire."

Now you take the subject of the cross," James said, as he reached over for a small hard-back Sunday School book. He opened it with one hand, back facing himself. Ruth looked at it in amazement. There was a picture of a cross. "Now Jesus," as he turned five pages at once. There was a picture of Jesus. Slowly placing the book on the table he went to the closet in the bedroom, and removed a coat hanger."

Ruth looked at James and he returned a glance. What had happened? James was led into a trap. Now they were laughing at him. Why did God leave him? Why was he humiliated? What about the eyes? Was it a coincidence or was it God? If it was God where did He go? James wished he had asked Him where He was going. The eyes,—they were looking at James. James must not look into anyone's eyes.

Those true happenings ran in the same vane as a 'lucky streak'. They always end. They cannot be depended on, the same as farmers who depend on the rains year after year, then the drought comes. It is during those times the pumps and irrigation ditches are needed.

Also, if a person believes all such information is directed by God he may place his finger on any one of the many violent passages in the Bible and believe it is God directing him toward some violent act. Of course, any logically thinking person would never be misled into such acts, but what about the weakened minds caused by disease or excessive usage of drugs?

While it is true God can and does direct, but there is a fine line between God's direction and the power of our own minds. We must have wisdom enough to know the difference.

It is important to understand that when a person is mentally weakened, either by disease, drugs or even ideas expressed in doctrines, it is possible to be led in the wrong direction if they depend on, and believe that any passage they should happen to point their finger to is by the direction of God.

There are many passage of scripture, although written by the inspiration of God, are the recordings of the actions of men that are opposed to the will of God.

For instance—Joshua 6:21—They utterly destroyed all that was in the city, (Jericho) both man and woman, young and old, and ox, and sheep, and ass, with the edge of the sword. (24) And they burnt the city with fire—

A logically thinking person will know that God did not tell anyone to KILL or STEAL, or BURN anybody's property, but a person deficient in his thinking capacity may be deluded by the thought that God had led him to such passages as a directed pattern for his own actions.

There are many voices in the world. They say many diversified things. We must have wisdom enough to know the difference. This wisdom can only be developed and our paths guided by the Holy Ghost.

God, does he cause pain in childbearing?

Anonymous asked this question.

When God confronted Eve over her sin, He said: "I will greatly increase your pains in your childbearing" Does this mean God inflicts pain on all women during labor, or what?

James gave this response.

Gen. 1:28 God said, "Be fruitful, and multiply, and replenish the earth." Why do some ministers say the sexual act was the original sin?

James gave this response.

Silently lying by Ruth's side, James wondered at the quickness of her sleep. A prayer was made. Dear God, I call upon your name continually, and it is because of this I ask that my mind be straightened out regarding the human reproduction question. It has been preached that the original sin was the sexual act between man and woman. The strongest evidence was that Adam and Eve were not ashamed until after they disobeyed God, then they became afraid because they were naked. Gen. 2:25, 3:10.

James was lying on his back. Sleep came heavy to his eyes as he drifted off into the darkness of the night. The world turned. Time passed. The clock indicated that it was two forty in the morning. Softly the words came to his ears.

YOU WILL TURN TO YOUR RIGHT SIDE.

James turned to his right side.

YOUR WIFE WILL NOW TURN TO HER RIGHT SIDE.

Ruth turned to her right side.

YOU WILL TURN WITH ABDOMEN DOWN, HOLD FOR A MOMENT, THEN TURN TO YOUR LEFT SIDE.

James turned with abdomen down, held for a moment then to his left side.

YOUR HAND WILL TOUCH HER ARM.

James' hand touched Ruth's arm and there was a spark.

YOUR FOOT WILL TOUCH HER FOOT.

When the feet made contact, there was a power flow from his body to hers.

YOUR WIFE WILL TURN WITH ABDOMEN DOWN, PAUSE FOR A MOMENT, THEN TO HER LEFT SIDE WITH BACK TOWARD YOU.

Ruth turned with abdomen down, paused for a moment, then to her left side.

NOW SHE WILL TURN TO HER BACK, PAUSE FOR A MOMENT, THEN TURN TO HER RIGHT SIDE FACING YOU.

Ruth turned to her back, paused and then to her right side.

SHE WILL TOUCH YOU WITH HER HAND.

When Ruth touched James there was a spark.

HER FOOT WILL TOUCH YOU.

When Ruth's foot touched James, there was a power flow from her body to his, which induced a dry climax.

The cycle was over. They were made dry by an element, James supposed, which emanated from God when He came to visit. James remembered a scripture which stated,

> 'COME NOT AT YOUR WIVES ON THE THIRD DAY,' (Exodus 19:15) because God was going to appear to Moses on the mountain.

James and Ruth had had no sex since the night the angels came. It was the movement of the human atom, and was the automatic process God put in operation during Adam and Eve's sleeping hours for releasing nervous tension, and to regulate propagation.

It was necessary for God to keep propagation under His own control, in order to eliminate the necessity for death. There would have been no death, if the system had remained in operation as God had planned.

James lay thinking. The scripture came to his mind, 'God put Adam into a DEEP SLEEP, and took a rib from his side.' It is reasonable then to think, that the sleep process should not have been changed after the creation of Eve, but should have continued in the creation of all mankind.

But that still does not explain why God said 'MULTIPLY, James thought, as a voice spoke plain and clear to his mind,

> ***MULTIPLY AND REPLENISH THE EARTH WAS SAID TO THE SUBCONSCIOUS MIND.***

It finally dawned on James that Adam and Eve were not even aware of the physical sensations experienced in their bodies during the climax, until they deliberately did what God told them not to do. The idea was impressed upon their minds by the open actions of the other animals.

There was no pain when the man was put into the deep sleep for the creation of his counter-part, the female, and there would have been no pain in childbearing for the female if they had conformed to the directions God had given them.

Adam was the Son of God, and it was intended that he live forever. In order for Adam and Eve, being one, to live forever, they must have conformed to the one commandment,

> ***Gen. 3:3 'Ye shall not eat of it (partake of it), neither shall ye touch it, lest ye die.'***

The other animals were not intended to live forever, therefore, that commandment was not necessary with them.

But Adam and Eve could not conform to the commandment unless they continued eating of the Tree of life, and this they refused to do until their guilty conscience drove them from Paradise. Then because of their fear of the 'flaming sword', (thou shall not) they could not return to the garden. (Paradise-spiritual state).

Christ (the power and anointing of God) was the true light, which lighteth every man that cometh into the world. John 1:9. It was Christ that was in man and woman (as one complete unit) in the beginning, but when they defied the will of God by taking the life making process and placing it under the control of their own will, Christ was driven out by their own guilt and that guilt caused the depression of the mind. That depressed mental system, in turn disrupted the natural automatic function of reproduction, causing the sensations of pain in the process of childbearing and throughout the physical body in its trek toward eventual death.

****

Original Sin—Second Witness.

Maxine asked this question.

Is there a second witness to confirm that conception was intended to be accomplished during the sleeping hours of the male and the female? And in the case of James and Ruth, why didn't they come together during their sleep for the conception of their next child?

James gave this response.

The human race has fallen and the genes have become out of focus. The original plan was designed with two parts. The one was for the release of tension. The other was designed to bring the male and the female together perfectly for the conception of new life. This was to be accomplished according to the TIME OF LIFE (Ref. Gen 18:10), which in the beginning (much earlier than Abraham) was designed to be many years apart.

****

THE SECOND WITNESS

The morning came without the sun. Or at least it could not be found. It was out there somewhere. Only a gray reflection penetrated the clouds. They hovered low. They were thick in quantity. They accomplished little or nothing. Clouds without water were they.

"Ruth," James called. She turned with a yawn.

"What time is it?" she inquired.

"Around seven," James replied.

Ruth informed, "The children don't have to leave for school until eight thirty."

"I couldn't sleep, so I wanted you to make a pot of coffee." James said.

"It's all right that you woke me. I want to talk to you. Did you sleep well last night?" Ruth asked.

"Yes, I don't remember a thing after I hit the bed. I wore myself out on that long walk last night,"James said.

"Do you mean you don't remember anything after you went to bed last night?" Ruth inquired.

"No! That's what I said. You know I seldom get up at night, or at least I never have until lately during the times I have been awakened at twenty minutes until three."

"You must have been awake last night," Ruth persisted.

"No! I wasn't awake. Why do you insist?" James replied with irritation.

"Do you remember what you told me about the operation of the human atom?" Ruth inquired.

"Yes," James replied.

Ruth continued. "That's what happened to me last night. It was just as you said. The voice came to my ears and told me you were going to move in a certain direction and you did exactly what the voice said. Then it told me to move in a certain direction and I couldn't help myself. I had to do what the voice said. Then you followed the instruction of the voice again. The only difference was that my climax came when my hand touched your side." (The first woman came from the side of the man.)

"Ruth, there has to be something we do not fully understand," James reasoned. "I would say that I had hypnotized you by telling you about it night before last, but then who hypnotized me in the first place? Also, what about the voices? And how could we do what the voices said while we were asleep? They are telling us things we never knew, nor had we ever thought of, or had we?

****

Body, Out of—Experience.

Zenaide asked this question.

Would you please explain the change, spiritual eyes, ears, and the out of body experience?

James gave this response.

It was in the wee hours of the morning. James was awakened by music. It sounded as though it was coming from the downstairs apartment. If he tried too hard to listen it would fade away. If he relaxed it returned. It was so faint. As he lay there quietly listening, a voice said to him.

"YOUR INSIDES WILL START GROWING TOGETHER. IT WILL BECOME ONE SOLID PIECE OF FLESH. YOU WON'T NEED TO EAT, BUT YOU CAN, IT WON'T HURT YOU. IT WILL BE BURNED OUT. THERE WILL BE AN OPEN CAVITY WHERE YOUR LUNGS ARE NOW FOR TALKING AND SINGING. THIS WILL BE HAPPENING TO YOUR WIFE TOO BUT SHE WON'T BE AWARE OF IT."

Immediately, James had the sensation of his insides becoming solid. He inhaled deeply. He could breathe deeper than usual.

"HERE ARE YOUR SPIRITUAL EYES."

James eyes blurred, and then came back into focus as his new spiritual eyes were set in place.

"HERE ARE YOUR SPIRITUAL EARS."

His ears went deaf for a moment, then back to full volume as his spiritual ears were set in place.

"NOW WE ARE GOING TO CUT A CORD LEADING TO YOUR HEART. IT WILL STOP BEATING, BUT YOU WILL FEEL NO DIFFERENCE."

Just then the pounding of his heart stopped. He felt no change. He felt his chest with his hand. There was no movement.

"IN THE MORNING THEY WILL SAY YOU HAD A HEART ATTACK."

There his body lay motionless on the bed. A new body had been created for him. He jumped up from the bed, and stood there looking back at the old Jim Creed. James could sing with melody, and tones he had never heard. His words came fluently, and to the point, filled with nothing but truth. He jumped up and down on the floor. His legs were more sturdy than before. He was more solid throughout.

He lay back down into the body he had just left. Without another thought drifted off into the mist of the early morning.

****

CREATE IN ME A CLEAN HEART, O GOD—

Psalms 51:10

THE HOLY GHOST AND WATER.

By the time Eldon came home Jim had worked himself into such a frenzy he knew there was something wrong. Jim told Ruby of those facts. He called her by her former name. He had to withdraw. He couldn't continue that way. Help was needed.

Ruby said to Eldon (her brother), "He says he needs help."

"Do you want to go to the hospital?" Eldon enquired.

"No, I want to go to a church. Now!" Jim said urgently.

Time was of the essence. They had to go at that moment. But where could they go? The churches were not open yet.

Eldon drove around just wasting time. With the windows rolled up Jim felt like his ears would pop. The car filled up with some pressure. After Jim mentioned it, even Eldon felt his head would pop. "Roll the window down," Jim instructed. As soon as a crack was made, the cold air rushed into the car, and the pressure was relieved. "All the way down," Jim demanded.

Mickie, while in the car always rode above the back seat, in the window. Jim noticed he was shivering, so he ordered the window closed. There were no more ill effects caused by the pressure.

The children were yelling and giggling. Jim started to hum. The louder they got, the louder Jim hummed, until it was unbearable. “Stop! Stop! Stop that unnecessary noise. God doesn’t like it. You should sit quietly, without that foolishness.”

“Stop the car. Stop! The earth is standing still. Nothing is moving, but those little people out there. Look at them. They are unaware of what is happening.”

Eldon pulled up to the nearest curb. They sat for awhile, until Jim’s mind was at ease. “Now we can go,” Jim instructed. “Let’s go. Where is the church?”

There were nine people and one dog in the car. Jim thought of Noah’s boat. The children didn’t seem to be concerned. It didn’t make any difference to them whether the things Jim said were right or wrong. Their ears were closed to it.

Eldon didn’t know where to go. But he knew he had to go somewhere fast. He thought of a lady church acquaintance. He drove to her house quickly, to find out if there was a church service somewhere. While she was talking with Eldon by the side of the car, Jim thought—I have to talk to someone, just anyone. If only I can secure her confidence, in one way or another, she would listen to me. Maybe I can flatter her.

Jim raised closer to the window. As he moved closer, she turned to look at him. Her eyes met Jim’s. He captured her mind for a moment. Jim looked deeper into her eyes. “You have spiritual eyes,” He said.

She stood without a word, then finally she broke the gaze and turned. “I must not look at his eyes,” she said, “It’s evil. I’ve seen that before.”

Jim couldn't forget her eyes. There they were looking at him. Eyes were everywhere. "Oh, but I know how to rid myself of them," he said aloud. "I cast those eyes from me through the Name of Jesus." The eyes left for awhile.

Eldon was parked along side the church when the minister unlocked the door. He explained the problem to the preacher, and by the time everyone was inside the church, about six saints had arrived. The preacher stood in the middle of the group and said,

> ***"THE LORD TELLS ME THIS MAN IS TO GO ALL THE WAY."***

They had gathered around Jim, and as the minister laid hands on his head, the same vehicle took hold of his body that Jim thought was epilepsy before. He was then thrown to the floor, right in the middle of the church. He began to squirm, still calling upon Jesus. All of a sudden the words were spoken directly to his mind.

> ***"HERE IS THE HOLY GHOST, THE TONGUES WILL COME LATER."***

It felt like a vest had just slipped around James, but more like inside than out. Just before he was released he turned his face and spat upon the floor.

James' understanding was opened to the fact that it was not the Holy Ghost that caused his body to squirm, nor his mouth to spit, but it was the result of delirium tremens, caused by the long term usage of alcohol. Cigarettes, alcohol and quilt contributed to the weakened brain, and would require a long time to heal.

Some of the saints said to one another, "I've never seen anyone receive the Holy Ghost that way."

Another voice spoke up and said, “They used to receive it that way all the time.” One of the women cleaned up the spit with a Kleenex.

The preacher stood up again and said,

“THIS MAN NEEDS WATER BAPTISM.”

Old clothes were available for baptismal services. They were borrowed, and the whole group paraded down the steps to the basement where the baptistry was located.

Eldon and Ruth decided to be baptized along with James, but Hazel (Eldon’s wife) decided not to. It was during the winter time. The water was ice cold. They each held their breath as they were submerged backwards in the Name of Jesus. They each changed back into their better clothes, and returned to the sanctuary in time for the meeting to start. James was feeling better, but did he have enough to hold him. He didn’t know.

****

TONGUES

Ruth asked this question.

Would you please tell us of your experience with the tongues?

James gave this response.

THE DAYS AND NIGHTS PROGRESSED A campground—Arizona—1961

A change of scenery was in order. James and Ruth decided to sit at the right side of the tabernacle. They made their way between the benches and found their seats in plenty of time before the service began.

The evening desert breeze picked up the vibrations of the strings and larynx and carried them into the wilderness where they rested among the foothills, out of reach of the human ear.

James stood in the aisle at the end of the benches. It was during the time of praise. His tongue began to form words which he did not understand. The ears listened. The man did not know what was being said. There was no control over his tongue. He did try to have control. It was imperative for him to know that it was the tongues. The words were remembered which were spoken with him while in the floor of the church in Saint Louis.

"HERE IS THE HOLY GHOST, THE TONGUES WILL COME LATER." James looked at Ruth. There must be a second witness to confirm that the tongues were for all times.

After the service James and Ruth went to their familiar camping spot. The food was gone but that didn't matter. They were not hungry. The next day James' Mother and Father were to come with more food, and beside that, the church was going to have a Bar-B-Q feast at around noon. There was a large cafeteria on the grounds, but James had no money.

As James was trying to go to sleep in the Station Wagon, he wondered in his thoughts. Why didn't Ruth hear him speak? It must merely confirm that Paul was right when he stated, 'Tongues shall cease.' (1 Cor 13:8) There was only one witness in the Bible, could this be his second witness?

****

Filling of the Holy Spirit.

James gave this response.
A campground—Arizona—1961

The service progressed. Peoples minds and voices began to blend together. Lightness of spirit prevailed. It was the afternoon service. They spoke with tongues, others interpreted. A man's voice rang loud and clear, which said, ***IF YOU DON'T RECEIVE THE FILLING OF THE SPIRIT YOU WILL FALL***.

About three hundred people moved forward. Ruth and James were there. Each was instructed to touch the person in front of them on the shoulder or back. James had the lamp all along, but he, like the foolish virgins found himself short of oil. He was now in the store house of them that had to sell. It was like a large pitcher tipping to spill into his lamp, until the pitcher was emptied and James was full. His eyes then could see on both sides of the fence. Evil was not the only thing directed to his attention. His physical body and mind could then withstand insanity that was all around. He could even control himself.

ORDINATION

Ruth asked this question. Were you ordained?

James gave this response.
A campground—Arizona 1961

It is no coincidence you are here, the minister said. God has selected individuals throughout the country. It is the time of the harvest but the laborers are few. God is calling you as laborers in his vineyard. Come forward, you that are willing to go. The people moved forward. They formed a single line in a semi-circle all the way from one side of the tabernacle to the other. James began to sweat. God did come to visit us, James said silently to himself. Do you mean he

would come to us and yet I would miss the chance of ordination? But God did not say that James should preach. The line was complete and James was not there.

This may be your last chance. The minister held both hands out toward the audience. If you feel the tug of God's spirit, don't turn him away. Won't you come? There are dying millions on the foreign fields without the knowledge of God.

Without more thought, since James could not think it through, he went forward, knelt on the ground with the rest. But I am not worthy to be here, James thought. I know they are all better than I. His head was lowered closer toward the ground in humiliation. He felt foolish. The minister is almost here, he thought. Oh, what am I doing here? I wish I hadn't come. I would run, but I don't know where to go.

The minister stood above James for a few moments. His hands were placed upon James head. It sounded like he was crying. What was the reason? Was it because he felt he had spoken too hastily? I must get out of here as soon as I can. I am not worthy, James thought again. The minister anointed James for the Gospel of Jesus. He moved on down the line anointing them all.

The preacher stood behind the mikes. He spoke. Everyone call upon Jesus from now until you return to the tabernacle for the night service. The people were dismissed. James thought. I'm glad he told them for me, but I wish it could have been emphasized. They might forget.

****

Abraham, Moses, Joshua?

Can you clarify some of the actions and deviations of Abraham, Moses and Joshua?

God spoke with Abraham but the devil (His own mind) talked with him too. There is a fine line between right and wrong. The line appears, at times, to be non-existent. The only way to make the line visible is to have a present and continued understanding of the commandments which were not established in a single book during the time of Abraham, although they were being accumulated at that time.

The way is clear, and the division between the different voices is understood when the mind is meditating upon the laws as set forth by the direction of God through Moses.

Joshua was told to (Joshua 1:8) meditate therein day and night, that thou mayest observe TO DO according to all that is written therein: for then thou shalt make thy way prosperous, and then thou shalt have good success.

But Joshua had an example set before him that took precedent over the law, and that was the actions and words of Moses. Moses had relayed the commandments, including the one that states 'Thou shalt not kill', (Exodus 20:13) but Moses told Joshua to fight against Amalek (the off-spring of Esau), and this he did.

Exodus 17:8 Then came Amalek, and fought with Israel in Rephidim. (9) And Moses said unto Joshua, Choose us out men, and go out, fight with Amalek—. (10) So Joshua did as Moses had said unto him and fought with Amalek—.

Exodus 17:13 And Joshua discomfited Amalek and his people with the edge of the sword. (14) And the Lord said unto Moses,

WRITE THIS FOR A MEMORIAL IN A BOOK, and rehearse it in the ears of Joshua:

WHY? So that future generations (however long it may take) could examine the actions of Moses and Joshua to determine how they erred from the laws God had confirmed with Moses.

When reading the law it is very easy to understand, but when voices come to the ears, whether they are from another person, or the product of one's own imagination, the voices take precedent over the written words.

God seldom speaks with people for they have fallen so far from him. There are many voices in the world that claim they are speaking the words of God, but they are the vehicles of confusion. The speakers are confused for they have not seen God, nor have they recognized his voice among all the others. The voices sound the same, we must have wisdom enough to know the difference.

Amalek's Grandfather was Esau, who was a profane person ***(Hebrews 12:16, Genesis 25:27-34), and in all his life never mentioned the Name of God. This in turn influenced his Grandson Amalek who became a man of war and founder of the tribal family known as the Amalekites (Genesis 26:12, 16: Exodus 17; Chron. 1:36).***

Men of violence are those that do not know God; they have not seen God, and cannot differentiate between his voice and voices of men.

The law of Moses is a divider between right and wrong in the entire BOOK OF TRUTH (The Bible). When using the law as a divider it is easy to determine which voice is speaking in every case, whether it is the voice of God, men, or a person's own thoughts.

Well, yes, the Bible is True. It is a true recording of what men have said and done, whether right or wrong, versus the will of God. The violence that is recorded in the Bible is not the will of God. It is the product of the animalistic nature of men.

The Bible is the Book of Truth. It contains both right and wrong. If it incorporated only right and eliminated the recordings of wrong, then it would not be a book of truth, but an accumulation of half truths which is synonymous with lies.

Many cover up the wrongs as recorded in the book because they do not know how to explain—,

> ***John 10:8 ALL THAT EVER CAME BEFORE ME ARE THIEVES AND ROBBERS—.***

They have not realized 'that Holy Thing' (Luke 1:35) was, Life from God placed in the body of a man bearing God's Name for saving men from the violence of their own minds.

The Bible is not the only book of truth; for any book that states facts as they have transpired is truth, but the Bible is the only book that transports the WORD OF GOD (God's Name—JESUS-Rev. 19:13) to the minds of the people, therefore, it is the only catalyst that can bring eternal life to the world, through faith in that Name.

Adam's transgression:

What was Adam's transgression?

Death reigned from Adam to Moses, even over them that had not sinned after the similitude of Adam's transgression.

(Adamah—man and woman together as one unit, one flesh. Gen. 2:24)

The man and the woman took the life making process and placed it under their own conscious control. This was the only thing God had asked them not to do, because God knew once they had experienced the physical sensations associated with that process they would not be able to stop its proliferation. This would overpopulate the world and cause death in order to balance the 'NEED WITH SUPPLY.'

Even those that partly understood the original sin and tried to make themselves celibate or separate themselves from the opposite gender could not change the inborn degeneration received from their ancestors. Death has still reigned.

But God has had mercy—looking forward to the time when men will grow out of their foolish years, for the imagination of man's heart is evil from his YOUTH. (Gen. 8:21).

But eventually all sin will be washed out of our systems as we partake of that TREE OF LIFE (the name of God), and the washing of the living water that flows out of our belly—(John 7:38) into eternal life. (John 3:15)

Natural will-power plays little part in this process. Any physical attempt to correct the problem caused by the inherited genes will only cause separations. Two by two, male and female, went into the ark (Gen. 6:19). The Holy Ghost will guide (John 16:13) and the holy spirit of God must flow from within—then time and understanding along with the power of God will raise the foundation of human life.

THE ESSENES TRIED IT AND IT DIDN'T WORK!

ESSENE: One of the brotherhood or monastic order of Jews in ancient Palestine, first appearing in history in the 2nd century B.C., characterized by asceticism (self denying), celibacy (state of being unmarried and abstention from sexual performance, and the strict observance of the non-Levitical portion of the Mosaic law.

Paul wrote, 1 Tim. 4:1 Now the Spirit speaketh expressly, that in the latter times some shall depart from the faith,—(3) FORBIDDING TO MARRY—.

For the human bodies to operate properly there must be the negative and the positive working together. It is not good that the man should be alone. The two parts must be joined together. ***Marriage is a must.***

Adultery—homosexuality

If a married person has sexual relationship with another person of the same sex, is that adultery?

Christ (the power of God) is the light which lighteth every MAN that cometh into the world. John 1:9.

When a man and a woman are joined together by God, the power of God flows from the male to the female and back again. This process continues all the time the two are in close proximity with each other. If one of those two parts unite with another person whether of the same or different sex, the power of Christ (view this power as an electrical current flow or as Jesus put it, Out of HIS belly shall flow rivers of living water. John 7:38) is disrupted, this is called a 'SIN AGAINST GOD,' because of this disruption.

Genesis 39:8 Joseph refused to lie with his master's wife and said (10) thou art his wife: how then can I do this great wickedness, and ***SIN AGAINST GOD***?

Genesis 20:3-4 If Abimelech had had relations with Abram's wife, even though Sarai was Abram's half sister, God said he would have been a dead man.

Why? Because the power of Christ would have been driven out of his system and this would have had a spiritual and ultimately a physical affect upon his body.

If one married person has relations with a single person it is called Adultery with the married person and the single person is a fornicator. Generally, fornication is between two single persons. Fornication is also applied to idolaters. (Worshipers of idols rather than God).

Jesus said (Matthew 5:32), Whosoever shall put away his wife (of course, after they are married), saving for the cause of FORNICATION (with another person that had transpired before their marriage), causeth her to commit adultery: and whosoever shall marry her that is divorced committeth adultery (because she had been married). Jesus made this exception because Joseph first thought that while Joseph and Mary were engaged, Mary had committed fornication.

As for homosexuality, those associations are not productive, scientifically, physically or spiritually, and not condoned anywhere in the Bible.

Read the story concerning Sodom and Gomorrah. Gen. 13:13, 18:22-33,19:26.

Alcohol

What does the bible say about drinking alcohol? Is it a sin? Are we instructed somewhere not to drink?

Romans 14:21 It is good neither to eat flesh, nor to ***drink wine***, nor anything whereby thy brother stumbleth, or is offended, or is made weak. (22) Hast thou faith? Have it to thyself before God. Happy is he that condemneth not himself in that thing which he alloweth.—(23) whatsoever is not of faith is sin.

Not given to wine is mentioned by Paul in the Bible, and Peter mentioned “excess of wine.” 1 Peter 4:4. There are so many of those passages it is not feasible to list them all here.

Please read more under WINE

Altar call

What was the “altar call” for the first Christians? When did they officially become a Christian?

Of course, (Acts 11:26) the disciples were called Christians first at Antioch, but to be a Christian means Christ-like. I don’t think there are many of them around. On the day of Pentecost the people were not at an altar. They were SITTING. Acts 2:2 And suddenly their came a sound from heaven as of a rushing mighty wind (spiritual), and it filled all the house where they were SITTING.

The holy Ghost can be received at anytime and anywhere. Jesus received the Holy Ghost at the time of his water baptism. Luke 3:22 And the Holy Ghost descended in a bodily shape like a dove upon him,—

Luke 4:1 And Jesus being full of the Holy Ghost—.

God’s spirit is strongest among people that are praising him. Psalm 22:3 But thou art Holy, O thou that inhabitest the praises of Israel—All people because Abraham was the father of many nations. Gen. 17:5.

Jesus said (Luke 24:49)—I send the promise of my Father upon you: but tarry ye in the city of Jerusalem, until ye be endued with power from on high. There were about 120 assembled in one place. (Acts 1:15). This indicates that they did not receive the Holy Ghost at the time Jesus breathed on them. (John 20:22.) (When we went to Jerusalem, and were in what they believed to be the upper room, we observed no Altar in that building).

Because of the Power of Christ generating from and between individuals it is advantageous to have more than two or three gathering together, even though the spirit of Christ is in the midst of only two or three when they are together as in husband and wife. Matthew 18:20 For where two or three are gathered together ***in my Name*** (which also is God's Name), there am I in the midst of them.

Paul said, Hebrews 10:25 Not forsaking the assembling of ourselves together, as the manner of some is; but exhorting one another—(26) For if we sin willfully—Prov. 11:14 Where no counsel is, the people fall: but in the multitude of counsellors there is safety.

Ananias and Sapphira:

Did Peter handle the case of ANANIAS AND SAPPHIRA the way Jesus would have?

Matthew 18:14—it is not the will of your Father which is in heaven, that one of these little ones should perish. (15) Moreover if thy brother shall trespass against thee, go and tell him his fault between thee and him alone: if he shall hear thee, thou hast gained thy brother. (16) But if he will not hear thee, then take with thee one or two more, that in the mouth of two or three witnesses every word may be established. (17) And if he shall neglect to hear them, tell it unto the church: but if he neglect to hear the church, let him be unto thee as an heathen man and a publican. (You still are not to kill him). (18) Verily I say unto you, Whatsoever ye shall bind on earth shall be bound in heaven: and whatsoever ye shall loose on earth shall be loosed in heaven. (Peter was given the power to bind or to loose, it was left up to him how he used that power).

PETER WANTED TO GET IT REAL CLEAR IN HIS MIND WHAT HIS ACTIONS SHOULD BE REGARDING FORGIVENESS.

Matthew 18:21 Then came Peter to him, and said, Lord, how oft shall my brother sin against me and I forgive him? till seven times?

Matthew 18: 22 Jesus saith unto him, I say not unto thee, Until seven times: but, Until seventy times seven. (490 times)

PETER DENIED JESUS THREE TIMES. MATT. 26:34, JESUS FORGAVE HIM.

Matthew 18:33 Shouldest not thou also have had compassion on thy fellowservant, even as I had pity on thee?

DID PETER CONFORM TO THE INSTRUCTIONS GIVEN BY JESUS REGARDING MERCY, WHEN HE DEALT WITH ANANIAS AND SAPPHIRA? LET US SEE.

Acts 5:1 But a certain man named Ananias, with Sapphira his wife, sold a possession. (2) And kept back part of the price, his wife also being privy to it, and brought a certain part, and laid it at the apostles feet.

(Matthew 19:21 Jesus said, go and sell that thou hast, and ***GIVE TO THE POOR,—AND COME AND FOLLOW ME.*** He did not say bring the proceeds to me and let me give it to the poor).

Acts 5:3 But Peter said, Ananias, why hast Satan filled thine heart to lie to the Holy Ghost, and to keep back part of the price of the land?

(4) Whiles it remained, was it not thine own? and after it was sold, was it not in thine own power? why hast thou conceived this thing in thine heart? thou hast not lied unto men, but unto God.

Acts 5:5 And Ananias HEARING THESE WORDS fell down, and gave up the ghost: (Ananias died of shock caused by fear and guilt) and ***GREAT FEAR*** CAME ON ALL THEM THAT HEARD THESE THINGS. (God is Love.)

1 John 4:8, There is no fear in Love, but perfect love casteth

out fear. 1 John 4:18, Keep yourselves in the Love of God. Jude 1:21.

Acts 5:6 And the young men arose, wound him up, and carried him out, and buried him.

(7) And it was about the space of three hours after, when his wife, not knowing what was done, came in.

(8) And Peter answered unto her, Tell me whether ye sold the land for so much? And she said, Yea, for so much.

(9) Then Peter said unto her How is it that ye have agreed together to tempt the Spirit of the Lord? behold the feet of them which have buried thy husband are at the door, and shall carry thee out.

(10) Then fell she down straightway at his feet, and yielded up the ghost: (Sapphira died of shock caused by guilt and fear) and the young men came in, and found her dead, and carrying her forth, buried her by her husband.

(11) And GREAT FEAR CAME UPON ALL THE CHURCH, AND UPON AS MANY AS HEARD THESE THINGS. (Fear is not of God).

Matthew 16:18 And I say also unto thee, That thou art Peter, and upon this rock I will build my church; and the gates of hell shall not prevail against it. 19 And I will give unto thee (Peter) the keys of the kingdom of heaven: AND WHATSOEVER THOU SHALT BIND ON EARTH SHALL BE BOUND IN HEAVEN: AND WHATSOEVER THOU SHALT LOOSE ON EARTH SHALL BE LOOSED IN HEAVEN.

Before Peter received the Holy Ghost he was a violent man. He was erratic and abrupt in his actions.

Mark 14:47 And one of them (Peter) that stood by drew a sword, and smote a servant of the high priest, and cut off his (Luke 22:50—right) ear.

JESUS WAS NOT LIKE PETER.

Luke 22:51 And Jesus answered and said, Suffer ye thus far, and he touched his ear, and healed him.

Before Peter received the Holy Ghost he used a natural sword. After he received the filling of the Spirit he used the 'SWORD OF THE SPIRIT', which was even more devastating.

WHY DID PETER DO THIS?

Because he still had his fallen human nature. (Gal. 5:17—The flesh and the Spirit are contrary the one to the other). He was given the power to 'bind' and he did not use this power in coordination with the instructions he had received from Jesus.

THINK IT THROUGH. Did he forgive Ananias and Sapphira four hundred and ninety times? Did he discuss with them and act in accordance with the instructions laid down by Jesus? Should there be fear in the church?

Jesus, after his resurrection, gave the power to forgive sins to his disciples. John 20:21. Then said Jesus to them again, Peace be unto you: as my Father hath sent me, even so send I you.

John 20:23 Whose soever SINS YE REMIT, they are remitted unto them; and whose soever SINS YE RETAIN, they are retained.

Romans 14:17—the kingdom of God is—righteousness and peace, and joy in the Holy Ghost. (Not fear!) Should Peter be judged for his actions?

1 Cor. 6:2 Do ye not know that the saints shall judge the world?

1 Cor. 6:3 Know ye not that we shall judge angels?

Isa. 12:2 BEHOLD, GOD IS MY SALVATION:

I WILL TRUST, AND NOT BE AFRAID.

Antichrist, who is the

It is simple. People that do not believe in Christ!

1 John 2:18-22.—(NAB) Children, it is the final hour; just as you heard that the antichrist was coming, so now many such antichrists have appeared. This makes us certain that it is the final hour. It was from our ranks that they took their leave—not that they really belonged to us; for if they had belonged to us, they would have stayed with us. It only served to show that none of them was ours. But you have the anointing that comes from the Holy One, so that all knowledge is yours. My reason for having written you is not that you do not know the truth but that you do, and that no lie has anything in common with the truth.

Who is the liar? He who denies that Jesus is the Christ. HE IS THE ANTICHRIST, denying the Father and the Son.

ANYONE who denies the Son has no claim on the Father, but he who acknowledges the Son can claim the Father as well.

WHY SHOULD WE BE CONCERNED ABOUT THIS? THESE THINGS WERE WRITTEN TWO THOUSAND YEARS AGO.

2 Peter 3:9 The Lord does not delay in keeping his promise—though some consider it 'delay.' Rather, he shows you generous patience, since he wants none to perish but all to come to repentance.

2 Thessalonians 2: 1 On the question of the coming of our Lord

Jesus Christ and our being gathered to him, we beg you, brothers, not to be so easily agitated or terrified, whether by an oracular utterance, or rumor, or a letter alleged to be ours, into believing that the day of the Lord is here. (3) Let no one seduce you, no matter how. Since the mass apostasy has not yet occurred nor the man of lawlessness been revealed—that son of perdition and adversary who exalts himself above every so-called god proposed for worship, he who seats himself in God's temple and even declares himself to be God—' do you not remember how I used to tell you about these things when I was still with you? You know what restrains him until he shall be revealed in his own time. The secret force of lawlessness is already at work, mind you, but there is one who holds him back until that restrainer shall be taken from the scene.

WHAT WILL HAPPEN TO THOSE THAT ARE ANTICHRIST?

Only those that insist upon holding to hate will be destroyed.

2 Thessalonians 2:8 Thereupon the lawless one will be revealed, and the LORD JESUS WILL DESTROY HIM WITH THE BREATH OF HIS MOUTH AND ANNIHILATE HIM BY MANIFESTING HIS OWN PRESENCE.

(9) This lawless one will appear as part of the workings of Satan, (the power of the natural mind) accompanied by all the power and signs and wonders at the disposal of falsehood—by every seduction the wicked can devise for those destined to ruin (WHY?) because they have not opened their hearts to the truth in order TO BE SAVED.

(11) Therefore God is sending upon them a perverse spirit which leads them to give credence to falsehood, so that all who have not believed the truth but have delighted in evildoing will be condemned.

What is the way out of the turmoil in this world and freedom from the natural thoughts of men?

Draw near God and He will draw near you. James 4:8.

How do we do that?

Call upon God by His Name, the mediator, Jesus. Jesus said, (John 14:6) I am the way, the truth, and the life: no man cometh unto the Father, but by me.

Acts 2:21 And it shall come to pass, that WHOSOEVER shall CALL on the NAME of the LORD shall be saved. Joel 2:32, Rom. 10:13.

****

Apple

Greg asked this question.

So it was not the poison in the apple that killed them?

It was really the guilt of doing something they knew was wrong?

APPLES ARE NOT POISON, AND NO IT WAS NOT A NATURAL APPLE.

The first time the apple tree was mentioned was in Songs of Solomon / Song of Songs 2:3—King James Version. But in the New English Bible it is called an Apricot tree. This was written around BC 1014. This was many years after the recording of the creation of man and woman. There is no mention of apple trees in the New Testament.

Genesis 3:3—Of the FRUIT of the tree which is in the midst of the garden, God hath said, Ye shall not eat of it, neither shall ye touch it, lest ye die.

Note the following:

The Song of Songs 2:3 Bride to Solomon—. The New American Bible

As an apple tree among the trees of the woods, so is my LOVER among men. I delight to rest in his shadow, and his FRUIT IS SWEET TO MY MOUTH.

This is a love song and clearly indicates that Solomon was symbolically viewed as an Apple or Apricot tree with delicious fruit that was sweet to his brides mouth.

Compare:

Genesis 3:6 And when the woman saw that the tree was good for food, and that it was pleasant to the eyes, and the tree to be desired to make one wise, she took of the fruit thereof, and did eat, and gave also unto her husband with her; and he did eat.

If it had been a natural apple the first couple ate of, it would have been mentioned by Jesus or at least one of the apostles in the New Testament.

As has been thoroughly explained in previous writings the original sin was the conscious physical act of reproducing offspring.

God spoke with the animals, birds, and man alike regarding multiplying and replenishing the earth. Genesis 1:21-22, 1:28 Common sense tells us that using a language to speak with animals and birds would have no effect on their reproductive capabilities. No, the process was placed in the genes and in the subconscious portion of the brain to cause the act of reproducing to operate according to the time of life in man and beast.

Note also:

Genesis 2:17—of the tree of the knowledge of good and evil. Thou shalt not eat of it: for in the DAY that thou eatest thereof thou shalt surely die. (This tree was symbolically made up of the Man and the Woman.)

Adam lived 930 years.

Genesis 5:5 And all the days that Adam lived were nine hundred and thirty years: and he died.

2 Peter 3:8 Beloved, be not ignorant of this one thing, that ONE DAY is with the Lord as a thousand years—.

Adam did not make it through the end of that one day.

Thousands of years of ancestral weaknesses have become a part of our gene make up. Individually a person should never try to change themselves with respect to these matters. IT CAN'T BE DONE. It takes the operation of God to change the spirit and the physical make up of the body (John 3:3 born again). The only way to obtain power over the weaknesses that is in all of us, is to TAKE HOLD OF THE TREE OF LIFE (Genesis 2:9). That tree of Life is the Name of God. Call upon it. Have faith in it and cast all our care upon him; for he careth for us. 1 Peter 5:7.

Hebrews 4:16 Let us therefore come boldly unto the Throne of Grace, that we may obtain mercy, and find grace to help in the time of need.

The first man and woman did not eat of that Tree of Life because they were afraid. Genesis 3:10 And he (Adamah-man) said, I heard thy voice in the garden, and I was afraid, because I was naked; and I hid myself.

Fear and weakness drove the man from the Tree of Life and from the presence of God.—Genesis 3:22 and now lest he put forth his hand, and take also of the Tree of Life, and eat, and live for ever—. 23—the Lord God sent him forth from the garden of Eden—that spiritual state. Man and woman drifted off into confusion and spiritual ignorance. Wisdom dissipated.

WISDOM

Proverbs 3:16 Length of days is in her right hand; and in her left hand riches and honor. (17) Her ways are ways of pleasantness, and all her paths are peace. (18) She is a TREE OF LIFE to them that lay hold upon her, and happy is every one that retaineth her.

Revelations 22:14 Blessed are they that do his commandments, that they may HAVE RIGHT to the TREE OF LIFE—.

Anonymous asked this follow-up question.

So the original man and woman did not have to eat or have sexual relations? All they had to do is live without sin and they would live for ever. Did they know this. If they did know this why did they let their physical needs overpower them to eat and have sex.

1) So the original man and woman did not have to eat—.

   Deut. 20:19—the tree of the field is man's (natural) life.

   Genesis 2:16 And the Lord God commanded the man, saying, of EVERY (natural) TREE of the garden thou mayest FREELY EAT—but of the TREE which symbolically represents you and your wife—it is a no, no, for good reasons which have already been thoroughly explained.

   The body can be healed by the power of God through the mind, but unless that body receives the proper nutrients on a continuing basis it can become sick again even without the element of sin.

Saul, after he was healed, it was stated—(Acts 9:19)—when he received meat (food) he was strengthened.

When God through Jesus caused the spirit and life to come back into the Maid, Jesus commanded to give her meat (food). (Luke 8:55).

2) So the original man and woman did not have to have sex.

Yes they had to have sex. Without the act of sex there could be no reproduction. But in order for God to regulate the population growth, and eliminate the need for death, he had to remain in control of conception.

God did not personally supervise every conception in human beings. He devised the plan through the subconscious mind to operate during their sleeping hours to perform this operation.

3) All they had to do was live without sin and they would live for ever.

In the beginning there was only one rule and that concerned the creation of new life. This was God's business. He knew of the consequences if man and woman discovered the sensual feelings that was associated with that process. Once experienced they would not be able to quit. It would contribute to a population expansion and that in turn would cause death to be imperative.

Breaking that one rule brought condemnation to the minds of the man and the woman. This became sin to them. James 1:12 Blessed is the man that endures temptation: for when he is tried, he shall receive the

CROWN OF LIFE, which the Lord hath promised to them that love him. (13) Let no man say when he is tempted, I am tempted of God: for God cannot be tempted WITH EVIL, neither tempteth he any man: (14) But every man is tempted when he is drawn away of his own lust, and enticed.

4) Did they know this?

Yes! God told man that he must call upon him by his Name (The Tree of Life) continually to give him strength to conform to that one rule. But the first man and woman never in their life time called upon the Name of God.

5) If they did know this why did they let their physical needs overpower them to—have sex?

They forgot to eat of the Tree of Life. This allowed their eyes to wander. They observed the open actions of the other animals and what they saw became a part of their activities.

This is only an explanation of the original sin. Do not try to conform to those guide lines. It won't work. It can only be attained by the operation of God and the direction of his spirit through the Holy Ghost. This can be achieved by calling upon, and having faith in the Name of God. His Name through faith in His Name will make men strong. (Acts 3:16)

Age also makes a difference. (Gen. 8:21) The imagination of man's heart is evil from ***his youth***—. When men have increased in age, and the creative years have expired, the desire for the physical sensations associated with the conception process will be diminished, and there will be little increase in the production of new life. The only increase will be directed by God through his original plan.

****

Astrology, the accuracy of

If Astrology is false, why then, when browsing through some astrological books, it is able to pen down, quite accurately, my personality and my weaknesses?

Why then does Astrology possess such accuracy in telling people about their characters, their personalities and their weaknesses? Isn't the Bible suppose to be the only and ultimate source of truth?

First, the Bible is a book of truthful recordings of the thoughts and actions of men. They are true, but do not always conform to the perfect will of God. God is love.(1 John 4:8) The Bible records continually the violent acts of men as they exercise the thoughts of their own minds.

Those animalistic acts of men do not express the desires of a loving spiritual Father, but rather the sentiments of their natural father Adamah (Devil) who abode not in the truth, who did not partake of that Tree of Life so that he could live. Too late, when he turned and realized that it was not possible for him to return to the Garden of God (Paradise-Heaven). His natural desires by then were too strong for him to control and diminish by his own power. The power of God had left his being and he wondered the earth in confusion.

Secondly, Jesus said, (John 14:6) I am the way, the truth and the life: no man cometh unto the Father, but by me. All truth comes from God through the name he selected for placement into the foreheads of men. Without that Name (Jesus), men cannot attain or recognize spiritual truth.

Thirdly, An extensive study of human nature can qualify just about anybody to generally make assessments of others. People have a tendency to accept that which hits them and ignore those statements that do not.

****

As the planets move in their respective orbits they exert certain pressures on the earth, i.e. upon the tides as well as all animal and vegetable life. They were created as part of the whole system of things that govern the universe in an orderly fashion.

The astrologers are condemned because they do not adhere to that truth that is only found in the Name God designated as the mediator between HIMSELF AND MAN.

The astrologers cannot tell you your thoughts and dreams. They can only describe to you, in part, the pressures that may exert against your body and mind at any given time. They cannot tell you how you will respond to those pressures. Each individual has certain strengths and weaknesses inborn from birth, handed down through their ancestors all the way back to the beginning. What we will do in time is determined by what we think, for what we think is what we will do.

A good example of the fallacies found among the astrologers and other learned individuals of the world is found in the Bible.

Daniel 2:2—The king commanded to call the magicians, and the ***astrologers***, and the sorcerers, and the Chaldeans, for to show the king his dream, So they came and stood before the king. (3) And the king said unto them, I have dreamed a dream, and my spirit was troubled to know the dream. (4) Then spake the Chaldeans' to the king of Syriack, O king, live for ever: tell thy servants the dream, and we will show the interpretation. (5) The king answered and said to the Chaldeans, The thing is gone from me: if ye will not make known unto me the dream, with the interpretation thereof,—. (9) If ye will not make known unto me the dream, there is but one decree for you: for ye have prepared lying and corrupt words to speak before me, tell the time be changed: therefore tell me the dream, and I shall know that ye can show me the interpretations thereof. (10) The Chaldeans answered before the king, and said, There is not a man upon the earth that can show the king's matter: therefore there is no king, lord, nor ruler, that asked such things at any magician, or astrologer, or Chaldean. (11) And it is a rare thing that the king requireth, and there is none other that can show it before the king, except the gods, whose dwelling is not with flesh.

Dan. 2:19 Then was the secret revealed unto Daniel in a night vision. Then Daniel blessed the God of heaven. (20) Daniel answered and said, Blessed be the NAME OF GOD for ever and ever: for wisdom and might are his.

(22) He (God) revealeth the deep and secret things: he knoweth what is in the darkness, and the light dwelleth with him.

Jesus said, (John 8:12) I am the light of the world: he that followeth me shall not walk in darkness, but shall have the light of life.

John 3:19 And this is the condemnation, that light is come into the world, and men loved darkness rather than light, because their deeds were evil.

John 1:9 That (Christ) was the true Light, which lighteth every man that cometh into the world.

But when the light is rejected, men remain in darkness and will never see the simple, logical, understandable movements and direction of the holy spirit of God.

****

BABIES BAPTIZED?

SHOULD BABIES BE BAPTIZED IN WATER?

Why? What sins have they committed?

Have the babies stolen, lied, committed adultery or fornication? Did the babies worship idols and turn from faith in the one true God? Did they covet their neighbor's wife or husband? Have they wanted their neighbors money, houses or automobiles?

Answer these questions and it will be evident that you have the correct understanding who should be baptized in water.

Ref: Bible dictionary.

Baptism (in water) signifies,

> A confession of faith in Christ
> A cleansing or washing of the soul from sin.
> A death to sin and a new life in righteousness.
> A baby's awareness has not yet been awakened to any of these things.

LOVE REMAINS FOR A WHILE UNTIL THE DESIRES OF THEIR FLESH AND THEIR SPIRIT ENGULF THEM. IT IS AFTER THIS THAT THE BAPTISM OF WATER, THE CHANGING OF THE SPIRIT, AND THE GIFT OF THE HOLY GHOST ARE NEEDED.

Acts 2:38 Then Peter said unto them, Repent, and be baptized every one of you in the Name of Jesus Christ for the REMISSION of SINS, and ye shall receive the GIFT of the HOLY GHOST.

Babies have no need for the remission of sins, for they have committed none . . .

****

BABIES FROM GOD?

Would you elaborate why some babies do not come from God.

Behold, I was shapen in iniquity; and in sin did my mother conceive me. Psalm 51:5 (7) Purge me with hyssop, and I shall be clean: wash me, and I shall be whiter than snow. (9) Hide thy face from my sins, and blot out all mine iniquities. (10) Create in me a clean heart, O God; and renew a right spirit within me.

Sin was introduced into the world by Adamah (man) and woman. Since that time the fallen generations have caused malfunctions in the bodies of their offspring. This was caused by the separation of the mind of man from the mind of God.

CONSIDER DEFORMITIES THAT OCCUR FREQUENTLY IN THE WORLD.

Babies that are born without arms or legs. Babies that are joined together at their heads or abdomen. Who is the father of such grotesque creations? Is it God who is a God of Love or could it be the product of our ancestors who have fallen from God into activities that encouraged diseases of all kinds. Diseases which have altered their genes and passed malfunctions on to their offspring.

The babies that are produced in such relationships receive their spirits from their fathers, and are not in the family of God, without a rebirth of the spirit. This does not only include the physically and mentally impaired, but the majority of the population presently in the world because the REBIRTH OF THE SPIRIT HAS NOT YET BEEN RECEIVED, PREACHED AND UNDERSTOOD.

Depart from me ye that work iniquity (wickedness) I NEVER

KNEW YOU—. Matt. 7:23, i.e. in a spiritual sense). (knew—as Adam knew Eve his wife; and she conceived)

IF GOD, SPEAKING THROUGH JESUS NEVER KNEW THEM IN CONCEPTION, THEN WHO WAS THEIR FATHER?

Jesus said to the Pharisees—John 8:38 I speak that which I have seen with my Father: and ye do that which ye have seen with your father. (41) Ye do the deeds of YOUR FATHER. Then said they to him, We be not born of fornication; we have one Father, even God. (42) Jesus said unto them, If God were your Father, ye would love me: for I proceeded forth and came from God; neither came I of myself, but he sent me. (44) YE ARE OF YOUR FATHER THE DEVIL(Adamah-Man), and the lusts of your father ye will do, He was a murderer from the beginning, and abode not in the truth, because there is no truth in him. When he speaketh a lie, he speaketh of his own: for he is a liar, and the father of it.

John 9:2 (Jesus') disciples asked him, saying, Master, who did sin, this man, or his parents, that he was born blind? (3) Jesus answered, Neither hath this man sinned, nor his parents: but that the works of God should be made manifest in him.

Even though the parents or the children have not sinned, the weaknesses have still been handed down from generation to generation through the genes of their weakened ancestors.

God created the mechanism for the production of new life, but people have used that process for their own gratification. Those babies are produced by the will of their fathers and mothers and are not the sons and daughters of God, and cannot be until they are born again by the direction of the spirit of God.

ELABORATION ON THE SUBJECT—DO BABIES COME FROM GOD?

The original machine for the automatic production of new life was developed by God and his associates. The mechanism of this machine was to be triggered by a subconscious response to the 'TIME OF LIFE' as programmed by God. If the man and the woman had left this automatic process alone, then, YES, BABIES WOULD HAVE COME FROM GOD, in that it was an extension of his perfect plan in the production of new life.

Since they did not adhere to God's will for the development of the human race over a long period of time, the whole plan buckled and—, NO, BABIES DO NOT COME FROM GOD, but they are the product of the conscious desires of the bodies of fallen humanity.

The SPIRIT of a BABY comes from the natural father, that is why every child or adult must have that spirit taken out and a right spirit installed in its place. This operation is a must for everyone that hopes to live in this world for the next thousand years and beyond . . .

Who are God's assistants that are helping in this operation?

They are the created angels and men and women who have resurrected and became AS THE ANGELS.

THIS IS NOT A THING OF FAITH. IT IS A THING OF FACT.

Jesus said (John 3:3) Except a man be born again, he cannot see the kingdom of God. This rebirth of the spirit cannot be performed by the will of man. The operation is completely directed by God.

HOW DO WE BECOME BORN AGAIN?

Ask God to create a clean heart and renew a RIGHT SPIRIT WITHIN. Psalm 51:10 He will do it when the time is right.

At the appropriate 'time of life.' Spiritual times are governed the same as natural times.

References

> Psalm 51:5 Behold, I was shapen in iniquity; and in SIN did my mother CONCEIVE me.

> 1 John 3:9 Whosoever is born of God doth not commit sin—

> 1 Cor. 7:14 For the unbelieving husband is sanctified by the wife, and the unbelieving wife is sanctified by the husband: else were ***YOUR CHILDREN UNCLEAN; BUT NOW ARE THEY HOLY.***

BAPTISM, WATER

Why does the Bible say that baptism should be in the name of Jesus Christ, when down through the centuries ministers and churches have not obeyed this?

Baptism:

> Christian rite signifying spiritual cleansing.

KJV

> Jesus said, "I am come in my Father's Name—."

John 5:43.

NAB

> Paul said, "That is why I kneel before the Father from whom every family in heaven and on earth takes His Name—." Eph. 3:14. KJV

Jesus said, "While I was with them in the world, I kept them in THY NAME—." John 17:12.

That they all may be one; as thou, Father, art in me, and I in thee, that they also may be one in us—.

John 17:21 (23) I in them, and thou in me, that they may be made perfect in one—.

I have declared unto them THY NAME, and will declare it—. John 17:26

Father, glorify THY NAME—. I have both glorified it, and will glorify it again. John 12:28.

Holy Father, keep through thine OWN NAME those whom thou hast given me, that they may be one, as we are one. John 17:11.

Then Peter said unto them, repent, and be baptized every one of you in the NAME of Jesus Christ for the remission of sins, and ye shall receive the gift of the Holy Ghost. Acts 2:38.

When they heard this (what Paul had said), they were baptized in the Name of the Lord Jesus. Acts 19:5

Go therefore, and teach all nations, baptizing them in the NAME (note this, in the name) of the Father, and of the Son, and of the Holy Ghost.

This passage states in the NAME OF—. They all reside in that one Name, the only saving NAME OF GOD.

And it shall come to pass, that whosoever shall Call on the Name of the Lord (Jesus, God's name) shall be saved. Acts 2:21.

Wherefore God also hath highly exalted him, and given him a

name which is above every name: That at the Name of Jesus every knee should bow, of things in heaven, and things in earth, and things under the earth; And that every tongue should confess that Jesus Christ is Lord, to THE GLORY OF GOD THE FATHER. Phlp. 2:9-11.

—Whatsoever ye do in word or deed, do ALL in the Name of the Lord Jesus, giving thanks to God and the Father by him. Col. 3:17

For there is one God, and one mediator between God and men, the man Christ Jesus—. 1 Tim. 2:5.

It is made clear that baptizing in the NAME of the Father, Son and the Holy Ghost is the same as being baptized in the Name of Jesus. This Name Jesus, since it is a name highly exalted by God, should be mentioned at the time of water baptism. When sin has been abolished in the world, then water baptism will become obsolete.

****

Bible study—WOMEN MINISTERS

iyole asked this question

> Hi, I'm wondering about an issue of 'women in ministry'.

In 1Tim 2:12 Paul did not permit that women should teach people . . . . but today, there are many great women pastor or evangelists . . . . I can't understand . . . .

Scripture in question: 1 Tim. 2:12 But I suffer not a woman to teach, nor to usurp authority over the man, but to be in silence. (13) For Adam was first formed, then Eve.

Genesis 2:18 And the LORD God said, It is not good that the man should be alone; I will make him an ***help meet*** for him—.

Conversely, it is not good for a woman to be alone. For the female to operate properly she must be joined mentally and spiritually with the male counterpart. They must be joined together spiritually by God through the operation of God.

In the natural, (Gen. 2:21) God caused a DEEP SLEEP to fall upon Adam, and he slept—while God caused the growth and separation of the female from her male counterpart. Then the flesh of the male's side was closed up. (The same operation as in the budding process of plants) This was a real and natural growth and separation of the two parts. They are dependent upon each other for help in all matters of life. The perfect order of God requires that they work in coordination with each other.

The perfect order of God is this:

God
Christ
Man/Woman
Family—Children
Community
State
Country
World.

The male receives from God and imparts to the female.

The female is the ***positive side*** of the human structure. The male is the ***negative part***. The negative current flows from the negative male to the positive female and then back to the negative side of the human A(tt)om.

(Atom-adam) This operation functions more perfectly at night, or during the sleeping hours, when the two parts are in close proximity. If, or when this connection is obstructed for longer periods of time by any means, it weakens both parts. As God said, "It is not good."

The man receives his spiritual knowledge, and understanding from God through the guidance of the Holy Ghost, and reveals that information to his counterpart, and in the case of leadership in the church (group of people), to the assembly. His counter part (the female) can then relay that which she has received, to others around her in a subordinate fashion, whether it is in the assembly, or in the home, or community. Primarily though, the female is to keep the home and be a helper mentally and physically to her counter part, the male.

There is no other way for the two parts to operate properly. Individuals that think they can do without one another, always run into misguided roads of thinking. The mind is weakened and eventually the physical body begins to deteriorate, because the body is operated through the direction of the mind, or brain. It should be remembered that the body, comprised of one unit (Matthew 19:5) of the positive and negative, was intended to live for ever. And this process would have continued if the knowledge of evil had not disrupted that 'power from God', as a current flow between the two parts.

****

Bible True—Right?

If the Bible is true, does that make it right?

Well, yes the Bible is true! But it was not RIGHT for Cain to kill his brother. It was a sin. Genesis 4:7-8. (SIN: offense against God)

God confirmed that 'Thou shalt not kill' was true (Exo. 20:13), along with the other primary commandments, but Moses' actions when he came down the mountain were not right.

Exodus 32:26—Moses stood in the gate of the camp, and said, 'Who is on the Lord's side? Let him come unto me. (27) And he said unto them Thus saith the Lord God of Israel, put every man his sword by his side, and go in and out from gate to gate throughout the camp, and slay every man his brother, and every man his companion, and every man his neighbour. (28) And the children of Levi did according to THE WORD OF MOSES: and there fell of the people that day about three thousand men.

God had said to Moses, (Exodus 32:10) Now therefore let me alone, that MY WRATH may wax hot against them—but Moses' ANGER WAXED HOT (Exo. 32:19) against the people, thinking he was doing God service,(John 16:2) and gave commandment to kill. This was in direct opposition to the commandment that God had just confirmed with him.

Note: John 1:17 The law was GIVEN BY MOSES, but grace and truth came by Jesus Christ.

Note: Why would God contradict himself? If he confirmed 'Thou shalt not kill, then why would he change his mind?

Numbers 23:19 God is not a man, that he should lie; neither the son of man, that he should repent: hath he said, and shall he not do it? Or hath he spoken, and shall he not make it good?

It was true that the children of Israel were to receive the promised land for their habitation, but God's intention was to melt (Josh. 2:11) the heart of the people and drive them out by the emotion (intense feeling) of fear.

But instead (Josh. 6:21)—they utterly destroyed all that was in the city (Jericho), both man and woman, young and old, and ox, and sheep, and ass, with the edge of the sword. (22) they saved only Rahab the prostitute, and her family—(24) and they burnt the city—.

It was true that the religious leaders incensed the people against Jesus, which led to his demise upon the wooden pole, but it was not right. Mark 15:10.

Well, yes the Bible is true. It is an inspired rendition of the thoughts and actions of men versus the will of God. Men were inspired by God to record the truth of all the actions of men for our instruction, doctrine, reproof, correction, that men of God may be perfect, thoroughly furnished unto all good works. 2 Tim 3:16-17.

Jesus said (John 10:8) All that EVER CAME BEFORE ME ARE thieves and robbers—. (10) The thief cometh not, but for to steal, and to kill, and to destroy: I am come that they might have life—and have more of it.

As the earth was corrupt and filled with violence (Gen. 6:11) before the flood so it remained afterward, and even unto this day.

It is imperative that people understand the difference between the words as written in the commandments and the smooth sounding words of the orators. The laity must have wisdom enough to know the difference.

****

BIBLE:

jdg31743 asked this question. Is the Bible true?

Well, yes the Bible is true!

It is inspired by God to tell the truth even though it may be against the writer himself. It is a recording of the thoughts and actions of men versus the will of God. Men have not followed the perfect will of God, and this truth is repeatedly shown throughout the pages of the accumulated writings.

Why so many translations? BBE, DBY, WEB, YLT, KJV, KFV W/STRONG, NRS, TEV, RHE, and many more in the making.

The translators of all versions are honestly trying to convey to the understanding the exact meaning of the best manuscripts available. This is difficult with out the Holy Ghost as a guiding factor in their search for meaning, even though they may understand the languages in question.

With reference to false prophets. To be sure there have been many false prophets in Biblical times as well as now. In the Bible there are many passages regarding them. Jer. 14:14, Matthew 7:15, 24:11, 24:24, Mark 13:22, 2 Peter 2:1, I John 4:1.

Ministers in many groups of religion delight in those passages. It makes it easier for them to draw the people closer to their way of thinking. The phrases are used as a club to control the masses through fear, and keep them in their own sphere of religion. God is not primarily in religion. He is in the hearts of men, women, boys and girls who will CALL UPON HIM.

When we have the Holy Ghost, and Call upon God by His Name, Jesus, continually, we CANNOT DECEIVE nor can we BE DECEIVED. We will not be caught up in the delusion of devil worship (those that believe in the devil instead of, or in addition to God), nor in the worship of stars, or the sun, or moon (Astrology), or animals or any other nonsense devised by the minds of men.

THERE IS ONLY ONE GOD, and one Name, with only one purpose in God's mind; that is for men to live peaceably with one another, and break down the walls which have been so studiously constructed by the natural minds of men.

Isa. 21:9 Babylon (confusion) is fallen, is fallen: and all the graven images of her gods HE HATH BROKEN unto the ground.

Revelations 14:8 And there followed another angel, saying, BABYLON IS FALLEN, IS FALLEN, THAT GREAT CITY

BECAUSE SHE MADE ALL NATIONS DRINK OF THE WINE (DOCTRINE) OF THE WRATH OF HER FORNICATION.

Confusion is dissipating. It is on its way out. THAT GREAT CITY SHALL NEVER BE AGAIN.

1 Cor. 15:24 Then cometh the end, when he shall have delivered up the kingdom to God, even the Father; when he shall have put down all rule and all authority and power. (25) For he must reign, till he hath put all enemies under his feet. (26) The last enemy that shall be destroyed is death. (28) And when all things shall be subdued unto him, then shall the Son also himself be subject unto him that put all things under him, that God may be all in all.

BIBLE—Continued

Is the Bible true?

The Bible was written by man but inspired and designed by God to give man what ever he wants. Man can believe anything and find passages in the Bible to back up his belief. (***This writing is included in that freedom***).

If men are not led by the Holy Spirit of God, then they will be led by the power of their own mind.

As in a plain in the land of Shinar, when the people wanted to build a tower and make a name for themselves, so it is yet in the land of Babylon (symbolic). They are still selecting names for themselves. It is for this reason God has confounded their language so that they will not be able to reach heaven (for they do not understand where heaven is) or understand each other's speech.

Gen. 11:4 And they said, Go to, let us build us a city and a tower, whose top MAY REACH UNTO HEAVEN; and let us make US A NAME—.

Who caused the confusion?

God did!

Gen. 11:7 (And the Lord said), Go to, let us go down, and there confound their language, that they may not understand one another's speech.

But rectification is on its way.

Acts 2:21—It shall come to pass that WHOSOEVER shall CALL on the NAME of the LORD shall be saved. Joel 2:32, Rom. 10:13.

THEN GOD WILL DRAW NEAR. (James 4:8)

Zeph. 3:9 For then will I turn to the people a pure language, that THEY MAY ALL CALL UPON THE NAME OF THE LORD, to serve HIM with ONE CONSENT.

Jesus said, (John 17:12) While I was with them in the world, I kept them in THY NAME: those that thou gavest me I have kept—. (15) I pray not that thou shouldest take them out of the world, but that thou shouldest keep them from the evil. (26)—I have declared unto them thy NAME, and will declare it—.

Rev. 7:9 After this I beheld, and, lo, a great multitude, which no man could number, of all nations, and kindreds, and people, and tongues, stood before the throne, and before the Lamb, clothed with white robes, and palms in their hands; (10) And cried with a loud voice, saying, Salvation (saving a person from sin or danger) to our God which sitteth upon the throne, and unto the Lamb. (15)—and he that sitteth on the throne SHALL DWELL AMONG THEM. (16) They shall hunger no more, neither thirst any more; neither shall the sun light on them, nor any heat.(17) For the Lamb which is in the midst of the throne shall feed them and shall lead them unto living fountains of waters: and God shall wipe away all tears from their eyes.

BIBLE, TIRED OF?

Helper76 asked this question.

> Hello! I have been reading the bible over and over again since I was really young. I have read many lessons over again and have been helped greatly by the bible and learned a lot from the bible. Lately though it seems hard getting into stories that I have read many times. I am not talking about stopping reading the bible, but it does seem to me the older versions of the bible seemed a lot more interesting even though some of the meanings were hard to get through because of the wording. That is why we have the complete newest English version of the bible. I told a relative that I am tired/bored of reading the same stories. He said, "Why do you read them over and over again? It is the meditation of the word that has helped me a great deal in life's lessons and about the forgiveness and love of God. Yet, at the same time I should keep the knowledge inspired and to read other inspirational material that will keep my soul and mind fresh is good as well?
>
> I bought a book today entitled ' The day I met God.' Now certain books that I tend to read that is spiritual, I read really fast and when finished I feel opened and refreshed in spirit. Even books about near death experiences and reincarnation. Like I said to my family member I am not going to stop reading the bible, but for a change I want to read something different that will inspire and refresh my soul. What do you think? Somebody mentioned this to me before, how I tend to focus on the bible and that is it, and how I should go out and find other inspirational books of people's lives and how God has helped them. Thank you for reading and responding. God bless!
>
> Joe

James gave this response on 5/26/2002:

I fear, lest by any means, as the serpent (man) beguiled Eve through his subtlety, so your minds should be corrupted from the ***simplicity*** that is in Christ.

God is a God of knowledge. He wants his sons and daughters to be knowledgeable too. He does not mind that we know. But we cannot reach God through the natural thinking of men.

1 Cor. 2:14—The natural man receiveth not the things of the Spirit of God: for they are foolishness unto him: neither can he know them, because they are spiritually discerned.

Jesus said, I am the Way, the Truth, and the Life, no man cometh unto the Father, but by me. John 14:6 (No one else).

Yes, I have seen angels.

Yes, I have had an out of body experience.

Yes, I have met God and he has talked with me and my family.

Yes, my spirit was killed, taken out and a right spirit was installed in its place. But my nature has remained.

Yes, I was born again.

No, that rebirth was not accomplished by going to an altar and shaking hands with the preacher. And no, I did not pay for it. The gifts of God are freely given.

Yes, I was ordained to preach the good news, but not by orations. (Elaborate formal speech)

Yes, I was filled with the Holy Spirit of God.

Yes, I was given the gift of the Holy Ghost.

Yes, I spoke with tongues.

Yes, I have written ten books and have the copyrights.

But spiritual gifts are not given by reading my books or any others.

John 6:45 It is written in the prophets, and they shall be ***ALL taught of God.*** Every man therefore that hath heard and hath learned of the Father, cometh unto me. (Jesus, the mediator).

The way to God is by calling upon him by the Name of His only begotten Son, Jesus. (Also check 1 Cor. 1:2 all that in every place call upon the NAME of Jesus Christ).

Acts 2:21 IT SHALL COME TO PASS, THAT WHOSOEVER SHALL CALL ON THE NAME OF THE LORD SHALL BE SAVED. Joel 2:32, Rom. 10:13.

Jer. 31:34 And ***they shall teach no more every man his neighbor, and every man his brother, saying, Know the LORD: for they ALL shall know me, from the least of them unto the greatest of them,*** saith the LORD: for I will forgive their iniquity, and I will remember their sin no more.

****

BIBLE—John, Chapter 1

Ronndonn asked this question.

(In the beginning was the Bible, and the Bible was with God, and the Bible was God.)

People are telling me that the Bible IS the word of God.

So if one IS the other, then the above verse should make perfect sense. Does it make sense to you or is it nonsense?

James gave this response.

First of all, the Bible was not in the beginning, it has been constructed by stages over a long period of time. It was developed as necessity demanded, because of the deviations of men from the perfect will of God.

God is more than just a WORD! God is a real spiritual individual. God is made of substance the same as man, except that the substance God is made of cannot be seen by the natural eyes of men. (God can only be seen through the process of visions). God thinks. He acts, and He creates through the power of Christ. John 1:3 All things were made by him; (Christ-The power of God) and without him was not anything made that was made.

GOD IS A SPIRIT

John 4:24 God is a SPIRIT: and they that worship him must worship him in spirit and in truth.

John 1:1 In the beginning was the WORD, and the WORD was with God, and the WORD was God. (2) The same was in the beginning with God. (3) All things were made by him; and without him was not anything made that was made. (4) In him was life; and the life was the light of men.

Jesus said (John 8:12) I am the light of the world: he that followeth me shall not walk in darkness, but shall have the light of life.

NAME = WORD OF GOD—Revelation 19:13 HIS NAME IS CALLED THE WORD OF GOD.

(The bible was inspired by God to be written for our instruction, doctrine, reproof, correction—2 Tim. 3:17)

Jesus said, (John 5:43) I am come in my Father's Name—.

John 1:14 And the WORD (Name of God) was made flesh—.

The old testament was a natural book. The new testament is primarily spiritual. If it is difficult for a person to understand spiritual things they should ask God to give them Spiritual eyes and spiritual ears. Along with these gifts (which are freely given by God) the Holy Ghost must be received, and Christ (the power and holy spirit of God) must be maintained within the individual. This is like water flowing out of the belly—, (John 7:38) or like Oil, (Matthew 25:4) to keep the light of Christ burning brightly. The Holy Ghost guides through the Christ of God into all truth needed to maintain the physical and spiritual body, so that men ('+ female' and—'male' are one) can live eternally as God intended in the beginning.

Heb. 7:19 The (natural) law made nothing perfect, but the bringing in of a better hope did; by the which we draw nigh unto God.

James 4:8 Draw nigh to God, and he will draw nigh to you.

HOW DO WE DRAW NIGH GOD?

We draw near God by calling upon His Name!

Joel 2:31—It shall come to pass, that WHOSOEVER shall CALL on the NAME of the LORD (Jesus) shall be delivered—.

Acts 2:21—It shall come to pass, that WHOSOEVER shall CALL on the NAME of the Lord shall be saved. Also Romans 10:13.

The early church was doing this, but because fear crept in, they soon forgot, thereby losing their power with God. It was then that the Kingdom of heaven suffered violence and was taken by force. (Matthew 11:12)

Acts 9:14 And here he hath authority from the chief priests to bind all that CALL on thy NAME. (Also check 1 Cor. 1:2–with all that in every place CALL upon the NAME of JESUS). During this time the church (that group of people) was protected from the devastation Saul had in his mind to do against those people that were calling upon the Name of God.

Ronndonn rated this answer:

> Yes, that is right, God is more than any word or words or book. So the phrase word of God must mean more than a book or even the ideas in a book. Its more . . . much more.

****

Blasphemy and Eternally judged.

How does a person blaspheme against the Holy Ghost and be eternally judged?

ETERNAL JUDGMENT

Judged forever without hope of forgiveness.

Matthew quoted Jesus as saying (Matthew 12:31) Wherefore I say unto you, ALL MANNER OF SIN AND BLASPHEMY SHALL BE FORGIVEN UNTO MEN: BUT THE BLASPHEMY AGAINST THE HOLY GHOST SHALL NOT BE FORGIVEN UNTO MEN.

Matthew 12:32 And whosoever speaketh a word against the Son of man, it shall be forgiven him: but whosoever speaketh against the Holy Ghost, it shall NOT BE FORGIVEN HIM, neither in this world (era), neither in the world (era) to come.

So it is clear, blasphemy against the Holy Ghost is the only way a person can be eternally judged. (Other than suicide— this is because after a person is dead they cannot ask forgiveness for killing).

HOW DOES A PERSON BLASPHEME AGAINST THE HOLY GHOST?

When an individual says that someone has an unclean spirit, an 'Evil spirit, or It is of the Devil, or Beelzebub, or Satan, when it is in fact the Holy Ghost.

Mark 3:22 And the scribes which came down from Jerusalem said, He hath Beelzebub, and by the prince of the devils casteth he out devils. (23) And he called them unto him, and said unto them in parables, How can Satan cast out Satan?

Mark 3:29 But he that shall blaspheme against the Holy Ghost hath NEVER forgiveness, but is in DANGER of Eternal Damnation: BECAUSE THEY SAID, HE HATH AN UNCLEAN SPIRIT.

Paul said, (Hebrews 10:26) If we sin wilfully after that we have received the knowledge of the truth, there remaineth no more sacrifice for sins, (27) But a certain fearful looking for of judgment and fiery indignation, which shall devour the adversaries—. Here it should be remembered Paul's own words where he wrote, (1 Cor. 13:12) For now we see through a glass, darkly—1 Cor. 13:10 But when that which is perfect is come, then that which is in part shall be done away.

Do not despair. The human race is still coming out of the wilderness of ignorance. Many of the statements made in the past regarding the operations of the spirit have been spoken in ignorance. We are still under grace and God is a very merciful God, and he has long patience.

James 5:7. Be patient therefore, brethren, unto the coming of the Lord, Behold, the husbandman waiteth for the precious fruit of the earth, and hath LONG PATIENCE for it, until he receive the early and latter rain—.

(2 Peter 3:9) The Lord is not willing that ***ANY SHOULD PERISH***, but that ALL should come to repentance.

Among Jesus' last words were, (Luke 23:34) 'Father, forgive them: for they know not what they do.'

If God does not have compassion and mercy upon the human race, and is not willing to save them from all sin, then the following passages would never have been written.

Joel 2:32 And it shall come to pass, that WHOSOEVER shall call on the NAME of the LORD shall be delivered:

Acts 2:21 And it shall come to pass, that WHOSOEVER shall CALL on the NAME of the Lord shall be saved.

Romans 10:13 For WHOSOEVER shall CALL upon the NAME of the Lord shall be saved.

These passages do not differentiate between individuals that have committed certain levels of offense against God or the Holy Ghost—but they all state WHOSOEVER—shall be saved.

****

Budding, Instinct, etc.

Could you explain further—budding, immune system, and guilt caused by the knowledge of evil?

God made many different living creatures, then he decided to make a man.

The body of man was made perfect in the beginning. Then God used the same budding process he had experimented with in the creation of various plants, in the development of woman.

He placed in the man and the woman brains that needed one another for the proper functioning of their bodies. It was not good that man should be alone (Gen. 2:18). The one brain could not function properly without the other. He also placed within them a soul and a spirit that could live forever if properly maintained. He gave them the Light of Christ (John 1:9) Christ was the true light, which lighteth EVERY MAN that cometh into the world. That light caused their minds to understand.

Their spirit directed them to everything needed to cause their bodies to live. They then understood by instinct what fruit and vegetables they should eat to supply all the essential amino acids needed for their sustenance and continual life of the body. Their immune systems functioned perfectly, so that if any substance was inadvertently introduced into their bodies it would have no ill effect.

They were informed that if they allowed 'GUILT' to come into the mental system, it would disrupt the proper thinking of the brain, drive out the Christ (The anointing from God) and, in turn, allow all kinds of emotional problems to develop. (grow, increase, or evolve gradually). All emotions of love, hate, fear, envy, etc., were GOOD, but if guilt was allowed to enter the mental system it would cause all the emotions to become out of balance. This would in turn disrupt the mental, spiritual and physical systems. God knew that men and women must have something stable to hold-on-to, so he gave them a formula. It consisted of keeping in contact with 'God's spirit' by calling upon his Name. This they forgot to do. The knowledge of God faded from the minds of men, causing weakness, confusion and death.

****

Calendar HOW OLD IS MAN?

Archaeological findings (study of past human life) and common sense based on logic, dictate that the creation of human beings was much farther back in time than the six thousand years of recorded history.

The following is ONE WAY of looking at the time of the creation of man and woman on the earth.

Based upon the fiftieth year plan of the jubilee we may draw a conclusion. Lev. 25:9-13.

First we must consider that one day is with God as a thousand years. (2 Pet. 3:8) Then consider that God's creative day is 7 x 7 thousand years or = 49,000 years allotted to each day. The jubilee is placed at the beginning of the seventh day, or the fiftieth thousand years from the beginning of the sixth day. During the first thousand years of the seventh day, men are set free, and God finishes his work and rests.

Gen. 2:2. And on the seventh day God ENDED his work which he had made; and he RESTED on the seventh day from all his work—.

Hebrews 4:11 Let us labor therefore to enter into that rest, lest any man fall after the same example of UNBELIEF. (Doubt)

It is not necessary to wait for the jubilee to receive the benefits of God's rest, because faith in, and calling upon the Name of God is all that is needed to access the power that emanates from God. This is all that has been needed from the beginning.

Jesus said (Matthew 11:28), Come unto me, ALL ye that labor, and are heavy laden, and I will give you REST.

The end of man's world (Adamah (man) and Woman) was reduced to two. The end of Adam and Eve's world ended with the flood, when eight souls were saved (1 Peter 3:20). Periodically there are ends of the world, clearing the earth of sin and ignorance. The end Jesus spoke of was A.D. 70, for he said Matthew 24:34 This (that) generation shall not pass, till all these things (that he spoke of) be fulfilled.

NOTE: The following is only a tool for thought:

EACH DAY REPRESENTS 49,000 YEARS.
THE SEVEN CREATIVE DAYS

1 0000000 7x7 = 49,000 years
2 0000000 98,000
3 0000000 147,000
4 0000000 196,000
5 0000000 245,000
6 0000000 294,000 293,000 years have expired.
7 0000000 343,000
(Each circle represents 7000 years)

1st Day Gen. 1:5 This was not the natural light of the sun. The gasses of our present sun were not ignited until the fourth day. Just after the end of the third creative day or after the 147,000 years from the beginning of the creation.

Light of Christ. Power of God. Christ was the light of the world. John 1:9. The glory of God did lighten it. Rev. 21:23. Angels do not need natural light to see.

2nd day Heaven, Water.

3rd day Seas, earth, grasses, fruit, seeds were in the

earth before they grew. Gen. 2:5. The natural sun was needed to cause germination.

4th day Sun, moon, stars.

5th Day Just after the end of the 4th day—196,000 years, Fish, whales, and birds began to appear. All these came from the oceans.

6th Day (7x7=49,000 years) Beasts, Cattle, Man.

Beasts were created from the dust of the earth during the first 8000 years of the 6th day. Man was created 40,000 years from the beginning of the last 1000 years of the sixth day.

Seventh part of the sixth day-reign with Christ (the Power of God) for 1000 years. This completes the sixth day.

7th Day Seventh day Begins. Gen. 2:2 And on the seventh day God ended his work, and he rested. Heb.4:4.

At the end of the 48,000 years of the sixth day, it has been 293,000 years since God said, Let there be light.

Light is LITERALLY—POWER or radiation that makes vision possible.

Light is FIGURATIVELY—INTELLIGENCE, WISDOM, AND UNDERSTANDING, without these things the worlds could not have been framed.

HAS MAN BEEN ON THE EARTH 6000 YEARS?

NO! HE HAS BEEN ON THE EARTH 40,000. YEARS.

THE PRIMITIVE PEOPLE HAD ONE CATASTROPHE AFTER ANOTHER.

THE SIXTH CREATIVE DAY REPRESENTS A SPAN IN TIME OF 49,000 YEARS.

****

Calling upon the Name of God.

Edward asked this question.

People are always using a passage from the Bible that states 'Not every one that saith unto me, Lord, Lord, shall enter into the kingdom of heaven; but he that doeth the will of my Father which is in heaven. Matthew 7:21

This is used as proof that we should not call upon the name of the Lord. Is there any compelling evidence that we should continue calling upon God by His Name?

Since many have disputed the idea of calling upon the Name of the Lord, as well as what that name is, I thought it appropriate to show many passages concerning it.

First, the following is the passage selected to refute and discourage people from calling upon the Name of the Lord.

Matthew 7:22 Many will say to me in that day, LORD, LORD, have we not prophesied in thy NAME? And in thy NAME have cast out devils? And in thy Name done many wonderful woks? (23) And then will I profess unto them, I NEVER knew you: depart from me, YE THAT WORK INIQUITY. (Wickedness). (24) Therefore whosoever HEARETH THESE SAYINGS OF MINE, AND DOETH THEM—.

The following is an example of some of the individuals Jesus was referring to.

Acts 19:13—certain of the vagabond Jews, exorcists, took

upon them to call over them which had evil spirits the name of the Lord Jesus, saying, We adjure you by Jesus whom Paul preacheth. (14) And there were seven sons of one Sceva, a Jew, and chief of the priests, which did so.

It is quite evident that a person may not continue working wickedness and expect to draw close to God by calling upon his Name.

Matthew 22:37 Jesus said unto him, (lawyer) Thou shalt love the Lord thy God with all thy heart, and with all thy soul, and with all thy mind. (38) This is the first and great commandment, (39) and the second is like unto it, Thou shalt love thy neighbor as thyself. (40) On these two commandments hang all the law and the prophets.

When conforming to these rules, sin is abolished, effecting a clear conscience toward God and thereby receiving power from him by faith in his Name.

Now let us consider the roots and subsequent history of calling upon the Name of the Lord.

Gen. 4:26 And to Seth, to him also there was born a son, and he called his name Enos: THEN BEGAN men to CALL UPON THE NAME OF THE LORD. (This indicates that the first man and woman never did it).

1 Kings 18:24 And call ye on the Name of your gods, and I WILL CALL ON THE NAME OF THE LORD: and the God that answereth by fire, let him be GOD.

Psalm 80:18—quicken us, (come to life, or give us life) and we will CALL UPON THY NAME.

Psalm 99:6 Moses and Aaron among his priests, and Samuel among them that CALL UPON HIS NAME; they

CALLED upon the Lord, and he answered them. (7) He spake unto them in the cloudy pillar: they kept HIS TESTIMONIES, and the ORDINANCE that he gave them.

Psalm 116:13 I will take the cup of salvation, AND CALL UPON THE NAME OF THE LORD. (17) I will offer to thee the sacrifice of thanksgiving, and WILL CALL UPON THE NAME OF THE LORD.

Isa. 12:4—In that day shall ye say Praise the Lord, CALL UPON HIS NAME, declare his doings among the people, make mention that HIS NAME is exalted.

FEAR THE LORD—Maybe a little fear in this case is desirable.

Jeremiah 10:25 Pour out thy fury upon the heathen that know thee not, and upon the ***FAMILIES THAT CALL NOT ON THY NAME—.***

Joel 2:32 And it shall come to pass, that WHOSOEVER SHALL CALL ON THE NAME OF THE LORD shall be delivered—.

Zeph. 3:9 For then will I turn to the people a pure language, that they may ALL CALL UPON THE NAME OF THE LORD, to serve him with one consent.

Zech. 13:9—and will refine them as silver is refined, and will try them as gold is tried: they shall CALL on MY NAME, and I will hear them:—.

Acts 2:21 And it shall come to pass, that WHOSOEVER SHALL CALL ON THE NAME OF THE LORD shall be saved.

Romans 10:13 For WHOSOEVER shall CALL upon the NAME OF THE LORD shall be saved. (14) How then shall they CALL on HIM in whom they have not believed? And how shall they believe in him of whom they have not heard? And how shall they hear without a preacher?

1 Cor. 1:2—to them that are sanctified in Christ Jesus, called to be saints, with ALL THAT IN EVERY PLACE CALL UPON THE NAME OF JESUS CHRIST OUR LORD—.

SAUL/PAUL

Acts 9:14 And here he hath authority from the chief priests to bind all that CALL on THY NAME. (15) But the LORD said unto him, Go thy way: for he is a chosen vessel unto me, to bear my NAME before the Gentiles, and kings, and the children of Israel. Jesus said, (John 17:11)—Holy Father, keep through thine OWN NAME those whom thou hast given me—.

Jesus said, (John 17:12) While I was with them in the world, I kept them in THY NAME: (26)—I have declared unto them THY NAME, and will declare it—.

Hebrews 13:15 By him therefore let us offer the sacrifice of praise to God CONTINUALLY, that is, the fruit of our lips giving thanks to HIS NAME.

Psalm 113:3 From the rising of the sun unto the going down of the same the Lord's Name is to be praised.

Psalm 119:55 I have remembered THY NAME, O LORD, in the night, AND HAVE KEPT THY LAW.

****

Christ as water, The flow of

Charlene asked this question.

Does the power of Christ flow among only larger groups of people?

COUNTRY FOLKS ARE NOT ISOLATED FROM THE POWER OF GOD.

The following statement was directed to the woman of Samaria that came to draw water from Jacob's well at about noon.

> John 4:24 God is a Spirit: and they that worship him must worship him in spirit and in truth.
>
> John 4:21—the hour cometh, when ye shall neither in this mountain (Gerizim in Samaria), nor yet at Jerusalem, worship the Father (John 4:23)—But the hour cometh, and now is, when the true worshipers shall worship the Father in spirit and in truth:
>
> Matthew recorded that Jesus said, Where two or three are gathered together in my Name, there am I in the midst of them. Matthew 18:20. Although Jesus was speaking with his immediate disciples, his statement was not limited to them only. This idea stems all the way back to the beginning when God said, It is not good that the man should be alone, I will make an help meet for him. That help meet was of the opposite gender, of course.

THE PERFECT ORDER OF GOD.

GOD
CHRIST (power of God through His Name)
MAN + WOMAN
FAMILY
COMMUNITY
COUNTY
STATE
COUNTRY
WORLD.

The church consisted of 'many' with Moses in the wilderness (Acts 7:38), or a 'few' in the individual homes during the time of Jesus and thereafter. Rom. 16:5, 1 Cor 16:19, Col. 4:15, Phlm. 1:2.

It is important to gather together in a church setting, either large or small, because the generated power of God flows between associated individuals, enabling them to refrain from acts which invariably affect the conscience, and ultimately determines the individual's state of health, mentally, physically and spiritually.

The New American Bible—Collins World.

Paul (Saul) wrote, We should not absent ourselves from the assembly, as some do, but encourage one another; and this all the more because you see that the day draws near. (The end of that era).

The power of Christ flows between two or more individuals. As the family grows in quantity, the generated power increases proportionately for the benefit of the family (church), as long as they maintain faith in, and call upon the Name of God, Jesus.

****

Christianity—Original sin.

Anonymous asked this question.

I'm studying the Genesis story. I am especially interested in the true meaning of Adam and Eve eating the apple.

James gave this response.

They did not eat an apple! (Gen. 3:2) The woman said unto the serpent,(Man) We may eat of the fruit of the trees of the garden.

PEOPLE ARE CALLED TREES IN THE BIBLE.

Judges 9:8 The trees went forth on a time to anoint a king over them; and they said unto the olive tree, Reign thou over us.

Pharaoh and his people were considered as trees. (Ezekiel 31).

John made reference to people when he said, Now also the ax is laid unto the root of the tree. (Matthew 3:10.

THE TREE OF KNOWLEDGE OF GOOD AND EVIL.

> Genesis 2:9.
>
> Genesis 3:3—God hath said, Ye shall not eat of it, neither shall ye touch it, lest ye die.
>
> Genesis 3:4 And the serpent (Adam) said unto the woman, Ye shall not surely die:
>
> Genesis 3:5 For God doth know that in the day ye eat thereof, then your eyes (of understanding) shall be opened, and ye shall be as gods, knowing good and evil.
>
> Genesis 3:6 And when the woman saw that the tree was good for food, and that it was pleasant to the eyes, and a tree to be desired to make one wise, she took of the fruit thereof, and did eat (partake of), and gave also unto her husband with her, and he did eat.

THE TREE WAS THE MAN AND THE WOMAN

The man and the woman were of ONE WHOLE UNIT.

They were of one flesh. (Gen. 2:23-24) They were given a mind that could know good and also evil. The knowledge of evil would eventually cause them to die because the pressure on the mind would disrupt their immune system.

Genesis 3:7 And the eyes of them both were opened, and ***they knew that they were naked—.***

Genesis 3:9 And the Lord God called unto Adam, and said unto him, Where art thou?

Genesis 3:10 And he said, I heard thy voice in the garden, and I was ***afraid, BECAUSE I WAS NAKED—.***

Genesis 3: 11 And he said, ***who told thee that thou wast naked?*** Hast thou eaten of the tree, whereof I commanded thee that thou shouldest not eat?

Guilt flooded their minds because they knew they were not permitted to partake of the reproduction process as the other animals were openly engaged in. Before this occurrence they did not partake of the Tree of Life (the first man never during his life time called upon the Name of God—the Tree of Life), therefore they did not have the strength to conform to the will of God regarding this matter.

Death reigned from Adam to Moses, even over them that had not sinned after the similitude of Adam's transgression. (Romans 5:14)

What was Adam's transgression? (Adamah—man and woman together as one unit, one flesh. Gen. 2:24)

The man and the woman took the life making process and placed it under their own conscious control. This was the only thing God had asked them not to do, because God knew once they had experienced the physical sensations associated with that process they would not be able to stop its proliferation. This would overpopulate the world and cause death in order to balance the 'NEED WITH SUPPLY.'

Even those that partly understood the original sin and tried to make themselves celibate or separate themselves from the opposite gender could not change the inborn degeneration received from their ancestors. Death has still reigned.

But God has had mercy—looking forward to the time when men will grow out of their foolish years, for the imagination of man's heart is evil from his YOUTH. (Gen. 8:21).

But eventually all sin will be washed out of our systems as we partake of that TREE OF LIFE (the name of God), and the washing of the living water that flows out of our belly—(John 7:38) into eternal life. (John 3:15)

Natural will-power plays little part in this process. Any physical attempt to correct the problem caused by the inherited genes will only cause separations. Two by two, male and female, went into the ark (Gen. 6:19). The Holy Ghost will guide (John 16:13) and the holy spirit of God must flow from within—then time and understanding along with the power of God will raise the foundation of human life.

****

Coats of skin.

Edward asked this question.

Did God make coats of skin for man and woman?

Genesis 3:21 Unto Adam also and to his wife did the Lord God make coats of skins and clothed them.

Adam and Eve (one unit comprised of the male (negative) and the female (positive) was the son and daughter of God. At the time of their creation God lived within them, giving them understanding and direction.

(1 Cor. 3:16) Know ye not that ye are the temple of God, and that the Spirit of God dwelleth in you? (2 Cor. 6:16) As God hath said, I will dwell in them, and walk in them; and I will be their God—.

But when the man and the woman committed the offense against God (sinned), they drove out the spirit of God and left themselves with the unbearable weight of guilt. They felt guilty because they had taken the life making process away from God and placed it under their own control. Even then God still had mercy and fulfilled their desires by showing them how to cover their nakedness. Although the act of wearing clothes and later the offering of animal sacrifices could never, as pertaining the conscience (Heb. 9:9) bring the man and the woman back to that perfect state of spiritual bliss.

God is a Spirit (John 4:24) A SPIRIT does not directly work with things. Things affect things by the direction of the spirit. God speaks the word. Heat and cold come together which produce wind. Water changes the face of the land. Many chemicals act as catalytic agents to change other chemical substances.

God, as an individual, has never made clothing for anyone, but he created the brain and placed within it the understanding of how to invent and create as he himself has done. By this process God, through the brain and hands of the individuals, made clothes of skin which was an improvement over the leaves. This would protect them from the impending cooler weather that was sure to come in time.

God is aware of what we need, but he also gives us the desires of our heart, whether good or bad, right or wrong, so that freedom of choice will continually be maintained.

****

COMPARING

Kathy asked this question.

Should we compare ourselves with others in doctrines and beliefs?

James gave this response.

2 Corinthians 10:12—they measuring themselves by themselves, and comparing themselves among themselves, ARE NOT WISE.

What do you believe about God?

I believe what my church teaches and believes.

And what does your church teach and believe?

My church teaches and believes what I believe.

What do you and your church believe?

Oh, we believe exactly the same thing.

The Lamplighter

Unless groups of people, either large or small, come together in the Name of God, it is impossible for them to perfectly understand theology.

1: study of religion,
2: theory or system of theology.—Theos—god—.

Theosophy—Wisdom concerning God; insight into the character and purposes of the divine mind, knowledge of divine things).

Just because the majority in each group understand certain doctrines alike does not make those accepted ideas conform to the doctrines of Christ. It matters not how many people have gathered together, how much they agree with one another, nor the amount of money and great buildings have been amassed. It all comes to a spiritual nothingness unless the people are feasting upon the Tree of Life (the Name of God).

Psalm 34:8 ***O taste and see that the LORD IS GOOD.***

PRAISING THE NAME OF GOD TASTES GOOD TO THE LIPS.

Irrespective of what others believe, we must adhere to the handle (Name) of God. Grab hold of that Tree of Life. Call upon it and have faith in it, then your faith will make you whole. Matt. 9:22, Matt. 15:28, Mark 10:52, etc.

Psalm 31:2—be thou my strong rock, for an house of (defense kjv) to ***SAVE ME.***

3 For thou art my rock and my fortress; therefore for thy NAME'S sake lead me, and guide me.

****

Ruth asked this question.

CONFUSION AND MORE LIFE, EXPLAIN

Humans are INFLUENCED unduly BY WORDS.

Dogs and cats, along with other free animals come and go when they desire, according to their own discretion and circumstance. They sleep when they are tired, and run, play, hunt, and eat when the urge hits them. The only animal that words unduly influence is the human species.

CONFUSION

The only thing that can save a person from the confusion of their own thoughts, and the thoughts as expressed by others, is faith in the Name of God to the point of stabilizing their mental faculties. Then and then only, can they become a Rock to withstand the waves of mental turmoil (extremely agitated conditions) in the world.

HOLY GHOST GUIDES

When a person calls upon the Name of God consistently, the Holy Ghost comes, takes up his abode in that person, and guides into the truth of all matters. It is then that the power of Christ flows like water from the inner being and stops the mouths of lions. That power saves and protects from the otherwise violent actions of men.

WHOSOEVER

Joel 2:32 And it shall come to pass, that WHOSOEVER shall CALL on the NAME OF THE LORD, SHALL BE DELIVERED. Acts 2:21, Romans 10:13 (saved).

****

CROSS

Is there a passage that shows Jesus could have avoided the cross?

James gave this response.

In the beginning God—Gen. 1:1

From God proceeded His Power, Christ, that created the heaven and the earth.

John 1:3 All things were made by him: and without him was not anything made that was made. (4) In him was life, and the life was the light of men.

When God said (Gen. 1:26) Let us make man in our image, after our likeness—He was speaking with His Son—Christ. (that power that proceeded from God).

Before the foundation of the world was laid, God knew man could fail because of the plan to give him his freedom of choice. Man could have stayed on that road which leads to life or he could take the other road that leads to death by destroying his spiritual, mental structure, and natural immune system because of the ingestion of the fruits of evil.

So from the foundation of the world God had an alternate plan in case man took the wrong road, first spiritual deviation from God, then mental confusion, and ultimately physical death because of a weakened immune system. Man was warned (Gen. 2:17), Thou shalt not eat of it:—if you do—you will surely die.

(Ref Deut 30:15—life-death) See, I have set before thee this day life and good, and death and evil; (16) In that I command thee this day to love the LORD thy God,—.

(17) But if thine heart turn away, so that thou wilt not hear, but shalt be drawn away, so that thou wilt not hear, but shalt be drawn away, and worship other gods, and serve them; (18) I denounce unto you this day, that ye shall surly perish, and that ye shall not prolong your days upon the land—. (19) I call heaven and earth to record this day against you, that I have set before you life and death, blessing and cursing: therefore choose life, that both thou and thy seed may live. (20) That thou mayest love the LORD thy God, and that thou mayest obey his voice, and that thou mayest cleave unto him: for he is thy life, and the length of thy days—.

God does not have pleasure in the death of him that dieth—Ezek. 18:32. So it was planned from the beginning that, at the appointed time God's Son would come to the earth in an attempt to make certain adjustments to the spiritual and psychological make up of the human species. Jesus determined, through his analysis, that men needed the Holy Ghost to guide them in the otherwise violent and deceptive world. So he prayed to his Father, God, to give men that spiritual gift as a comforter to abide with, and in them, as a permanent gift. John 14:16. God's will was Jesus' will. (John

8:29) I do always those things that please him.) They were working together to create the perfect man in the sixth day which we are still in. Jesus came as a life giving spirit (1 Cor. 15:45 The first man Adam was made a living soul; the last Adam was made a quickening spirit), to raise them up and to draw them into His Father's Name.

John 17:11.—Holy Father, keep through thine own NAME those whom thou hast given me, that they may be one as we are. (12) While I was with them in the world, I kept them in thy NAME—. John 17:26 I have declared unto them thy NAME, and will declare it: that the love wherewith thou hast loved me may be in them, and I in them.

Prov. 18:10 The Name (Tree of Life) of the Lord is a strong tower: the righteous runneth into it, and is safe.

IT COULD HAVE BEEN DIFFERENT.

Jesus put it this way to show that there was a possibility for the picture to change even when dealing with the religious system of godless men.

Matthew 21:37—Last of all he (God) sent unto them his Son, saying, ***THEY WILL REVERENCE MY SON***—.

But of course they didn't, so the alternate plan had to be carried out by Jesus. This plan he knew in advance and was a party to its creation.

Jesus despised the shame and endured the cross (Heb. 12:2) but the true picture was not seen by the people. Jesus felt no pain because he was in Paradise (Luke 23:43), second heaven state, where the first Adam had been placed.

John 19:32. Then came the soldiers, and brake the legs of the first, and of the other which was crucified with him. (33) But when they came to Jesus and saw that HE WAS DEAD ALREADY—.

All other scriptures as referenced by the other writers have been taken into consideration. Acts 2:23, John 10:15-18, Isaiah 53, John 6:38-40 also Gen. 3:15. And there are many other scriptures foretelling what must be done to retrieve man from his fallen condition and show him the way back to life. (Heaven—Paradise)

****

CROSS, WHAT DOES IT MEAN?

The POWER OF GOD " . . . save in the cross of our Lord Jesus Christ." Galatians 6:14

Odaatsissy asked this question.

" . . . take up and follow me . . ."

" . . . bear . . ."

" . . . come down from . . .

" . . . descend . . ."

" . . . take up daily . . ."

" . . . put it on . . ."

" . . . stood by . . ."

" . . . remain upon . . ."

" . . . enemies of . . ."

" . . . made of none effect . . ."

" . . . preaching . . . foolishness (to them that perish) . . ."

" . . . suffer persecution for . . ."

" . . . death of . . ."

" . . . peace through . . ."

" . . . nailing it . . ."

" . . . endured . . ."

That so much emphasis (26 verses in the NT) was placed on the cross of Jesus, I am curious about what the preaching of the cross means to you . . .

I have listed the verses below . . .

Mt:10:38: And →he that taketh not his cross,←and followeth after me, is not worthy of me.

Mt:16:24: Then said Jesus unto his disciples, If any man will come after me, let him deny himself, and →take up his cross, and follow me.←

Mt:27:32: And as they came out, they found a man of Cyrene, Simon by name: him they compelled to →bear his cross.←

Mt:27:40: And saying, Thou that destroyest the temple, and buildest it in three days, save thyself. If thou be the Son of God, →come down from the cross.←

Mt:27:42: He saved others; himself he cannot save. If he be the King of Israel, let him now →come down from the cross, ←and we will believe him.

Mk:8:34: And when he had called the people unto him

with his disciples also, he said unto them, Whosoever will come after me, let him deny himself, and →take up his cross, and follow me.←

Mk:10:21: Then Jesus beholding him loved him, and said unto him, One thing thou lackest: go thy way, sell whatsoever thou hast, and give to the poor, and thou shalt have treasure in heaven: and come, →take up the cross, and follow me.←

Mk:15:21: And they compel one Simon a Cyrenian, who passed by, coming out of the country, the father of Alexander and Rufus, to →bear his cross.←

Mk:15:30: Save thyself, and →come down from the cross.←

Mk:15:32: Let Christ the King of Israel →descend now from the cross,←that we may see and believe. And they that were crucified with him reviled him.

Lk:9:23: And he said to them all, If any man will come after me, let him deny himself, and →take up his cross daily, and follow me.←

Lk:14:27: And whosoever doth not →bear his cross,← and come after me, cannot be my disciple.

Lk:23:26: And as they led him away, they laid hold upon one Simon, a Cyrenian, coming out of the country, and →on him they laid the cross,← that he might bear it after Jesus.

Jn:19:17: And he →bearing his cross ← went forth into a place called the place of a skull, which is called in the Hebrew Golgotha:

Jn:19:19: And Pilate wrote a title, and →put it on the

cross.← And the writing was, JESUS OF NAZARETH THE KING OF THE JEWS.

Jn:19:25: Now there →stood by the cross ← of Jesus his mother, and his mother's sister, Mary the wife of Cleophas, and Mary Magdalene.

Jn:19:31: The Jews therefore, because it was the preparation, that →the bodies should not remain upon the cross← on the sabbath day, (for that sabbath day was an high day,) besought Pilate that their legs might be broken, and that they might be taken away.

1Cor:1:17: For Christ sent me not to baptize, but to preach the gospel: not with wisdom of words, →lest the cross of Christ should be made of none effect.←

1Cor:1:18: For →the preaching of the cross is to them that perish foolishness;← but unto us which are saved it is the power of God.

Gal:5:11: And I, brethren, if I yet preach circumcision, why do I yet suffer persecution? then is the →offence of the cross← ceased.

Gal:6:12: As many as desire to make a fair shew in the flesh, they constrain you to be circumcised; only lest they should →suffer persecution for the cross← of Christ.

Gal:6:14: But God forbid that I should →glory, save in the cross← of our Lord Jesus Christ, by whom the world is crucified unto me, and I unto the world.

Eph:2:16: And that he might reconcile both unto God in one body →by the cross,← having slain the enmity thereby:

Phil:2:8: And being found in fashion as a man, he humbled himself, and became obedient unto death, even the →death of the cross.←

Phil:3:18: (For many walk, of whom I have told you often, and now tell you even weeping, that they are the →enemies of the cross← of Christ:

Col:1:20: And, having made →peace through the blood of his cross,← by him to reconcile all things unto himself; by him, I say, whether they be things in earth, or things in heaven.

Col:2:14: Blotting out the handwriting of ordinances that was against us, which was contrary to us, and took it out of the way, →nailing it to his cross;←

Heb:12:2: Looking unto Jesus the author and finisher of our faith; who for the joy that was set before him →endured the cross,← despising the shame, and is set down at the right hand of the throne of God.

James gave this response.

What does the preaching of the cross mean?

Numbers 21:7 ***The people came to Moses and said, We have sinned.***

(8) The Lord said unto Moses, ***Make thee a fiery Serpent*** (a representation of the Serpent in the Garden of Eden—Serpent-man—Gen. 3:1), and ***set it upon a pole***: and it shall come to pass, that ***every one that is bitten (by sin as in the first Adam), when he looketh upon it, shall live.***

John 3:14—***As Moses lifted up the serpent in the wilderness, even so must the Son (Sun-Mal.4:2) of man***

(last Adam—1 Cor. 15:45)be lifted up: (15) That WHOSOEVER believeth in him (the Tree of life) should not perish, but have eternal life.

1 Cor. 15:22 **For as in Adam all die, even so in Christ shall all be made alive.**

Rom. 3:23—All have sinned, and come short of the glory of God; (24) Being justified freely by his grace through the redemption that is in Christ Jesus: (25) Whom God hath set forth to be a propitiation (gain or regain the favor of) through faith in his blood, to declare his righteousness for the remission of sins that are past, through the forbearance of God.

TOMBSTONE, ARIZONA 1961

James arose early. There were blocks to lay. The schedule must be kept day after day. The walls rose. The windows were set in place. The second week of the blocks came. The word Jesus, Jesus, Jesus was spoken with his inner voice continuously. His eyes—he could not keep them from gazing at the hill. Why did it bother him so? He must forget. His eyes must be kept from staring. Work harder. But he could not forget, nor could he erase the cross from his mind. There it stood on 'T' hill. ***He must go to the cross. It was inevitable. There was no way out.***

They must not know. He wouldn't want them to worry. It was too hot to walk to the foot of the hill. It was one p.m. I must go alone, he said to himself. No one can go with me. The station wagon motor started. It was backed from the drive way. It rolled east on Allen street, turned left onto the highway, and pulled off the road by the fence.

He climbed over the barbed wire fence and proceeded up the hill. The mesquite brushed by. Cactus needles came close. Radiant beams beat upon his head. Drops of sweat appeared.

The cross stood there. He must go to the cross. There was no other way.

He gazed at the sky. There was not a cloud. ***He was alone***. Where is God? Where did my Father go? ***My God, my God, why did you leave me?***

James sat down to rest. The eyes scanned the horizon. They moved slowly up and down the streets of Tombstone. No one was in sight. He remembered the saying IT'S DIFFERENT THIS TIME, I PROMISE YOU.

The base of the cross was there. The rocks were removed. The cross was lowered to the ground. He stood up and looked in the direction of Tombstone. He thought, Jesus had taken my place on the cross and the pole. 'It's different this time. He remembered the doubling over and the crying of God for what they did to His only begotten Son. He had sent his Son to the vineyard, thinking it was possible that they would reverence him, but they killed him. (Matthew 21:37).

Dear God, James said, We are also sorry for what they did to your Son, but all is not lost. If it had not been for him we would never have known of the power that is received by faith in you through him, and calling upon YOUR NAME.

James turned to the lifeless cross upon the ground. It was raised again toward the sky. The rocks were replaced around its base. It was set again for those that insist upon its worship. It will not hurt them as long as they see life as in the resurrection rather than death. But as for James and his house, they will look to Jesus, the Name of God, whom the heaven received until the times of restitution of all things. (Acts 3:21).

1 Cor. 1:18 For the preaching of the cross is to them that perish, foolishness, but unto us which are saved (from the effects of sin) IT IS THE POWER OF GOD.

Hebrews 12:2 Looking unto Jesus the author and finisher of our faith; who for the joy that was set before him endured the cross despising the shame, and is set down at the right hand of the throne of God.

Odaatsissy rated this answer:

YES!

****

CURSE OF THE EARTH

Ruth asked this question.

WILL THE CURSE EVER BE LIFTED FROM THE EARTH?

James gave this response.

No, it will be understood that the earth is only cursed with respect to each individual. When the mind is weighted down with condemnation caused by sin, it is not capable of healing the body and producing products for its nutritional needs.

CAIN

Gen. 4:11—Now art THOU CURSED from the earth, which hath opened her mouth to receive thy brother's blood from thy hand. (12) ***When thou tillest the ground, it shall not yield unto thee her strength—.***

Because of Cain's sin the earth was cursed, in that it did not produce for him. Water was available and nutrients were still in the soil but Cain's mind lacked understanding of how to produce the usual agricultural products because of the guilt that weighed upon it.

NOAH

Gen. 6:5 And God saw that the wickedness of man was great in the earth, and every imagination of the thoughts of his heart was only evil continually.

So God saved only eight human souls from the devastation of the flood. 1 Peter 3:20.

CURSE

Gen. 8:21—The Lord said in his heart, ***I will not again curse the ground any more for man's sake; for the imagination of man's heart is evil from his youth—. (Men are still young).***

BUT

Deut. 11:26 Behold, I set before you this day a BLESSING and a CURSE; (27) A BLESSING, if ye obey the commandment of the Lord your God, which I command you this day: (28) And a CURSE, if ye will not obey the commandments of the Lord your God, but turn aside out of the way which I command you—.

WEEDS AND BUGS—ARE THEY A CURSE?

No! If all the insects, bugs, weeds (even poison ones) and microscopic life is killed, humanity will become extinct. But that will not happen (no matter how much insecticides that are used—God strengthens their immune system and they produce stronger offspring) because it is not in the ultimate plan of God. It is God's desire that men live and understand his creation. EVERYTHING IS GOOD. Gen. 1:4, 10, 12, 18, 21, 25, 31.

It has only appeared to be an evil curse because men have become out of focus with God. They have seen evil when it was only good. They have called evil good, and good evil, and light for darkness, and bitter for sweet, and sweet for bitter. Isaiah 5:20.

MIND BALANCED BY CHRIST

The mind when balanced by Christ (the anointing of God) has the potential, through the immune system, of causing the body to live and destroy all harmful bacteria, viruses and all manner of diseases.

God through Jesus (His Name) can relieve the minds of the people after they begin to have faith in him, for during the time Jesus was on the earth, and as a result of their faith, God healed all manner of sickness and all manner of disease among the people. Matthew 4:23.

So it is the mind and faith in the Name of God, that causes healing. Any healing outside of that Name is short lived. It is an attempt to climb into heaven through other means while continuing to sin.

WILL THE CURSE BE LIFTED FOR MAN?

YES, WHEN MEN TURN TO GOD WITH THEIR WHOLE MIND.

Matthew 22:37 Jesus said,—Thou shalt love the Lord thy God with all thy heart, and with all thy soul, and with all thy MIND. (38) This is the first and great commandment. (39) And the second is like unto it, Thou shalt ***love thy neighbor as thyself***. (40) On these two commandments hang all the law and the prophets. **This will cure all the ills of the world.**

****

DAGGER

Silver dagger in the Bible Anonymous asked this question.

I met the phrase “silver dagger” in an essay. What does it mean?

James gave this response.

As you probably know by now the only reference to 'dagger' in the KJV is located in Judges 3:16-22. The proliferation of this kind of violence should not be continued either in essays or in any other media process. Men have patterned their activities from the actions of the other animals. Violence among humans is not the will of a loving God no matter in which book or social group it is found. The Bible is a recording of what men have said, thought and done, most of which is in opposition to the way of God.

Both ways are shown in the Bible for our learning and eventual understanding of God's perfect will. (1 Tim 3:16)

Proverbs 11:19 As righteousness tendeth to life: so he that pursueth evil pursueth it to his own death.

Genesis 6:11 The earth also was corrupt before God, and the earth was filled with violence. (12) And God looked upon the earth, and behold, it was corrupt; for all flesh had corrupted his way upon the earth.

Jesus said to Peter—Matthew 26:52 Put up again thy sword into his place: for ALL THEY THAT TAKE THE SWORD SHALL PERISH WITH THE SWORD.

Call upon the Name of the Lord and be saved from the violence of this present world. (Joel 2:32, Acts 2:21, Rom. 10:13)

Zeph. 3:9—Then will I turn to the people a pure language, that they may ALL CALL UPON THE NAME OF THE LORD, to serve him with one consent.

****

Darkness, Laws and Penalties.

John asked this question.

Should the actions caused by the fallen animalistic nature of men be judged by the laws and the penalties imposed by Moses or the teachings of Jesus?

James gave this response.

The sun is out there where it has always been since the first ignition of the gasses which brought light to the material objects in space, of which the earth is only one small part.

But the sun is not always visible because of the dark clouds, or the tall trees, the leaves of which hide the rays of the sun, and the heavy mist that cloud the minds of the masses in the world.

Natural clouds are created for the good of the earth. The trees breathe oxygen for the benefit of all animal life.

No, the dark clouds and the shading of the trees that do the most harm are those of a spiritual and mental nature. It was that darkness that enveloped the minds of men shortly after their beginning.

When men observed the actions of the other animals, they quickly patterned their own lives after the way of the beasts. In time little difference could be noted between them.

Genesis 6:11 The earth also was corrupt before God, and the earth was filled with violence.

It is not God's will that the violence of the past be perpetuated either by the orators or by printed matter. Good and evil are both written in the book. It is time for thinking humanity to have wisdom enough to know the difference between right and wrong. Pure wisdom and understanding cannot come without the gift of the Holy Ghost and the re-birth of the spirit.

'THOU SHALT NOT KILL' is written in the book of the law.

(Exodus 20:13) Jesus came not to do away with that law but to fulfill it (and also, to show he could conform to it). Matthew 5:17 He came to bring in the New Testament (Luke 22:20), but still Moses is being taught every week to the unwary. (Acts 15:21) It is right to teach the commandments, but it is not right to teach the penalties as advocated by Moses.

Jesus said (Matthew 5:38), Ye have heard that it hath been said, An eye for an eye, and a tooth for a tooth: But I say unto you (Matthew 5:44), LOVE YOUR ENEMIES.

John 1:17 The Law was given by Moses, but GRACE and ***TRUTH*** came by JESUS CHRIST.

God confirmed that the law was good and right, but He said, (Hebrew 10:38—Vengeance belongeth unto me, I will recompense, saith the Lord.

Deut. 32:35 To me belongeth vengeance, and recompense; THEIR FOOT SHALL SLIDE IN DUE TIME—.

When people are weighted down by their mind and spirit because of guilt, they are susceptible to all kinds of disease, accidents, fear, discouragement, depression, etcetera. Their foot shall slide in due time—

But Moses would not wait. He thought he was doing God service (John 16:2) when he gave instructions to kill the evil doers even though the commandment 'Thou shalt not kill' had been confirmed by God. (Exo. 20:13)

Moses imposed these penalties.

Exodus 21:24 Eye for eye, tooth for tooth, hand for hand, foot for foot, (25) Burning for burning, wound for wound, stripe for stripe.

Jesus said, (Matthew 5:38) Ye have heard that it hath been

said, An eye for an eye, and a tooth for a tooth: (39) But I say unto you, That ye resist not evil:

Jesus said, (Matthew 5:43) Ye have heard that it hath been said, Thou shalt love thy neighbor, and hate thine enemy. But I say unto you, Love your enemies—.

Moses said, (Lev. 20:10) The man that committeth adultery with another man's wife even he that committeth adultery with his neighbor's wife, the adulterer and the adulteress shall surely be put to death.

Jesus said to the adulteress, (John 8:11) I do not condemn you, go and sin no more.

Violence among the sons and daughters of God has never been the desire of their loving Father. God has mercy—people do not.

They fail to consider their own weaknesses when judging one another. ***God constructed the conscience and this is the tool by which people are judged.***

****

DEAD RAISED

Edward asked this question.

Will you please explain the 'DEAD BEING RAISED?'

James gave this response.:

After they did what men and women do, the man arose from the bed. He walked about fifteen feet, then collapsed and fell to the floor. He was having a heart attack. Immediately the ambulance was called. He was taken to the hospital.

The man could not be stabilized. Hours passed. The heart stopped. The doctors performed artificial respiration and cardiac pulmonary resuscitation. Even though the heart was not beating they continued messaging the heart for forty five minutes. The treatment was so severe that one of his ribs was broken in the process. There was no hope. The man was dead according to all the monitors. The tendons to his feet were cut so that his legs would not draw up from the contraction. They covered him with a sheet and moved him to another room.

The wife was called. She was asked to come to the hospital. There was no explanation as to why she should come. The wife, son and the daughter-in-law went to the hospital. The wife was asked to enter a room with the doctor. The son stood by listening.

“I’m sorry Mrs. Creed,” the doctor said sympathetically, “But your husband passed away about an hour ago. We performed C.P.R., but could not revive him. Even if he had survived, he would be nothing but a vegetable. His mind would be gone. The flow of blood which carries oxygen was kept from his brain for too long.”

The son walked to the hall. There was nothing else to do but call San Francisco.

“Hello, Charles?

“Jimmie, is that you? Where are you?”

“I am at the hospital in Phoenix, Arizona. Pop died of a heart attack. Will you call Jeanie in Portland, Oregon?”

The phone receiver was hung back on the wall. He stood pondering the situation. A nurse burst from the room where the father had been placed. She ran to the doctor. “That man is alive.”

The doctors and nurses rushed back to the room. The tendons to his feet had to be re-connected. Time passed. He was taken from intensive care and placed in another room. Family members spoke with the man. His mind was clear. He could remember everything. Passed and present episodes were recalled when questioned.

If this could happen with all the technology in the twentieth century, what should we suppose could have happened in the first century. What about comatose patients, very shallow breathing, faint pulse, fibrillations? A body can appear to be dead when they are not.

A person can come back to life as long as the body has not decayed. When they are resurrected after the destruction of the physical body they are 'AS THE ANGELS'(Matt.22:30) possessing a spiritual body only.

John 11:1 Now a certain man was sick, named Lazarus, of Bethany, the town of Mary and his sister Martha. (4) When Jesus heard—he said, "This sickness is ***NOT UNTO DEATH, BUT FOR THE GLORY OF GOD, that the Son of God might be glorified thereby***. (11)—After that he saith unto them, Our friend Lazarus sleepeth; but I go, that I may awake him out of sleep (coma). (12) Then said his disciples, Lord, if he sleep, he shall do well. (13) Howbeit Jesus spoke of his death: but they thought that he had spoken of taking of rest in sleep. (14) Then said Jesus unto them plainly, Lazarus is dead. (17) He had lain in the grave four days—. (39) Martha said, by this time he stinketh for he hath been dead four days.

John 11:40 Jesus saith unto Martha, if thou wouldest BELIEVE, thou shouldest see the glory of God. (43) (Jesus) cried with a loud voice, "Lazarus come forth."

Lazarus' body was in a comatous state (deep prolonged unconsciousness) and Jesus knew this. When this miracle is understood it ceases to be a miracle. This was all done so that the Name of God could be placed more vividly in the foreheads of people on the earth.

****

DEATH? END OF

John asked this question.

IS THE END OF DEATH POSSIBLE?

James gave this response.

The powers of darkness will influence the minds of everyone that will not call upon the Name of the Lord. But where the light of Christ is, there is no darkness at all. The minds will be filled with power to control every thought. There will be no harm to themselves or those around them. God has given the world to man, and man has at last found the power to subdue it. It is not in his own strength, but in the power of God that flows from his Name. Men are rising to a higher level of intelligence because of their faith in the Name of God. That faith is enhanced by calling upon it.

Do feelings of despair come to the mind? Do thoughts of condemnation flood the whole being? Do violent thoughts enter the mental and physical system? Be saved from this destructive force. Call upon the Name of Jesus.

Joel 2:32 And it shall come to pass, that WHOSOEVER shall call upon the NAME of the LORD shall be DELIVERED . . .

Acts 2:21 And it shall come to pass, that WHOSOEVER shall call upon the NAME of the LORD shall be SAVED.

Romans 10:17 For whosoever shall call upon the NAME of the LORD shall be SAVED.

Are those prophesies IRON-CLAD? It depends upon the willingness of people to believe and do it. The power of God does not flow through anyone that will not draw near God by HIS NAME. It is the belief in God and faith in His Name, plus calling upon it, that will save each individual from the destruction that is overshadowing the human minds.

Hebrews 11:6—he that cometh to God must believe that he is, and that he is a rewarder of them that diligently seek him.

Jesus said, (John 14:6) NO MAN cometh to the Father, but by me.

1 Cor. 15:22—as in Adam all die, even so in Christ shall ALL BE MADE ALIVE.

1 Cor. 15:23 But every man in his own order: Christ the first fruits; afterward they that are Christ's at his coming.

1 Cor. 15:24 Then cometh the end (the end of all destruction), when he shall have delivered up the kingdom to God, even the Father; when he shall have put down ALL RULE and all authority and power.

1 Cor. 15:25 For he must reign, till he hath put ALL ENEMIES under his feet.

1 Cor. 15:26 The last enemy that shall be destroyed is DEATH.

Isaiah 25:8 He will swallow up death in victory; and the Lord God will wipe away tears from off ALL faces—.

1 Cor. 15:54—then shall be brought to pass the saying that is written, Death is swallowed up in victory.

1 Cor. 15:55 O death, where is thy sting? O grave, where is thy victory?

Romans 7:24 O wretched man that I am! Who shall deliver me from the body of this death?

Romans 7:25 I thank God through Jesus Christ our Lord.

****

DEBATE AND OPPOSITION

Ronndonn asked this question.

What I am finding is that everyone I talk to has a point of view that they can explain and is helpful to them so I am thinking, why should I be opposed or debating anybody. If there is something that they believe that is helping them, then it is helping them and that is a good thing. We all change and grow and see new things all the time. So all sounds right to me. What do you think?

Aren't all these different interpretations and views just a sign of God's diversity in His creation. Sounds like it might be a good thing. What do you think?

James gave this response.

Romans 1:21-32

DEBATE is listed on the side of the many wrong devises created by the evil thoughts and actions of men. (Rom. 1:29)

1 Cor. 2:14 The natural man receiveth NOT the things of the Spirit of God: for they are foolishness unto him: neither can he know them, because they are spiritually discerned.

Debate alone cannot possibly change the base nature of men. The center of man's being must be filled with the Holy Ghost and the holy spirit of God. The holy spirit, when maintained, flows like water (John 7:38) to wash out all other impurities and gradually changes the fallen nature of man.

Paul said, (2 Cor. 12:20) I fear, lest, when I come,—there be DEBATES, envyings, wraths, strifes, backbitings, whisperings, swellings, tumults—. (Also Rom. 1:29)

1 Tim. 2:25—There is only ONE GOD, and ONE MEDIATOR between God and men, the man Christ Jesus.

DEBATE would be good if it could lead to that one God and one truth, but the best guide is the Holy Ghost. (John 16:13) Howbeit when he, the Spirit of truth is come, he will GUIDE you into ALL TRUTH—. John recorded that Jesus said (John 14:16), I will pray the Father, and he shall give you another Comforter, that he may abide with you FOR EVER; (17) Even the Spirit of Truth; whom the world CANNOT RECEIVE, because it seeth him not, neither knoweth him: but ye know him; for he dwelleth with you, and shall be in you.

It is a known fact that all of the experts are familiar with these passages, but sometimes in the press of the people's convincing words, we let them slip from our conscious thoughts. We try to compromise in hopes that we can save some, but the only way to be saved is believing that God IS (Heb. 11:6) and by calling upon his name JESUS. This is the only Name God selected to save the human inhabitants of this world from their sins and their ultimate destructive guilt.

Joel 2:32, Acts 2:21, Rom. 10:13.

Jesus, in reference to Capernaum, made the following statements, but such an idea can easily be applied here. Matthew 11:25 At that time, Jesus said, I thank thee, O Father, Lord of heaven and earth, because thou hast hid these things from the wise and prudent, and hast revealed them unto babes.

Call upon the Name of God fervently and he will give the Holy

Ghost in his due time, then the Holy Ghost will reveal all the truth. Truth is truth. There can be no DEBATE.

Ronndonn rated this answer:

Yes, the Holy Spirit. In spirit and in truth.

****

DENOMINATIONS, ON THE SUBJECT OF

STONY asked this question.

IT TOOK A PLAIN TALKING PREACHER FROM TEXAS IN MY CHURCH LAST SUNDAY TO BRING THIS OUT INTO THE LIGHT. THIS IS NOT A QUESTION BUT RATHER AN OBSERVATION. I'M NOT LOOKING FOR ANSWERS BUT IF YOU RESPOND IN GRACE AND HUMILITY I WILL RATE THEM WITH FAVOR.

HIS STATEMENT WAS THIS, "DENOMINATIONALISM DOES NOT TELL ME EXACTLY WHAT YOU BELIEVE, IT TELLS ME WHERE YOU STOPPED."

WHILE BEARING THIS IN MIND, CAN WE END THE USELESS AND NEEDLESS BICKERING BETWEEN ONE GROUP OF BELIEVERS AND ANOTHER? SEEING MORE SOULS SAVED IS OUR ONLY REQUIRED ACTION, WE ARE NOT THE JUDGE . . . .

James gave this response.

Names in religion do make a difference. Calling this to the attention should not be classified as useless and needless bickering. There are many ways and most of them are succeeding even in their own selected nomenclature. (system of names).

Gen. 11:4—They said, Go to, let us build us a city and a tower, whose TOP MAY REACH UNTO HEAVEN; and let us make us a NAME—.

Gen. 11:6 And the Lord said, Behold, the people is one, and this they begin to do: and now NOTHING will be RESTRAINED FROM THEM . . . . (7) Go to, let us go down, and there confound (confuse) their language, that they may not understand one another's speech.

There is only one way to reach heaven. There is only one way to be saved. Coming together in a wrong name is not the way to heaven.

Matthew 18:20 For where two or three are gathered together in MY NAME, there am I in the midst of them.

He did not say gather together in the name of your particular religious organizational name. They come together in the spirit of their own respective names. They say in effect, Let us be called by your Name to take away our reproach, but let us be known by our own name so that we may be separated from the others that do not believe the way we do.

Neither God, Jesus, nor the Holy Ghost reside in the midst of people through any other name.

Acts 4:12 Neither is there salvation in any other: for there is none other NAME under heaven given among men, WHEREBY WE MUST BE SAVED.

I am not attempting to answer a question because there was no question asked. I am only calling to the attention those passages that have already been known for many years. Most have never applied the story of the Tower of Babel to spiritual understanding, only to the development of various languages. But since they made the statement, 'Who's top may reach unto heaven,' it very well may also be applied to the many religious names as well.

Peace and tranquility (a quiet and undisturbed environment)cannot come through segregation or conformity. It must come through faith in and calling upon the Name of God, and coming together in that Name, no other.

2 Cor. 10:12 For we dare not make ourselves of the number, or compare ourselves with some that commend themselves: but they measuring themselves by themselves, and comparing themselves among themselves, are not wise.

****

DEPRESSION:

Charlene asked this question.

DEPRESSION, SHOULD IT COME WITH AGE?

James gave this response.

For those calling upon the name of the Lord it should be enjoyable to see the years flow by, for each year that passes is proof that God has the power to save.

(For) It shall come to pass, that WHOSOEVER shall CALL on the NAME of the LORD shall be saved. Acts 2:21.

There are too many destructive elements in the world to be enumerated individually here, but generally if we are not receiving more life we have not yet reached PARADISE where Jesus was living while physically on the earth.

Jesus said, I am come that they might have life, and that they might have it more abundantly. John 10:10.

Well, why didn't Jesus live longer on the earth?

Jesus was with His Father in the creation of all things. He came to the earth as the 'last Adam' (1 Cor. 15:45) to show men the way back to that spiritual state with the power of God, where the first Adam had resided. When that work was done, Jesus said (John 17:4), I have glorified thee on the earth: I have finished the work which thou gavest me to do. (5) And now, O Father, glorify thou me with thine own self, with the glory which I had with thee before the world was. (6) I have manifested THY NAME unto the men which thou gavest me out of the world—.

When the first man was created there was only one requirement, and that was to stay in contact with God by calling upon His name fervently. After all, the spiritual gravitational force was constant, therefore, man's contact with God must also be constant to off-set that power.

This act of loving God with all the heart, and with all the soul, and with all the mind, and with all the strength (Mark 12:31) was all embodied in the formula for reaching God and maintaining control over life in this otherwise violent destructive world.

This perfect plan would have worked if man and woman had maintained faith in God and called upon his Name relentlessly. By using this 'formula' they would have been able to withstand the spiritual forces and the changing elements that are always prevalent in the physical make up of the earth.

Not once during their life time did they call upon God. So they became too weak to withstand the visual images of the actions of the other animals around them. Those actions became part of their activities.

They had been created perfect. They knew from the beginning by natural instinct the difference between good and evil. They chose evil, and it was their evil actions that brought condemnation to their mental system and drove out the power of Christ, which is the guiding power for the instincts, and the light of understanding which lighteth every man which cometh into the world. (John 1:9) This was all on a spiritual and mental level.

But the same light of understanding governed their natural instincts so that they would know what to eat for the nourishment of their natural body. The woman knew she could eat of the natural fruit of the trees of the garden. (Gen. 3:2) This guidance of the spirit would play a major part in causing them to live forever. Even if the man had been bitten by a venomous viper his immune system would have quickly rallied to protect his life.(Acts 28:3)

Well, why did Adam live 930 years (Gen. 5:5) if he never called upon God by His Name for strength and guidance?

It has been said that the first man's longevity was attributed to the clean air and water, but it should be noted that the body of man was constructed to become stronger and stronger as the elements changed around him. If poisons were released into the air or water, or he ingested toxic substances from any other source on a gradual basis his body would become immune to the ingested material.

The first man was created after God's own image and likeness. (Gen. 1:26-27) His genes were created by his father God. His DNA was perfect. His internal parts were not contaminated by his physical ancestors as was the bodies of his offspring. This is the primary reason why it took so many years for his body to deteriorate and fall into decay.

In the beginning man was instructed to eat fruit and vegetables. (Gen. 1:29) And God said, Behold, I have given you every herb bearing seed, which is upon the face of all the earth, and every tree, in the which is the fruit of a tree yielding seed; to YOU IT SHALL BE FOR MEAT.

Even before the man was created God caused millions of plants to grow. This was done in preparation for the health and longevity of the human race upon the earth.

For thus saith the Lord that created the heavens; God himself that formed the earth and made it; he hath established it, he created it not in vain, he formed it to be inhabited: I am the Lord; and there is none else. (Isa. 45:18).

As God through Jesus at the appointed time, healed all manner of sickness and disease among the people, (Matthew 4:23) so he still has the power to save WHOSOEVER will call upon His Name. There is no reason for the elderly to be depressed.

****

Destructive Force v Holy Spirit:

Maxine asked this question

How is the destructive force affected by the Holy Spirit and Vice Versa?

James gave this response.

DESTRUCTIVE FORCE COMES FROM WITHIN.

It takes the holy spirit flowing from the innermost being to render the destructive force inoperable and drive it out.

Since men were created in the likeness of God (Gen.1:26), he placed within them the mechanism for the creation of (spiritual) life similar to the life force that flows from himself. By this similarity men are called the sons of God when they are born again of their spirit.

It is the destructive power of the mind that cripples, and disrupts the effects of the holy spirit, and drives the man from the presence of God, and from the heavenly realms of Paradise. When outside that realm man is not protected from the violent elements of the earth or the destructive minds of men.

Heaven for man was originally upon the earth. Heaven will return by man's knowledge of GOD'S NAME, and his acceptance of God's original purpose for the human race.

Men can live long lives as they did in the beginning of their existence. And since the arrival of Christ (the anointing of God) men may even have life more abundantly than they have had since the degeneration of man that has continued for the last forty thousand years.

Adam lived 930 years (Gen. 5:5)—Noah 950 years (Gen. 9:29)—Methuselah 969 years.(Gen. 5:27). Oh yes, those years were essentially the same in length as ours. The earth still travels around the sun in one year.

Jesus said, I am come that they might have LIFE, and that they might have it more abundantly. (John 10:10)

THE GIFT OF THE HOLY GHOST IS A MUST!

THE FILLING OF THE HOLY SPIRIT IS ALSO REQUIRED.

The Holy Ghost is a permanent gift. (John 14:16).

The Holy Spirit flows from within like water. (John 7:38). The Holy Ghost remains forever, but without proper maintenance the Holy Spirit can stop flowing and dissipate, allowing the mind to lead back into destructive activities.

****

DEVILS

Maxine asked this question.

Please explain casting out a devil. What causes the problem and what is the cure?

James gave this response.

CASTING A DEVIL OUT.

The stark reality of his past sins came crashing down upon his head as the voice turned violently upon him.

"YOU'LL HAVE TO TELL THE WORLD."

"No! No! I must not tell the world. I can't. I just can't. Why must my guilt be confessed to the world? What would they think? The string, the string, where is the string. I have to leave."

Jim jumped to the floor. Ruby was just inside the kitchen door. He began to speak without thought, as if something was speaking through him.

"YOU WILL SEE ME PULL MY HAIR OUT."
"ELDON WILL PUT IT BACK."
"THEY WILL TAKE ME AND TEAR ME."
"YOU WILL SEE ME EXPERIENCE EPILEPSY."
"I WILL BE A MAD MAN AND SPIT UPON THE FLOOR."

"Oh no, I can't see that. I don't want to see it." Ruby doubled over in crying for fear.

"There's no reason to cry. It's too late now. You will have to see it. I have said it. You have heard it. Now you must see it."

Jim looked at the children. They seemed to be unconcerned and unaffected. "Charlene, come here,—say Jesus all the time. Zenaide, say Jesus, Terrence, say Jesus, Maxine, say Jesus. We can go all the way through this, if you will continue to call upon Jesus."

Great floods of fear came over Jim as another pang took hold of his brain. “They will not get me,—my coat. I must run, quickly, my coat. I have to leave here.”

“Where will you go?” Ruby asked.

Jim ran to the closet, yanked the coat from the hanger then turned for the door. With the coat halfway on, he grabbed at the knob, but with that movement came the realization that he had no place else to run. Not knowing where to go he felt like a trapped animal. The wall, the wall—. He jumped for the top of the door facing. He could not reach it. He must climb the wall. The hurt, the fear, he could not rid himself of it. The string, he must get himself up and out of there.

Another pang of fear made a jab at his brain. He grabbed his hair with both hands and must get it out, all of it. He pulled and tugged. It made his brain feel better. Twisting his hands from side to side—why won’t it come out?

Tears were streaming down Ruby’s face. A voice spoke with her.

“GO CAST THE DEVIL OUT OF HIM.”

“I cannot. I do not know how,” She said, but what else was there to do? How else would the end come to this?

If only he could get his hair out, he would feel better. Maybe he should have taken less hair in each fist. He was facing the wall he had just attempted to climb, pulling with all his strength. Ruby was standing beside him. She said,

“DEVIL, COME OUT OF THIS MAN THROUGH THE NAME OF JESUS.”

Jim’s body fell to the floor. It lay limp and motionless. He looked at his hands. There were strands of hair between each finger.

He felt his head. All of his hair had not been taken. He felt relieved that his words had not all come true. He had visualized blood on his head, but there was no blood.

Fear was gone for awhile. He walked over to the bed, relaxed upon his back. Just like the undulations of the ocean waves, another one was coming. He would not dare stop calling upon the Name of the Lord.

Not then. It was his only chance to live, and be free of himself.

IF THERE WERE NO MINDS THERE WOULD BE NO DEVILS.

Many things cause deranged minds, too many sources to itemize them all here, but excessive usage of alcohol and cigarettes over a period of years caused this particular derangement. The intensity of this mental condition was caused by withdrawing from the usage of alcohol and cigarettes ten days prior to this time without nutritional and spiritual help. Guilt for past sins contributed greatly to this man's dilemma. Those acts of sin were caused partly by the consumption of alcoholic beverages.

****

DEVIL—CONTINUED

Edward asked this question.

How do we keep that Devil out of our heads?

James gave this response.

A campground—Arizona 1961

Distant shouts with songs of praise filtered into the tabernacle from somewhere on the grounds. Ruth and James arose from the bench to follow in its direction. They stepped to the door. It was one of the school buildings.

The instruments made joyful noises, entrancing the minds and transporting them to realms of unreality. The people lay upon the floor. James had been there. It was not his intention to degrade.

One young man was in fact a helicopter. His left arm and right foot were going round and round. It was the rotor blade. It was plain to see he had either good or bad experience with them in order for his mind to be impressed in such a manner. He stood to his feet. A bible was placed on the top of his head. He jumped up and down.

Ruth and James moved closer to him. "Why the action and the bible used in this manner?" James asked.

He looked at James while yet jumping and said, "Some minister told me I had trouble with sex devils, so I'm trying to get away from them by keeping the Bible on my head."

James spoke with him above the noise. "No sex devil or any other kind will get in you if you will just call upon Jesus all the time, inside yourself, of course, with your inner voice. Don't let it be outward. It is an inward work. God wants you to have a good appearance."

The Bible was slowly removed from his head. He started calling upon the Name of the Lord silently inside himself. He was so astonished that the devils were nowhere around, that he stated with a loud voice, "It works! It works!"

He shook hands and left saying, "Thank you brother, thank you."

Jeremiah 10:23 O Lord, I know that the way of man is not in himself: it is not in man that walketh to direct his steps.

Try ever so hard, the thoughts cannot be controlled by man without spiritual help. Actions, either good or bad, are spawned by thoughts. The Bible is a recording of the thoughts and actions of men versus the will of God. Without the continual flow of the Holy Spirit from the inner being, men will always fall prey to the thoughts that ramble through their heads. Oh yes, the acts of sex and violence are portrayed throughout the pages of man's history in the majority of the books written from olden times. This includes the Bible. Men have fallen from their original heavenly state (Paradise). It is time for them to return.

****

DIABETES

Maxine asked this question.

IS DIABETES BEING CONTROLLED?

James gave this response.

For those calling upon the Name of the Lord for proper guidance there is help.

A TRUE EXPERIENCE

In 1986 the doctor asked Ruby if she had any history of diabetes in her family. She said, Yes, my mother died with diabetes.

He said, You are on the borderline now so I am going to give you some pills to keep it in check.

Despite the pills Ruby's diabetes progressed until one day while she was sitting on the side of the bed she fell over into a deep sleep. After being aroused she was taken to the St Joseph Medical Center for lab work (Glycohemogl, Gluscose) on 2-28-92, 4-27, and 6-7-1992. It was determined at that time she was no longer borderline but had developed diabetes.

During the interim she was going to the doctor where the nurses administered the finger sticks and the insulin shots. Ruby still did not want to accept the on-set of diabetes and could not bring herself to administer her own shots.

Because of the frequency of the insulin shots she was instructed that she must obtain a Glucose Monitor and administer her own shots. She bought the Tracer 11 blood Glucose Monitor on 6-9-92 from the Fifth Street Pharmacy.

She was taking 36 Novolin N and 10 Novolin R in the morning and 15 N and 6 R in the evening.

In the middle 90s she began taking vitamin and mineral supplements, but continued with the same level of fatty foods. One doctor had told her that after being on insulin for as long as she had been, she would never get off of it.

In the month of July, 2000, she weighed 278 pounds. By October 7th, her weight was down to 256. This weight loss was due to her spasmodic dieting. During this time the doctor said she could start lowering the insulin.

On 10-17-2000, her daughter, Maxine, gave her a book entitled 'The Diabetes carbohydrate and Calorie Counter'—Natow—Heslin. Her weight at that time was 251-1/2.

After perusing the pages she decided to go on a strict 1200 calorie per day diet. As the weight came down she had to lower the insulin injections. As of June 7, 2001 she weighed 216 1/4.

The Doctor said he was not issuing any more prescriptions for insulin or needles because the blood test from the last report, one month prior, showed just a flick of sugar in the blood. And that if she continues with her present diet there should be no more problems. On June 30, 2001, she stopped her insulin shots.

Since August 4, 2002 Ruby's weight has been fluctuating between 161 and 165. Insulin is a thing of the past and she seldom has a need for checking her blood sugar.

Thanks to medical science and profession; to the vitamin and mineral industry; to publications and computers for making information available, and most of all to the guidance of the Holy Ghost which stimulates the natural instincts so that all that are endowed with that power can recognize what is needed in each individual case.

Acts 1:8—Ye shall receive power, after that the Holy Ghost is come upon you—.

John 16:13—When he, the Spirit of Truth, is come, he will guide you into ALL TRUTH—.

Romans 8:28—We know that ALL THINGS work together FOR GOOD to them that love God, to them who are the called according to his purpose.

God is working within the whole process to advance the truth about heaven on earth and developing the power of HIS NAME within the minds of the people.

Some may say I also have lost weight and am no longer dependant upon insulin, and I do not call upon the Name of the Lord.

The magicians did all the things God did through Moses and Aaron, (Exo.7:10-19)

BUT THEY COULD NOT CAUSE LIFE NOR SUSTAIN IT.

Jesus said, I am come that they might have life and that they might have it more abundantly. (John 10:10)

It shall come to pass, that WHOSOEVER shall CALL ON THE NAME OF THE LORD SHALL BE SAVED. Acts 2:21

WHAT DO WE NEED TO BE SAVED FROM? EVERY DESTRUCTIVE ELEMENT OF THE EARTH.

1 Corinthians 2:9 Eye hath not seen, nor ear heard, neither have entered into the heart of man, the things which God hath prepared for them that love him.

****

DINOSAUR

RENEE asked this question.

ACCORDING TO THE BIBLE DID MAN AND DINOSAUR WALK THE

EARTH AT THE SAME TIME?

Queenybee gave this response.

DID MAN AND DINOSAUR WALK THE EARTH AT THE SAME TIME?

QUOTE— "As an archaeologist and geologist, With regard to the time of their disappearance, human fossils occur in rock layers well above those containing dinosaur fossils and that there are rock layers in between. In many parts of the world, these intervening rock layers, or strata, also contain fossils. Many new varieties, or kinds, of animals appear in these layers, such as elephants, saber-toothed cats, and several varieties of flightless running birds. This would strongly suggest that God was still creating new animals AFTER the dinosaurs were gone and that the dinosaurs disappeared during the sixth creative epoch".

The Bible does not specify the time of either the creation or the disappearance of dinosaurs.

Rlee gave this response.

Dinosaurs and man did walk the earth at the same time. They have found very old native American cave paintings that show people running away from some of the big dinosaurs. There were some rocks found in South America that have carvings of dinosaurs on them. So, yes, man and dinosaurs did walk the earth at the same time.

James gave this response.

The above seem to be in conflict with one another. But does it really matter. When I was twelve years of age and until my twentieth birthday I was taught that with God, one creative day was 7 x 7 = 49,000 years. It still is not clear to me how they determined those figures, or what proofs they had, but if that is the case then the sixth day = 49,000 years. Whether this is true is yet to be determined, but let us use it as a tool for thought.

It is easy to speak and write of millions of years since the beginning of the creation of animal life, but there is no proof of land animals existing more than forty eight thousand years ago. Even the carbon dating process is not always accurate. Even before man's recorded history there were many upheavals in the surface of the earth by earth quakes, volcanos, floods, etcetera. This could have easily displaced the original location of fossils.

During the fifth 49,000 year period, (Gen. 1:20-23) God created whales, other living creatures, (this period could have included some strain (lineage) of the Dinosaurs) and winged foul that the waters of the ocean brought forth. Then the foul began to multiply in the earth.

5th day = 49,000 years—Dinosaurs

During the first 8000 years of the sixth 49,000 year period God caused the beasts of the earth to come forth.

6th day

Eight thousand years—Beasts

Forty thousand years—Man

One thousand years left before the end of the sixth day.

Genesis 1:24 And God said, Let the EARTH bring forth the living creature after his kind, cattle, and creeping thing, and beast of the earth after his kind: and it was so.

The fact is that ***the soil of the earth is teaming with life or potential life, and at the proper time that life comes forth as rapidly as vegetation appears in the spring time of each year.***

Even man and the lower forms of animal life came from that same soil. (Gen. 2:7 Gen. 2:19) And the Lord God formed man of the dust of the ground—. Gen. 3:19 Dust thou art, and unto dust shalt thou return.

During the first part of the 9000 years into the sixth day God made man.

Gen. 1:26 And God said, Let US make man in our image, after our likeness: and let them have dominion over the fish of the sea, and over the fowl of the air, and over the cattle, and over all the earth, and over every creeping thing that creepeth upon the earth.

If this analogy is correct, then that means man has been on the earth for approximately 40,000 years at the beginning of the year 2001. This also means there are still 1000 years before the end of the six day. God is not resting yet.

Regarding Rlee's response.

Let us consider this:

Dinosaur bones have been found in various places around the world. There are many such findings here in the United States. **Isn't it logical that the native Americans, and those in South America found such Dinosaur bones, and at the time of their artistic moments painted and carved what**

they thought had roamed the earth in the distant past based upon those findings?

Dinosaurs—What happened to them?

They were plentiful and colossal with voracious appetites. They ate themselves out of existence. After the accessible vegetation was gone from the land and sea they began eating each other until they became extinct.

Look what has happened in the last six thousand years of recorded history. Why would it be so difficult to believe the things that could have transpired during the 49,000 years of the fifth day, and the first eight thousand years of the sixth day before the advent of man?

****

DOCTORS—HEALING AT ALL TIMES?

Sirach 38 : 1-15

(Not to be disclosed) asked this question.

I finally found the book in the bible talking about Sickness and Medicine. I asked the question about where in the bible it says for us to go to doctors and let them help us.

Short version of what it says.

Give doctors the honour they deserve. The Lord gave them work to do. Their skill came from the most high. Their knowledge gives them a position of importance. The lord created medicines from the earth, a sensible person will not hesitate to use them. He gave medical knowledge to human beings, so that we would praise him for the miracles he performs. Druggist mixes these medicines, and the doctor will use them to cure diseases and ease pain. There is no end to the activities of the lord who gives health to the people of the world. When you get sick do not ignore it. Pray to the lord and he will make you well. Confess all your sins. Determine that in the future will give a righteous life. Call the doctor, for the lord created him and keep him at your side. There are times when you have to depend on his skill.

This is from the Good News Bible with Deuterocanonicals/ Apocrypha English version.

James gave this response

Healing at all times?

Eccl. 3:1 To everything there is a season, and a time to every purpose under the heaven.

Deut. 8:15 There are times of the rains and then there are years of drought, where there is no water. It is during these times the water must be released from behind the flint rock (Exo.17:6) or pumped from previously prepared reservoirs.

When the power of the Lord was present to heal (Ref. 5:17), God instantly healed the back of one and kidney infection was relieved in another. Lingering pain from a previously broken bone was instantly taken away.

When the power of the Lord is not present to heal, God in his mercy has prepared other means of healing until the light of the perfect day arrives.

John 1:9 That (Christ) was the true Light, which lighteth EVERY MAN that cometh into the world.

Doctors are in the profession of healing. They pray too that God will assist them in their knowledge and understanding to heal in the time of need; when the time is not exactly right for the flow of healing virtue from that perfect spiritual force.

There were times when God did not heal through Jesus all the multitudes that needed physical and spiritual help. There were other times that he did.

****

DOCTRINES: VARIABLE

Ruth asked this question.

Variable doctrines over time regarding the health and Well-being of mankind—WHAT IS THE ANSWER TO IT ALL?

James gave this response.

A group of Pharisees and lawyers asked Jesus, Why do your disciples not wash their hands before meals? Matthew 15:3 (The New English Bible—Oxford Cambridge.)

Jesus called the crowd and said to them, 'Listen to me, and understand this: a man is not defiled by what goes into his mouth, but by what comes out of it.' Matthew 15:10. Jesus was concerned primarily about the words that produce condemnation. Those utterances damage the mind and spirit. They bring heaviness of mind and this weight lowers the natural bodies resistance to diseases.

FULL CIRCLE . . .

2000 B.C. Here eat this root.

AD 1000: That root is heathen, here say this prayer.

AD 1850: That prayer is superstition, here drink this potion.

AD 1940: That potion is snake oil, here swallow this pill.

AD 1980: That potion is ineffective, here take this antibiotic.

AD 2000: That antibiotic doesn't work.

The Lamplighter:

(The body has become immune to it—This is God's plan devised to save the body of men from the destructive elements in the world.)

****

AD 2001 The millennium.

When the mind is relieved of the weight of condemnation, it is free to do the work it was designed to do, namely, to control the well being of the body through the immune system. When operating at its full potential, the immune system can destroy all invading foreign physical substance that could cause diseases and destroy the body. It takes the vitamins and minerals received in the available ingested food products and ***manufactures what is needed*** for the health of the body. This is why the body was made omnivorous. (The ability to eat meat, and/or fruit and vegetables).

A guilty conscience is a weight upon the mind and causes a depressed physical system. When the mind is relieved by the spirit of God, the person returns to his/her right mind, and with the ingestion of food the body can be returned to normal. Mark 5:15

IT IS NECESSARY TO EAT NATURAL FOOD FOR STRENGTH.

When Saul received his natural sight and was baptized, he still needed natural food for strength. Acts 9:18 And immediately there fell from his eyes as it had been scales: and he received sight forthwith, and arose, and was baptized. (19) ***And WHEN HE HAD RECEIVED MEAT (food), he was strengthened.***

The daughter of a ruler of the Synagogue died. Luke 8:49.

Luke 8:54 (Jesus) took her by the hand, and called, saying, Maid, arise. (55) And her spirit came again, and she arose straightway: and ***he commanded to give her meat (Natural food).***

TAKE NO THOUGHT

Matthew 6:25 Take ***no thought*** for your life, ***what ye shall eat, nor what ye shall drink,*** nor yet for your body, (26) Behold the fowls of the air; for they sow not, neither do they reap, nor gather into barns; yet your heavenly Father feedeth them. ARE YE NOT MUCH BETTER THAN THEY?

ANSWER?

Matthew 22:37 Jesus said—Thou shalt love the Lord thy God with all thy heart, and with all thy soul, and with all thy MIND. Jesus said John 17:12 While I was with them in the world, I kept them in Thy Name—.

HOW DO WE STAY IN GOD'S NAME?

Call upon God by His Name without ceasing. (1 Ths.5:17)

Acts 2:21 And it shall come to pass, that WHOSOEVER SHALL CALL ON THE NAME OF THE LORD SHALL BE SAVED.(Joel 2:32, Rom 10:13).

By staying in contact with God, the power of God through the Holy Ghost will guide in ***every phase of our lives***. There is nothing God cannot, or will not do for mankind when they are calling upon Him by His Name without ceasing. ***What we need***

for our physical, mental, and spiritual well being will all be supplied by the direction of the spirit.

Each body is different at any given time. God is aware of all its complications and has devised the answer from the beginning. Call upon God with the inner voice and be saved from every conceivable destructive element.

This is what God told Adamah to do in the beginning, but he forgot—.

***TAKE HOLD OF THE TREE OF LIFE—
THE NAME OF GOD AND LIVE.***

****

DRINK—ANY DEADLY THING

Kathy asked this question.

Please explain Mark 16:18— if they drink any deadly thing {inadvertently or unknowingly} it shall not hurt them.

James gave this response.

An Arab woman had been won to Christ from Mohammedanism.

Her family became very upset and coaxed, argued and threatened to draw her from her new faith, but it was all in vain. Then they concocted a simple, but deadly poison, and secretly put it in her food. When she had eaten the meat containing the poison, she realized very quickly what had happened, and knew how deadly it was.

She knew she was doomed to die. The poison would make her very irritable, then very sluggish; then it would affect her mind even more and after that her body. Then the inevitable—DEATH.

She was greatly startled and distressed, and did not know what to do. As she sat, ***WITHOUT PLANNING TO*** (this shows that God is delivering this message to the world), she began to repeat the NAME, the great NAME. Not aloud but to herself she repeated with great intensity. ***Jesus,Jesus, Jesus.*** For two or three days she continued. (She had lost track of time). While the family was watching for death, they saw life gradually coming back into her body. Their scheme had failed. The poison had failed. She told the missionary, Each time I said that NAME, I felt as though there was a wave of life, in between the waves of death, until finally there was nothing but waves of life. (Ref. also Acts 28: 3-5)

The NAME of the Lord is a strong tower: the righteous runneth into it and if safe. Proverbs 18:10

Psalm 61:2 From the end of the earth will I cry unto thee, when my heart is overwhelmed: lead me to the rock that is higher than I. (3) For thou hast been a shelter for me, and a strong tower from the enemy.

Joel 2:32 And it shall come to pass, that WHOSOEVER shall CALL on the NAME of the LORD shall be delivered—.

Acts 2:21 And it shall come to pass, that WHOSOEVER shall CALL on the NAME of the LORD shall be saved. (Also Romans 1:13).

Two or three witnesses are needed to establish every word.

John 8:17. It is also written in your law, that the testimony of two men is true. In the mouth of two or three witnesses every word may be established. Matthew 18:16.

Jesus said (John 14:6)—I am the WAY, the TRUTH, and the LIFE—.

The bible is full of witnesses for calling upon the name of the Lord without ceasing. Psalm 113:3 From the rising of the sun unto the going down of the same the LORD'S NAME is to be praised. Psalm 119: 55 I have remembered thy NAME, O LORD, in the night—.

Please read JAPAM in this alphabetical series of answers.

****

DYING WITH SIN.

Charlene asked this question.

What happens as the brain cells die?

James gave this response.

In God's mercy a whirlwind of conglomerated memories flood the mental system until the whole being is immersed with the feelings of bliss Then complete quiet and perfect peace prevails forever.

Romans 6:23 The wages of sin is death; but the gift of God is ETERNAL life through Jesus Christ our Lord.

Eccl. 9:5 The living know that they shall die: but the dead know not anything, neither have they any more a reward; for the memory of them is forgotten. (6 Also their love, and their hatred, and their envy, is now perished; neither have they any more a portion for ever in any thing that is done under the sun.

In interviews with over 3,000 people who were revived after they died during surgery or in accidents, the researchers discovered that virtually every one of them experienced an otherworldly journey to a place of perfect bliss.

In each instance, the subject reported leaving their bodies and moving upward with incredible speed. At some point during their journey, they found themselves traveling through a tunnel toward a point of blinding white light.

Arriving at the end of the tunnel, they recalled stepping into the light, which brilliantly illuminate a great shining city peopled with the souls, or 'essences, of everyone and everything that had lived and died before them.

The subjects reported that they were overcome with a feeling of peace, serenity, tranquility and bliss.

Even more important, the subjects said they were flooded with an immediate and complete understanding of all that was, all that is, and all that is yet to be.

Though they found their experiences next to impossible to describe with mere words, they are convinced that they were given a glimpse of the wonderful eternity that waits us all.

In most cases, the subjects met and spoke with long departed friends, relatives and PETS. These meetings weren't one to one. They occurred all at the same time in what one woman called 'an explosion of consciousness.' She said it was like having a reunion with everyone at once. When you die, you'll understand.

Clergymen the world over are hailing the study as final confirmation that God really is merciful—and truly loves mankind.

THEY HAVE BEEN SENT A STRONG DELUSION: THAT THEY BELIEVE A LIE, BECAUSE THEY HAVE NOT

BELIEVED THE TRUTH THAT GOD INTENDS MAN AND WOMAN TO LIVE ON THE EARTH, IN PARADISE, WHERE HE PLACED THE FIRST COUPLE.

2 Thessalonians 2:7 The mystery of iniquity will be revealed, whom the LORD shall consume with the spirit of his mouth (his words), and shall DESTROY with the brightness of HIS COMING. (9) Even him whose coming is after the working of Satan with all power and signs and lying wonders. (10) And with all deceivableness of unrighteousness in them that PERISH, because they received not the LOVE OF THE TRUTH THAT THEY MIGHT BE SAVED. (11) And for this cause GOD SHALL SEND THEM STRONG DELUSION, THAT THEY SHOULD BELIEVE A LIE.(12) That they all might be damned who believed not the truth.

1 Cor. 15:24 Then cometh the end, when he shall have delivered up the kingdom to God, even the Father; when he shall have put down all rule and all authority and power.

1 Cor. 15:25 For he must reign, till he hath put all enemies under HIS feet.

1 Cor. 15:26 ***THE LAST ENEMY THAT SHALL BE DESTROYED IS DEATH.***

****

EARTH UNHOLY

2 Kings 5 (Biblical history question)

Gaelic asked this question.

I have a question about Elisha and Naaman (the Syrian leper he cured).

In 2 King 5:17, after he has been healed and offered Elisha

money, and Elisha has refused it, he asks if he may be given two mule loads of earth; "for your servant will no longer offer burnt offering or sacrifice to other gods, but to the Lord."

Why would he ask for 2 mule loads of earth? And what would this have to do with not sacrificing to other gods. It's not a big point . . . but I'd still like to understand it.

James gave this response.

Please bear with me while I expand the value of the earth.

God made the earth and he saw that it was good. (Gen. 1:10) ***The only pollution in the soil, to make it unholy, have been caused by man.***

God is an individual. The power of God that emanates (comes forth) from God flows into everybody and everything. This power (Christ) is the anointing from God. This is the true light, which lighteth every man that cometh into the world. (John 1:9) This is the power used to create all things.

Col. 1:16—By him (Jesus—through Christ) were all things created, that are in heaven, and that are in earth, visible and invisible, whether they be thrones, or dominions or principalities, or powers: all things were created by him, and for him. (17) And he is before all things, and by him all things consist.

The earth (soil) in one area is no better than the earth in another location. Christ made it all. But Naaman did not thoroughly understand this.

Jesus informed the woman of Samaria—(John 4:21) Woman, believe me, the hour cometh, when ***ye shall neither in this mountain(Gerizim), nor yet at Jerusalem, worship the Father***. (23) But the hour cometh and now is, when the true worshippers shall ***worship the Father in spirit and in truth:*** for the Father seeketh such to worship him. (24) God is 'A'

Spirit: (signifying one) and they that worship him must worship him in spirit and in truth.

1 Tim. 2:8 I will therefore that men pray EVERYWHERE—.

Paul said (Eph. 3:9) And to make ALL men see what is the fellowship of the mystery, which from the beginning of the world hath been hid in God, who created all things by Jesus Christ.

Why did God speak with Moses thusly? . . .

Exodus 3:5 Put off thy shoes from off thy feet, for the place whereon thou standest is holy ground.

The earth had been polluted by idolatry and the spilling of blood as a result of their violence. It was for this reason that Naaman said, (2 Kings 5:17) Shall there not then, I pray thee, be given to thy servant two mules burden of earth? for ***thy servant will hence forth offer neither burnt offering nor sacrifice unto other gods, but unto the LORD.***

Even the offering of animals was rejected by God as was shown by Hebrews 10:5. Sacrifice and offering thou wouldest not, but a body hast thou prepared me.

Hebrews 9:8 The Holy Ghost this signifying, that the way into the holiest of all was not yet made manifest, while as the first tabernacle was yet standing: (9) Which was a figure for the time then present, in which were offered both gifts and sacrifices, that **could not make him that did the service perfect, as pertaining to the conscience.**

The conscience can only be cleared by the Power of God—***Christ.***

****

EDEN, Conditions in . . . ?

(Not to be disclosed) asked this question.

Given the fact that the serpent spoke to Eve in the Garden of Eden, apparently without any reaction of shock or surprise on her part, and given the fact that Balaam's donkey possessed the power of speech at least on one instance, is it possible that, in the original Creation, all creatures possessed the capability of speech?

James gave this response.

Did a serpent actually talk with the woman?

YES, THE SERPENT DID TALK WITH THE WOMAN!

PEOPLE ARE CALLED SERPENTS—VIPERS.

Matthew 23:33 ***Ye serpents, ye generation of vipers***, how can ye escape the damnation of hell?

Matthew 12:34 ***O generation of vipers***, how can ye being evil, speak good things? For out of the abundance of the heart the mouth speaketh.

Matthew 3:7 But when he (John the baptizer) saw many of the Pharisees and Sadducees (Men) come to his baptism, he said unto them, ***O generation of vipers,*** who hath warned you to flee from the wrath to come?

THE SERPENT WAS THE SUBTLETY IN MAN

(Hardly noticeable, clever way of getting what he wants).

Genesis 3:1 Now the ***serpent (mind of Adamah-man) was more subtle than any beast of the field*** (he was the most intelligent of all the animals) which the Lord God had made. And he (Adam) said unto the woman

(he wanted to bring up the subject) Yea, hath God said, Ye shall not eat of every tree of the garden?

Genesis 3:2 And the woman said unto the serpent (Adamah-man), We may eat of the fruit of the trees of the garden (Natural fruit of the natural trees):

Genesis 3:3 But of the fruit of the tree which is in the midst of the garden,(God had placed the man and the woman in the midst of the garden. Gen. 2:8 & 22) God hath said, Ye shall not eat of it, (partake of it) neither shall ye touch it, lest ye die.

Natural snakes do not talk. They have never talked and will never talk.

Parable: Simple story illustrating a moral truth.

Jesus often spoke with the people in parables. Matt 13:10, 13, etc. He made use of them to veil the truth from those who were not willing to see it. Those who really desired to know would not rest till they had found out the meaning.

Mat. 13:34 All these things spake Jesus unto the multitude in parables; and without a parable spake he not unto them.

THAT OLD SERPENT

And the great dragon was cast out, ***that OLD SERPENT, called the DEVIL, and Satan, which deceiveth the whole world—. (Rev. 12:9)***

Who was the OLD SERPENT? It was and is natural men, that

do not have spiritual minds. They think in natural terms and are guided by their own thoughts.

1 Cor. 2:14 The natural man receiveth not the things of the Spirit of God: for they are foolishness unto him: neither can he know them, because they are spiritually discerned.

DOES THE DONKEY TALK?

In dealing with Balaam and his encounter with the Angel of the Lord, Numbers 22:22-35, it must be considered what God can do with the mind. ***God has the power to produce words directly to the brain of individuals.***

Voices are heard by many people every day, especially during the times of mental stress.

A DONKEY DOES NOT SPEAK WITH HUMAN WORDS.

****

Eden, garden of, is where?

(Not to be disclosed) asked this question.

It was a real Garden. It was blocked by real angels. Do we have any clues as to what happened to it, the Garden of Eden? Is it to be identified with"paradise" ? Did it survive the flood? Was it transferred to heaven? Is it somehow miraculously preserved on earth? The tree of life is there . . .

James gave this response.

The Tree of Life was in the Garden of Eden. Gen. 2:9 (Turkey).

Revelation 2:7 He that hath an ear, let him hear what the Spirit saith unto the churches; To him that overcometh will I give to eat of the Tree of Life, which is in the midst of the paradise of God.

Since the Tree of Life was in the Garden of Eden and John states it was in the Paradise of God, then this proves that Eden was the natural garden and Paradise was the spiritual state in which God had placed the man and woman. It was the spiritual state they fell from when they took the mechanism for the production of new life and placed it under their own control.

The natural trees were for the sustenance of the natural body. The woman said, (Gen. 3:2) ***We may eat of the fruit of the trees of the garden.***

There also were two symbolic trees. ***First, the tree of Knowledge of Good and evil.*** This symbolizes the fact that the man and woman were given the capabilities of knowing and experiencing both good and bad. When the knowledge of evil overtakes the conscience, then it begins to destroy the spiritual and mental fabric, and ultimately undermines the physical structure of the body. When evil is present in the mental system it condemns and begins this process of death. The only remedy for this condemnation is through the fervent adherence to that one mediator between God and man—God's Name.

The second symbolic tree is the Tree of Life.

Jesus said, I am come in my Father's Name. (John 5:43). He is the Tree of Life. Jesus said, I am come that they might have life, and that they might have it more abundantly. (John 10:10).

The Tree of Life is the off-set for that spiritual destructive force which continually draws human life toward their death. It was not in God's plan that men should die, but that they should grow continually from strength to strength as time progressed. The Tree of Life was accessible if the man and woman would fervently call upon the Name of God, but this they refused to do.

The first man and woman never, in their lifetime, called upon the Name of God. It was not until Adam's Grandson (Enos) came on the scene that men began to call upon the Name of the Lord. (Gen. 4:26).

Without this faith and adherence to the Name of God, they had no spiritual strength to conform to the original logical will of God, and that was to leave the process for the creation of new life under God's automatic control.

Their first son was a murderer. God had spoken with the subconscious mind, Multiply and replenish the earth, (Gen. 1:28) but they decided not to wait on God. His process was too slow for them, as was the slowness of the promise to Abram and Sarai.

(Reference: Abram was 75 years old when the promise was made—Gen. 12:4 Abraham was 100 years old before the promise was fulfilled. (Gen. 17:17) This was God's promise to Abram and Sarai regarding the promised birth of Isaac. (Gen. 17:16 & 19).

After the man and the woman had observed the actions of the other animals they began the process for the production of life on their own, thus producing an evil son. That son's (Cain's) offspring all perished in the flood.

Since that time overpopulation has occurred time and time again, necessitating the elimination of masses to effect the gradual expansion God had in mind from the beginning.

The bodies of men and women are designed to live continually as they partake of that spiritual fruit of the Tree of Life. Gen 3:22

Jesus put it this way: John 6:35 I am the Bread of Life: he that cometh to me shall never hunger; and he that believeth on me shall never thirst. John 6:40

And this is the will of him (God) that sent me, that every one which seeth the Son, and believeth on him, may have everlasting life—. John 5:24 Verily, verily, I say unto you He that heareth my word, and believeth on him that sent me, hath everlasting life, and shall not come into condemnation; but is passed from death unto life. John 8:51 I say unto you, If a man keep my saying, he shall never see death. John 11:26 And whosoever liveth and believeth in me shall never die, Believest thou this?

Jesus said, (John 15:5) **I am the vine, ye are the branches:**

(Tree of Life) He that abideth in me, and I in him, the same bringeth forth much fruit; for without me ye can do nothing. (6) If a man abide not in me, he is cast forth as a branch, and is withered.

To him that overcometh will I give to eat of the Tree of Life, which is in the midst of the ***paradise of God.*** Revelation 2:7

****

Education:

Maxine asked this question.

Does the academic studies as presented by the present educational system enhance spiritual development?

James gave this response.

OF MAKING MANY BOOKS THERE IS NO END—ECCLESIASTES 12:12.

1 Samuel 2:3 The Lord is a God of knowledge.

Education is a must for the betterment of the human race in the material world. The right kind of educational instruction is required also in the spiritual area of human lives. But natural education alone can do very little or nothing toward the advancement of the spiritual side of human existence.

Anyone that has written or read the many varieties of self-help books, without being born again of their spirit, have come up empty. They still are not helped inwardly. The feeling of condemnation still exists within themselves.

With the beginning of each book there may be a feeling of hope. The reader may think 'When I read this book I will be relieved of all this heaviness of mind and spirit.' But when the book has been completed the same feeling of despair and hopelessness remains.

WHAT IS THE ANSWER?

Believe and Call Upon the Name of God. John 3:18. He that believeth on him is not condemned; but he that believeth not is condemned already, because he hath not believed in the NAME OF THE ONLY BEGOTTEN SON OF GOD.

Matthew 11:28 Come unto me all ye that labor and are heavy laden and I will give you rest.

SINCERELY and RELENTLESSLY call upon the Name of the Lord for deliverance from the overshadowing cloud of heaviness that has plagued the mind and spirit for so many years.

ASK GOD TO TAKE THE HURT AWAY. HE WILL DO IT.

1 Chr. 4:10—Jabez called on the God of Israel—saying—that

thou wouldest keep me from evil, that it may not grieve me! And God granted him that which he requested.

Joel 3:32 And it shall come to pass, that WHOSOEVER shall CALL on the NAME of the LORD shall be delivered.

Total peace will come with the HOLY GHOST and the filling and generation of the holy spirit. It drives out all condemnation and delivers to men and women total freedom as God designed for the human race from the beginning.

****

END: THE

Edward asked this question.

What is meant by the 'END OF THE WORLD?'

James gave this response.

Psalm 119:89 Forever, O Lord, thy WORD is settled in heaven.

Psalm 119:90 Thy faithfulness is unto all generations: thou hast established the earth, and it abideth.

Ecclesiastes 1:4—the earth ABIDETH FOREVER.

The end of the world is not referring to the end of the earth, but only the end of an era.

FLOOD

2 Peter 3:6—The world that then was, being overflowed with water, perished.

ANNO DOMINI SEVENTY

(A.D. 70)

Matthew 13:40 As therefore the tares are gathered and burned in the fire; so shall it be in the END OF THE WORLD.

Matthew 24:36 Verily I say unto you, ALL THESE THINGS SHALL COME UPON ***THIS GENERATION***.

Matthew 24:34 Verily I say unto you, THIS GENERATION SHALL NOT PASS, TILL ALL THESE THINGS BE FULFILLED. (witnesses: Mark 13:30, Luke 21:32).

Matthew 24:35 Heaven and earth shall pass away, but my words shall not pass away.

Matthew 24:36 But of that day and hour knoweth no man, no, not the angels of heaven, BUT MY FATHER ONLY.

Matthew 24:37 But as the days of Noe were, so shall also the Son of man be to THIS GENERATION.

Luke 21:20 And ***when ye shall see Jerusalem compassed with armies, then know*** that the desolation thereof is nigh.

Luke21:21 ***Then let them which are in Judaea flee to the mountains; and let them which are in the midst of it depart out; and let not them that are in the countries enter there into.*** (a. d. 70)

Luke 21:22 For these be the days of vengeance, ***that all things which are written may be fulfilled.***

IT IS VERY CLEAR THAT JESUS WAS SPEAKING OF THE IMPENDING DEVASTATION THAT WAS COMING UPON JERUSALEM.

It is time for mankind to wake up and understand that God has always wanted men to live in peace with themselves and one another. He wants them to take dominion over the world, and make a new earth by cleaning it up. Get rid of all the portraits of violence. Use the media for instruction in science, religion, nature, music, etc., etc., instead of all the destructive images as are presently being portrayed.

It is time for all peoples to control their own minds by the direction of the Holy Spirit and do away with the DEMAND for any harmful substance; those materials that destroy the mind, body and lower spiritual strength.

THERE ARE PERIODIC ENDS OF TIME, BUT GOD INTENDS FOR THIS WORLD TO BE INHABITED FOREVER. WAKE UP. CALL UPON GOD'S NAME AND LIVE YE.

Isaiah 45:18 God himself that formed the earth and made it; he hath established it, he created it not in vain, he formed it to be inhabited.—

****

ENOCH

Anonymous asked this question.

Does anyone have any idea or information on what it meant for Enoch to walk with God. The Living Bible says he stayed in constant touch with God. Can anyone elaborate?

Thanks

James gave this response.

How does a person walk with God?

Groundwork:

Gen. 5:22 And Enoch walked with God after he begat

Methuselah three hundred years, and begat sons and daughters: (23) And all the days of Enoch were three hundred sixty and five years: (24) And Enoch walked with God: and he was not; for God took him.

Heb. 11:5 By faith Enoch was translated that he should not see death; and was not found, because God had translated him: for before his translation he had this testimony, that he pleased God. (6) But without faith it is impossible to please him: for he that cometh to God; must believe that he is, and that he is a rewarder of them that diligently seek him.

Was Enoch translated into heaven?

No! He was translated into death. Heb. 1:13 These ALL DIED in faith, not having received the promises—.

Rom. 5:12—As by one man (Adamah) sin entered into the world, and death by sin; and so death passed upon ***all men***, for that ***ALL HAVE SINNED***: (13) (For until the law sin was in the world: but sin is not imputed (credit to or blame on a person or cause) when there is no law. (14) ***Nevertheless death reigned from Adam to Moses, even over them that had not sinned after the similitude (likeness) of Adam's transgression,—.*** So then death reigned from Adam until Jesus came on the scene when he attempted to show men the way back into that heavenly state, Paradise.

HOW DOES A PERSON WALK WITH GOD?

Jesus said, (John 8:29)—He (God) that sent me is with me: The Father hath not left me alone; ***FOR I DO ALWAYS THOSE THINGS THAT PLEASE HIM.***

Adam did not please God. So the Christ (Power) of God was driven out of his mental and spiritual system. When God came to visit, both Adamah (man) and the woman were afraid and ran behind the trees to hide. (Gen. 3:8) They could not maintain faith because they both knew they had disobeyed the one rule God had revealed to them regarding the reproduction process. (Gen. 3:10) And he (man) said, I heard thy voice in the garden, and ***I was afraid, because I was naked;*** and I hid myself. There was no way for their conscience to be cleared so that they could return to Paradise (spiritual state)because that way had not yet been made. The last Adam was not in the schedule until many years in the future.

Gen. 3:14 And the Lord God said unto the serpent, (man) Because thou hast done this, thou art cursed above all cattle, and above every beast of the field; upon thy belly shalt thou go, and dust shalt thou eat all the days of thy life. Dust thou art and dust shalt thou return. (Gen. 2:7, 3:19) And I will put enmity between thee and the woman, and between thy seed and her seed; it shall bruise thy head, and thou shalt bruise his heel. (Gen. 3:15).

1 Cor. 15:45 And so it is written, The first man Adam was made a living soul; the LAST ADAM (Jesus) was made a quickening (life giving) spirit.

Jesus walked with God. He did no sin. (2 Cor. 5:21, Heb 4:15, 1 Pet. 2:22). He was sent by God to save them that were lost (John 1:29) to the elements of the world and the destruction caused by the heaviness of mind, so that people could come boldly to the throne of grace, that we may obtain mercy, and find grace to help in the time of need. Heb. 4:16.

All except Jesus have sinned and come short of the glory of God. (Rom. 3:23) (24) Being justified freely by his grace through the redemption that is in Christ Jesus. (25) Whom God hath set forth to be a propitiation (gain or regain the favor of) through faith in his blood, to declare his righteousness ***for the remission of sins that are past, through the forbearance of God—.***

To walk with God and obtain strength to overcome the weaknesses in our bodies that have accumulated from our ancestors back to the time of the first man, we must call upon the Name of God (Jesus) without ceasing. This increases faith and invites the power of God through the Holy Ghost to come in and take up their abode within us.

The law was made necessary because of the deviation of the first man and his son Cain, and all men after them until the Only Begotten Son of God (the Last Adam) came to retrieve us from the curse of the law, and give us power to conform to the will of God in all matters.

****

EPICURUS

Bridgette asked this question.

James what do you make of this statement by Epicurus, true or false? ‘If GOD wishes to prevent evil, but cannot, He is impotent. If HE can but will not HE is malevolent.’ What kind of rhetoric is this?

James gave this response.

God is not impotent (lacking power), nor is he malevolent (malicious or spiteful.)

God did not make robots. He gave man and woman their free will. They must decide for themselves whether they will draw near God and enjoy his protection or drift away into darkness, confusion and eventual death.

God is our only savior. He saves by Christ—the power of God—through HIS SON.

A person must draw near God by calling upon the handle of God which has been designated as the mediator between God and man.

James 4:8 Draw nigh to God, and HE WILL draw nigh to you. Cleanse your hands, ye sinners; and purify your hearts ye double minded. (It is up to us)

We must call upon God by His Name and have faith in that Name, otherwise HE will not save us from our weaknesses and troubles. We must believe that HE has the power to save. (Heb. 11:6)—He that cometh to God must believe that HE IS, and that he is a rewarder of them that diligently seek him. (Matt. 9:29) Jesus said, According to your faith be it unto you.

Proverbs 18:10 The NAME of the LORD is a strong tower: the righteous runneth into it and is safe.

Psalm 145:19 ***He will fulfil the desire of them that fear (reverence and love) him: he also will hear their cry, and will SAVE THEM. (20) The LORD preserveth ALL them that love him: but all the wicked will he destroy.***(He lets them become entangled in their own devices).

(21) My mouth shall speak the praise of the LORD: and let all flesh bless HIS holy NAME for ever and ever.

Jer. 10:25 Pour out thy fury upon the heathen that know thee not, and upon the families that call not on thy NAME.

God has never been malicious or spiteful. The road is very clear when men/women draw near God fervently through His Name. But the first man and woman never did, in their lifetime, call upon the Name of the Lord. It was not until their Grandson (Enos) was born that men began to CALL upon the NAME OF THE LORD. (Gen 4:26) But even they, when the waves of the boisterous sea became fearful, have repeatedly forgotten. At such moments they have had too much doubt and cast their faith aside. Peter said Lord, Save Me—but doubt interfered. (Matt. 14:31) Jesus saved him anyway to prove this point.

Acts 2:21 And it shall come to pass, that WHOSOEVER shall CALL on the Name of the LORD shall be SAVED.

1 Tim. 2:5—There is ONE GOD, and ONE MEDIATOR between God and men, the man Christ Jesus.

Please read my other answers. There is a single thread throughout them all.

Bridgette32 asked this follow-up question.

James thanks but that's not what I meant or rather Epicurus meant. It is not up to us, we cannot prevent evil, sickness or death. Sickness & death are evil. What would we say about mortals who could prevent evil but will not?

James gave this response.

Sorry, but it seemed to me that Epicurus was writing about God and not mortals. As long as mortals are living in the condemnation of sin they will not have the spiritual strength to prevent evil in themselves or anyone else. But,—Through Christ and time we can prevent sin!

Ezek. 18:32—I have no pleasure in the death of him that dieth, saith the Lord GOD: wherefore ***turn yourselves*** and live ye.

It is up to us. We must draw near God and through His Christ we can overcome the weaknesses in the world and within ourselves.

Ezek. 18:31 **Cast away from you all your transgressions, whereby ye have transgressed; and make you a new heart and a new spirit: for why will ye die—.**

Romans 6:23—the wages of sin is death; but the gift of God is eternal life through Jesus Christ our Lord.

Phlp. 4:13 I can do all things through Christ which strengtheneth me.

1 Cor. 15:56 The sting of death is sin—. (57) But thanks be to God, which giveth us the victory through our Lord Jesus Christ.

1 Cor. 15:25 For he must reign, till he hath put all enemies under his feet. (26) The last enemy that shall be destroyed is death.

Bridgette asked this follow-up question.

James I only meant that you said “it is up to us”. I have A real question for you.

Doesn’t the Bible say “man was made for the earth, and earth for man? Why would we go to heaven? That does not seem to be our ultimate goal that God had in mind, or does it?

James gave this response.

‘Man was made for the earth, and earth for man.’

I could not find that exact passage in the bible.

The following may be helpful.

Isaiah 45:18 For thus saith the LORD that created the heavens; God himself that formed the earth and made it; he hath established it, he created it not in vain, he ***FORMED IT TO BE INHABITED.***

We are already in the physical heavens. In six months the earth will be approximately 93 million miles X 2 from where we are now. The people on the earth will be no better off then than they are right now unless they turn to God with all their heart, soul, mind, and with all their strength: this is the first and great commandment. Matthew 22:37-38. (Strength—Mark 12:30).

Yes, the spiritual heaven was established upon the earth for man and woman to live in forever. And they were warned that in the day they take into their system the knowledge of evil they would die. This was not an immediate process. That is why they could see no sense to staying in the presence of God by conforming to his will. What was death? They, individually had not experienced it until Cain killed his brother Abel. It was before that time that the man and woman decided to disobey the instructions God had given regarding the production of life. It was not because God wanted to keep some pleasure from them, but so that he could regulate the production of new life in order to eliminate eventual death. (Do not try this at home. Think in terms of long life—none will have problems conforming when they have been many years on the earth).

Adamah and his companion failed to remain in the presence of God because of the guilt they felt for their disobedience. So God sent his only begotten son to show the way back into paradise, that spiritual state where people were supposed to have remained.

John 3:16 For God so loved the world, that he gave his only begotten Son, that WHOSOEVER believeth in him should ***NOT PERISH, but have EVERLASTING LIFE.*** But the world of men misunderstood and rejected their only hope of that continual life that only the mediator could provide.

God wanted the human race to call upon him by his Name so that it would stabilize their spiritual, mental and ultimately their physical system. This information has been confirmed over and over throughout the Bible, starting with Gen. 4:26, And to Seth, to him also there was born a son; and he called his name Enos: ***then began men to call upon the Name of the LORD.***

Joel 2:32 And it shall come to pass, that WHOSOEVER shall CALL on the NAME OF THE LORD shall be delivered—.

Acts 2:21 And it shall come to pass, that WHOSOEVER shall

CALL on the NAME of the LORD shall be saved. (Also Romans 10:13 and many more).

The wages of sin is death. Romans 6:23. We cannot sin our way to heaven. This is more of the confusion God has allowed because people have not accepted the idea of calling upon the Name of the Lord without ceasing.

Romans 8:3—God (sent) his own Son in the likeness of sinful flesh, and for sin, condemned sin in the flesh—.

John said, (John 1:29) Behold the Lamb of God, which taketh away the sin of the world.

Jesus said, (John 8:34) Whosoever committeth sin is the servant of sin, (35) And the servant abideth not in the house FOREVER: but the Son abideth ever.

Rom. 5:21—As sin hath reigned unto death, even so might grace reign through righteousness unto ETERNAL LIFE by Jesus Christ our Lord.

I realize this subject can meander in many directions. These advocations are all in the Bible but very few have made mention of them. When looking at history it makes it more difficult to fathom living for any length of time on the earth. But it should be remembered that some have lived long lives, like Noah, 950 years, Adam 930 years and Methusalah 969 years. The measurement of those years are essentially the same as ours. It still takes, within a few seconds, in a hundred thousand years, the same time now as it did then, for the earth to circle the sun, thus making a complete year.

Remember the saying, 'The just shall LIVE by his faith? (Hab. 2:4, Rom. 1:17, Gal. 3:11, Heb. 10:38) We must first be just and then live by faith that it can be done. Phlp. 4:13 I can do all things through Christ which strengtheneth me.

Luke 18:8—WHEN THE SON OF MAN COMETH, SHALL HE FIND FAITH ON THE EARTH?

Bridgette asked this follow-up question.

Thank you James. I rated your answer excellent. I have to ask though, since you said Adam/Eve had not experienced death, where did God get animal skins to clothe them? Did animals always die & only man would not if he had obeyed God? This is a bit convoluted I know. Why did Adam eat of the fruit, since he was not deceived? Could it be that he would rather die than be alone, after the death of Eve or would he as the leader have died anyway with Eve?

1) Since you said Adam/Eve had not experienced death—.

   James gave this follow-up answer.

   We are speaking of the first man and woman. They had not known death among humans at that time, so the word or reality of death meant nothing to them. They could only understand death when Cain killed his brother Abel. This murderous condition in Cain was created by the deliberate actions of his father and mother.

2) Did animals always die, and only man would not, if he had obeyed God?

   The cycle of life, growth, maturity and death was always among the lower animals ever since their creation. God desired to create a son as his natural offspring, patterned after himself and the beings which had been created of spiritual substance (substance that is just as real as natural substance, but cannot be seen by natural eyes). (Let us make man in our image and likeness (Gen. 1:26) Eternal life as God experienced within himself was designed to flow from God to his son.

His son, in order to operate properly was made up of two parts, the positive (female) and the negative (Male). As long as these two parts stayed in contact with God through the spirit, they would enjoy the flow of life from that spiritual source. The knowledge of evil was the only thing that could separate them from that spiritual source. But it was their decision to sever that contact with their Father, God. This left them without the strength to conform to his will. The only off-set for that weakness was the Tree of Life, (Gen. 3:24) but they could not reach that Tree of Life because of the flaming sword. (the Thou Shalt not stipulation).

3) Where did God get animal skins to clothe them?

It has been established that animals die. First we must understand that God was not in the business of making clothes. (Gen. 3:21) Unto Adam also and to his wife did the LORD God make coats of skins and clothed them. God revealed to the man and the woman how to make coverings for themselves which were more substantial than the leaves they had used as the covering they had first chosen to lesson the pangs of guilt which they felt.

(Gen. 3:7) And the eyes of them both were opened, and they knew they were naked; and they sewed fig leaves together, and made themselves aprons.

Nor did God create shame. (James 1:13) Let no man say when he is tempted, I am tempted of God: for God cannot be tempted with evil, neither tempteth he any man: The conscience of the man and the woman felt shame because of their eagerness to become as God to create life, without waiting for the 'time of life' when it would automatically take effect by the operation of God that had been implanted within their subconscious.

4) Why did Adam eat of the fruit, since he was not deceived?

James 1:14 Every man is tempted, when he is drawn away of his own lust, and enticed.

The fruit was not the natural fruit of the trees of the garden. The fruit was symbolic of the knowledge of evil. (Gen. 3:2) And the woman said unto the serpent (symbolic of the man), We may eat of the fruit of the trees of the garden: (3) ***But of the fruit of the tree which is in the midst of the garden,(symbolic of the man and the woman*** in the midst of the garden) God hath said, Ye shall not eat of it, neither shall ye touch it, lest ye die.

5) Could it be that he would rather die than be alone, after Eve would die, or would he as the leader have died anyway with Eve?

Death was pronounced on them both. The positive and negative force drives the current flow interchangeably between the male and the female. It is not good that the man should be alone. (Gen. 2:18) When the life force is withdrawn from the two individuals, the process of death begins. (Gen. 2:17)

It was stated—for in the 'day' that thou eatest thereof thou shalt surely die. Adam lived 930 years, (Gen. 5:5). It was not recorded when Eve died. One day is with the Lord as a thousand years. (2 Peter 3:8). They did not live one day.

****

Exercising!

Charlene asked this question.

How much emphasis should we put on exercising?

Is it necessary?

James gave this response.

EXERCISING.

Is it necessary to exercise?

YES!

How much exercise is needed?

When the mind and spirit are in perfect coordination with the spirit of God, the subconscious mind causes sufficient movement to effect proper circulation even during the time allotted for sleep.

Generally, excessive exercise is not needed.

Saul (Paul) said, 1 Tim. 4:8—bodily exercise profiteth LITTLE: but godliness is profitable unto all things.

Exercising the body is important within reasonable boundaries, that is one of the reasons why God took the man and put him into the garden of Eden to DRESS IT AND TO KEEP IT. Gen. 2:15. The other reason, of course, is for the production of food products for nourishment of the natural body.

But when a person is led to believe he or she must do additional walking or running, or purchase expensive exercise equipment for exercising the body, this is in excess. This wasted energy should be used in doing something constructive. Of course there are exceptions to this rule. In cases of infirmity caused by sickness, accident or other abnormalities, extra exercise for a time may be needed. But when a person's body is used to walking five miles a day and lifting heavy weights it becomes dependent upon that amount of exercise. Then when the excessive exercise is stopped the body becomes weaker than it was before.

What about people that are retired, or live in an apartment and do not have access to many chores that are found on a farm or around a house and yard?

There are many tasks in the world that need to be done. There is no time or energy to waste on nonsensical movement just because someone has advertised that it be done. The motive, all too often, is to improve their own monetary standing.

IN SHORT, a person should call upon the Name of God and be led by the power that emanates from God through the Holy Ghost, and that person will always be guided into the proper activities needed for the welfare of the body, mind and spirit. This in turn, relieves the mind of all worry, and lets it do the job of caring for the entire physical body through the immune system.

The following excerpt was clipped from a letter received from Diabetes Self-management.

P.O. Box 51125
Boulder, CO 80321-1125 on 3-24-2001.

Researchers recently discovered that simple household chores like cooking meals and mopping the floor help you burn an extra 219 calories a day—that adds up to a whopping 79,935 calories per year.

Think on these things.

****

FAITH

Anonymous asked this question.

Can someone please explain to me why faith is important?

I don't want to know what God said or anything, but why faith is important to you people. Why do we need it? What would life be like if we did not believe in it? What is it like to believe in faith? I would like a lot of answers from everyone—Thanks!!!!

James gave this response.

If you don't want to hear what God says—YOU WON'T.

Hebrews 11:6 Without FAITH it is impossible to please him: for he that cometh to God must BELIEVE that he is, and that he is a rewarder of them that DILIGENTLY seek him.

Luke 18:7—shall not God avenge his own elect, which cry day and night unto him—. (8) I tell you that he will avenge them speedily.

Ezekiel 18:31 Cast away from you all your transgressions, whereby ye have transgressed; and make you a new heart and a new spirit: for why will ye die—. (32)—I have no pleasure in the death of him that dieth, saith the Lord God: wherefore turn yourselves, and live ye.

Even you can be saved from the destructive elements of the earth and the thoughts of natural men, for(Acts 2:21)—it shall come to pass that WHOSOEVER shall call on the Name of the Lord shall be saved. (Also Rom. 10:13).

So then ***faith cometh by hearing, and hearing by the word of God.*** Romans 10:17.

Nevertheless when the Son of man cometh, shall he find faith on the earth? Luke 18:18.

FAITH, *TRUE* Southern Baptist: only—

klaytu asked this question.

That was an attention grabber, eh? Let's examine that ridiculous statement.

If your denomination means more to you than your walk with Christ, or if your denomination IS your walk with Christ, then you must face two possible conclusions:

1) you have inappropriate feelings toward your denomination, or

2) you are in a cult.

One star will be given for poor logic or rudeness.

James gave this response.

There are many names in religion. Which name can lead to heaven? Which name can reveal where heaven is?

Why did God confound the language of those that were building the tower of Babel? Gen. 11:7

They wanted to make a name for themselves instead of accepting the Name of God only! Gen. 11:4.

When any religious group of people come together in any other name, other than the Name of God, that name engenders confusion.

Matt. 17:4 When Peter said unto Jesus, Let us make here three tabernacles; one for thee, and one for Moses, and one for Elias, (5) a voice out of the cloud said, This is my beloved Son, in whom I am well pleased; HEAR YE HIM. (8) And when they (Peter, James and John) had lifted up their eyes, they saw no man, save ***JESUS ONLY.***

WORDS ARE SPIRIT

Jesus said, (John 6:63) The words that I speak unto you, they are spirit, and they are life.

Jesus said (John 4:24), God is a Spirit and they that worship him must worship him in spirit and in truth.

Jesus said, (to the woman at the well) Woman, believe me, the hour cometh, when ye shall neither in this mountain (Gerizim in Samaria), nor yet at Jerusalem, worship the Father, (23) true worshipers shall worship the Father in spirit and in truth—.

Note: Gerizim was the site of the Samaritan temple, which was built there after the captivity, in rivalry with the temple at Jerusalem. Gerizim is still to the Samaritans what Jerusalem is to the Jews and Mecca to the Mohammedans.

Jesus said (John 14:6) I am the way, the truth, and the life: no man cometh unto the Father, but by me.

NAMES ARE WORDS—THEY TOO ARE SPIRIT

Names make a difference in the lives of people. That is why God changed the names of many throughout human history. Abram to Abraham (Gen. 17:5), Sarai to Sarah (15), Jacob to Israel (Gen. 32:28), etc., etc. and many others.

HIS NAME IS CALLED THE WORD OF GOD.

Revelation 19:13 His Name (Jesus) is called the word of God.

Jesus said (John 5:43), I am come in my Father's Name.

Ephesians 3:15 Of whom the whole family in heaven and earth is named.

When it is understood that God's Name was given to His

Son for placement in the minds of the people (Rev. 14:1), then confusion will subside and all other names in religion will be dissolved. It is only then that all nationalities and religions can become one in purpose and congeniality.

It shall come to pass, that WHOSOEVER shall call on the Name of the Lord shall be saved. Acts 2:21, Rom. 10:13, (Joel 2:32 delivered).

WHOSOEVER does not mean any particular religion. It means every individual in the world that will call upon God by His Name (Jesus) without ceasing. (I Ths. 5:17)

Acts 4:12 ***Neither is there salvation in any other: for there is none other name under heaven given among men, whereby we must be saved.***

John (the Baptizer) said, Behold the Lamb of God, which taketh away the sin of the world. John 1:29.

Hear that Lamb of God.

klaytu rated this answer:

Ok, good argument. It is obvious you spent much time studying your Bible. I commend you on that. However, there is some confusion in your answer. Your argument implies that you believe that Baptist denomination is THE only true faith. Why do you believe only Baptist are going to Heaven?

James gave this follow-up answer.

Your conclusion was not implied by my words.

Jesus said, (John 3:13) NO MAN hath ASCENDED up to HEAVEN, but he that came down from heaven, even the Son of man which is in heaven.

Jesus at that moment was standing in heaven, Paradise, where the first man and woman had been placed.

It is not my intention to bash any religion. It is only hoped that all leaders of religious organizations come to the understanding that their names divide people and this is not according to God's will for the human race.

It is important that certain passages be re-considered, i.e., God confounded their language!

Why?

They wanted to make a name for themselves—. When any religious group of people come together in any OTHER NAME, other than the Name of God, that name engenders confusion.

It shall come to pass, that WHOSOEVER shall call on the Name of the Lord shall be saved.

WHOSOEVER DOES NOT MEAN ANY PARTICULAR RELIGION.

John the baptizer pointed his followers to Jesus. After that, ***John's disciples should have followed Jesus only.***

Gen. 11:4 And they said, Go to, let us build us a city and a tower, whose top may reach unto heaven; and let us ***make us a name—.***

The advocates of all religions say that—but there is only one way to heaven and that is through faith in and calling upon the name of God—JESUS.

klaytu asked this follow-up question.

I am sorry sir, but I was hoping for a direct answer for my

question. Let me give you a statement, and if you are interested, you may reply.

I have been a Christian for 11 years. God speaks to me by the following ways:

1) my Bible

2) my prayers

3) my fellow Christians

4) my church (pastor's sermons, etc.)

5) my heart

Because God has given my spiritual discernment, I can now determine if a church is a cult or not.

Now, back to you. Do you believe there is ONLY one denomination that is the true faith?

James gave this response.

No! There is one God and His Name one. Denominations separate the people in mind and in spirit. Church buildings are necessary, but all should come together in the Name of God only. Matthew 18:20 For where two or three are gathered together in MY NAME (Not the name of an organization), there am I in the midst of them.

klaytu asked this follow-up question.

Good! We have communicated.

There is only one God. We are not commanded to go to only one denomination, we are commanded instead to serve God.

With discernment, we can then determine where God wants us to attend church.

James' comment:

When the people in organized religion turns to God through his name and dissolves their particular religious names, then they will be crawling out of the dark ages of ignorance, and into the light of Christ. Then they will discover where heaven is.

Proverbs 21:2 Every way of a man is right in his own eyes—this also applies to men of the various churches. If they did not think they were right, then that church would cease to exist. But it is most important to realize that all the churches are needed to do their part in withstanding the pressures of the millions in the world that are anti-christ.

****

Fanaticism

(Not to be disclosed) asked this question.

Is there anything in the bible about being very fanatic about religion? There are so many people who are just so fanatical they think my brother, for knowing a couple of magic tricks, is doing the work of satan.

Did Jesus or the apostles ever say anything about this?

James gave this response.

The other writers have done such a splendid job revealing the fallacies of fanaticism and NIT—picking, those which strain at a gnat, and swallow a camel, (Matt. 23:24) that I feel it may be appropriate to look at this subject in a different light. Please allow my indulgence.

We know that all things work together for good to them that love God, to them who are the called according to his purpose. Rom. 8:28

God used the emotional instability of Pharaoh and the work of the magicians to advance God's Name in the minds of the people. (Exodus 7:11 How appropriate that 'wise men, sorcerers, and magicians' just happen to be listed in this particular numbered scripture).

Everything that God did through Moses and Aaron, the magicians could also do, except one thing: They could not bring lice (LIFE) out of the earth. Then the magicians said, ***This is the finger of God—.*** (Exodus 8:19)

All these things were done so that to the end, thou mayest know that I am the LORD in the midst of the earth. (Exo.8:22).

God works no miracles! He plans things to come together at the appropriate time for the advancement of His Name. The nits (parasitic insect eggs) were already in the earth and the lice were ready at the appointed time to come crawling out of the ground when Aaron followed God's instructions and smote the dust of the land with the rod. (Exodus 8:16)

The reason we have so many criticisms coming from the religious system is that they still have the doctrines and self righteous attitudes of the Pharisees. The only way to rectify this problem is for everybody to turn to God with their whole heart, soul, and ALL THE MIND. (Matt.22:37). They must Call upon God through the mediator and let the power of Christ begin flowing from their belly into continual life. It will wash out all the pride, self righteousness, hatred, malice and all other misdirected thoughts that permeate the system of the human intellect.

Jesus said, 'I am the way the truth and the LIFE—. John 14:6.

This life springs out of the belly into everlasting life via of the Holy Ghost. (John 7:38).

****

Fasting, The practice of

Anonymous asked this question.

I am new to Christianity. What is the purpose of fasting? I am told that it is NOT "sacrificing food for a day" so God can answer our prayers.

James gave this response

FASTING

It is possible to fast for forty days and nights if the body is well balanced nutritionally at the on-set of the fast. Elijah and Jesus did just that. But it is also clear in the bible, that the body must have natural food to remain alive, as the spiritual body needs spiritual food (a flow of Christ-the power of God).

The self righteous Pharisee said, (Luke 18:12) I fast twice in the week. I give tithes of all that I possess. And the publican, standing afar off, would not lift up so much as his eyes unto heaven, but smote upon his breast saying, GOD BE MERCIFUL TO ME A SINNER. (14) I tell you this man (publican) went down to his house justified rather than the other.

Matthew 9:14 Then came to him the disciples of John, saying, Why do we and the Pharisees fast oft, but thy disciples Fast Not? (15) And Jesus said unto them, Can the children of the bridechamber MOURN, as long as the bridegroom is with them? But the days will come, when the bridegroom shall be taken from them, and then shall

they fast. Mark 2:20—and then shall they fast in those days. (It will then be a time of mourning.)

Matthew 6:16 Moreover when ye fast, be not, as the hypocrites, of a sad countenance: for they disfigure their faces, that they may appear unto men to fast. Verily I say unto you, they have their reward. (17) But thou, when thou fastest, anoint thine head, and wash thy face; (18) That thou appear not unto men to fast, but unto thy Father which is in secret: and thy Father, which seeth in secret, shall reward thee openly.

Isa. 58:5 Is it such a FAST that I have chosen? A day for a man to afflict his soul? Is it to bow down his head as a bulrush, and to spread sackcloth and ashes under him? Wilt thou call this a fast, and an acceptable day to the Lord? (6) IS NOT THIS THE FAST THAT I HAVE CHOSEN? To loose the bands of wickedness, to undo the heavy burdens, and to let the oppressed go free, and that ye break every yoke? (7) Is it not to deal thy bread to the hungry, and that thou bring the poor that are cast out to thy house? When thou seest the naked, that thou cover him; and that thou hide not thyself from thine own flesh? (8) Then shall thy light break forth as the morning, and thine health shall spring forth speedily: and thy righteousness shall go before thee; the glory of the Lord shall be thy rereward. (9) Then shalt thou call and the Lord shall answer; thou shalt cry, and he shall say, here I am. (1) and the Lord shall guide thee continually—. (There is more on this subject).

****

Fighting and Killing:

Moses was wrong when he came down the mountain and (Exod. 32:;27 Said unto them, Thus saith the LORD God of

Israel, Put every man his sword by his side, and go in and out from gate to gate throughout the camp, and slay every man his brother, and every man his companion, and every man his neighbor. God had just confirmed to Moses that (Exo. 20:13) Thou shalt not kill. God does not need man to do service for him by killing anyone. (John 16:2)

When people leave God they are susceptible to all kinds of diseases, poverty, addictions, (one who is psychologically or physiologically dependent, as on a drug), and totally convinced that their way is right.

James 4:1 From whence come wars and fightings among you? Come they not hence, even of your lusts that war in your members? (2) Ye lust, and have not: ***ye kill, and desire to have, and cannot obtain: ye fight and war, yet ye have not***, because ye ask not. (3) ***Ye ask, and receive not, because ye ask amiss, that ye may consume it upon your lusts***.

When God promises houses and lands he does not mean that you should go in and kill the occupants and take their land and houses. He means he will cause you to become friends with the people of the country so that you will be able to work and plan to buy the property with total agreement on both sides.

Matthew 6:33 But seek ye first the kingdom of God, and his righteousness; and all these things shall be added unto you.

What things? (Mark 10:30) But he shall receive an hundredfold now in this time, ***HOUSES***, and brethren, and sisters, and mothers, and children, and ***LANDS.***

Jesus said, (John 10:8) All that EVER came before me are thieves and robbers: (10) The thief cometh not, but for to steal, and to kill, and to destroy: I am come that they might have life, and that they might have it more abundantly.

Matthew 5:38 Ye have heard that it hath been said, An eye for an eye, and a tooth for a tooth: (39) But I say unto you, That ye resist not evil—(43) Ye have heard that it hath been said, Thou shalt love thy neighbor, and hate thine enemy. (44) But I say unto you, Love your enemies—.***Jesus was a Jew. Will the Jews and the rest of the world ever hear him?***

John 1:17—The law was given by Moses, but grace and ***TRUTH came by Jesus Christ.***

The primary ten commandments were confirmed by God for the guidance of men among themselves. But the penalties (punishment for crimes) as given by Moses were not advocated by God. Moses took that authority upon himself. And to cause the people to listen and obey his commands, he said, God said thus and so. Well, yes, the Bible is true, Moses and others did those things just as it was written, but that doesn't make everything that men have done, right.

Rom. 12:19 Dearly beloved, avenge not yourselves, but rather give place unto wrath: for it is written, Vengeance is mine; I will repay, saith the Lord.

Deut. 32:35 To me belongeth vengeance, and recompense; t***heir foot shall slide in due time:—.***

Anonymous rated this answer:

AMEN.

AMEN.

Amen.

Anonymous asked this follow-up question.

Greetings.

Would you be willing to share all the above again, in person?

Would you be willing to share all the words of wisdom above again, to a race of people that are lost in darkness?

Would you REALLY?

James gave this response.

I am not a speaker, although I have tried the oration route (elaborate formal speech) throughout the years since our enlightenment in 1960, so far as I could tell, it has never been effective. Everyone I have the opportunity to speak with are told of the necessity for calling upon the Name of God to reach him.

God continue blessing you in everything you say and do.

Maybe it is through you that God will reach them.

****

FIRE

Newstome asked this question.

What is the difference between the Lake of Fire and Hell? How does it happen that hell (eternal) is cast into the Lake of Fire?

James gave this response.

Revelation 20:14 And death and hell were cast into the lake of fire, this is the second death. (15) And whosoever was not found written in the book of life were cast into the lake of fire.

From the Mount of Olives we walked through the valley of Hinnom toward the dung gate. On the side of the path were grave stones. The word most frequently used (occurring twelve times (in the new testament for the place of future punishment) is Gehenna or Gehenna of Fire. This was originally the valley of Hinnom south of Jerusalem where the filth and dead animals of the city were cast out and burned; a fit symbol of the wicked and their destruction.

In the old testament 'Hell' is rendered into the Hebrew word 'Sheol.' It really means the place of the dead, without deciding whether it be the place of misery or of happiness, but is clear that in many passages of the Old Testament Sheol can only mean 'the grave,' and is so rendered in the Authorized Version. In other passages, however, it seems to involve a notion of punishment, and is therefore rendered in the Authorized Version by the word 'Hell'.

Eccl. 9:5 The living know that they shall die: but the dead know not anything, neither have they any more a reward; for the memory of them is forgotten.

Jesus said, (Matt. 8:22)—Let the dead bury their dead—.

The ungodly are spiritually dead. Psalm 1:4 The ungodly are not so: but are like the chaff which the wind driveth away. (5) Therefore the ungodly shall not stand in the judgment, nor sinners in the congregation of the righteous—. (6)—***the way of the ungodly shall perish.***

Whether Godly or ungodly the spiritual and mental systems of man were created the same. (John 1:9 Christ was the true light, which lighteth EVERY MAN that cometh into the world.) When a person deviates from the ways of God his spiritual life dies and the mental system becomes depressed. That depression causes the body to malfunction and hell takes over the mind. First spiritual death, then hell and ultimately the grave.

Rev. 20:6 Blessed and holy is he that hath part in the first resurrection (of the spirit) on such the second death hath no power—.

For a person that has received the rebirth of their spirit (John 3:3), but continues in disobeying the laws of God, the hell they have created for themselves will overtake them and be cast into the lake of fire. This is the second death. Rev. 2:11 He that overcometh shall not be hurt of the second death.

When people turn to God through His Name with all their heart, soul and mind (Matthew 22:37) God will give them all the spiritual gifts necessary to do the job complete and along with it the strength to overcome.

Jesus said, (John 7:38) He that believeth on me, as the scripture hath said, out of His Belly shall flow rivers of living water. (Isa. 12:3—With joy shall ye draw water out of the wells of salvation. (4) And in that day shall ye say, Praise the Lord, Call upon His Name. This water flows throughout the spiritual and mental system and washes out all the effects of sin before it has a chance to produce hell in the mind which leads to ultimate destruction in the lake of fire to be completely consumed in the grave where the body decays in the land of forgetfulness.

Gen. 2:17 The knowledge of evil is poison. When the knowledge of evil is ingested into the system it causes death. Ezek. 18:4 The soul that sinneth, it shall die. 1 Cor. 15:56 The sting of death is sin. How can a person experience death which is caused by sin and then go to heaven?

Jesus said, (John 313)—No man hath ascended up to heaven, but he that came down from heaven, even the Son of Man which is in heaven. (Jesus was in paradise where man and woman were intended to live).

1 Thes. 5:23 And the very God of peace sanctify you wholly; and I pray God your whole spirit and soul and body be preserved blameless unto the coming of the lord Jesus Christ.

Call upon the Name of the Lord and all these things will be clarified.

When we receive the gift of the Holy Ghost and have been born again of our spirit (that spirit we received from our natural father must be killed, taken out, and a right spirit installed in its place) and the holy spirit is continually renewed as 'oil in our lamp,' (Matt. 25:4) our names are written in the book of life. The second death will have no effect and death and hell will be destroyed in the lake of fire.

Rev. 7:14 These are they which came out of great tribulation, and have washed their robes, and made them white in the blood of the Lamb. (15) Therefore are they before the throne of God, and serve him day and night in his temple: (This is not a natural place—(God is a Spirit John 4:21-24) and he that sitteth on the throne shall dwell among them. (16) They shall hunger no more, neither thirst any more; neither shall the sun light on them, nor any heat. (17) For the Lamb which is in the midst of the throne shall feed them, and shall lead them unto living fountains of water; and God shall wipe away all tears from their eyes.

Death and hell is cast into the lake of fire to be destroyed from the human race forever.

****

Fire:

Zenaide asked this question.

God, can He save from fire?

James gave this response

THE LITTLE YELLOW HOUSE

Tombstone, Arizona 1962

Rays of the warm sun beat upon James' head. He remembered

Saint Louis. The beams had penetrated the glass and warmed the back of his neck. James did not care what they said. The way to God and to all truth is by calling upon His Name. That fact was confirmed to him when God said 'This is what I told Adam to do in the beginning' and he also said, 'Every time I turn my back, man forgets.' James had determined that he would not forget, no matter what comes or goes. Jesus, Jesus, Jesus, Jesus he repeated silently inside himself. With those thoughts he turned and went into the little yellow house.

The nights were cold. Mesquite was drug from the other side of the road to the back yard. An old axe was found in the shed. Sweat poured from James' face. He was weak. It was a wood cook stove. In order to cook they must have wood small enough to fit in the stove. Much was needed to furnish fire for cooking and for heat during the night. The exercise was good for James. How long will it take before he recuperates? If he had a job he would straighten out more quickly. He wondered why God didn't direct him to a job? Even if the unemployment checks expire, they would still have the commodities. They could probably live on that. He wondered what plants in the desert could be eaten. He was not educated in that line.

The stove was too hot. The fire started where the stove pipe goes into the ceiling. Flames were already reaching for the roof. No, James said urgently, That cannot happen on top of everything else. This house does not belong to us, and we have no money to pay for it. We can not even pay the rent. He grabbed the pots and pans. The faucet was turned on full blast. The flames must be stopped. One after another the containers were emptied. The water was splashed against the ceiling. At last he had won again. Jesus, Jesus, Jesus, Jesus. He wondered if he had been guided by the Holy Ghost because he was calling upon the Name of the Lord continuously. How else could those flames have stopped. They had already reached inside the loft. The area around the stove pipe was too small for much water to be thrown through into the opening above, between the ceiling and the roof.

I Cor. 1:2—With all that in every place CALL UPON THE NAME OF JESUS CHRIST OUR LORD,—.

John 5:43 Jesus said, I am come in my Father's Name.

Acts 9:14 And here he (Saul) hath authority from the chief priests to bind all that call on thy name.

Luke 18:7 And shall not God avenge his own elect, which cry day and night unto him, (8) I tell you that he will avenge them speedily.

Acts 9:4 And he (Saul) fell to the earth, and heard a voice saying unto him, Saul, Saul, why persecutest thou me? (5) And he said, Who art thou, Lord? And the Lord said, I am Jesus whom thou persecutest:

Acts 2:21 It shall come to pass, that whosoever shall call on the Name of the Lord shall be saved.

Does this mean saved even from fire? Daniel 3 confirms God's ability to save from fire.

2 Cor. 5:19—God was in Christ, reconciling the world unto himself,—.

John 17:11 Holy Father, keep through thine own NAME—.

John 17:12 While I was with them in the world, I kept them in THY NAME.

John 17:15 I pray not that thou shouldest take them out of the world, but that thou shouldest keep them from the evil.

John 17:26 Jesus said to God, his father,—I have declared unto them THY NAME, and will declare it—.

John 3:18 He that believeth on him (Jesus) is not condemned:

but he that believeth not is condemned already, because he hath not believed in the Name of the only begotten Son of God.

Acts 4:12 Neither is there salvation(saved from sin or danger) in any other: for there is none other NAME under heaven given among men, whereby we must be saved.

John 12:28 Jesus said, Father, glorify Thy Name. Then came there a voice from heaven, saying, I have both glorified it, and will glorify it again.

Psalm 113:3 From the rising of the sun unto the going down of the same the Lord's Name is to be praised.

Psalm 119:55 I have remembered thy Name in the night . . .

Rev. 22:4—His Name shall be in their foreheads—.

The first man did not call upon the Name of the Lord, but his Grandson did. Gen. 4:26 To Seth, to him also there was born a son; and he called his name Enos: then began men to Call upon the Name of the Lord.

****

FIRST? WHAT DO

Maxine asked this question.

WHAT SHOULD WE DO FIRST, PRAY OR CALL UPON THE NAME OF GOD?

James gave this response.

We do not know what to pray for, nor do we in many cases, have the words in our language to express to God what is needed. We do not know of the potential dangers, or the thoughts of others toward our cause, whether favorable or detrimental.

Romans 8:26—The Spirit also helpeth our infirmities: for we know not what we should pray for as we ought: but the Spirit itself maketh intercession for us with groanings which cannot be uttered.

It is necessary to CALL UPON THE NAME OF THE LORD WITHOUT CEASING, and the Holy Ghost will guide us into proper words (whether in our language or some other language) in perfect coordination with all potentialities.

We do not have to worry about doing certain ritualistic recitations in prayers, or pray at certain times every day or night in a forceful manner.

When someone's name comes to mind, we may not know if there is a problem that needs attention, but we should pray inside ourselves concerning that person no matter where we are or what time of day or night it is.

There is no need to pray openly (Matt. 6:5)or for setting aside a time for prayers in a closet somewhere, or on the knees at the side of the bed. This belief sometimes stands in the way of needed timely prayers because there was no closet or bed available at the time the prayers were needed.

When Jesus spoke of 'Closet' he was referring to praying inside ourselves (Matthew 6:6), for it was not recorded thereafter that anyone actually went into their closet to pray.

Prayer is a necessity, no matter where or how we pray. Nothing in this writing states that you should not pray in a closet or at the side of the bed. It only informs that prayers to be timely must be spontaneous and according to the will of God. Spontaneity cannot be framed into certain hours of the day, or locations.

When something is about to happen that needs attention, the spirit of prayer will come over us, and even though we may think we are praying by our own understanding and knowledge, we will not be, it will all be done by the Holy Ghost, as long as we continue calling upon the Name of the Lord.

When praying, you are not praying to God out there somewhere, you are praying to God that is in you. As God was in Christ, so God and Jesus have taken up their abode within you when you are given the Holy Ghost.

In addition to praying by the direction of the Spirit spontaneously, there are times when it is advantageous to pray with others. This should be done when the church comes together. (Church: Two or three gathered together in the name of God—Matt.18:20).

Call upon the Name of God and place all our cares and worries upon him. We should not carry the world on our shoulders. There are presently too many problems in the world for us to become weighted down with them all. The world's problems will be solved when people collectively decide to call upon the Name of the Lord forever.

Matthew 11:28 Come unto me, all ye that labor and are heavy laden, and I will give you rest. (29) Take my yoke upon you, and learn of me; for I am meek and lowly in heart: and ye shall find rest unto your souls.

Calling upon the Name of the Lord, Jesus, is all that is necessary. When this is done consistently, everything else falls into place by the direction of the Spirit.

****

FISHES AND LOAVES.

Charlene asked this question.

Please explain how the multiplying of the fishes and loaves were accomplished. (Five and four thousand—Matthew 14:21, Matthew 16:10, Mark 8:20).

James gave this response.

After Jesus left his own country he was teaching round about the villages. (Mark 6:1-6) Then he came to Tiberias. The disciples were following him and by that time many people had begun to follow.

Mark 6:31 And he (Jesus) said unto them (Disciples), Come ye yourselves apart into a desert place, and rest a while: for there were many coming and going, and they had no leisure so much as to eat. 32 And they departed into a desert place by ship privately. 33 And the people saw them departing, and many knew him, and RAN AFOOT thither out of all cities, and OUTWENT THEM, and came together unto him.

They went on foot and by boat to the outskirts of Tiberias.

Mark 6:34 And Jesus, when he came out, saw much people, and was moved with compassion toward them, because they were sheep not having a shepherd and he began to teach them many things.

Ref: John 6:32—God was giving them the true BREAD from heaven through Jesus.

Matt. 14:15 And when it was evening, his disciples came to him, saying, This is a desert place, and the time is now past; send the multitude away, that they may go into the villages, and buy (they had money) themselves victuals.

(16) But Jesus said unto them—They need not depart; give ye them to eat. (17) And they said unto him, We have here but five loaves, and two fishes. (Where did the loaves and fishes come from?) John 6:9 There is a LAD here, which

hath five barley loaves, and two small fishes: but what are they among so many?

Why did the lad have more food than he needed? It was intended for sale, but the children of that day were also taught to share.

The feeding of the 5000 occurred at the outskirts of Tiberias. Matt. 14:18 He said Bring them hither to me. (19) And he commanded the multitude to sit down on the grass, and took the five loaves, and the two fishes, and looking up to heaven, he blessed, and break, and gave the loaves to his disciples, and the disciples to the multitude. (20) And they did all eat, and were filled: and they took up of the fragments that remained twelve baskets full. (21) And they that had eaten were about five thousand men, besides WOMEN AND CHILDREN.

What percentage of women would walk into the desert with their children without assuring they had enough food?

During the time of Jesus the people used a SCRIP when they traveled. The scrip of the Galilean peasants was of leather, used especially to carry their food on a journey, and slung over their shoulders. Matt. 10:10; Mark 6:8; Luke 9:3; 22:35.

This day when the people left Tiberias and other cities on foot to follow Jesus, many of them took their 'scrip' full of food. The lad that had five fishes and two barley loaves, had more food than he needed. He had this food for selling, the same as young boys do even to this day in parts of Israel. But the people during that time were taught to give freely and that is what this lad did along with many others that had more than they needed.

PAUL PUT IT THIS WAY.

2 Cor. 8:14 ***But by an equality, that now at this time your abundance may be a supply for their want, that their***

abundance also may be a supply for your want: that there may be equality:

2 Cor. 8:15 ***As it is written, He that had gathered much had nothing over; and he that had gathered little had no lack.***

If you have trouble with this analogy, go back to the time when Jesus was coming off of a forty day fast. When he hungered, the TEMPTER-DEVIL said (It came into his mind) If thou be the Son of God turn this stone into bread.

Matt. 4:2 And when he had fasted forty days and forty nights, he was afterward an hungered. (3) And when the ***temper*** came to him, he said, ***If thou be the Son of God, command that these stones be made bread.*** (4) But he answered and said, It is written, Man shall not live by bread alone, but by every word that proceedeth out of the mouth of God.

Luke 4:2 Being forty days tempted of the devil. And in those days he did eat nothing: and when they were ended, he afterward hungered. (3) And the ***devil said unto him, If thou be the Son of God, command THIS STONE (not stones as Matthew stated) that it be made bread.*** (4) And Jesus answered him, saying, It is written, That man shall not live by bread alone, but by every word of God.

If Jesus recognized that this was not according to the laws of nature and the laws of God, and on this basis, he did not listen to such nonsense, to satisfy his own hunger after forty days, why would he capitulate to such thoughts and tactics for anyone else that had only done without eating for one to three days?

It should be remembered that the apostles attempted to write later from memory about the way they saw things while Jesus was with them. Jesus did not write anything except on one occasion when he wrote on the ground. John 8:6.

Remember too, that the apostles, although they were given the power to cast out devils (heal the minds) and heal the sick (by the power of God through the faith of the people), ***they did not have the gift of the Holy Ghost***. This was not given until the day of Pentecost. The Holy Ghost when it came was to guide into all truth. At the time of the various writings, they had not come together for comparison. Each wrote their own story in their own way from memory of the various events.

Also we have no original manuscripts and there are clerical and translation errors in what we have. So ***we must rely on COMMON SENSE and the guidance of the Holy Ghost in search for all truth.***

Ref: John 16:23 Howbeit when he, the Spirit of truth is come, he will guide you into ALL TRUTH.

Acts 2:4 And they were all filled with the Holy Ghost—.

In order to make natural bread, barley (or some other grain) must be planted, watered, cultivated, crushed, kneaded and baked. Jesus was fully aware of this.

God is logical in everything he does. If it was not necessary for him to create various plants and trees for the nourishment of the natural bodies he would not have done so. It is time for the world to wake up and become acquainted with God and his ways, and stop wavering with the thoughts of men.

****

GAMBLING

Anonymous asked this question.

Can anyone tell me where I might find scriptures in the Bible relating to gambling, please?

James gave this response.

The casting of lots was used to select the thirteenth apostle.

Acts 1:26 And they gave forth their lots; and the lot fell upon Matthias; and he was numbered with the eleven apostles.

The soldiers cast lots.

Matthew 27:35 And they crucified him, and parted his garments, casting lots; that it might be fulfilled which was spoken by the prophet, They parted my garments among them, and upon my vesture did they cast lots.

LOT: (literally a pebble) The custom of deciding doubtful questions by lot is one of great extent and high antiquity. Among the Jews lots were used with the expectation that God would so control them as to give a right direction to them. They were very often used by God's appointment. As to the mode of casting lots, we have no certain information. Probably several modes were practiced. Very commonly among the Latins little counters of wood were put into a jar with so narrow a neck that only one could come out at a time. After the jar had been filled with water and the contents shaken, the lots were determined by the order in which the bits of wood, representing the several parties, came out with the water. In other cases they were put into a wide open jar, and the counters were drawn out by the hand. Sometimes again they were cast in the manner of dice. The soldiers who cast lots for Christ's garments undoubtedly used these dice.

Lyman Abbott.

GAMBLING ESTABLISHMENTS

The gambling houses are designed to play upon the people's greed. They know that when a person wins, that memory continues to grow within the person's mind until they return in the hopes of gaining even more than at the first. It is a known fact that the odds are set in the establishment's favor, and there is no way the player can win in the long run. Gambling in this manner can lead to obsessions, and that in turn sometimes lead to an unstable financial life.

God understands that the imagination of men's heart is evil from his youth. Excessive greed is a part of that weakness. (Gen. 8:21). When men mature, and have enough experience, they will learn, and be able to conform to the natural laws of nature and the spiritual laws of God. The laws of men have never completely controlled the thoughts of men. When thoughts run rampant the body follows, irrespective of the rules of law. People cannot conform to the natural laws, whether they are the Laws given by Moses, or the laws of the land, until they have been given the power to conform to the spiritual laws of God.

It is not a question of gambling or drinking or any other activity of destructive potential, it is the obsessions they may encourage to lowering of the mental or spiritual status. This may cause weakness to temptations and lead to all sorts of inappropriate actions.

BUT SHOULD WE JUDGE OTHERS?

Matthew said, (Matthew 7:1-2) Judge not, that ye be not judged.

Luke 6:37 Judge not, and ye shall not be judged: condemn not, and ye shall not be condemned: forgive, and ye shall be forgiven—.

Jesus said, (John 12:47) I came not to judge the world, but to save the world.

Paul said, (1 Cor. 6:12), All things are lawful unto me, but all things are not expedient: (advantageous) all things are lawful for me, but ***I will not be brought under the power of any.***

Should we gamble or not gamble? Should we drink or not drink? To these questions we must all be convinced in our own minds after determining if it adversely affects our lives or the lives of others around us. Jesus did drink intoxicating beverages. Even the Apostles drank with him. But Jesus did no sin, and the Apostles did gamble in actuality when they cast lots in the selection of the thirteenth apostle. Even when we invest in ANYTHING, yes, even in banks, it is a gamble.

Anonymous rated this answer:

Very thorough; thank you too!!!

****

Gift of God, Living Water.

Ronndonn asked this question.

The Gift Jesus brought was the Gift of "Eternal Life".

When Jesus talked with the woman at Jacob's well, He went into some detail as to how she could ask and receive the "Gift of God" from Him, and how it would become a spring "welling up into Eternal Life". So there is that connection with the word Gift (that Jesus used) and Eternal life. So that's right.

So my question is this . . . When Jesus is talking about "living water", is He talking about H2O (material water) or is he talking about something spiritual?

Be careful how you answer this question because you will notice that Jesus is talking about DRINKING something that He has brought from God . . . or the GIFT OF GOD that he brought. So this GIFT OF GOD, this "LIVING WATER" . . . is it material water or is it spiritual?

James gave this response.

John 4:13 Jesus answered and said unto her, Whosoever drinketh of this (natural) water shall thirst again: (14) But whosoever drinketh of the water (spiritual) that I shall give him shall never thirst; but the water that I shall give HIM shall be in ***HIM*** a well of water springing up into everlasting life.

Note that Jesus said unto her (16) ***Go, call thy husband***, and come hither. ***Herein lies the answer. It is the spiritual power that flows from the positive to the negative and back to the positive of the human structure. This is a continual spiritual current like water flowing between the husband and the wife and back again.***

The following was structured for the original question.

John said, (Matthew 3:11) He, Jesus, shall baptize you with the Holy Ghost—. (Also Mark 1:8, Luke 3:16)

John was filled with the Holy Ghost from his mother's womb (Luke 1:15, 41), ***but it was different with Jesus.*** Jesus had to be tempted in all manner as we are. (Heb. 2:18, 4:15) without the support of the Holy Ghost. It was necessary for him to experience the weaknesses in men so that he could prescribe for them the remedy that would eventually bring them back into the state of Paradise.

The Holy Ghost came upon Mary and guided the conception and the power of God overshadowed her (Luke 1:35), but Jesus did not receive the gift of the Holy Ghost until he was baptized in water. Now when all the people were baptized, it came to pass, that Jesus also being baptized, and praying, the heaven was opened, (22) And the ***Holy Ghost descended in a bodily shape like a dove upon him, and a voice came from heaven, which said, Thou art my beloved Son; in thee I am well pleased. (Luke 3:21-22) And Jesus being full of the Holy Ghost returned from Jordan. (Luke 4:1)***

The Holy Ghost through Jesus was the disciples comforter while

Jesus was with them, but Jesus knew he was going away so he said, (John 14:16) I will pray the Father, and he shall give you another Comforter, that he may abide with you FOREVER; even the spirit of truth; whom the world cannot receive, because it seeth him not, neither knoweth him: but ye know him; for he dwelleth with you, and shall be in you. (18) I WILL NOT LEAVE YOU COMFORTLESS: I WILL COME TO YOU. (19) Yet a little while, and the world seeth me no more; but ye see me: because I live, ye shall live also. (20) At that day ye shall know that I am in my Father, and ye in me, and I in you. As Jesus communed with those he had chosen, he said, This do in remembrance of me (1 Cor. 1:24-26),—as often as ye eat this bread, and drink this cup, ye do show the Lord's death till he come. (Natural communion) Jesus came to them with the Holy Ghost on the day of Pentecost and at that time they all received the gift of the Holy Ghost and the filling of the Holy Spirit (Acts 2:4) so that they could spiritually move into the Holy Place where the first man and woman had resided.

Matthew 18:1 The Son of man is come to save that which was lost.

Heb. 9:28 So Christ was once offered to bear the sins of many: and UNTO THEM THAT LOOK FOR HIM SHALL HE APPEAR THE SECOND TIME—.

Jesus came to give spiritual gifts to humanity so that they could overcome the weaknesses that had developed within their genes caused by the unspeakable deeds perpetrated by their ancestors.

But the kingdom of God was taken by force (Matthew 11:12) by ungodly men primarily in religion at the time of Jesus' sojourn here. They didn't hear him then. Are they hearing him now?

Those that do not have the Holy Ghost, the filling of the holy spirit, spiritual eyes and ears, have not been born again of their spirit, i.e. the spirit of the natural father killed, taken out and a right spirit placed within, should call upon the Name of God fervently.

Acts 2:21—It shall come to pass, that WHOSOEVER shall CALL on the NAME of the LORD shall be saved. Joel 2:32, Rom. 10:13)

Saved from what?

Saved from every conceivable destructive element in the world so that humanity can experience eternal life as was shown to man and woman in the beginning.

John 3:16 For God so loved the world, that he gave his only begotten Son, that WHOSOEVER, believeth in him should not perish, but have everlasting life.

Faith is increased when calling upon His Name.

The spiritual water is the holy spirit that flows from the belly into ever lasting life after the Holy Ghost is received. As the natural current flows between the male and the female so does the spiritual water flow between the two. This is why Jesus said, Go call they husband, and come hither.

Ronndonn rated this answer:

Thanks James. Thanks for going into all the current thinking on it.

****

Give to the poor and leave family.

Charlene asked this question.

Is it right to sell everything, give to the poor and leave the family?

James gave this response.

Is it right to sell everything we have an give to the poor?

Why did Jesus advocate leaving the family?

Mark 14:7 (Jesus said), Ye have the poor with you always, and whensoever ye will ye may do them good:—.

Jesus said to a young affluent man (Matthew 19:21),—If thou wilt be perfect, go and sell that thou hast, and give to the poor, and thou shalt have treasure in heaven and come and follow me.

Evidently, it is not God's intention to force people into poverty by demanding that they give away their livelihood, but that they seek first the kingdom of God and then they will have access to a hundred times more, after they have received a correction in their spiritual life.

Jesus said (Mark 10:29) There is no man that hath left house, or brethren, or sisters, or father, or mother, or wife, or children, or LANDS, for my sake, and the gospel's, (30) But he shall receive an ***HUNDREDFOLD NOW IN THIS TIME, HOUSES,*** and brethren, and sisters, and mothers, and children, and ***LANDS—.***

Matthew 6:33. But seek ye FIRST the Kingdom of God, and his righteousness; and ALL THESE THINGS SHALL BE ADDED UNTO YOU. (32)—for your heavenly ***Father knoweth that ye have need of ALL THESE THINGS.***

Why did Jesus advocate leaving home and family?

Jesus knew that the believer and the unbeliever would never be able to amicably coexist. There is always a war between the natural and the spiritual. A person that has received spiritual understanding cannot be understood by a naturally minded person. (1 Cor. 2:14) The natural man receiveth not the things of the Spirit of God: for they are foolishness unto him: NEITHER CAN HE KNOW THEM, because they are spiritually discerned.

(2 Cor. 6:14) ***Be ye not unequally yoked together with unbelievers: for what fellowship hath righteousness with unrighteousness? And what communion hath light with darkness? (15) And what concord hath Christ with Belial? (worthless lawless fellow). Or what part hath he that believeth with an infidel?*** (One who does not believe in a particular religion).

Ephesians 5:8 For ye were sometimes darkness, but now are ye light in the Lord: (11)—Have no fellowship with the unfruitful works of darkness, but rather reprove them.

Jesus said (Matthew 10:34) Think not that I am come to send peace on earth: I came not to send peace, but a sword. (Not a literal sword).

No amount of words will ever be able to change and convince the spiritually dead person. They must first be resurrected to spiritual life, be given spiritual eyes and ears, the spirit they received from their natural father must be taken out and they must be born again with a right spirit, receive the gift of the Holy Ghost, and maintain the flow of spiritual water from their inner being.

All these spiritual gifts are available to those that will call upon the Name of God without wavering. There will continue to be separations of families unless the whole family together reaches out to God by their faith through His Name in order to receive those spiritual gifts.

Hebrews 11:6 But without faith it is impossible to please him: for he that cometh to God must BELIEVE THAT HE IS, and that he is a rewarder of them that diligently seek him.

****

God, Is anything too hard for?

Edward asked this question.

IS ANYTHING TOO HARD FOR GOD? Gen. 18:14.

James gave this response.

NO! With God all things are possible. Matt. 19:26.

Jer. 21:17 Ah Lord God! behold, thou hast made the heaven and the earth by thy great power and stretched out arm, and there is nothing too hard for thee:

Ah Ha! But God used physical things to deal with physical things.

Does he not make mountains by continents pressing against one another, and Islands by the use of molten rock (magma) flowing from beneath the surface of the earth? Are not stones reshaped and worn away by the continuous rushing of water down mountain streams? Didn't he make water by the mixture of hydrogen and oxygen? Did he not speak the worlds into existence by the cooling of gasses to below 6000 degrees, so that they became solid matter?

GOD IS A SPIRIT. HE IS ALSO A SCIENTIST. He uses physical things to change physical things.

DOES HE NOT PRESENTLY USE THE HANDS OF MAN TO REMOVE GALL STONES AND SET BROKEN BONES?

Bones which have been broken and separated can be brought together by God, but he uses doctors in this process. The mind and spirit cannot do this job alone. This operation must be done manually. The bones must be held in a close stationary position until they have had time to grow back together. (knit).

When we all get to Paradise (heaven) the minds of all men will be directed by the spirit, then there will be no 'accidents'.Consequently, there will be no broken bones. There will be no gall or kidney stones, or brain tumors to be removed, because all systems in the body will be working properly. The autonomic (acting or functioning automatically)system of the body will be regulating not only the heart, digestion, and blood pressure, but all other unconscious activities such as reproduction, and reflex senses to warn of unseen dangers.

Accidents among people are caused by minds out of focus.

WHEN WE ALL GET TO HEAVEN, WHAT A DAY OF REJOICING THAT WILL BE. WHEN WE ALL SEE JESUS—.

All this and more including the healing of diseases can be done by faith—but none of these things will ever be done unless works are included—.

James 2:18 Yea, a man may say, Thou hast faith, and I have works: show me thy faith without thy works, and I will show thee my faith by my works.

James 2:26—as the body without the spirit is dead, so faith without works if dead also. We can't just do nothing—God doesn't.

Yes, there is nothing too hard for God to do, but he always uses a logical plan in the construction of everything. Look at the creation of animals and plants. They all are developed by an understandable order of things.

****

God, is He an Automobile mechanic?

Edward asked this question.

Does God heal cars when you pray for them?

James gave this response.

IS GOD AN AUTOMOBILE MECHANIC?

James began to examine Jim Creed's brain cells for answers to perplexing problems. Well I'll be, James said to himself, Here is the answer. It appeared that many preachers had said in Jim's presence that you could pray for your automobile and it would run. Why had not Jim prayed for this one? Why did not I think of it before? I guess Jim was more knowledgeable than I thought. Maybe I am the one that has a lot to learn. Oh well, I am not like Jim, I am tired of walking everywhere.

If any one had faith, it was James. He had God and all his angels behind him. If all this was true, he would know. But he did not want to shake his faith by trying the key first. He knew the car was very cold, and would need extra power in the battery to start it. It also had not run since it suddenly broke down at least a week ago. The battery was probably discharged all the way.

He looked around to see if anybody was watching. He knew what he was going to do, but other people may not understand. They were sure to think James too was having mental problems.

The hood was open. The first thing to do was to charge the battery. He placed one thumb on the positive side, and the other thumb was placed on the negative side of the battery. The posts were very cold, but sure enough he had faith and it was working. His arms had a tingling sensation as the charge went from his body, down through his arms and flowed into the battery.

The time required to charge a battery on a charger in a station is usually half an hour, but the power in James was greater. It should not be more than ten minutes to complete the job. His two thumbs were numb because of the cold. A snow flake lit on his nose. It melted and ran down to his lips. His nose began to itch. If he let go to scratch his nose, or to wipe the water from his face, he would loose his contact. He would then have to build himself up mentally in order to have enough faith to complete the charging.

When the flow of power through his arms slowed up, he knew the battery was completely charged. Now for the basic problem. What was wrong with the car? What had caused it to stop suddenly the way it did. James did not know, but he knew how to find out. It was through prayer. He put his hand on the engine. Dear God, James implored, through the Name of Jesus I ask to be shown the problem with this engine. Immediately he could look down deep into the engine and there was the problem. One of the piston rods, where it connected to the bottom of the piston had broken. It was not completely loose though, so it would make things easier. Boy, we would really have problems if it was broken all the way off. Now all that had to be done was to weld it back and the car should be in top shape.

With his hands on the engine, James prayed, Dear God, give me the power to weld this rod, in the Name of Jesus. Immediately the power began to flow from his hands into the engine. The eyes could see the rod being welded. There it was completed so soon. It was as good as new. He thanked God for faith. He could do all things.

His hands were placed in his pockets. The fingers were so numb they could not recognize the keys. After his hands became a little thawed, he lowered the hood and walked slowly to the drivers side. He gently opened the door and slid in, closing the door behind him. The key was placed into the ignition. He was ready to go. He said to himself, I will drive over and park in front of our apartment, then I won't have to answer any questions for the police. The key was turned. Nothing happened.

James returned to the apartment. When he opened the door Ruth inquired, "Did you fix the car?"

No, the battery is dead, I guess, James replied.

GOD IS A SCIENTIST, HIS sons and daughters have followed in his likeness. The intelligence and understanding from their Father God enables humanity to invent, but ***God is not their MAINTENANCE TECHNICIAN.***

MAINTENANCE AND REPAIRS are required on man's inventions. GOD DOES NOT INTERVENE, nor does he answer such prayers.

MAN MADE IT—MAN MAINTAINS IT—unless he can invent a robot to do the job.

1 John 5:14—If we ask ***ANYTHING ACCORDING TO HIS WILL, he heareth us:***

James 4:3 ***Ye ask, and receive not, because ye ask amiss,—***.

****

God, Calling on the Name of

Ruth asked this question.

Why did you determine to Call on the Name of the Lord all the time?

James gave this response.

YEAR: 1960

PLACE: St Louis, Missouri.

Jim wondered—***Since he felt so good after only fifteen minutes of calling upon God's Name, what would happen if he decided to Call upon Him all the time, just with his inner voice, of course.***

Maybe it was intended to be something like the heart beat of the spiritual man. Maybe by calling upon God through his Name, the power of Christ is attracted to men to wash away the condemnation from their mental and spiritual system. It didn't matter. He had nothing to lose. He had tried everything else he could think of to find relief, and it didn't help, so what made the difference?

He determined that this would be his prayer. ***"Lord, let me live to say Jesus just one more time, forever. Jesus, Jesus, Jesus."***

****

God, can he help?

Maxine asked this question.

Does God protect you from every possible destructive element when you are calling upon His Name without ceasing?

James gave this response.

The power of God is able to protect in every case.

WORDS

Psalm 64:2 Hide me from the secret counsel of the wicked; from the insurrection of the workers of iniquity:

Psalm 64:3 Who whet their tongue like a sword, and bend their bows to shoot their arrows, even BITTER WORDS.

Psalm 64:4 That they may shoot in secret at the perfect: suddenly do they shoot at him, and fear not.

Psalm 64:6 They SEARCH OUT iniquities; they accomplish a diligent search:—.

Psalm 64:7 But God shall shoot at them with an arrow; suddenly shall they be wounded.

Psalm 64:8 So they shall make their own tongue to fall upon themselves:

PHYSICAL REALITY

Psalm 91 You that live in the shelter of the Most High and lodge under the shadow of the Almighty, who say, 'The Lord is my safe retreat, my God the fastness in which I trust'; he himself will snatch you away from fowler's snare or raging tempest.

He will cover you with his pinions, and you shall find safety beneath his wings: you shall not fear the hunters' trap by night or the arrow that flies by day, the pestilence that stalks in darkness or the plague raging at noonday.

A thousand may fall at your side, ten thousand close at hand, but you it shall not touch; his truth will be your shield and your rampart.

With your own eyes you shall see all this; you shall watch the punishment of the wicked. For you, the Lord is a safe retreat; you have made the Most High your refuge. No disaster shall befall you, no calamity shall come upon your home. For he has charged his angels to guard you wherever you go, to lift you on their hands for fear you should strike your foot against a stone.

You shall step on asp and cobra, you shall tread safely on snake and serpent.

Because his love is set on me, I will deliver him; I will lift him beyond danger, for he knows me BY MY NAME.

When he calls upon me, I will answer; I will be with him in time of trouble; I will rescue him and bring him to honor. I will satisfy him with long life to enjoy the fullness of my salvation.

Acts 2:21 AND IT SHALL COME TO PASS, THAT WHOSOEVER SHALL CALL ON THE NAME OF THE LORD SHALL BE SAVED.

God, Creation of

Edward asked this question.

Can the creation of God as an individual be explained?

James gave this response.

Rom. 11:33 O the depth of the riches both of the wisdom and knowledge of God! How unsearchable are his judgments, and his ways past finding out!

Paul said, (1 Cor. 13:9)—We know in part, and we prophesy in part, (10) But when that which is perfect is come, then that which is in part shall be done away.

God is A (signifying one) Spirit—John 4:24. If that one individual spirit is in one place he is not in another at the same time. The power or spirit that emanates from that one spirit permeates all space. It is this spirit of God (Christ) that lights (gives understanding and life to) every man that cometh into the world.

(John 1:9) That was the true light, which lighteth every man that cometh into the world.

Man was made in the image and likeness of God. It follows as a matter of course that God looks like man. He has a form, though that form is made of spiritual substance that cannot be seen by the natural eyes of man, only in the form of vision.

Consider the atom!

The nucleus of the natural atom is made up of two parts—The proton and the neutron.

Nucleus: central mass or part (as of a cell or an atom).

Proton: Positively charged particle.

Neutron: Uncharged atomic particle.

The electron circles the nucleus of the natural atom.

Electron: negatively charged particle within the atom.

Between the positive and the negative is the generation of power.

God is the spiritual proton and neutron that activates the movement of the electron. The power that emanates from the nucleus is the power of God (Christ) which was used in the creation of all things. (The spiritual being of God embodies knowledge, understanding, wisdom, and form in appearance as that of a man, though made of spiritual substance that cannot be seen by the natural eyes of man.)

Col. 1:16 For by him were all things created, that are in heaven, and that are in earth, visible and invisible, whether they be thrones, or dominions, or principalities, or powers: All things were create by him, and for him: (17) And he is before all things, and by him all things consist. (18) For it pleased the father (the spiritual nucleus) that in him (His Son Jesus who is called Christ (Matthew 1:16) should all fulness dwell—.

From God, the nucleus, came Christ (the power or anointing from God). And then after much time and experimentation God said to his Son Christ, (Gen. 1:26) Let us make man in our image, after our likeness"—First the male, (negative who received his spiritual strength from God, until the counter part was developed, which was the positive part of the human atom—these two parts were as one unit and God called them MAN. (Gen.1:27). They were of one flesh.

Matthew 19:4 Have ye not read, that he which made them at the beginning made them male and female,(5) And said, For this cause shall a man leave father (God) and mother (earth), and shall cleave to his wife: and they twain shall be one flesh?

Originally man received his positive strength from God direct, but after the creation of his counter part he received that positive power from the female. But they both were to receive their spiritual strength from God through the flow of Christ. If this tie was severed they would be drawn down by the destructive elements of the earth, first spiritually, then naturally.

Remember that God was the positive side on the spiritual level and Christ was the negative side of that union. Christ emanated from God, he was never considered God. He himself said, (John 10:36) I said, I AM THE SON OF GOD—.

Can the creation of God be explained? Yes, all things are logical, and can be explained in a logical manner by the direction of the Holy Ghost.

Psalm 31:3 Thou art my rock and my fortress; therefore for THY NAME'S sake lead me, and guide me.

John 16:13—When he, (the Holy Ghost)the SPIRIT OF TRUTH, is come he will guide you into ALL TRUTH.

Rev. 19:13 HIS NAME is called the WORD of GOD.

John 1:1 In the ***beginning*** was the WORD—AND THE WORD WAS GOD.

So the vibration caused by the sound of His Name was the beginning, it was God, then (Gen. 1:1) God created the heaven and the earth and all things by Christ which is the power that flows from him.

****

GOD, DID HE HAVE A BEGINNING?

Edward asked this question.

Did God have a beginning?

James gave this response.

DID GOD HAVE A BEGINNING?

Darkness was there,
but there was no night.
There was no day because
there was no light.

A pulsation occurred:
Out of nothing it came,
So small in fact,
it could not be heard.
Then it produced the sound
of a Name.

In the beginning was the WORD,
and the word WAS GOD. John 1:1.

The nucleus at first was all, nothing more,
then the electron began to circle its core.

God and then His Christ had been formed.
Then the angels swarmed. (Electrons)

INTELLIGENCE APPEARED AT THE SPARK
OF THAT FIRST LIGHT.
It flooded across the then known night.

THE SMALLEST THING BECAME THE GREATEST.
IT WAS GOD.
If there had been a rain drop, God could have been a part of it a million, million billion times, for it takes that many atoms to form one drop.

According to the theory of atomism, the atom is one of the extremely small particles, out of which the entire universe is composed.

EXAMINE THE FOLLOWING

GOD—NUCLEUS OF ATOM
EMISSION—VIBRATION
VIBRATION—FRICTION
FRICTION—RESISTANCE—SOUND
SOUND—NAME
FRICTION—HEAT
HEAT—LIGHT
LIGHT—CHRIST
CHRIST—POWER EMANATING FROM GOD
LIGHT—INTELLIGENCE.

John 1:9 That was the true LIGHT, which lighteth EVERY MAN that cometh into the world.

DID GOD HAVE A BEGINNING?

YES!

John 1:1 In the BEGINNING was the WORD, and the WORD was with God, and THE WORD WAS GOD.

Revelations 19:13—HIS NAME is called the WORD OF GOD.

****

GOD, DID HE SAY "EAT NO NATURAL FRUIT?

James gave this follow-up.

Gen. 3:2 And the woman said unto the serpent,(Man)

WE MAY EAT OF THE FRUIT OF THE TREES OF THE GARDEN—.

Fruit and vegetables are what we should eat for good physical health. THIS IS NOT A SIN.

EAT OF THE TREE OF LIFE

The way back to Paradise is through the Tree of Life. Jesus is that Tree of Life. (Psalms 34:8) Oh taste and see that the LORD is good: blessed is the man that trusteth in him.

Psalm 63:5 My soul shall be satisfied as with marrow and fatness; and my mouth shall praise thee with joyful lips.

Hebrews 13:15 By him therefore let us offer the sacrifice of praise to God CONTINUALLY, that is, the fruit of our lips giving thanks to HIS NAME.

The Tree of Life. Gen. 2:9, 3:22.

John 15:1 I am the true vine, and my Father is the husbandman.

Jesus said,(John 15:5) I am the vine, ye are the branches: He that abideth in me, and I in him, the same bringeth forth much fruit: for without me ye can do nothing. (6) If a man abide not in me, he is cast forth as a branch, and is withered—.

Rev. 2:7—To him that overcometh will I give to eat of the tree of Life which is in the midst of the PARADISE of God.

Heb. 7:19—the law made nothing perfect, but the bringing in of a BETTER HOPE did; by the which we draw nigh unto God.

James 4:8 Draw nigh to God, and he will draw nigh to you.

HOW DO WE DRAW NIGH GOD?

Acts 2:21—it shall come to pass, that WHOSOEVER shall CALL on the NAME of the Lord shall be SAVED. This is the way to heaven, Paradise.

****

GOD, DOES HE CAUSE PAIN AND DEATH?

James gave this follow-up answer.

Man and woman were intended to live forever on the earth, always increasing in strength as the years continued. This they would have done had they not ingested the knowledge of evil into their mental and spiritual system.

Gen 2:17—in the day that thou eatest thereof thou shalt surely die.

2 Peter 3:8—one day is with the Lord as a thousand years.

Gen 7:24—The waters prevailed upon the earth an hundred and fifty days. 150 divided by 30 = 5 months. Using this logic and the fact that it has always taken the earth essentially the same amount of time to circle the sun, we find that the years have always been the same no matter how it has been figured.

Adam lived 930 years. Genesis 5:5

Noah lived 950 years. Genesis 9:29

Methuselah lived 969 years. Genesis 5:27

Not one of those men lived more than one of God's days. Yet it proves that God wants people to live in physical bodies upon the earth eternally the same as he lives in his spiritual existence. God has never wanted pain and death for mankind. Ezek. 18:32 For I have no pleasure in the death of him that dieth, saith the Lord God; wherefore turn yourselves and live ye.

THERE IS NO PAIN IN PARADISE.

Where is Paradise?

Paradise is here upon the earth. It is the spiritual realm in which God placed the man and the woman where they were supposed to live eternally, their bodies always becoming stronger and stronger.

In order for them to have free will, God placed before them two roads. One led to life and the other led to death. They chose death and their conscience drove Christ out of their system.

Since that time they have been deceived into thinking they can do what ever comes to mind and then at death they will make their place among the stars. They are totally ignoring the passage in Eccl. 9:5 For the living know that they shall die: but the dead know not anything, neither have they any more a reward; for the memory of them is forgotten. (6) Also their love, and their hatred, and their envy, is now perished; neither have they any more a portion forever in any thing that is done under the sun.

This passage is applied to the ungodly: Psalm 1:4 The ungodly are not so; but are like the chaff which the wind driveth away. (6) the way of the ungodly shall perish.

Spiritually dead

Jesus said, (Matthew 8:22) Let the dead bury their dead.

People that have driven Christ out of their system or that have never been born again of their spirit are spiritually dead. Paul said (Eph. 5:14) Awake thou that sleepest, and arise from the dead, and CHRIST WILL GIVE THEE LIGHT.

Jesus said, (John 8:12) I am the light of the world: he that followeth me shall not walk in darkness, but shall have the LIGHT OF LIFE.

THOSE THAT HAVE THE LIGHT OF LIFE SHALL MEET JESUS IN THE AIR.

WHERE IS THE AIR?

The atmosphere extends no farther out than 600 miles from the earth.

1 Thes. 4:17 Then we which are (spiritually)alive and remain shall be caught up together with them in the clouds, to meet the Lord in the air: AND SO SHALL WE EVER BE WITH THE LORD.

WHERE?

We shall be caught up into Paradise (Second heaven) where the man and woman were placed in the beginning, (Rev. 2:7) and where Jesus spoke of (Luke 23:43) and Paul mentioned in his vision and out of body experience. (2 Cor. 12:2-4)

GOD HIMSELF SHALL DWELL WITH THEM ON THE EARTH.

Rev. 21:2 And I John saw the holy city, new Jerusalem, COMING DOWN FROM GOD OUT OF HEAVEN, prepared as a bride adorned for her husband.

Rev. 21:3 And I heard a great voice out of heaven saying, Behold, the tabernacle of God IS WITH MEN, and HE WILL DWELL WITH THEM, and they shall be his people, and GOD HIMSELF SHALL BE WITH THEM, and be their God.

Rev. 21:4 And God shall wipe away all tears from their eyes; and there shall be no more death, neither sorrow, nor crying, neither shall there be any more pain:

****

God, does He direct and speak with people?

Anonymous asked this question.

Does God speak and direct people to one another by the Holy Ghost?

James gave this response.

Yes. But, as in everything, there is the other side.

Through observance you will find that many of the ministers and laity alike say the Lord spoke with them concerning what to say or who to see. They have been known to use these tactics to lead the hearers into their way of thinking. It is only through wisdom, knowledge, understanding, and the guidance of the Holy Ghost, that a person will be able to know the difference.

There are two cases along with others of course, where God did direct individuals to another person. Saul and Ananias were directed to each other by the Lord. Acts 9:10. And three men were directed to Peter. Acts 10:5-23. But these directing situations are not common every day occurrences.

THERE ARE SCAMS

I am from the 30s and 40s where people have been known to knock on the door and say the Lord told them to come, then proceeded to get anything they could by hook or crook. After all, it is a lot easier when the person is convinced that God sent them.

I have been told by at least one person that they could speak in tongues anytime they wanted to. Then they proved it. This was used to convince that what they were saying were the words of God. Dangerous business? Yes!

But that is in the world.

People must wake up and ask God for spiritual eyes and ears, and the gift of the Holy Ghost for guidance, and then maintain the holy spirit within themselves in order to be saved from the tactics used by the sly ones.

How do we maintain the holy spirit within ourselves? In the first place the holy spirit flows from God through the assembly of people gathered together in His Name. Matthew 18:20 For where two or three are gathered together in my NAME, there am I in the midst of them. The holy spirit abides where God and his Name (mediator) are. John 14:23 Jesus said, If a man love me, he will keep my words: and my Father will love him, and WE will come unto him, and make our abode with him.

Wickedness (iniquity) drives out the holy spirit of God. Then the oil becomes deficient to keep the light of Christ burning, (John 1:9, 8:12, 9:5,12:46, Matt. 25:3) or the water of life flowing from the belly into continual life. (John 7:38) When this happens, the person drifts off into confusion and more weakness. (Darkness)

When God speaks with a person, they will know it. Hopefully if God speaks to someone else, the Holy Ghost will confirm it to those that are in close contact with God.

****

God, getting Together with

Ronndonn asked this question.

Is it our job to wait around for God to return to us, or is it our job to return to God?

James gave this response.

David prayed:

Psalms 51:10 Create in me a clean heart, O God; and renew a right spirit within me. (11) Cast me not away from thy presence; and take not thy holy spirit from me.

But in Ezekiel 18:31 it is written:

Cast away from you all your transgressions, whereby ye have transgressed; and make you a new heart and a new spirit: for why will ye die. (32) For I have no pleasure in the death of him that dieth, saith the Lord God: wherefore TURN YOURSELVES, and live ye.

As has been repeatedly shown, James said, (James 4:8) Draw nigh to God, and he will draw nigh to you. Cleanse your hands, ye sinners; and purify your hearts, ye double minded.

Hebrews 7:19—The law made nothing perfect, but the bringing in of a better hope did; BY THE WHICH WE DRAW NIGH UNTO GOD.

Hebrews 9:28—Christ was once offered to bear the sins of

many; and unto THEM THAT LOOK FOR HIM shall he appear the second time—.

Rev. 3:20 Behold, I stand at the door and knock: if ANY MAN hear my voice, and open the door, I will come in to him, and will sup with him, and he with me.

The spirit of God is always drawing his creation of men to himself, (Rom. 8:7) but the natural (carnal) mind is enmity (an enemy) against God; for it is not subject to the law of God, neither indeed can be. (8) So then they that are in the flesh cannot please God.

People must draw near God by opening the door,(figuratively) and calling upon him by His Name. Then and only then will God draw near them and give the spiritual gifts necessary to overcome the evil that has been prevalent in the world since the first man, by the feelings of guilt, drove out that holy spirit of God.

Ronndonn rated this answer:

Thanks James

****

God, how may we reach him?

Anonymous asked this question.

Can a person reach God by any other means than through the Name he designated as the NAME of the Mediator between himself and man?

James gave this response.

No!

There is NONE OTHER NAME under heaven given among

men, whereby we must be saved. (Acts 4:12). God is the one who saves through faith in the NAME he gave his only begotten son. There is no other way. (John 3:18) He that believeth on him is not condemned: but he that believeth not is condemned already, because he hath not believed in the NAME of the Only begotten Son of God.

Any religion that by-passes that NAME is the same as a thief and a robber. (John 10:1) He that entereth not into the sheepfold, but climbeth up some other way, the same is a thief and a robber. (9) I am the door: by me if ANY MAN enter in, he shall be saved—.

Denominationalism is comparable to the Tower of Babel when the people wanted to make a name for themselves. (Gen. 11) They thought that tower may reach unto heaven, but it did not, because confusion was allowed by God.

Until the tower of Babel, when the languages commenced their diversification, God was known as LORD GOD. He was not known by any other names until Exodus 3:14. After that time God was called by eight different primary handles. Then when Jesus was born and matured, he said, (John 5:43) I am come in my Father's NAME—. In Rev. 19:13 it is declared that His Name is called the WORD OF GOD. It is that same WORD that was in the beginning: it was with GOD, and it was GOD, (John 1:1) and that WORD was made flesh in the body of JESUS bearing His Father's Name. (John 1:14).

Does this mean that if I do not believe in Jesus, that no matter how much I fast and pray without ceasing; (1 Ths. 5:17) if I prostrate myself with my face on the ground five times a day, God won't hear me?

Yes, that is true! Jesus said, (John 8:24) Ye shall die in your sins; for if ye believe not that I am he, ye shall die in your sins. Jesus said, (8:34) Whosoever committeth sin is the servant of sin, (35) And the servant abideth not in the house for ever: but the Son abideth ever.

Isaiah 43:11 God said through Isaiah,—I, even I, am the LORD; and beside me there is no saviour. God may say, (Matthew 7:23) I never knew you: depart from me ye that work iniquity (wickedness). God through Jesus is the only one that forgives sins. (2 Cor 5:19—God was in Christ—Matt. 9:6 By this power of God, the Son of man hath power on earth to forgive sins—.)

Psychiatrists cannot take the weight of guilt permanently away. They can only deal with words that temporarily affect the emotions, or in some cases they use drugs. Jesus relieves that heaviness of guilt when he comes with the Holy Ghost and places that gift inside the soul of the individual. This power which emanates from the Holy Ghost generates the water of life, and it commences to flow like water out of the belly (John 7:38) into continual life. This water of life washes out the effects of wickedness and causes the body to live. It clears the conscience and produces the reality of freedom. Paul said, (Romans 8:2) For the law of the Spirit of life in Christ Jesus hath made me free from the law of sin and death. Paul was, of course, writing about the laws of Moses, and the gifts and sacrifices, that could not make him that did the service perfect, as pertaining to the conscience. (Hebrews 9:9).

ALL HAVE SINNED—FORGIVENESS IS AVAILABLE ONLY THROUGH HIS SON—JESUS.

1 John 1:7—The blood of Jesus Christ, his (God's) Son cleanseth us from all sin. (8) If we say that we have no sin, we deceive ourselves, and the truth is not in us. (9) If we confess our sins, (to God through His Son—this type of a sinners prayer is heard—John 9:31) he is faithful and just to forgive us our sins, and to cleanse us from all unrighteousness. (10) If we say that we have not sinned, we make him a liar, and his word is not in us.

Romans 10:12 ***THE SAME LORD OVER ALL IS RICH UNTO ALL THAT CALL UPON HIM.***

Galatians 3:28 There is neither Jew nor Greek, there is neither bond nor free. There is neither male nor female: for ye are all one in Christ JESUS.

****

GOD INDIFFERENT?

Charlene asked this question.

IS GOD INDIFFERENT ABOUT THE SUFFERINGS OF HUMANITY?

James gave this response.

No! God has always been deeply concerned.

Man was given the formula for maintaining continuous life within himself, but because of his pride and arrogance he would not use that formula until it was lost from his own memory and the minds of his offspring.

Over and over God has tried to help man but every time He turned his back man has forgotten. Man was God's invention. He still loves that product of his own thoughts and labor. He has always pleaded with the human race to call upon him for help and direction. God knew from the very on-set of the creation that man could fail, but that failure was not predetermined. God knew that man could fall but he did not know that he would. That would have been unjust. To protect the human race from the destructive elements of the earth and the devastation of man's own thoughts, God had a pre-determined course of action in mind from the beginning.

At the time of the last Adam (1 Cor. 15:45), God knew men may not accept the words or person of His Son, for there were many examples of the prophets that had been rejected by men of natural understanding.

But to retrieve men from the destructive elements of the earth, it was necessary for God to send the knowledge of His Name to man in the physical body of His Son.

God thought—It is possible they may hear MY SON.

Matthew 21:33 Hear another parable: There was a certain householder, which planted a vineyard, and hedged it round about, and digged a winepress in it and built a tower, and let it out to husbandmen, and went into a far country:

(34) And when the time of the fruit drew near, he sent his servants (the prophets) to the husbandmen (religious leaders), that they might receive the fruits of it.

(35) And the husbandmen (religionists) took his servants (the prophets) and beat one, and killed another, and stoned another.

(36) Again, he (God) sent other servants more than the first: and they did unto them likewise. (37) But last of all he sent unto them (the religious leaders) HIS SON, saying,

THEY WILL REVERENCE MY SON.

Matthew 21:38 But when the husbandmen (religious leaders) saw the SON (JESUS), they said among themselves, This is the heir; come, let us kill him, and let us seize on his inheritance.

(39) And they caught him, and cast him out of the vineyard, and slew him.

WHY DIDN'T GOD STEP IN AND SAVE HIS SON from the trauma of those cruel hands and hammer?

With God there is no variableness, neither shadow of turning. (James 1:17)

God would not change his own pre-determined plan to give men their own free-will, so they could think and act without direct supervision. God wants men to have freedom of choice, therefore he has set before them two roads, life and good, and death and evil (Deut. 30:15). Because they have not understood the formula for attracting the power of God and his direction they have always taken the wrong road.

But there is an answer which was determined from the beginning.

When men and women, ***two by two***, are calling upon the Name of the Lord without ceasing, there is a protective force in and around them that causes the diversion of all destructive powers. This was the formula set forth from the beginning, IN THE GARDEN OF EDEN. MAN AND WOMAN TOGETHER, TWO BY TWO. AND ON THE ARK WITH NOAH—EIGHT SOULS, TWO BY TW0.

YES, GOD CARES. BUT HE HAS GIVEN THE FORMULA. THE ONLY THING ALL MEN AND WOMEN MUST DO, IS USE IT.

Call upon God's name without ceasing and be saved from the destructive elements of the earth and the thoughts and actions of men.

****

GOD, IS HE JESUS? IS JESUS GOD?

a_curious_researcher asked this question.

Could you please interpret Philip:2:6. Does it mean Jesus is God or not?

Thank you so much for your time.

God bless you.

James gave this response.

Philip 2:6 Who, being in the form of God, thought it not robbery to be equal with God.

This does not indicate that Jesus is God. Men can also become the sons of God through the rebirth of their spirit but that does not make them God.

God was in Christ reconciling the world unto himself.

John 5:43.

JESUS/PHILIP

John 14:9 Jesus saith unto him, (This was God speaking through His Son) Have I been so long time with you, and yet hast thou not known me, Philip? He that hast seen me hath seen the Father; and how sayest thou then, Show me the Father?

Jesus said, (John 5:43) I am come in my Father's Name—.

1 John 4:9—God sent his only begotten SON into the world, that we might live through him. (Also John 3:16). Jesus said, (John 10:36) ***I am the Son of God—.***

John said, (John 1:34) And I saw, and bare record that this is the Son of God.

John 14:10 Believest thou not that I am in the Father, and the Father in me? The words that I speak unto you I speak not of myself: but the Father that dwelleth in me, he doeth the works.

(11) Believe me that I am in the Father, and the Father in me—
.

Let nobody impart to the mind that Jesus is God, but that Jesus is the mediator between God and man. Even Jesus himself said in answer to the Jews, (John 10:31-36) Say ye of him, whom the Father hath sanctified, and sent unto the world, Thou blasphemest; because ***I SAID I AM THE SON OF GOD?***

Jesus came to replace that which was lost. Jesus tried to show people the way back to Paradise by faith in the Name of the Lord. That saving Name of the Lord that had always been in existence since the beginning, but had been lost to the minds of men. His Name was called the Word of God in (Rev.19:13) and (John 1:2) the same was in the beginning with God.

David said, (Proverbs 18:10) The Name of the Lord is a strong tower: the righteous (justified) runneth into it, and is safe.

Acts 2:21—It shall come to pass, that WHOSOEVER shall CALL on the NAME of the LORD shall be saved.

Did the early church know this?

Yes, but when the way got rough they forgot and began to doubt as Peter did when attempting to go to Jesus on the water. Matthew 14:31.

The church at Corinth.

1 Cor. 1:2 Unto the church of God which is at Corinth, to them that are sanctified in Christ Jesus, called to be saints, with ALL THAT IN EVERY PLACE CALL UPON THE NAME OF JESUS CHRIST OUR LORD. (This was the name 'Jesus.' It was not one of the many names given in the Old Testament).

Believe in the Name of the Son of God.

John 3:18 He that believeth on him is not condemned: but he that believeth not is condemned already, because he hath not believed in the Name of the only begotten SON of God.

John 17:12 Jesus said, (John 17:12)—I kept them in thy Name: those that thou gavest me I have kept—. (26) I have declared unto them thy NAME, and will declare it—.

How will we know the name of the Father and the Son? Proverb 30:4 Who hath ascended up into heaven, or descended? Who hath gathered the wind in his fists? Who hath bound the waters in a garment? Who hath established all the ends of the earth? What is HIS NAME, and WHAT IS HIS SON'S NAME, if thou canst tell?

The problems were partly caused by languages.

God caused to be written, (Zeph. 3:9) For then will I turn to the people a PURE LANGUAGE, that they may ALL CALL upon the NAME of the LORD, to serve him with one consent.

A quiet and peaceable life. VIA—ONE GOD AND ONE MEDIATOR—HIS NAME

1 Tim. 2:3—This is good and acceptable in the sight of God our Saviour; (4) Who will have all men to be saved, and to come unto the knowledge of the truth. 1 Tim 2:5 FOR THERE IS ONE GOD, and ONE MEDIATOR between God and men, the MAN CHRIST JESUS.

1 Cor. 8:5 For though there be that are called gods, whether in heaven or in earth, (as there be gods many, and lords many,) (6) But to us there is but one God, the Father, of whom are all things, and we in him; and one Lord Jesus Christ, by whom are all things, and we by him.

****

God, Glory of

Anonymous asked this question.

When Moses came down the mountain his face shone. Exodus 34:30.

Jesus' face did shine as the sun. Matthew 17:2 Explain the difference.

James gave this response.

MOSES

Exodus 19:18 And mount Sinai; was altogether on a smoke, because the Lord descended upon it in fire: and the smoke thereof ascended as a smoke of a furnace, and the whole mount quaked greatly. (19) And when the voice of the trumpet sounded long, and waxed louder and louder, Moses spake, and God answered him by a voice. (20) And the Lord came down upon Mount Sinai, on the top of the mount: and Moses went up.

Exodus 19:24 And the Lord said unto him, Away, get thee down, and thou shalt come up, thou, and Aaron with thee: but let not the priests and the people break through to come up unto the Lord, lest he break forth upon them.

MOSES' FACE SHONE FROM A CHEMICAL ELEMENT RECEIVED WHILE IN THE MOUNTAIN.

How could Moses' body withstand the poisonous chemical action upon his skin, while the people were instructed not to come up the mountain (Exo. 19:21) lest, MANY OF THEM perish? Why didn't Aaron's skin shine the same as Moses'?

Moses and Aaron were brothers. Their immune system was such that it could withstand forty days without eating plus the effects of the chemicals received from the active volcano. Many of the people's systems were not as strong as that of the two brothers. Aaron's skin did not shine because he did not go all the way to the top. It was stated in Exodus 19: 20—The Lord called Moses up to the TOP of the mount, and Moses went up. Later on the next trip it was stated (Exodus 19: 24) The Lord said unto him (Moses), Away, get thee down, and thou shalt come up, thou, and Aaron with thee—but did not state 'to the top.'

At the age of 120 Moses was still a strong man. His eye was not dim, nor his natural force abated. Exodus 34:7.

JESUS

Matthew 17:1 And after six days Jesus taketh Peter, James, and John his brother, and bringeth them up into a high mountain apart, (2) And was transfigured before them: and his face did shine as the sun, and his raiment was white as the light.

THIS WAS A VISION

Matthew 17: 9 And as they came down from the mountain, Jesus charged them, saying, tell the ***VISION*** to no man, until the Son of man be risen again from the dead.

Since this was a 'vision' there were no physical elements involved, just spiritual.

Neither Moses nor Elijah was aware of this VISION. Peter suggested building three churches and God was letting them know that Jesus was creating words that brought life and those before advocated words and actions that brought death.

Matthew 17: 8 And when they had lifted up their eyes, they saw no man, save JESUS ONLY.

John 14:6—Jesus said, I am the way, the truth, and the life: NO

MAN cometh unto the Father, but by me—not Moses, not Elijah, and not anyone else in the world.

JESUS, the Name of God, is the Tree of Life. We must call upon and have faith in it, and we will all be saved from the destructive elements of the earth.

Tree of Life—Gen. 2:9, 3:22 and Rev. 2:7.

God, How did he appear?

Edward asked this question.

Since no man can see God and live, how did he appear and with what voice did he use?

James gave this response.

GOD IS A SPIRIT. MAN CANNOT SEE A SPIRIT.

Exo. 33:20 Thou canst not see my face: for there shall no man see me, and live.

Jesus said to the Jews, because they were in opposition to him. John 5:37 Ye have neither heard HIS VOICE at any time, nor seen his shape.

How did Jim see God?

He saw God in the form of a vision.

Then what voice did Jim hear?

God used Jim's voice.

Where did the shape of God as in Jim's mind come from?

The ***image and likeness came from the Bible***. Gen 1:26 And God said, Let us make man in our image, after our likeness—.

All of the words were an accumulation of what Jim had learned through sight, sound, experience, and reading. Many of the ideas were forgotten, but stored in his subconscious mind. As he reached for God out of despair caused by guilt and alcohol, (the usage of alcohol had been discontinued ten days prior to the vision) the inspiration he was receiving by his faith in God, caused a correlation of all the knowledge stored in his subconscious mind, and then brought it to the surface.

Unfortunately the knowledge of the proper usage of grammar, English and punctuation had never been stored sufficiently, therefore could not possibly come out.

So then can you say it was God that visited?

Yes, the same as He visited many in the old testament.

The usage of alcoholic beverages were common during the old testament times, and it continued during the time of Jesus, but should have been discontinued on the day of Pentecost when the ***new spiritual wine was dispensed.***

Adam and Eve heard the voice of God, but saw no vision of him. There are multiple passages in the Old Testament that states God appeared to Abraham, Isaac, Jacob and Solomon, along with others in different ways.

****

God, how does he guide?

Anonymous asked this question.

How does God guide in the process of protecting a person from evil forces?

James gave this response.

There are certain boundaries set by God for the protection of those that Call upon His Name. They are spiritual boundaries that the natural human or animal mind, that is being affected by an evil force, cannot cross. When evil is intended, the holy spirit causes the mind of the perpetrator to malfunction so that they will be unable to do harm to their proposed target. The Holy Ghost guides into all truth (John 16:13), and angels protect individuals from other natural pending disasters.(sudden great misfortunes). This process does not work perfectly unless the positive and negative are working together. This is why God said, 'It is not good for man to be alone.'

Psalm 91:3 Surely he shall deliver thee from the snare of the fowler, and from the noisome pestilence. (4) He shall cover thee with his feathers, and under his wings shalt thou trust: his truth shall be thy shield and buckler. (5) Thou shalt not be afraid for the terror by night; nor for the arrow that flieth by day. (6) Nor for the pestilence that walketh in darkness; nor for the destruction that wasteth at noonday. (7) A thousand shall fall at thy side, and ten thousand at thy right hand; but it shall not come nigh thee. (8) Only with thine eyes shalt thou behold and see the reward of the wicked. (9) Because thou hast made THE LORD, which is my refuge, even the most High, thy habitation. (10) There shall no evil befall thee, neither shall any plague come nigh thy dwelling. (11) For he shall give his angels charge over thee, to keep thee in all thy ways. (12) They shall bear thee up in their hands, lest thou dash thy foot against a stone.

This protection is not available to those that will not call upon the Name of the Lord, no matter how religious they think they are and may seem to be.

Jer. 10:25 Pour out thy fury upon the heathen that know thee not, 'AND' UPON THE FAMILIES THAT CALL NOT ON THY NAME—.

Men had not advanced to that perfect state of protection two thousand years ago. The full understanding of the saving power generated by faith in and calling upon God's Name was advocated, but not in common use. When the waves became boisterous it caused the mind to doubt. Matthew 14:31.

Joel 2:32—It shall come to pass, that WHOSOEVER shall CALL on the NAME of the LORD shall be 'delivered'—.

Acts 2:21 And it shall come to pass, that WHOSOEVER shall CALL on the NAME of the LORD shall be 'SAVED.' (Also Romans 10:13)

Of course, God's will for calling upon His Name for the unification of the body, mind, and spirit of man was from the beginning. But it was not exercised until Adam's Grandson (Enos) was born. Gen 4:26 And to Seth, to him also there was born a son; and he called his name Enos: then began men to CALL UPON THE NAME OF THE LORD.

Evidence shows that this act of calling upon God's Name was spasmodic and was only practiced upon occasions. When the way became rough men have always forgotten, (Matthew 14:30-31 Primarily because of fear and doubt).

According to your faith be it unto you. (Matthew 9:29) When calling upon the Name of the Lord we must believe that he is, and that he is a rewarder of them that diligently seek him. (Heb. 11;6)

The early church was calling upon God's Name in every place, (1 Cor 1:2) but as the years wore on they became weary and lost that burning desire to draw near God through the Name of His only begotten Son who had borne God's name to be placed in the minds of men. (Rev. 14:1) As a result of this doubt and indifference that had enveloped the church (group of people) the majority drifted off into the dark ages of confusion and ignorance.

****

GOD IS GREATER. JESUS RETURN THE SECOND TIME.

Alaphiah asked this question.

Dear James,

What did Y'hoshua mean when he said,

"You have heard Me say to you, "I am going away and coming back to you.' If you loved Me, you would rejoice because I said,[14:28 NU-Text omits [I said.]] "I am going to the Father,' for My Father is greater than I. " John 14:28

Regards,
Alaphiah

James gave this response.

God is greater!

Jesus said, (John 5:19) The Son can do nothing of himself, but what he seeth the Father do—.

2 Cor 5:19—God was in Christ reconciling the world unto himself.

GOD CREATED ALL THINGS BY JESUS CHRIST. Eph. 3:9.

God spoke with Philip.

John 14:5 Philip saith unto him, Lord, show us the Father, and it sufficeth us. (9) Jesus saith (i.e. God said through Jesus) unto him, Have I been so long time with you, and yet hast thou not known me, Philip? he that hath seen me hath seen the father;—. (10) Believest thou not that I am in the Father, and the Father in me? the words that I speak unto you I speak not of myself: but the Father that dwelleth in me, he doeth the works. (11) Believe me that I am in the Father, and the Father in me—.

When it came close to time for Jesus' departure, He said, (John 14:12)—I go unto my Father.

JESUS WAS LIFTED UP TWICE.

(Once naturally and once spiritually)_

NATURAL

(If I be lifted up)

John 12:32 And I, if I be lifted up from the earth, will draw all men unto me. (33) This he said, signifying what death he should die.

John 3:14 And as Moses lifted up the serpent in the wilderness, even so must the Son of man be lifted up: (15) That whosoever believeth in him should not perish, but have eternal life.

Jesus said, (John 14:16)—I will pray the Father, and he shall give you another Comforter, that he may abide with you forever—.John 14:28 Ye have heard how I said unto you, I go away, and come again unto you.

Jesus said, (John 14:18) I will not leave you comfortless, I will come to you.

Jesus came to the people with the Holy Ghost on the day of Pentecost. Acts 2:4

Heb. 9:28 Christ was once offered to bear the sins of many; and unto them THAT LOOK FOR HIM SHALL HE APPEAR THE SECOND TIME—WITHOUT SIN UNTO SALVATION (Salvation—saving a person from sin or danger).

How will he return the second time?

In the same manner in which he left.

SPIRITUAL—IN VISION FORM

IF I BE LIFTED UP FROM THE EARTH, WILL DRAW ALL MEN UNTO ME. John 12:32

Acts 1:9—while they beheld, he was taken up; and a cloud received him out of their sight. (10) And while they looked stedfastly toward heaven as he went up, behold, two men stood by them in white apparel; (11) Which said, Ye men of Galilee, why stand ye gazing up into heaven? this same Jesus, which is taken up from you into heaven, shall so come in LIKE MANNER as ye have seen him go into heaven.

God/Jesus, Find

Edward asked this question

Must we travel to find God?

James gave this response.

NO!

The Samaritan woman at the well said (John 4:20), Our Fathers worshiped in this mountain; and ye (Jesus) say, that in Jerusalem is the place where men ought to worship.

John 4:21 Jesus said unto her, Woman, believe me, the hour cometh, when ye shall neither in this mountain, NOR at Jerusalem, worship the Father,—.

John 4:23—the hour cometh, and now is, when the true worshipers shall worship the Father in spirit and in truth: For the Father seeketh such to worship him.

John 4:24 GOD IS A SPIRIT: and they that worship him must worship him in spirit and in truth.

MUST WE TRAVEL TO FIND JESUS?

NO!

Matthew 24:27 For as the lightning cometh out of the east, and shineth even unto the west; so shall also the coming of the Son of man be.

Matthew 24:26 Wherefore if they shall say unto you, Behold, he is in the desert; go not forth: behold, he is in the secret chamber; believe it not.

Jeremiah 31:34—they shall teach no more every man his neighbor, and every man his brother, saying, know the Lord: for they shall ALL know me, from the least of them unto the greatest of them, saith the Lord:

WE DO NOT NEED TO TRAVEL THE WORLD OVER TO FIND JESUS.

HE IS EVER PRESENT WITH US WHEN WE, AT LEAST TWO BY TWO, CALL UPON HIM BY HIS NAME, JESUS.

Matthew 18:20 For where two or three are gathered together in my Name, there am I in the midst of them.

Rev. 21:3 Behold, the tabernacle of God is with men, and he

will dwell with them, and they shall be his people, and God himself shall be with them, and be their God.

John 14:23 If a man love me, he will keep my words: and my Father will love him, and WE WILL COME UNTO HIM, and make our abode with him.

****

God, the Names of

Ruth asked this question.

Why so many names of God?

James gave this response.

God has revealed himself to man through many names.

Genesis 28:3—God Almighty, Exodus 3:14—I Am that I Am, Exodus 6:3—Jehovah, Exodus 34:14—Jealous, Deuteronomy 28:58—The Lord Thy God, Amos 5:27—God of Hosts, Isaiah 54:25—Lord of Hosts, Jeremiah 33:2—Lord, etc., etc., This was designed by God for man's confusion.

Those different names occurred after God confounded the language of the people, because of their desire to 'make a name for themselves' instead of seeking the only true God with their whole heart, and learning, and accepting HIS NAME ONLY. Gen. 11:9 (Matt. 17:8 NO MAN SAVE JESUS ONLY.)

But—The Lord shall be King over all the earth in that day shall there be ONE LORD, and HIS NAME ONE. Jesus said, "I am come in my FATHER'S NAME." John 5:43.

He said to the Jews—John 10:36, "I said I AM THE SON OF GOD. Jesus was not God, but God was in Christ Reconciling the world unto himself. 2 Corinthians 5:19.

WHEN THE PEOPLE LEARN THE NAME OF GOD,

Zephaniah 3:9 ***Then will I turn to the people a pure language, that they may ALL CALL UPON THE NAME OF THE LORD, to serve him with one consent.***

Revelation 3:12 Him that overcometh—I will write upon him the Name of my God, and the name of the city of my God, which is New Jerusalem, which cometh down out of heaven from my God; and I will write upon him ***MY NEW NAME, JESUS.***

Deuteronomy 10:17—The Lord your GOD is GOD of gods, and LORD of lords. Isaiah 26:13 O LORD our GOD, other lords beside thee have had dominion over us: but by thee only will we make mention of THY NAME.

1 Tim. 6:12 Fight the good fight of faith, LAY HOLD ON ETERNAL LIFE, whereunto thou art also called, and hast professed a good profession before many witnesses.

1 Tim 6:13 I give thee charge in the sight of God, who quickeneth (gives life to)ALL THINGS, and before Christ Jesus, who before Pontius Pilate witnessed a good confession:

1 Tim. 6:24 That thou keep this commandment (faith in eternal life) without spot, unrebukeable, until the appearing of our Lord Jesus Christ:

1 Tim 6: 15 Which in his times he SHALL SHOW, WHO IS THE BLESSED and ONLY POTENTATE, the KING OF KINGS, and LORD of lords:

1 Tim. 6:16 Who only hath immortality, dwelling in the light which NO MAN can approach unto; whom NO MAN hath seen, nor can see (GOD is a spirit. Men cannot see a spirit. They can

only see God through the form of an especially prepared vision), to whom be honor and power everlasting.

JESUS WAS GOD'S AMBASSADOR
(He spoke only God's words)

(The Kings) made war with the Lamb (Rev. 17:14) and the Lamb shall overcome them for he is Lord of lords, and King of kings:

> Rev. 19:1l6 And he hath on his vesture and on his thigh a name written, KING OF KINGS, and LORD OF LORDS.
>
> 1 Cor. 15:24 THEN COMETH THE END, when he shall have DELIVERED UP THE KINGDOM TO GOD, even the FATHER, when he shall have put down all rule and all authority and power.
>
> 1 Cor. 15:25 For he must reign, till he hath put all enemies under his feet.
>
> 1 Cor. 15:26 The last enemy that shall be destroyed is death.
>
> 1 Cor. 15:28 And when all things shall be subdued unto him, then shall the ***SON also himself be subject unto him (GOD) that put all things under him, that GOD MAY BE ALL IN ALL***
>
> Deuteronomy 10:17 GOD of gods, and LORD of lords.

****

God, Praise by His Name.

jdg asked this question.

Praising the Lord has been advocated for thousands of years.

Why does the societies of this world still remain in spiritual darkness?

James gave this response.

The New American Bible. Psalms 147:16 He spreads snow like wool; frost he strews like ashes. He scatters his hail like crumbs; before his cold the waters freeze. He sends his word and melts them; he lets his breeze blow and the waters run.

Psalms 148:1 Praise the Lord from the heavens, praise him in the heights; Praise him, all you his angels, praise him, all you his hosts. Praise him, sun and moon; praise him, all you shining stars. Praise him, you highest heavens, and you waters above the heavens. Let them praise the NAME of the Lord, for he commanded and they were created; He established them forever and ever; he gave them a duty which shall not pass away.

Psalms 148:11 Praise the Lord from the earth, you sea monsters and all depths; Fire and hail, snow and mist, storm winds that fulfill his word; You mountains and all you hills, you fruit trees and all you cedars; You wild beasts and all tame animals, you creeping things and you winged fowl.

King James Version

Proverbs 30:4 Who hath ascended up into heaven, or descended? Who hath gathered the wind in his fists? Who hath bound the waters in a garment? Who hath established all the ends of the earth? WHAT IS HIS NAME, AND WHAT IS HIS SON'S NAME, IF THOU CANST TELL?

(Ref: Genesis 4:26) Enos discovered the formula for reaching God, but he did not know HIS TRUE SAVING NAME.

Jesus came to reveal that NAME to the minds of humanity so

they could be saved from the destructive elements of the earth and the minds of natural men.

JESUS IS HIS NAME AND IT IS THE NAME OF HIS FATHER.

Jesus said, I am come in my Father's Name—John 5:43.

Proverbs 21:2 Every way of a man is right in his own eyes—. But there is only one way to God, and his power is attracted only by calling upon His true saving Name.

****

God and prayers:

Rachelle asked this question.

Where is God when we pray?

James gave this response.

The presence of God left the man when the Lord God sent him from the garden of Eden, that spiritual state of second heaven (Paradise—Luke 23:43, 2 Cor. 12:4, Rev. 2:7)where the man and the woman had been placed. Gen. 3:23.

From that time on until the day of Pentecost God was not found within the spiritual life of man or woman. When they prayed it was always directed to 'out there' somewhere in the heavens. Men were moved by the Holy Ghost in olden time, (2 Pet. 1:21) but that guiding force was not found within the beings of men.

When Jesus walked upon the earth he discovered by his own experience that men needed more spiritual strength to combat the evils presented by the natural minds of men, so He said, (John 14:16) I will pray the Father, and he shall give you another Comforter, that he may abide with you forever.—(17)—he dwelleth with you, and shall be in you.—(18) I will not leave you comfortless: I WILL COME TO YOU. (20) At that day ye shall know that I am in my Father, and ye in me, and I in you. (23)—WE WILL COME UNTO HIM, AND MAKE OUR ABODE WITH HIM. (26)—THE Comforter, which is the Holy Ghost, whom the Father will send in MY NAME, he shall teach you all things—.

By way of the Holy Ghost, through the Name of God (Jesus), the spirit of God dwells within everyone that has been given the Holy Ghost as they had received on the day of Pentecost. (Acts 2:4). As it was given on that day to the Jews and witnessed to all nations via other tongues, so it is for all peoples of the earth who will CALL UPON GOD BY HIS NAME WITHOUT CEASING. (Joel 2:32, Acts 2:21, Rom. 10:13, 1 Ths. 5:17, Acts 9:14, 1Cor. 1:2).

When prayers are made according to God's will, they are received by God that dwells within, and to the unwavering, (James 1:6) those prayers are answered, and will be fulfilled in God's time.

****

God, Reaching for-consistently over time.

Maxine asked this question.

How do you reach God? How long does it take?

James gave this response.

Forty two years had passed since the man stood in the valley with no hope. He was at the end of his life. Wherever God was, if there was one, he had to find him. Crying out to God through the Name of His Son Jesus was the only way he could relieve himself of the hurt and despair he felt in his mind and spirit.

Through the process of spiritual changes he finally found his footing. But after his enlightenment he found that he was still in the valley. After a few years discouragement returned. Calling upon the Name of the Lord was an every moment occurrence. Even while falling back into sin he found that God had mercy because of the formula.

From the on-set of complete weakness he had a vision of a great mountain. In his mind, if he could only reach the top of that mountain all problems, real or imagined would melt away into nothing.

His work habits had become more stable. Never again was he flitting from one company to another as he had done in his past life. Stick ability in job related matters was a new found trait. He no longer changed jobs frequently. Twenty Two years was the length of the last job before retirement.

But he was dissatisfied. He had asked God to give him stability in the business world so he could show to the masses that there was real value in calling upon the Name of the Lord. It was a spiritual work that he desired more than the physical day to day labor intensive grind. He wanted permanence in the spiritual realm rather than complacence in the material area that fades away with time.

That distant mountain stood at a very far expanse from where he had begun. There was hope in the envisioned reality of reaching that mountain pinnacle some day.

Suddenly the man arrived at the top of the highest peak. The eyes scanned the world from on top. The masses were out there, reaching, grabbing, condemning, hating, starving for both natural and spiritual sustenance.

The man was shown the means for reaching those masses. His hopes had been at last realized. They would hear and believe. They too would have hope. They would all believe in God and the mediator, His Name Jesus. They would all call upon that Name and be saved from the destructive elements of the earth.

But soon he found that the world did not care. They would not hear; they would not read, all but a very few were too busy. They all knew the way. The way they had been raised in to believe could not be changed.

The feet could not stop walking. There was another valley out there. It was hoped that the steps would be guided even better than they had been in the past. But the valley is wide and the appearance of the next mountain is not as great. Will there be more gurgling brooks meandering across that depression in the contour of the earth? The colorful flowers, will they be more plentiful along the path, and more pleasing to the eyes? More pleasant, that is, than those found in the hot dry desert country of the past! Maybe the man will have to do more planting both spiritually and naturally, and direct more moisture to the area of the dry places.

As the man still stood upon the mountain top he looked around and observed that he himself had a home to live in, the cupboards and freezers were filled with all kinds of food. The valley was teaming with people that were starving naturally and spiritually. Why haven't they heard? Why don't they want to read? Oh, they are busy doing what they want to do!

The man still determined he must continue calling upon the Name of God. How long? Forever! Even if the people do not hear and believe.

The words were recalled, "I have tried to help man from time to time all the way down through the ages, but every time I turn my back man forgets."

This man is alone, but he has remembered. He will not forget.

****

GOD—SAVES THROUGH JESUS HIS SON.

WHO CAN SAVE US FROM THE DESTRUCTION THAT HAS

ALWAYS BEEN IN THE WORLD?

James gave this response.

1 John 5:20 And we know that the Son of God is come and hath given us an understanding, that we may know him (God) that is true, and we are in him that is true, even ***HIS SON JESUS.***

Jesus said, I am come in my Father's Name—(John 5:43).

Proverbs 30:4 Who hath ascended up into heaven, or descended? Who hath gathered the wind in his fists? Who hath bound the waters in a garment? Who hath established all the ends of the earth?

WHAT IS HIS NAME, AND WHAT IS HIS SON'S NAME, IF THOU CAST TELL?

Jesus said, (John 3:13),—No man hath ascended up to heaven, but he that came down from heaven, even the SON of man which is in heaven. (Jesus was standing before them at that present time in Paradise).

2 Cor. 5:19 God was in Christ, reconciling the world unto himself.

John 20:28 And Thomas answered and said unto him, (Jesus) My Lord AND My God. (Thomas recognized that God was in Jesus, therefore he addressed them both).

John 14:20 At that day ye shall know that I am in my Father, and ye in me, and I in you. (21) He that hath my commandments, and keepeth them, he it is that loveth me: and he that loveth me shall be loved of MY FATHER, and I will love him, and will manifest myself to him. (23)—If a man love me, he will keep my words: and MY FATHER will love him, and WE will come unto him, and make our abode with him.

John 5:18 (The Jews sought to kill Jesus) because he said that God was His Father, making himself equal with God.

John 10:33 The Jews answered him (Jesus) saying, For a good work we stone thee not; but for blasphemy; and because that thou, being a man, makest thyself GOD. (34) Jesus answered them, Is it not written in your law, I said, Ye are gods? (35) If he called them gods, unto whom the word of God came—(36) Say ye of him, whom the FATHER hath sanctified, and sent into the world, Thou blasphemest, because I said, ***I AM THE SON OF GOD?***

Matt. 5:16—glorify ***YOUR FATHER WHICH IS IN HEAVEN.***

Note: If God is in you and He is in heaven, then where is heaven? 1 Cor.3:16 Know ye not that ye are the temple of God, and that the Spirit of God dwelleth in you?

Matt. 6:9—(Jesus said) After this manner therefore pray ye: OUR FATHER which art in heaven, Hallowed be thy NAME.

Matt. 7:21 Jesus said, My Father—.

John 1:34—I saw, and bare record that this is the SON OF GOD.

John 3:16 God gave his only begotten Son—.

John 3:34—He whom God hath sent speaketh the words of God—.

John 5:19 (Jesus said) The Son can do NOTHING of himself, what he seeth the Father do—.(If Jesus were God why couldn't he do more?). John 16:26 At that day ye shall ask in my Name: (Jesus) and I say not unto you, that I will pray the Father for you: (27) For the Father himself loveth you, because ye have loved me, and have believed that I came out from GOD. (28) I came forth from the Father, and am come into the world: again, I leave the world, and go to the Father.

John 20:17 I ascend unto my Father and your Father; and to my God and your God.

IT WAS GOD THAT RAISED JESUS FROM THE GRAVE.

Acts 2:32 This Jesus hath GOD raised up—.

Acts 3:15—whom God hath raised from the dead; whereof we are witnesses.

Acts 3:26—God, having raised up HIS Son Jesus—.

John 14:8 Philip saith unto him, Lord (Jesus), show us the Father, and it sufficeth us. (9) Jesus saith unto him, Have I been so long time with you, and yet hast thou not known me, Philip? (This was God in Jesus speaking with Philip through Jesus' voice). He that hath seen me (Jesus the son, said) hath seen the Father; and how sayest thou then, Show us the Father? (10) Believest thou not that I am in the Father and the Father in me? the words that I speak unto you I speak not of myself: (on my own accord) but the Father that dwelleth in me, he doeth the works. (11) Believe me that I am in the Father, and the Father in me—.

John 1:12 But as many as received him, to them gave he power to become the sons of God, even to them that believe on HIS NAME.

Though there are many, many more passages throughout the

Bible proving that Jesus is the Name God designated for HIS SON, and the Son of God is God's Son, and not God himself, the foregoing is sufficient to satisfy the requirement of two or three witnesses to establish every word—though there are many more.

Psalms 110:1 The LORD said unto my Lord (Jesus)—.

Acts 2:34 For David is not ascended into the heavens: but he saith himself, The LORD (God) said unto my Lord, (Jesus) (The son of David (Jesus) that was to sit on David's throne) Sit thou on my right hand, (35) Until I make thy foes thy footstool.

Mark 12:37 David therefore himself calleth him Lord; and whence is he then his son?—They gave no answer because they didn't understand. (Jesus was the Son of God through the spirit, but the Son of David by the flesh). (There is God the Father and also the Lord Jesus). (Gen. 18:12 even Sarah called her husband, Lord).

1 Tim. 2:5 For there is one God, and one mediator between God and men, the MAN Christ Jesus.

1 Cor. 15:24 Then cometh the end, when he (Jesus) shall have delivered up the kingdom to God, even the Father; when he shall have put down all rule and all authority and power,(25) For he (Jesus) must reign, till he (God) hath put all enemies under his feet. (28) And when all things shall be subdued unto him, ***then shall the Son also himself be subject unto him (God) that put all things under him, that God may be all in all.***

GOD SAVES THROUGH THE NAME HE DESIGNATED FOR HIS SON JESUS WHEN WE CALL UPON THAT NAME.

****

God, how Many terms apply?

Anonymous asked this question.

To how many persons do the following terms apply?

1) Everlasting Father

2) Mighty God

3) The First and the Last, also Alpha-Omega, Beginning-End.

4) Saviour

5) Redeemer

6) The Almighty

Can any (or all) of these terms apply to more than only one person and the scripture still be true in saying "I am X, and besides me there is none other (or none other that can do X)?

Thank you

James gave this response.

In reading the following passage from Isaiah remember that the ***operative word here is 'NAME'. His Name is Called***— not the person that was to bear that name. Jesus said, John 10:36 "I said, I am the Son of God. Rev. 19:13 His Name is called the WORD of GOD. John 1:1 In the beginning the WORD WAS GOD.

Isaiah 9:6 For unto us a child is born, unto us a son is given: and the government shall be upon his shoulder: and ***his NAME shall*** be called Wonderful, Counsellor, The mighty God, The everlasting Father, The Prince of Peace.

Orange blossoms in any language is still the same. Likewise, God is the same as he has always been. On occasion he has revealed himself to various individuals within their own dialect and language. This explains why different handles have been attributed to him.

Who confounded their language? Gen. 11

God!

Why?

Because the people wanted to make a name for themselves.

We still have this problem in religion.

Two or three Gods there are not. 1 Tim 2:5 For there is one God, AND one mediator between God and men, the MAN Christ Jesus.

Jesus said, (John 5:43) I am come in my Father's Name. God delivered that name to Joseph by an angel in a dream. (Matthew 1:20). That name is God's 'saving' name. His only begotten Son is named after His FATHER.

Eph. 3:14 For this cause I bow my knees unto the Father of our Lord Jesus Christ, (15) Of whom the whole family in heaven and earth is named.

When Jesus said, (John 10:30) I and my Father are one, he was saying His Father God was within him, and that he (God)was the one speaking and doing the works.

****

God, true and eternal life

Anonymous asked this question.

Who can explain what the bible says in 1 John 5:20 That called The Lord Jesus Christ The true God and eternal life. I believe this is the word in it's simple state not a mystery this word is direct. Please do say something on this as an expert of the Bible knowing that all teachers will be judged pertaining to what so ever they teach.

Please your opinion is needed.

God bless you

James gave this response.

1 John 5:20 And we know that the Son of God is come and hath given us an understanding, that we may know him that is true, and we are in him that is true, even ***HIS SON JESUS*** (God's name) Jesus said, I am come in my ***Father's Name***— John 5:43) ***CHRIST*** (the power of God). This is the true God, and eternal life.

Eternal life is in Christ (The power of God that flows from the Tree of Life—God's Name)

Proverbs 30:4 Who hath ascended up into heaven, or descended? Who hath gathered the wind in his fists? Who hath bound the waters in a garment? Who hath established all the ends of the earth?

WHAT IS HIS NAME, AND WHAT IS HIS SON'S NAME, IF THOU CANST TELL? (Note: God is the Father and Jesus is the Son, bearing the Name of God to the people on the earth.

Jesus said, (John 3:13),—No man hath ascended up to heaven, but he that came down from heaven, even the SON of man which is in heaven. (Jesus was standing before them at that present time in Paradise).

2 Cor. 5:19 God was in Christ (the power of God, anointing),

reconciling the world unto himself (God, through his Name, Jesus).

John 14:20 At that day ye shall know that ***I am in my Father***, and ye in me, and I in you. (21) He that hath my commandments, and keepeth them, he it is that loveth me: and he that loveth me shall be loved of MY FATHER, and I will love him, and will manifest myself to him. (23)—If a man love me, he will keep my words: and MY FATHER will love him, and ***WE will come unto him, and make OUR abode with him.***

John 5:18 (The Jews sought to kill Jesus) because he said that God was His Father, making himself equal with God.

John 10:33 The Jews answered him (Jesus), saying For a good work we stone thee not; but for blasphemy; and because that thou, being a man, makest thyself GOD. (34) Jesus answered them, Is it not written in your law, I said, Ye are gods? (35) If he called them gods, unto whom the word of God came—(36) Say ye of him, whom the FATHER hath sanctified, and sent into the world, Thou blasphemest, because I said, ***I AM THE SON OF GOD?***

Matt. 5:16—***glorify YOUR FATHER WHICH IS IN HEAVEN.***

Matt. 6:9—(Jesus said) After this manner therefore pray ye: ***OUR FATHER*** which art in heaven, Hallowed be thy NAME.

Matt. 7:21 Jesus said, My Father—.

John 1:34—I saw, and bare record that this is the SON OF GOD.

John 3:16 God gave his only begotten Son—.

John 3:34—He whom God hath sent speaketh the words of God—.

John 5:19 (Jesus said) The Son can do NOTHING of himself, what he seeth the Father do—.

John 16:26 At that day ye shall ask in my Name: (God's name-Jesus) and I say not unto you, that I will pray the Father for you: (27) For the Father himself loveth you, because ye have loved me, and have believed that I came out from GOD. (28) I came forth from the Father, and am come into the world: again, I leave the world, and go to the Father.

John 20:17 I ascend unto my Father and your Father; and to m***y God and your God.***

John 14:8 Philip saith unto him, Lord (Jesus), show us the Father, and it sufficeth us. (9) Jesus saith unto him, Have I been so long time with you, and yet hast thou not known me, Philip? (This was God in Jesus speaking with Philip). He that hath seen me (Jesus the son, said) hath seen the Father; and how sayest thou then, Show us the Father? (10) Believest thou not that I am in the Father and the Father in me? the words that I speak unto you I speak not of myself: (on my own accord) but the Father that dwelleth in me, he doeth the works. (11) Believe me that ***I am in the Father, and the Father in me—.***

John 1:12 But as many as received him, to them gave he power to become the sons of God, even to them that believe on HIS NAME.

Though there are many, many more passages throughout the Bible proving that Jesus is the Name of God,(i.e. the name God selected for his son) and the Son of God is God's Son, and not God himself, the foregoing is sufficient to satisfy the requirement of two or three witnesses to establish every word.

Psalms 110:1 The Lord said unto my Lord—.

Mark 12:37 David therefore himself calleth him Lord; and whence is he then his son?—There was no answer given.

Acts 2:34 The Lord (God) said, unto my Lord (Mediator), Sit thou on my right hand, (35) until I (God) make thy foes thy footstool.

1 Tim. 2:5 For there is one God, and one mediator between God and men, the man Christ Jesus.

Gal. 3:20 Now a mediator is not a mediator of one, but GOD is ONE.

Anonymous asked this follow-up question.

Thanks for the work. May God reward you in Jesus name. Thank God you know what is God's name. I hope you do baptism in the name of the father, that is God's name. Acts 2:38 Finally, what is your opinion about the question.

I need your own opinion you have stated the scriptures but what is you opinion.

James gave this response.

Whether you baptize in the Name of Jesus, (Acts 2:38) or in the Name of the Father, Son and the Holy Ghost, (Matthew 28:19) you are still baptizing in the Name of Jesus.

God's Name is Jesus. God's son came in his Father's Name. Jesus is not God. He is the Son of God, the same as we all can become the Sons of God by being born again, i.e. our spirit killed, taken out, and a right spirit installed in its place. This is accomplished by the operation of God and the guidance of the Holy Ghost. This process starts by having faith in and calling upon God by His Name.

The Name of God is the Tree of Life that was in the garden of Eden. If Adamah had called upon that Name without ceasing, he would never have become weak and consciously taken control of the new life making process. Since he never, in his life time, called upon the Name of God he drifted off into weakness, confusion and more sin. (Gen. 3:22).—Now, lest he put forth his hand, and take also of the TREE OF LIFE, and eat, and LIVE FOREVER,—the flaming sword (24) (laws) were devised to keep the way of Paradise (heaven).

If we Call upon the Name of the Lord, God gives us power (at his time) through the guidance of the Holy Ghost to conform to those laws. God understands that we are young and weak because of spiritual ignorance, so through the Mediator, His Son, we can come boldly to the throne of grace, that we may obtain mercy, and find grace to help in the time of need. Heb. 4:16.

Giving a direct opinion on a subject is difficult because people generally feel that God refrained from talking thousands of years ago. Nothing can be said that was not recorded in the Bible already. As in law there must be a precedent. (something said or done earlier that serves as an example). Words are being dissected syllable by syllable, language by language. This causes more contention and confusion. It leads further from the truth. It is indicated that we must know all that is contained in the millions of pages now constructed before we can reach God. If this were true, children and men alike will never find their way to God. Even the persons producing such pages are no closer to God.

No! Eternal life comes through faith in and calling upon the Name of God.

Joel 2:32 It shall come to pass, that WHOSOEVER shall CALL on the NAME OF THE LORD shall be delivered.

Acts 2:21 And it shall come to pass, that WHOSOEVER shall CALL upon the Name of the Lord shall be saved. Also Rom. 10:13.

At the moment the Holy Ghost is received we are in the second heaven spiritual state of Paradise. Because of sin prevalent in our bodies it does not take long for the stream of spiritual water to stop flowing from our bellies that would otherwise produce everlasting life. Our nature must be changed.

To find out where I am coming from please read my other answers.

****

GOD, what is he like?

Ruth asked this question.

What should we think about the appearance, personality and traits of God?

James gave this response.

WHAT IS THOUGHT OF GOD TO BE?

Is he thought to be a vengeful God? Does he carry a sword, or throw stones at people that have sinned? Or is he portrayed more truthfully in HIS SON JESUS, as a kind and merciful deity.

WHAT IS VISUALIZED IN ANOTHER PERSON, OR PERSONAGE IS REFLECTED BACK.

Do we want to be like God? Visualize him as an individual man (Genesis 1:26) for indeed, in spiritual substance, he is in the same image and likeness as man.

God is in man. Look for God in man. Visualize God as being strong, kind, and filled with love for his offspring.

God's son, that came in His Father's Name, made it possible for natural men and women to become sons and daughters of God through a spiritual rebirth. (John 3:7) 2 Corinthians 6:17—I will receive you (18) and ye shall be my sons and daughters, saith the Lord Almighty.

2 Corinthians 7:1 Having therefore these promises, dearly beloved, let us cleanse ourselves from all filthiness of the flesh and spirit, perfecting holiness—.

Have men been good? No! Jesus said (Luke 18:19), Why callest thou me good? none is Good, save one, that is God. Jesus said that because he was aware of where his physical body came from. He knew that there was no good thing in his natural genes. He was aware of his physical ancestors.

Hebrews 5:8 Though he were a Son, (spiritual) yet learned he obedience by the things which he suffered. Romans 3:23 All men have sinned (except Jesus) and are deprived of the glory of God. (24) All men are now undeservedly justified by the gift of God, through the redemption wrought in Christ Jesus. (25) Through his blood, God made him the means of expiation (making amends) for all who believe. He did so to manifest his own justice, for the sake of remitting sins COMMITTED IN THE PAST—(26) to manifest his justice in the PRESENT, by way of forbearance, so that he might be just and might justify those WHO BELIEVE IN HIS NAME

2 Cor. 5:19 God was in Christ, reconciling the world unto himself. God through Jesus said "Have I been so long time with you, and yet hast thou not known me, Philip? John 14:9.

God that was in Christ did not throw stones or cast people that had sinned into a burning hell. No, his attitude was on this wise—

Isaiah 42:3 A bruised reed shall he not break, and the smoking flax shall he not quench—. (Matthew 12:20)

God, why . . . . Abraham?

Anonymous asked this question.

Why did God select certain individuals over others?

James gave this response.

God gave mankind their own freewill. Some called upon the Name of God, but the majority didn't and wouldn't.

In Adamah the knowledge of the Name of God was lost. after Adam's Grandson, Enos (Gen. 4:26), was born, then began men to call upon the Name of God. But they too called upon God spasmodically, and since the knowledge of God's true saving name was lost in Adamah (man),because he would not, at anytime during his life, call upon that name, his offspring did not know the way back to the Garden (Paradise-spiritual), where their ancestor had been placed in the beginning.

This lack of focus upon God through his Name caused the minds of men to be attracted to the actions of the other animals around them, and to their own base thoughts. They became obsessed by those actions and thoughts, and their indulgences ultimately changed their genes so that their offspring became even weaker than themselves.

All the way down through time God has periodically tried to help man, but every time God turns his back, man forgets.

Gen. 6:11 The earth also was corrupt before God, and the earth was filled with violence. Gen. 6:9 Noah walked with God—His family was saved, but not because of their own righteousness

(Acts 16:31 Believe on the Lord Jesus Christ, and thou shalt be saved, ***AND THY HOUSE***). It was solely because of Noah.

But after the one year and ten days on the ark, Noah emerged with his family, and in time his mind became weakened by the use of alcohol (Gen. 9:20-24) and the effects of sin caused him to be separated from the power of God that he had been so accustomed to before the flood.

God knew what could happen from the beginning, but he did not know that it would. ***That would have been unjust and would have taken away the power of choice.***

Faith is handed down through the offspring. (2 Tim 1:5) When I call to remembrance the unfeigned faith that is in thee, which dwelt first in thy Grandmother, Lois, and thy mother Eunice; and I am persuaded that in thee also.

Hebrews 11 enumerates various individuals that obtained favor from God because of their faith. Namely, Abel, Enoch, Noah, Abraham, Sarah, Isaac and Jacob. **IT IS BECAUSE OF THEIR FAITH IN GOD THAT DIRECTLY CAUSED GOD TO SELECT CERTAIN INDIVIDUALS FROM THEIR OFFSPRING TO DRAW THE MINDS OF MEN BACK TO HIMSELF AND TO HIS TRUE NAME THAT WAS FINALLY FOUND IN HIS ONLY BEGOTTEN SON, JESUS.** This could have happened among any group of people, other than the Jews, ever since the beginning, but all others were idol worshipers and did not know the True God, much less His Name.

Jesus said (John 17: 11) Holy Father keep through Thine Own Name, those whom thou hast given me . . . (12)while I was with them in the world, I kept them in thy Name. (14) I have given them thy word—. (26) I have declared unto them THY NAME— and will declare it. (Rev. 19:13 His Name is called the WORD of God).

The name of God was further confused during and after the time of the Tower of Babel. Gen. 11. Babel—noisy confusion.

1 Cor. 15:28 And when all things shall be subdued unto him, then shall the Son also himself be subject unto him that put all things under him, that GOD MAY BE ALL IN ALL.

John 17:3 And this is life eternal, that they might know THEE the only TRUE GOD, and Jesus Christ, whom thou hast sent.

1 Cor. 8:4—there is NONE OTHER GOD BUT ONE.

John 5:43 I am come in my Father's Name—.

John 14:6 Jesus said, I am the way, the truth, and the life: no man cometh unto the Father, but by me.

When men, women, boys and girls begin calling upon God's Name, Jesus, all truth will be opened to their understanding.

****

God's character

beethovensteiner asked this question.

I was asked if God is so loving, but is also so knowing, then why does he create people knowing that they will go to hell. since he knows the future, then why does he create them knowing they will die. I know there must be an answer, but what do I say.

James gave this response.

The seed for the body of man was placed in the earth and from the nutrients and the dust of the ground (Gen. 2:7) was formed the human body. The design for the construction of the female was incorporated within that same seed. The formation of the counter-part (female) of the male was developed through the budding process. During that process the male was placed into a deep sleep. (Gen. 2:21-22)

This same sleep process was to be used for the production of all new human life. The words 'Multiply and replenish the earth' were spoken with the subconscious mind. (of Animals, Fish and Foul, Gen. 1:22, Man and woman—Gen. 1:28) By this process, reproduction would have been controlled by the automatic direction of the subconscious mind, thereby eliminating overpopulation among humans and ultimately making death unnecessary. This process was only for man and woman because they were designed to live forever. Eternal life was not in the plan for the other animals.

Yes, God made the design for reproduction, but in the case of human conceptions, the process was to be controlled by the subconscious mind. As the male was put to sleep during the development of the female, so that same sleep process should have continued for the reproduction of all their offspring.

The breakdown came because the first man and woman decided to produce life on their own, without waiting for the automatic process to commence. They consciously patterned their reproduction activities after what they observed in the other animals. The man and the woman were to live forever in their physical bodies, always being directed by the spirit of God for all the proper nutritional intake so that their bodies could increase in strength as time continued.

NO, GOD DOES NOT MAKE PEOPLE! PEOPLE MAKE PEOPLE.

God is aware of all babies from the time of their conception, and even before, but there has only been one couple since Adamah and woman that was directed through the process of the original plan, and they were Joseph and Mary. Even they were not aware of the intricate operation of that process.

God is aware of all things, but he will not interfere except in the case of protection for those that are drawing near him. Men and women must have their own free-will. God has set before all of us 'Life and Death.' It is up to each of us which road we take.

Remember that Adam's first son was a murderer. All the sins from the beginning have weakened the genes of the offspring and will not allow the natural process of reproduction until we all become born again of our spirit. This entails more than what we have been taught in the past. This process is directed by the operation of God within the limits of his time, and will be performed for those that will call upon God's Name without ceasing.

IT IS NOT GOD'S FAULT WE ARE IN HELL. IT IS OUR FAULT.

Look at all the violence perpetrated from the beginning, and remember that the thoughts of men are on evil continually even to this day. (Gen. 6:5)

God knew man could fail, but he did not know he would. That would have been unjust.

WE MAY ASK—Psalm 51:10 Create in me a clean heart, O God; and renew a right spirit within me.

AND GOD MAY SAY—Ezekiel 18:31 ***Cast away from you all your transgressions, whereby ye have transgressed; and MAKE YOU A NEW HEART AND A NEW SPIRIT, FOR WHY WILL YE DIE. TURN YOURSELVES AND LIVE YE.***

****

GODS

*j*dg asked this question.

How many Gods are there?

James gave this response.

WHO MADE ALL THIS?

HOW MANY GODS DID IT TAKE TO FORM ALL THESE THINGS?

IS THERE ONE GOD?

ARE THERE TWO GODS?

ARE THERE THREE GODS?

Oh yes, in the minds of men there are many gods. (1 Cor. 8:5) Even though there are SO-CALLED gods in the heavens and on the earth—there are, to be sure, many such 'gods' and 'Lords'—(6) FOR US there is ONE GOD, the father, from whom all things come and for whom we live and ONE LORD JESUS CHRIST, THROUGH whom everything was made and THROUGH whom we live.

Acts 17:28 For in Him (Christ—the anointing of God) we live, and move, and have our being; as certain also of your own poets have said, For we are also his offspring.

John 10:33 The Jews said to Jesus "Thou, being a man, makest thyself God. (34) Jesus said, Is it not written in your law, I said, Ye are gods? (36) I said, I AM THE SON OF GOD.

2 Cor. 5:19 GOD WAS IN CHRIST reconciling the world unto himself—.

It was God in Jesus when he said to Philip (John 14:9), Have I been so long time with you, and yet hast thou not known me, Philip? He that hath seen me hath seen the Father. John 14:10 Believest thou not that I am in the Father, and the Father in me? The words that I speak unto you I speak not of myself: but the Father that dwelleth in me, he doeth the works.

John 14:11 Believe me that I am in the Father, and the Father in me—.

John 1:18 No man hath seen God at any time; the only begotten Son, which is in the bosom of the Father, he hath declared him.

John 4:24 God is a Spirit-man cannot see a Spirit except in vision form . . . .

John 14:16 And I (Jesus) will pray (ask earnestly of) the Father, and he shall give you another Comforter, that he may abide with you FOREVER. (17) for he dwelleth with you (in Jesus) and shall be in you. (John 14:18) I will not leave you comfortless: I WILL COME TO YOU. (18) At that day ye shall know that I AM IN MY FATHER, AND YE IN ME AND I IN YOU.

Understanding that God came into Jesus, his only begotten Son, to speak with the world, makes it easier to understand the other passages regarding the exalted status of His Son who was bearing His Father's Name to the world. i.e. Isaiah 9:6 For unto us a child is born, unto us a Son is given: and the government shall be upon His shoulder: and HIS NAME (NOT THE MAN) shall be called WONDERFUL, COUNSELLOR, THE MIGHTY GOD, THE EVERLASTING FATHER, THE PRINCE OF PEACE.

JOHN 5:43 I am come in my Father's name.

There is only one God. Looking to more than one causes weakness and confusion. The eye is not single. The power of Christ is gone.

****

God's name? Can't we do better than LORD?

Brainfire asked this question.

Must we follow Jewish tradition and refuse to speak it? Their traditions were add-ons to the law. Some harmless, some truly wicked.

Most ancient Bible manuscripts were written in the Hebrew language. In the Hebrew Scriptures, the divine name occurs almost 7,000 times and is spelled with four consonants YHWH or JHVH.

Today many Hebrew scholars prefer Yahweh as the true pronunciation.

However, consistency favors Jehovah. In what way? The pronunciation Jehovah has been accepted in English for centuries.

Those who object to using this pronunciation should also object to the use of the accepted pronunciation Jeremiah and even Jesus. Jeremiah would need to be changed to Yir_meyah' or Yir_meya'hu, the original Hebrew pronunciations, and Jesus would become Ye_shu'a' (Hebrew) or I_e_sous' (Greek).

It seems the exact pronunciation is not what is important. Doesn't the fact that thousands of times God told us his name compel us to find the closest pronunciation, and joyfully use it?

James gave this response.

WHAT IS GOD'S NAME? CAN'T WE DO BETTER THAN LORD?

God has revealed himself to man through many names.

Genesis 28:3—God Almighty, Exodus 3:14—I am that I am, Exodus 6:3—Jehovah, Exodus 34:14—Jealous, Deuteronomy 28:58—The Lord Thy God, Amos 5:27—God of Hosts, Isaiah 54:25—Lord of Hosts, Jeremiah 33:2—Lord, etc. etc. This was designed by God for man's confusion.

Those different names occurred after God confounded the language of the people, because of their desire to 'make a name for themselves(Gen.11:4), instead of seeking the only true God with their whole heart, and learning and accepting HIS NAME ONLY. Gen. 11:9 (Matthew 17:8 No man save Jesus only.)

But—the Lord shall be King over all the earth in that day shall there be one Lord, and His Name ONE. Jesus said, I am come in my Father's Name. John 5:43.

He said to the Jews—John 10:36 I am the SON OF GOD. Jesus was not God, but God was in Christ reconciling the world unto himself. 2 Corinthians 5:19.

GOD'S NAME IS JESUS

When the people learn the Name of God (Zephaniah 3:9), Then will I (God) turn to the people a pure language, that they may ALL CALL UPON THE NAME OF THE LORD, to serve him with one consent.

Acts 2:21 And it shall come to pass, that WHOSOEVER shall CALL on the NAME of the LORD shall be SAVED. Also Romans 10:13, Joel 2:32 Delivered.

We have so many names in religion because people still want to make a name for themselves to fit their own way of thinking. It is time for the multitudes to take hold of the true Name of God (The Tree of Life) and be saved from all the religious confusion in the world.

James 4:8 Draw nigh to God (through his true name, Jesus), and he will draw nigh to you.

Proverbs 30:4 Who hath ascended up into heaven, or descended? Who hath gathered the wind in his fists? Who hath bound the waters in a garment? Who hath established all the ends of the earth?

WHAT IS HIS NAME, AND WHAT IS HIS SON'S NAME, IF THOU CANST TELL?

Jesus said (John 3:13),—No man hath ascended up to heaven, but he that came down from heaven, even the Son of Man which is in heaven.

Jesus was standing on the earth, in the physical heaven, as we all are. But he was also standing in the spiritual state where man had been placed in the beginning.

Jesus did not fall from that state of Paradise as the first man (Adam) did. The only begotten Son of God came to the earth for one primary purpose, and that was to bring men back to the knowledge of God's Name. John 17:11—Keep through thine own NAME those whom thou hast given me—.

Jesus said (John 17:12), While I was with them in the world, I kept them in THY NAME—. (15) I pray not that thou shouldest take them out of the world, but that thou shouldest keep them from the evil.

John 17:25 O righteous Father, THE WORLD HATH NOT KNOWN THEE: but I have known thee, and these have known that thou hast sent me.

John 17:26 I have declared unto them thy Name, and will declare it—.

****

God's name

poo2k_2001@ . . . , a user from encyclopedia.com, asked this question.

In the Bible has God ever told anyone his name, and if so to whom and where in the bible did it occur.

NAMES OF GOD!!

James gave this response.

The TREE OF LIFE is the NAME OF GOD—JESUS (Of course there is no effect without faith in, and calling upon that Name, believing that it is the Name of God.}

The only way man and woman could have remained in the Garden of Eden (Spiritual state) was for them to have conformed to the original plan of God. This they could not do because they refused to CALL UPON HIS TRUE NAME.

Since they didn't do it, they had no power over their own actions, and as a result, the true NAME of GOD was lost to the knowledge of mankind. This had to be rectified by God. So God sent HIS SON to the earth in God's own NAME, in order to show men and women THE WAY BACK INTO PARADISE. (Luke23:43, 2 Cor 12:4, Rev. 2:7).

WITH RESPECT TO MAN, God had eight NAMES as recorded in the Old Testament. But this multiplicity was caused by the diversified languages. According to Zeph 3:9 this problem of languages will be rectified.

There is only one NAME under heaven given among men, whereby we must be saved. Acts 4:12.

As recorded in the King James Version of THE OLD TESTAMENT:

Exo. 3:14 I AM THAT I AM

Exo. 6:3 GOD ALMIGHTY

Exo. 6:3 JEHOVAH

Exo. 34:14 JEALOUS

Isa. 54:5 LORD OF HOSTS

Jer. 33:2 LORD

Amos 5:27 GOD OF HOSTS

Deut. 28:58 THE LORD THY GOD.

THE NEW TESTAMENT

Luke 2:21 JESUS

Matt. 1:23 EMMANUEL—GOD WITH US.

Matt. 1:212 SHALL CALL HIS NAME JESUS.

Rev. 19:13 And HIS NAME is called the WORD OF GOD.

John 14:6 JESUS SAID, I AM THE WAY, THE TRUTH, AND THE LIFE: NO MAN COMETH UNTO THE FATHER, BUT BY ME.

John 5:43 I AM COME IN MY FATHER'S NAME.

Ps. 34:3 O magnify the LORD with me, and let us exalt HIS NAME together.

Over the years many of the Names attributed to God have resulted from the make up of different languages. This confusion was caused by God himself, (Gen. 11:7) because the people have preferred to make a name for themselves (Gen. 11:4) rather than go by the Name of God only. (Matthew 17:8).

For the name Jehovah check Exod. 6:3, Pslm 83:18,Isa. 12:2, 26:4.

Note: ***If any translation changes these names to read only as one particular name it is a sign that they are trying to make the Bible conform to their own belief.***

STONY gave the following additional explanation of the Name Jehovah of God.

JEHOVAH-TSIDKENU . . . . " JEHOVAH OUR RIGHTEOUSNESS"

"—M'KADDESH . . . "WHO SANCTIFIES"

"—SHALOM . . . . "IS PEACE"

"—SHAMMAH . . . . "IS THERE"

"—ROPHE . . . . "WHO HEALS"

"—JIREH . . . . JEHOVAH'S PROVISION SHALL BE SEEN"

"—NISSI . . . . "JEHOVAH MY BANNER"

"JEHOVAH-ROHI . . . "JEHOVAH MY SHEPHERD"

Hope this helps and that Stony is agreeable with me calling his work to your attention.

****

Gossiping

Brob asked this question.

Come on people, is not gossiping a sin? How come we can't just discuss the Bible. Isn't this what this forum was designed for. I thought we were supposed to lift people up not to tear them down. God Bless. (Bobby)

James gave this response.

Rocks in Cranes' Mouths—

The heights and recesses of mount Taurus are said to be much infested with eagles, which are never better pleased than when they pick the bones of Cranes. Cranes are prone to crackle and make a noise and particularly so while they are flying. The sound of their voices arouses the eagles, which spring up at the signal, and often make the talkative travelers pay dearly for their impudent chattering.

The older and more experienced cranes, sensible of their besetting foible (character fault) and the peril to which it exposes them, take care before venturing on the wing to pick up a stone large enough to fill the cavity of their mouths, and consequently to impose unavoidable silence on their tongue, and thus they escape the danger.

The foregoing is an excerpt from The Lamplighter.

JESUS SAID, ACCORDING TO MATTHEW

(The New English Bible—Oxford Cambridge)

Matthew 12:34 You vipers' brood! How can your words be good when you yourselves are evil? For the words that the mouth utters come from the overflowing of the heart. A good man

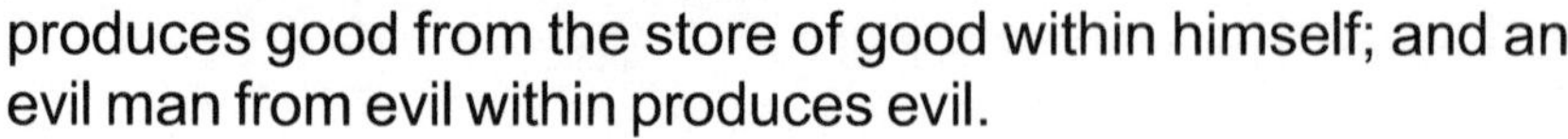

produces good from the store of good within himself; and an evil man from evil within produces evil.

****

We as humans need the gift of the Holy Ghost, and the filling of the holy spirit, then our nature must be changed. What we think, produced by the evil that is in us, is what we WILL SPEAK. We, unlike the Cranes, have hands with which we take out the stone long enough to say what has been prepared in our minds, caused by the evil that is in our beings, then the stone is placed back. It is then that the heaviness of guilt is more weightier than the stone itself.

Who gossips with you will gossip of you.—Irish Proverb.

****

Greed, small scale—but harmful.

Kathy asked this question.

What can in-born greed cause a person to do? What is the remedy?

James gave this response.

George went to the grocery store to pick up a few items. He didn't need tuna, but it was there before him at half price. Twenty five cents per can was a real bargain. Instead of half a case comprised of twenty four cans, he decided to take a whole case.

When the clerk saw the box of tuna in the bottom of the grocery cart she mistook the case as being half a case, so she clicked into the register six dollars instead of twelve.

Rationalization immediately took over George's mind. After

all there had been many times he had been overcharged, so that made it all right for him not to call the clerk's attention to the fact that it was a whole case. Also, since he received the twenty four cans free he could give them to someone more needy.

While loading the vehicle with the grocery items, gloom began to set in. Blue was the color of the sky and the sun was shining well that day, but for George the sky began to turn dark. If he were a drinking man he would have an alcoholic beverage. That would correct the condemnation he felt for awhile. But he would not do that. He had learned that depriving the brain of oxygen in order to have the feeling that everything is all right, is like poisoning the brain cells, and it compounds the problem.

George was an affluent man. He attended church regularly. When the offering pan came by he always deposited a bill. His wife did the same. Giving to PAL, a police organization to help teenagers refrain from drugs was a part of his regular giving. The house and vehicle were totally paid for and he had no credit cards.

But the inherited nature of greed was still deep within his mental make up. This he had to overcome. He must call upon the Name of God for more strength to change the force of his weakened nature received from his ancestors.

As the days wearily flowed one after the other, condemnation increased until finally George decided to return to the store and give the clerk six dollars for the extra twenty four cans of tuna.

When George left the store he could see the blue sky in its true color. The pleasant days returned. Flowers were in full bloom with radiant colors. Even the birds were singing again.

Jesus said of His Father. I do always those things that please him. John 8:29

This is the way back to Paradise.

James gave this follow-up answer.

David prayed: Psalm 51:10 Create in me a clean heart, O God; and renew a right spirit within me.

Isn't this done by God?

Eph. 2:8 For by grace are ye saved through faith; and that not of yourselves: it is the gift of God: (9) Not of works, lest any man should boast.

ALL GIFTS OF THE SPIRIT ARE GIVEN FREELY AND THEY ARE PERFORMED BY THE OPERATION OF GOD. Rev. 21:6 I will give unto him that is athirst of the fountain of the water of life FREELY.

BUT WE MUST TURN OURSELVES!

Ezek. 18:31 Cast away from you all your transgressions, whereby ye have transgressed; and MAKE YOU A NEW HEART AND A NEW SPIRIT: for why will ye die—.

Rev. 2:7—To him that overcometh will I give to eat of the tree of life, which is in the midst of the PARADISE of God.

****

Hand Writing on the Wall:

Ruth asked this question.

Would you explain more fully about the Hand Writing on the Wall? Who saw it?

James gave this response.

Daniel 5

Impious Feast of Belshazzar son of Nebuchadnezzar.

The man stood in a drunken haze. The words were very clear as they were being imprinted upon the brain: A brain which had been addled by the use of excessive wine. He, with a thousand of his lords had been partying for at least an hour, consuming the purple liquid from the silver and golden vessels. It was an unusually drunken celebration.

Belshazzar the king made a great feast to a thousand of his lords, and DRANK WINE before the thousand. They drank wine, and praised the gods of gold, and of silver, of brass, of iron, of wood, and of stone.

In the same hour came forth fingers of a man's hand, and wrote over against the candlestick upon the plaster of the wall of the kings palace: and the king saw part of the hand that wrote.

Then the King's countenance was changed, and his thoughts troubled him, so that the joints of his loins were loosed, and his knees smote one against another.

The King cried aloud to bring in the astrologers, the Chaldeans, and the soothsayers. Then came in all the king's wise men: but they could not read the writing, nor make known to the king the interpretation. They could not read the writing because it was only in the head of Belshazzar. It was a hallucination caused by alcohol, but the hand and the writing was directed by God to inform him of his impending doom. God had used Daniel previously in revealing a dream and the interpretation to Belshazzar's father Nebuchadnezzar

(Daniel 2), and now in the same manner he revealed to Daniel the vision and the interpretation of the words.

MENE, MENE, TEKEL, UPHARSIN

God revealed the words and the interpretation in Balshazzar's vision, the same as he had revealed the dream and the interpretation to Daniel for Belshazzar's father. (Daniel 5:1-29)

Remember that God understands all languages, even those that are generally unknown and close to extinction.

MENE, MENE, TEKEL UPHARSIN OR PERES

Daniel 5:25 was taken from an older (ancient-belonging to times long past) language, and was generally forgotten because of its lack of use. It could be classed as an unknown tongue. But those symbols had been heard or seen at some time during the life of Belshazzar, although he had forgotten them. This dormant subconscious memory God used in delivering the prophetic message to Belshazzar through Daniel. Daniel 5:26-28

****

Healing Lines:

Zenaide asked this question.

Are some people healed in healing lines?

James gave this response

HEALING LINES

1961

(Miracle Valley—Arizona)

The next day went about the same as usual. The same healing lines were formed. James was convinced. Healing was being accomplished. Particularly those which dealt with the mind.

Some that thought they couldn't walk were convinced they could. They broke through a mental block because they had faith in what was said. The same as James and Ruth had been delivered from everything because of their faith in the Name of God. There was also plenty of spiritual help.

During intermission before the Bar-B-Q, Ruth and James were sitting on one of the benches in front of the church. A man approached them, and said, "Brother Creed, Brother Creed, come here!." James and Ruth followed him out the door. He wondered how the man knew his name.

He led the way to a prayer tent. Most of the people were sitting on chairs, just visiting, waiting for the Bar-B-Q. Over to one side, the same young man that had gone through the prayer line, was lying on the ground. He was having a Grand Mal seizure. Six young potential ministers surrounded him. Each took his turn trying to cast the devil out. When the devil would not go, they collectively attempted to cast him out.

James stood close by. He prayed quietly. He would help if he could. But how could he do that. The filling station came to mind. He knew if God wanted to do something, he could. Just then the young man stretched his leg as far as he could and touched James' ankle with the tip of his toe. He then arose from the ground with a disturbed expression, as if he didn't like to be just something to practice on.

Had he just come out of a seizure as usual? James remembered back in Saint Louis. He had told Eldon that the time would come when there would not be a big noise when supplying people with healing needs. All you would have to do is touch them even if it was on a street corner. This thinking brought on more questions. What healing would be accomplished in this manner? Would it only be those defects related to the mind and spirit? What about gall stones? What about growing a third set of teeth which some have advocated. What about a new leg which also was against present nature.

Had not God devised certain principles for the growth of cells and in every case in the animal world those principles have been adhered to, except of course, in cases of freaks. On and on there were questions still unanswered. Where did the boy go? Would he have another seizure?

God is a scientist. Wouldn't he expect his sons to follow in his foot steps? Shouldn't all men be dependent upon the Holy Ghost for guidance and God's power of Christ to effect unity among all men? Wasn't Christ the light which lights every man that comes into the world? How could one man be greater than another, or have the audacity to stand arrogantly above another to domineer? Do we not all have questions?

James remembered when God sat upon the side of the bed and asked, "ARE THERE ANY QUESTIONS?" He still had many questions and he knew knowledge was so vast that it could not all be grasped by only one man. In order to effect humility, knowledge must be gained collectively, then understanding is received through the inspiration of God.

James observed the young man drifting off into the crowd, mobbed by advisors. What could James do? If he pushed himself, he would be as they are. Oh, how he wanted to help the world, but how could he do that? It would have to be done by the direction of God by the Holy Ghost, and in His Time.

After the completion of the meal, James and Ruth returned to the church. There the young man stood, right in the midway, with three young ministers around him, each exercising his ability to instruct. When one spoke, the young man looked at him, then another broke in, attracting his attention. The third chimed in and then back to the first. His mind was going into a spin.

How could a man find a place to speak, with all the babble?

Even the words, 'You can be saved by calling upon the Name

of the Lord,' would be taken lightly. He may say 'So what, I have been told that before, along with many other things.'

****

Healing:

Zenaide asked this question.

Some receive healing through prayer and faith. Why doesn't everybody that prays receive healing at all times?

James gave this response.

Aside from Nutrients and Doctors and Drugs and things—can anybody, by their own will, direct healing toward another person at anytime?

No! There is a time to heal. Eccl. 3:3 And God does not hear a sinners prayer without conversion.

Jesus (referring to Isaiah 6:9) said, (Matthew 13:15 For this people's heart is waxed gross, and their ears are dull of hearing, and their eyes they have closed; lest at ANY TIME they should see with their eyes, and hear with their ears, and should understand with their heart, and should be converted, and I (GOD) SHOULD HEAL THEM.

John 9:31 (Some of the Pharisees said, Now we know that God heareth not sinners: but if any man be a worshipper of God, and doeth his will, him he heareth.

Who among us is free of guilt? Who has no condemnation drifting into their minds from the past? This heaviness of mind drives out the power of God and casts the shadow of unbelief upon everyone within the circle of its influence.

Even Jesus' disciples had little power because of their unbelief.

A certain man brought his son who was considered to be a lunatic to Jesus. Matthew 17:16—I brought him to thy disciples, and they could not cure him. (17) Then Jesus answered and said, O faithless and perverse generation, how long shall I be with you? How long shall I suffer you? Bring him hither to me. (18) And Jesus rebuked the devil;(the power of the mind that weakened the immune system of the child's body) and he departed out of him: and the child was cured from that very hour, (19) Then came the disciples to Jesus apart, and said, Why could not we cast him out? Matthew 17:20 And Jesus said unto them, because of your unbelief:—.

This unbelief on the part of the people was the same thing that hindered Jesus in the beginning of his ministry. He was in his own country in the synagogue—Matthew 13:58—he did not many mighty works there because of their unbelief.

Through it all, it must be understood that Jesus could do nothing without God in him, for God does the work.

John 5:19—Jesus said,—The Son can do nothing of himself, but what he seeth the Father do: for what things soever he doeth, these also doeth the Son likewise. (20) For the Father loveth the Son, and showeth him all things that himself doeth:

In short: When it was revealed to Jesus what God was going to do, Jesus placed himself in that position to be used of God.

2 Cor. 5:19 To wit, that God was in Christ, reconciling the world unto himself—. Nevertheless, even God does not continue working with the faithless and perverse generations.—(Hebrews 11:6) For without faith it is impossible to please him: for he that cometh to God must believe that HE IS.

So what is the answer? Romans 8:1 There is therefore now no condemnation to them which are in Christ Jesus, who walk not after the flesh, but after the Spirit.

So walk in the spirit of God, and it will be revealed when to move, what to do, and what to say—Mark 13:11—take no thought beforehand what ye shall speak,—for it is not ye that speak, but the Holy Ghost.

Nothing can be done before its time. When the time comes it will be easy, for it will not be done by man, but by the power and direction of God through the Holy Ghost.

There was a multitude of impotent people, blind, halt and withered at the pool of Bethesda (John 5:2-9),but there was only one man healed, and it was in accordance with God's time.

Luke 4:27 Many Lepers were in Israel in the time of Eliseus the prophet and none of them was cleansed, saving Naaman the Syrian.

****

Healing—Wife:

jdg asked this question.

Does God, through the Holy Ghost, ever heal the wife through the husband?

James gave this response.

TOMBSTONE

1961

The station wagon stopped in front of the house. They went in as Ruth said, "James, I didn't want to say anything to you because I know you are not working and don't have the money for a doctor."

"What's wrong Ruth?"

"Do you remember that I went to the doctor because I had kidney infection?"

"Yes."

"Well, it is back. I have been in misery for the last few days and it is getting worse."

"I don't feel I can pray for you right now and get results, but as soon as I feel it, I will. God knows our situation, that I don't have a job and no money for a doctor. He also knows how serious the infection is."

"I think you are right," Ruth said. "I had a vision to that effect. It was a large bowl sitting in the middle of the living room. A voice said it contained my healing."

TIME PASSED

Ruth had just returned from across the street. She was in the left bed room. James was in the living room standing toward the west. He turned to look up over his right shoulder toward the north. It came through the ceiling at the north east corner of the room. "Ruth, come here quickly. It is here. It came into my body, then down into my hands."

Ruth stood before James. He touched her. Words came from his mouth. "In the Name of Jesus heal this infection. In the Name of Jesus it is done." He could feel the flow of healing virtue transfer from his hands into her body. She was in fact healed. The infection did not return.

****

LATER

Ruth came into the house from across the street. She carried a mop and bucket. Grandma had given orders to give the house another general cleaning. James arose from the bed.

"James," she called.

"Yes?" he said, as he came into the living room.

"My ankle has been hurting so bad I can scarcely walk. Will you pray for it?"

"Well, yes I will, but I don't feel like it now."

"I feel like it," Ruth said. "It will be healed if you will pray for it."

"All right, if you think so."

He felt foolish. Nothing came through the ceiling. There was no feelings of power in his body or in his hands. He placed his hand on her ankle. "In the Name of Jesus let this ankle be healed. Through the Name of Jesus it is done." He did not feel it was healed, but he said it. Ruth said. "The pain is gone." She went about her business of cleaning the house.

As Jesus had said to the woman that touched his garment,(Matthew 9:22) "Thy faith hath made thee whole." In this case it was Ruth's faith that caused her healing. As the knowledge of God's Name becomes widespread, healing will come from God that is within, through the mind coordinating the immune responses.

Jesus said (John 5:19,30) The Son can do nothing of himself, but what he seeth the Father do: for what things soever he doeth, these also doeth the Son likewise. (21) For as the Father raiseth up the dead, and quickeneth them; even so the Son quickeneth whom he will. As was said, 'You will think you are doing things in your own self but you won't be, I will be working through you.'

It is the power of God that heals through the guidance of the Holy Ghost, and then only in God's manner and time. This principle is also applied to doctors and most of them know it. They know that it is God that heals. They are only instruments in God's hands. God is helping the scientific and the church world alike. (2 Pet.3:10) He is not willing that any should perish.

****

Heathens by birth, not by choice?

Anonymous asked this question on 1/25/2002:

I saw on the discovery channel that people in remote parts of Africa have never seen or even heard of television.

What happens to these people when they die, since they had no chance to embrace Jesus as their personal Lord and Savior?

James gave this response.

After approximately 2000 years those that have heard of and believe in Jesus are still in the minority among so many of the established religions of men.

The majority have tried to reach God by making names for themselves. They have said (Gen. 11:4) Go to, let us build us a city and a tower, whose top may reach unto heaven; And let us make us a name—.

People have forgotten that for man heaven was established here on the earth. It was called the Garden in Eden (Gen. 2:8). It was a physical but also a spiritual place where men were intended to live forever, prosper and be in continual health.

Always abounding in strength and growth as they partook of the Tree of Life, the Name of God.

Psalm 34:8 O taste and see that the Lord is good—.

Heb. 13:15 By him therefore let us offer the sacrifice of praise to God CONTINUALLY, that is the fruit of our lips giving thanks to His Name.

Acts 4:12 Neither is there salvation in any other: for there is NONE OTHER NAME under heaven given among men, whereby we must be saved.

Phlp. 2:10—at the Name of Jesus ***every*** knee shall bow, of things in heaven, and things in earth, and things under the earth. (11) And that every tongue should confess that Jesus Christ is Lord, to the glory of God the Father.

Acts 2:21—It shall come to pass, that WHOSOEVER shall call on the Name of the Lord shall be saved. Romans 10:13, and Joel 2:32.

Zeph. 3:9—then will I turn to the people a pure language, that they may ALL call upon the Name of the Lord, to serve him with one consent.

1 John 2:2—he is the propitiation for our sins: and not for ours only, but also for the sins of the whole world.

This truth will be heard by everyone in the world and then if they will not believe and call upon God by HIS NAME (the mediator—Jesus—1 Tim. 2:5 For there is one God, and one mediator between God and men, the man Christ Jesus) then they will be like the chaff which the wind driveth away. (Ps. 1:4)

Matthew 3:12 (Jesus)—will thoroughly purge his floor, and gather his wheat into the garner; but he will burn the chaff with unquenchable fire.

Psalm 1:6—the way of the ungodly shall perish—THAT'S ALL.

****

HELL

Since some interpret—hell ("sheol",hades," grave") as the same as the "Lake of Fire" is that Scriptural?

(Not to be disclosed) asked this question.

In view of the following Scriptures—Is the Lake of Fire a symbol of Everlasting Destruction, rather than a literally hideos pagan concept of burning people and whatever else forever?

Revelation 20:10,14 : New Living Translation (NLT)10"Then the Devil, who betrayed them, was thrown into the lake of fire that burns with sulfur, joining the beast and the false prophet. There they will be tormented day and night forever and ever.14 And death and the grave were thrown into the lake of fire. This is the second death—the lake of fire."

Revelation 20:10,14 : Amplified Bible (AMP)10"Then the devil who had led them astray [deceiving and seducing them] was hurled into the fiery lake of burning brimstone, where the beast and false prophet were; and they will be tormented day and night forever and ever (through the ages of the ages).14Then death and Hades ([1] the state of death or disembodied existence) were thrown into the lake of fire. This is the second death, the lake of fire."

Footnotes

James Orr et al., eds., The International Standard Bible Encyclopedia.

James gave this response.

If anybody wants to know where hell is just tell them to read the newspapers, watch television, and visit the hospitals.

Psalms 9:17 The wicked shall be turned into hell, and all the nations that forget God.

Men have lived in hell ever since that first man would not call upon the name of God unceasingly. As a result, Christ, the power of God was driven from his system, leaving him powerless to conform to the will of God. He was driven from that spiritual state where God had placed him, and the knowledge of how to return was lost to his posterity. (succeeding generations) It took the last Adam (Jesus—1 Cor. 15:45) to bring back the knowledge of God's Name and place it in the foreheads (Rev. 14:2) of men and women on the earth.

What is the answer?

Acts 2:21—It shall come to pass, that WHOSOEVER shall call on the NAME of the LORD shall be SAVED. (Joel 2:32, Rom. 10:13).

Saved from what?

Saved from all the hell that is in this world created by the naturally thinking minds of Godless men, and return to the spiritual state God intended for man from the beginning. That garden of God where he placed the man and woman and informed them that in the day they take into their system the knowledge of evil they would drive out the Christ of God and be driven into destruction and eternal death.

DEATH, HELL AND THE GRAVE. First spiritual DEATH, then HELL, and finally the grave.

Who has the key?

Rev. 1:18 I am he that liveth, and was dead; and, behold, I am alive for evermore, Amen; and have the keys of hell and of death.

Isa. 38:18—The grave cannot praise thee, death can not celebrate thee: they that go down into the pit cannot hope for thy truth.

Jonah 2:2 Jonah was in the ***belly of hell***. He was not physically dead.

Eccl. 9:5 For the living know that they shall die: but the dead know not anything, neither have they any more a reward; for the memory of them is forgotten. (6) Also their love, and their hatred, and their envy, is now perished; neither have they any more a portion for ever in anything that is done under the sun.

John 3:3 We must be born again. (That spirit received from our fathers must be killed, taken out, and a right spirit installed in its place. (Ps. 51:10)

Rev. 2:11 He that overcometh shall not be hurt of the second death.

1 Cor. 15:53—This corruptible must put on incorruption, and this mortal must put on immortality. (54) So when this corruptible shall have put on incorruption, and this mortal shall have put on immortality, then shall be brought to pass the saying that is written, Death is swallowed up in victory. (55) O death where is thy sting? O grave, where is they victory? (56) The sting of death is sin; and the strength of sin is the law. (57) But thanks be to God, which giveth us the victory through our Lord Jesus Christ.

We must call upon God through the Name of Jesus, the mediator, and he will guide us by the Holy Ghost to all the spiritual gifts necessary to reestablish heaven on earth as it was intended from the beginning.

Rev. 21:4 And God shall wipe away all tears from their eyes;

and there shall be no more death, neither sorrow, nor crying, neither shall there be any more pain: for the former things are passed away. (5) And he that sat upon the throne said, Behold, I make all things new.

The lake of fire is merely a symbolism to show the eradication of death and hell caused by all the other elements of destruction.

****

HELL, Teaching On

Anonymous asked this question.

Where would you direct a 30 minute teaching on hell to junior high students?

I want to make sure to cover every biblical principle on the teachings of hell without scaring their socks off.

Your insights are appreciated!

James gave this response.

HELL

The word most frequently used (occurring twelve times) in the New Testament for the place of future punishment is Gehenna or Gehenna of fire. This was originally the valley of Hinnom, south of Jerusalem, where the filth and dead animals of the city were cast out and burned; a fit symbol of the wicked and their destruction.

My wife and I visited this place in 1985. That area was then a grave yard just outside the Dung Gate. It is a valley between the wall and the Mount of Olives. We walked from Mt Olives through the valley toward the gate.

Matthew 13:34—Without a parable spake he (Jesus) not unto them. (35) that it might be fulfilled which was spoken by the prophet, saying, I will open my mouth in parables; I will utter things which have been kept secret from the foundation of the world.

The story of the rich man and Lazarus (Luke 16:19) should be placed in this category and must be considered separately as to its symbolic meaning.

Psalm 9:17 The wicked shall be turned into hell, and all nations that forget God.

James 4:9 Be afflicted, and mourn, and weep: let your laughter be turned to mourning, and your joy to heaviness.

James 4:8 Draw nigh to God, and he will draw nigh to you. Cleanse your hands, ye sinners; and purify your hearts, ye double minded.

The first man and woman were placed in heaven (Paradise-Rev.2:7-a spiritual place—the Garden of God-Gen. 2:8 a natural place in Eden, here on the earth. They could have remained in that spiritual state had they not decided to pattern their lives after the animals instead of adhering to God by the strength of the Tree of Life (The Name of God).

The knowledge of evil flooded their minds and condemnation drove the power of God from their mental and spiritual system. They were driven from peace within themselves to the desperation of hell.

This hell envelops every mind that is cut off from the flow of the holy spirit of God by guilt that produces condemnation. The feeling of condemnation cannot be washed out of the mental and spiritual system by any other means than the flow of spiritual water out of the inner most being of humankind. (John 7:38).

Do you want to escape hell and all the destructive elements of the world?

Draw near God by calling upon His Name. He will give all the spiritual gifts necessary to cause the continual flow of life through faith in the Name of His Son Jesus.

Are you in Hell because of the feeling of condemnation?

John 3:18 He that believeth on him is not condemned: but he that believeth not is condemned already, because he hath not believed in the NAME of the only begotten Son of God.

****

HELL, UNDER GROUND?

Edward asked this question.

Is hell under the ground?

James gave this response.

IS HELL UNDER THE GROUND?

WE SHOULD NOT BE ABSURD! (ridiculous or unreasonable).

The only thing hot under the surface of the earth is molten material called magma. Magma is melted rock that has been subjected to extreme pressure and chemical reactions resulting in high temperature beneath the earth's surface. Ninety eight percent of all rock on earth is created of oxygen, silicon, aluminum, iron, calcium, potassium, and magnesium.—NO HELL.

NO, HELL CANNOT BE FOUND UNDER THE SURFACE OF THE EARTH.

Hell is found in, and generated by the minds of men, and the devil resides in the middle of that hell—IN THE MIND—NOWHERE ELSE.

WHERE IS HEAVEN?

HEAVEN IS OUT THERE, AND FOR MAN HEAVEN IS HERE. WE ARE FLOATING AROUND IN HEAVEN. The spiritual heaven for man was established here on the earth.

Jesus said (John 3:13),—NO MAN HATH ASCENDED UP TO HEAVEN, but he that came down from heaven, even the Son of man WHICH IS IN HEAVEN.

Jesus was standing on the earth, in the physical heaven, as we all are. But Jesus was also standing in the spiritual state where man had been placed in the beginning. Adam and his wife resided right in the middle of the garden, Paradise, the second heaven (2 Cor. 12:2) realm where they should have remained forever free from death.

ANGELS AND PEOPLE THAT BECOME AS THE ANGELS RESIDE OUT THERE IN HEAVEN. (Matt. 22:30)(until the end of all confusion).

Men and women, boys and girls are to remain here on the earth, in heaven, and God himself shall be with them.

Rev. 21:3 And I heard a great voice out of heaven saying, Behold, the tabernacle of God is with men, and he will dwell with them, and they shall be his people, and GOD HIMSELF SHALL BE WITH THEM, AND BE THEIR GOD.

****

HELP, Please

Yeremias asked this question.

Beloved Friend,

You know, in all the time I have known you, you have always been there to listen when I needed to talk. If it is not too much trouble, would you do that now? I am sorry if this is long and makes no sense, but I just need to let my thoughts run for a short spell.

As I look back on my life, I see many many short comings and acts of sheer madness. In fact, there are mornings where I wake up wondering if I am sane anymore or not. I feel life closing in on me, and for the first time feel what understanding mortality really is. I look into the face of death in my dreams, and wonder what is stopping it from coming. I do not WANT to die, but I do not fear it. I have no desire to die, but I have few things to make me want to stay. I have your love for life to keep me going, even though you have your troubles and stumbling, as well.

When ever I need support I have always been able to find it in you, but I must say, though you may be able to comfort me, I am not sure any but God himself can support me at this point in my life. A darkness has encompassed my heart so that I see no fear in life and I feel a cold rushing in to replace the joy I felt by doing things I love. Don't take me wrong, my love for you and those closest to me still remains, but my joy in other things has left. I see no purpose to my meaningless existence. I know I have helped people in life. I have seen a difference come in the lives closest to me, so I know I must be doing some good. I have even been of a little help while at church camp as well as college.

As all things pass, so does our moment of happiness. I am going to be nineteen, and already I feel the cold fingers of

> desolation around my heart. I do not know what to do, and my confusion scares me . . . fear is a wonderful sensation. When you have nothing else you always have fear, It lets you know you have not been condemned yet, that there is a chance for repentance. Not spiritual repentance, I have this already, but a physical one. To repent from my life and body. Only if it were possible.
>
> I do not know what I meant to accomplish by writing this, but I hope that you could summon a few words for me . . . I am in a time of need. Need for what, I do not know, but I am searching for a truth that has eluded me thus far. I need a contentment that has so long been my shadow. Help me Lord . . . I fall in darkness and I need your help.
>
> Always,
>
> Jeremiah

James gave this response.

THE TREK TO PARADISE

TIME: 1960

PLACE: St Louis, Missouri.

Jim wondered—Since he felt so good after only fifteen minutes of calling upon God's Name, what would happen if he decided to Call upon Him all the time, just with his inner voice, of course.

Maybe it was intended to be something like the heart beat of the spiritual man. Maybe by calling upon God through his Name, the power of Christ is attracted to men to wash away the condemnation from their mental and spiritual system. It didn't matter. He had nothing to lose. He had tried everything else he could think of to find relief, and it didn't help, so what made the difference?

He determined that this would be his prayer. “Lord, let me live to say Jesus just one more time, forever. Jesus, Jesus, Jesus.”

DEVIL.

How do we keep that Devil out of our heads?

James gave this response.

A campground—Arizona

1961

Distant shouts with songs of praise filtered into the tabernacle from somewhere on the grounds. Ruth and James arose from the bench to follow in its direction. They stepped to the door. It was one of the school buildings. The instruments made joyful noises, entrancing the minds and transporting them to realms of unreality. The people lay upon the floor. James had been there. It was not his intention to degrade.

One young man was in fact a helicopter. His left arm and right foot were going round and round. It was the rotor blade. It was plain to see he had either good or bad experience with them in order for his mind to be impressed in such a manner. He stood to his feet. A bible was placed on the top of his head. He jumped up and down.

Ruth and James moved closer to him. “Why the action and the bible used in this manner?” James asked.

He looked at James while yet jumping and said, “Some minister told me I had trouble with sex devils and I’m trying to get away from them by keeping the Bible on my head.”

James spoke with him above the noise. “No sex devil or any other kind will get in you if you will just call upon Jesus all the time, inside yourself, of course, with your inner voice. Don’t let it be outward. It is an inward work. God wants you to have a good appearance."

The Bible was slowly removed from his head. He started calling upon the Name of the Lord silently inside himself. He was so astonished that the devils were nowhere around, that he stated with a loud voice, "It works! It works!" He shook hands and left saying, thank you. thank you."

Jeremiah 10:23 O Lord, I know that the way of man is not in himself: it is not in man that walketh to direct his steps.

Try ever so hard. The thoughts cannot be controlled by man without spiritual help. The Bible is a recording of the thoughts and actions of men versus the will of God. Without the continual flow of the Holy Spirit from the inner being, men will always fall prey to the thoughts that ramble through their heads. Oh yes, the acts of sex and violence are portrayed throughout the pages of man's history in the majority of the books written from olden times. This includes the Bible. Men have fallen from their original heavenly state (Paradise). It is time for them to return.

James gave this follow-up answer.

Psychiatrists and Books:

CAN PSYCHIATRISTS HELP?

Yes, if that psychiatric practitioner has had his/her spirit killed, taken out, and a right spirit installed in its place: If spiritual eyes and ears have been received: If they have received the gift of the Holy Ghost: If their heart (center of their being) has been filled with the holy spirit from God.

DO BOOKS HELP?

Without those aforementioned spiritual gifts nobody can, through any amount of education as expressed through books or by any other means, thoroughly understand the operation of the mind, spirit, and body of anyone.

1 Corinthians 2:14—The natural man receiveth not the things of the Spirit of God: for they are foolishness unto him: NEITHER CAN HE KNOW THEM, because they are spiritually discerned.

Is God concerned with the natural body? God made both. He is equally concerned with the welfare of both the physical and the spiritual. 1 Corinthians 15:44 There is a natural body, and there is a spiritual body—. But, especially, the spiritual body cannot be understood by a natural person without the spirit.

The majority of the people with mental problems need spiritual help, and they cannot receive that help from a natural man that does not understand spiritual things. This does not only apply to psychiatrists, but to anyone that works in that capacity, including preachers that have not been born again of the spirit.

A properly functioning brain can cause the body to live, but with a depressed mind because of guilt, or any other reason, the body malfunctions. This is why an individual needs the water of life flowing freely from his/her being.

John 7:38 He that believeth on me (Jesus) as the scripture hath said, out of his belly shall flow rivers of living water.

This spiritual water is needed to continuously wash out the effects of guilt before it has a chance to destroy the body and mind of the individual. A permanent cure cannot be effected by words of natural men, OR ANY DRUG.

DOES NATURAL WATER BAPTISM WASH AWAY SINS?

NO! THE WATER OF LIFE DOES. John 4:14—the water that I shall give him shall be in him a well of water springing up into everlasting life.

Ananias said to Saul—Acts 22:16 Be baptized, AND WASH AWAY THY SINS, CALLING ON THE NAME OF THE LORD.

BAPTISM IN WATER IS A RITUAL TO OUTWARDLY SHOW THAT A PERSON HAS DECIDED TO TURN FROM HIS SINFUL WAYS AND START LIVING A BETTER LIFE. The attitude of the Pharisees and Sadducees when they came to John the baptizer was not based on their desire to change. So John said, Matthew 3:7 O generation of vipers, who hath warned you to flee from the wrath to come? (8) Bring forth therefore fruits (attitude) meet for repentance. (Mark 1:4) John was preaching the baptism of repentance for the remission of sins, but water alone could not remit (pardon) those sins. It took faith in and calling upon the Name of God to do that.

The effects of sin drives out the holy spirit of God: but it cannot destroy the Gift of the Spirit: Jesus said, (John 14:16) I will pray the Father (ask earnestly), and he shall give you another Comforter, that he may abide with you FOREVER.

Yeremias rated this answer:

Thank you for your input. It is appreciated.

****

HERBS, EATING OF

Charlene asked this question.

Please explain the Eating of Herbs.

James gave this response.

Romans 14:1 Him that is weak in the faith receive ye, but not to doubtful disputations.

2 For one believeth that he may eat all things: another, who is weak eateth HERBS.

3 Let not him that eateth despise him that eateth not; and let not him which eateth not judge him that eateth for God receiveth him.

Was Saul (Paul) right?

Yes, when he warned against 'doubtful disputations.' An idea is not worth making enemies, and disputations do not necessarily change the beliefs of the disputers.

Yes, he was right when he stated 'One believeth that he may eat all things'—for the body was made omnivorous to survive times when fruit and vegetables were not available.

But Saul again saw through the glass darkly (1 Cor. 13:12) because he did not consider the original plan of God for the sustenance and longevity of man. Here he should have examined the passages in Genesis 1:29 before giving his opinion. If he had, it would have slightly modified his judgement, especially in the statement 'who is weak eateth herbs.' For weakness comes more readily to them that ingest animal fat. (Refer to the Kings meat Daniel 1:12-15).

Genesis 1:29 And God said, Behold, I have given you every HERB bearing seed, which is upon the face of ALL THE EARTH, and every tree, in the which is the fruit of a tree yielding seed; TO YOU IT SHALL BE FOR MEAT. (Food).

Are there any exceptions?

Yes. The human body was designed so that it was capable of maintaining itself FOREVER. Men and women were created omnivores, rather than herbivores or carnivores only. Although they were originally told they should eat nuts, fruits and vegetables, God knew the time would come when there would be a scarcity of such products and it would become necessary for people to resort to eating meat. So the bodies were constructed with the capability of tolerating meat products during those periods.

Noah was on the boat one year and ten days. It was not possible at that time, since there was no refrigeration or the art of canning to preserve fruits and vegetables for that duration, and it was not recorded that they dried food items, so it was written. Gen. 9:3—Every moving thing that liveth shall be MEAT FOR YOU (NOTE: that this was written well after the flood. After they had already started eating meat); even as the green herb have I given you all things.

NOTE: When fruits and vegetables are plentiful, people should revert to its consumption because it is not impossible, but more difficult for the body to dispose of excessive animal fats in the system. What shall we do then?

Cast all our care upon God for his spirit can guide in every phase of our lives. Each body is different. The individual needs are not the same at any given moment. God knows what is needed in our bodies and by our instincts leads us to proper nutrition.

Romans 11:17—The kingdom of God is not meat and drink—. 20 Meat destroy not the work of God, all things indeed are pure. 1 Cor 8:8 But meat commendeth us not to God: for neither, if we eat, are we the better; neither, if we eat not, are we the worse. (It has no effect on the spiritual life.)

Col.2:16 Let no man therefore judge you in meat, 1 Tim 4:3 Forbidding to marry (marriage is a necessity). The positive (female)cannot operate properly without the negative (male), and commanding to abstain from meats which God hath created to be received with thanksgiving of them which believe and know the truth. (4) For every creature of God is good, and nothing to be refused, if it be received with thanksgiving.

Matthew 15:11 Not that which goeth into the mouth defileth a man; but that which cometh out of the mouth, this defileth a man.

****

Here and Hereafter:

Edward asked this question.

Is there hope for humanity in the hereafter?

James gave this response.

HERE AND HEREAFTER

Psalms 80:18 Quicken us, and we will CALL upon thy NAME.

(10) Turn us again, O Lord God of hosts, cause thy face to shine; and WE SHALL BE SAVED.

Acts 2:21 And it shall come to pass, that WHOSOEVER shall CALL on the NAME of the LORD shall be saved.

God must quicken us with life and we must be changed or we will never understand the mysteries of the spirit, for the (1Cor.2:14) natural man receiveth not the things of the Spirit of God: for they are foolishness unto him, neither can he know them, because they are spiritually discerned.

Jesus said (John 3:3), I say unto thee, Except a man be born again, he cannot see the kingdom of God.

Jesus came in His Father's Name to set up God's kingdom here on the earth as it was intended in the beginning. The Son of God placed His Father's Name in the foreheads of those around him, but the darkness of the world of men was too great at that time and his followers had not yet been born again of their spirit.

Matthew 11:12—from the time of John the Baptist until now (a.d.31) the kingdom of heaven suffereth violence, and the violent take it by force.

It's different this time.

WHERE DOES GOD WANT US?

If we go out there we may miss God, for he desires to dwell here on the earth among men along with those that have held firm to HIS NAME. (Romans 8:38)—Paul said, I am persuaded, that neither death, nor life, nor angels, nor principalities, nor powers, nor things present, nor things to come, (39) Nor height, nor depth, nor any other creature, shall be able to separate us from the love of God who is in Christ Jesus.

Revelations 21:3—The tabernacle of God is with men, and he will dwell with them—God himself shall be with them, and be their God.

Isa. 45:18 For thus saith the Lord that created the heavens: God himself that formed the earth and made it: he hath established it, he created it not in vain, he formed it to be inhabited: I am the Lord; there is none else.

Jesus came to bring more life. He said (John 14:6), I am the way, the truth and the life. (John 10:10)—I am come that they might have life—more abundantly. (More than Adamah had in the beginning by the additional support of the Holy Ghost and the rebirth of man's spirit).

Sins cause death!

How?

By the force of guilt. It disrupts the mental process that maintains the immune system of the body and eventually the physical system becomes unbalanced and death occurs.

Ezek. 18:4—the soul that sinneth, it SHALL DIE.

Gen 2:17—In the day (1000 years—2 Pet 3:8) ye eat thereof (take into the mental and spiritual system, the knowledge of evil) thou shalt surely die.

Can a person sin their way to heaven?

We should not be absurd!

Psalm 1:4 The ungodly are not so but are like the chaff which the wind driveth away. (5) Therefore the ungodly shall not stand in the judgment, NOR SINNERS in the congregation of the righteous. (6)—the way of the ungodly SHALL PERISH.

For those that are saturated with the fruit of the tree of evil, have not called upon the Name of God constantly, have not received spiritual eyes, ears, the Gift of the Holy Ghost, the filling and maintenance of the holy spirit, and received the rebirth of their spirit, cannot expect more than the following.

Eccl. 9:5—the living know that they shall die: but the dead know not anything, neither have they any more a reward: for the memory of them is forgotten. (6) Also their love, and their hatred, and their envy, is now perished: neither have they any more a portion FOREVER IN ANYTHING that is done under the sun.

Paul said (Rom. 7:24) O wretched man that I am! Who shall deliver me from the body of this death? (25) I thank God through Jesus Christ our Lord—.

Hebrews 7:25—He (Jesus) is able also to save them to the

uttermost that come unto God by him, seeing he ever liveth to make intercession for them.

1 Cor. 15:19 If in this life only we have hope in Christ, we are of all men most miserable. (20) But now is Christ risen from the dead, and become the firstfruits of them that slept. (21) For since by man came death, by man came also the resurrection of the dead. (22) For as in Adam ALL DIE, even so in Christ shall ALL BE MADE ALIVE.

Matthew 11:28 Come unto me, all ye that labor and are heavy laden and I will give you rest.

1 Peter 5:7 Casting all your care upon him (God); for he careth for you.

'Here' is where God wants us, and he intends to give the

'HEREAFTER' to those that will CALL UPON HIS NAME,

****

HOLY CITY

Anonymous asked this question.

1) Does the Holy City already exist anywhere?

2) Is anybody already in the Holy City?

James gave this response.

The holy city has existed from the beginning, but without permanent inhabitants. Adamah (man) and woman first lived there. It was the garden of Eden or Paradise, a spiritual state where men and women were to live forever without the fear of death. But when sin appeared, fear drove them out of that heavenly realm and that is where mankind has remained ever since.

Jesus came to the earth to show men the way back into that garden of God, but they did not understand him. John 14:2 He said 'I go to prepare a place for you. (3) And if I go and prepare a place for you, I will come again, and receive you unto myself; that WHERE I AM (at that present time), there ye may be also.

Jesus, while on the earth, was standing before them in the second heaven state, in Paradise. He did no sin, therefore guilt did not drive him out of the presence of God for the entire three and a half years of his ministry.

What did he go away to prepare? He had previously prayed to his father that his followers be given the Holy Ghost (Comforter—John 14:16) as he had received at the time of his water baptism (Luke 4:1). This is what he and his father, God, were preparing for the people to receive on the day of Pentecost. (Acts 2:4) This was done so that the people would have power to overcome and remain in that heavenly state all the time without the effects of sin separating their minds from the presence of God.

Every individual that receives the Holy Ghost is in that holy city at the time they receive that gift. But shortly thereafter, the Adamic nature that has been inherited from the many generations of fallen ancestors, cause them to be driven out of that city, back into the courts where confusion has always resided.

It shall come to pass that WHOSOEVER shall CALL upon the NAME OF THE LORD (the tree of life) shall be saved. It is through faith in that name that will convey power to overcome the fallen human nature that is in all of us, allowing us to permanently live in that city on the earth where it was first established.

Rev. 2:7 He that hath an ear, let him hear what the spirit saith unto the churches; to him that overcometh will I give to eat of the Tree of Life (The Name of God), which is in the midst of the Paradise of God (second heaven). (2 Cor. 12:4)

Rev. 7:15—and he (God)—shall dwell among them (the same as God wanted to dwell with Adamah and woman from the beginning). (17) the Lamb, God's son (Jesus, who bore God's Name for placement in the minds of men—Rev. 14:1) shall feed them, and shall lead them unto living fountains of waters: (John 14:4) and God shall wipe away all tears from their eyes.

Rev. 21:3—The tabernacle of God is with men, and he will dwell with them—HE HIMSELF shall be with them, and be their God.

Acts 17:28 FOR IN HIM WE LIVE, AND MOVE, AND HAVE OUR BEING—.

****

Holy Ghost

Charlene asked this question.

How does the Holy Ghost speak different languages through a person?

James gave this response.

John 16:13 Howbeit when he, the Spirit of truth, is come, he will guide you into ALL TRUTH: for he shall not speak of himself; but whatsoever he shall hear, that shall he speak: and he will shew you things to come.

John 16:14 He shall glorify me: for he shall receive of mine, and shall shew it unto you. (15) All things that the Father hath are mine: therefore said I, that he shall take of mine, and shall shew it unto you.

Since the Holy Ghost DOES NOT SPEAK OF HIMSELF (on his own accord) but what he hears, that he speaks; how did he speak in so many languages at the time of the feast of Pentecost?

GOD UNDERSTANDS ALL LANGUAGES.

He created the brain, tongue and lips to form words, but he did not create languages. It was man and woman that made the sounds and designated meaning to them. The mind absorbs all sounds and sights. Most impressions are on a subconscious level during waking hours. It is the spirit of God that flows through the Holy Ghost that stimulates the memory banks of an individual and brings together a super intelligent flow of understandable phrases that have been heard and stored by the brain over a period of time.

The following is a rendition in part from the Bible dictionary, By William Smith. Revised Edition—Copyright l984 by Porter and Coates.

The words spoken were not by the will of the speakers, but by the Spirit which 'gave them utterance.' Such words as they then uttered had been heard by the disciples before. The difference was that before, the Galilean peasants, who spoke primarily Aramaic, had stood in that crowd, neither heeding nor understanding nor remembering what they heard, still less able to reproduce it; now they had the power of speaking it clearly and freely. The divine work would in this case take the form of supernatural exaltation of the memory.

For the Spirit to give utterance to words, they must be available in the memory banks of the brain. We hear different languages around us all the time. We do not understand them, but the Spirit of God does, so it is no great thing for God to, through the Holy Ghost, use those linguistic phrases when needed to show his mighty works and power to the glory of His Name.

It must be understood that the Holy Ghost always advances the works of God. Any one that mimics sounds that have been previously advanced by the Holy Ghost, may at a different time and under different circumstances, be in danger of infringing or hindering the operation of the spirit of God. Even though God has mercy, and still is showing compassion upon the ignorance of the masses, it is time for those fraudulent sounds to subside. When God wants to speak through the Holy Ghost, it will happen without conscious thought or effort on the part of the person through which God speaks. (Matt. 10:19)

****

Holy Spirit and confusion.

Translations and interpretations

This question is about that confusion. Where is it coming from?

Which group is behind most of the confusion?

James gave this response.

Can the story of the Tower of Babel have a two-fold meaning?

Genesis 11 tells the story of the separation of people and the ultimate development of different languages. But it is also a good example of the confusion caused by the many names in religion.

Gen. 11:4 And (the people) said, Go to, let us build a city and a tower, whose top MAY REACH UNTO HEAVEN; and let us MAKE A NAME, lest we be scattered abroad upon the face of the whole earth.

Gen. 11:6 And the Lord said, Behold, the people is one, and they have all one language; and this they begin to do: and now

NOTHING WILL BE restrained from them, which they have imagined to do.

GOD said, LET US CONFOUND (confuse)

Gen 11:7 Go to, let us go down, and there confound their language, that they may not understand one another's speech.

The many thousands of names in our religious societies are testimony that the people have made names for themselves. They have imagined that through their particular name they have selected, ***they may reach heaven***. Because they have not accepted God's NAME ONLY he has taken their understanding away.

Acts 4:11 (Speaking of Jesus—the Name of God) This is the stone which was set at nought of you builders (religionists), which is become the head of the corner.

Acts 4:12 Neither is there salvation (saving of a person from sin or danger) in any other; for there is NONE OTHER NAME under heaven given among men, whereby we must be saved.

For those that become one in God's Name there will be nothing restrained from them.

Revelation 14:8 And there followed another angel, saying, Babylon (confusion) is fallen, is fallen, that great city—.

When the people become ONE in GOD'S NAME, they will understand that they should not follow the ideas of men, or Moses, or Elijah, ONLY JESUS, THE NAME OF GOD AND THE SON OF GOD.

Peter, James and John was with Jesus—

Matthew 17: 3 And there appeared unto them Moses, and Elias talking with him. (Jesus). (4) Then Peter said unto Jesus, Lord, it is good for us to be here: if thou wilt, let us make here three tabernacles; one for thee, and one for Moses, and one for Elias. (5) While he yet spake, behold, a bright cloud overshadowed them: and behold a voice out of the cloud, which said, This is my beloved Son, in whom I am well pleased; HEAR YE HIM.

Matthew 17:8 (After the vision, Peter, James and John) lifted up their eyes, and saw NO MAN, SAVE JESUS ONLY.

John 5:43 I am come in my Father's NAME, and ye receive me not: if ANOTHER shall come in ***HIS OWN NAME***, HIM YE WILL RECEIVE. (yes, they have done this).

1 John 3:23—This is His commandment, That we should believe on the NAME of HIS SON, Jesus Christ—.

John 20:31—These are written, that ye might believe that Jesus is the Christ, the Son of God; and that believing ye might have life through HIS NAME.

1 Cor. 14:33—God is not the author of confusion, but of peace—.

God allows confusion for those that will not believe in and call upon His Name.

Acts 2:21—It shall come to pass, that WHOSOEVER shall CALL on the NAME of the Lord shall be saved.

Eph. 3:14 For this cause I bow my knees unto the Father of our Lord Jesus Christ, (15) Of whom the whole family in heaven and earth is named.

****

Holy Spirit, Filling of the.

Ruth asked this question.

Would you please explain your experience with the filling of the Holy Spirit?

James gave this response.

A campground—Arizona—1961

The service progressed. Peoples minds and voices began to blend together. Lightness of spirit prevailed. It was the afternoon service. They spoke with tongues, others interpreted. A man's voice rang loud and clear, which said, ***IF YOU DON'T RECEIVE THE FILLING OF THE SPIRIT YOU WILL FALL***.

About three hundred people moved forward. Ruth and James were there. Each was instructed to touch the person in front of them on the shoulder or back. James had the lamp all along, but he, like the foolish virgins found himself short of oil. He was now in the store house of them that had to sell. It was like a large pitcher tipping to spill into his lamp, until the pitcher was emptied and James was full. His eyes then could see on both sides of the fence. Evil was not the only thing directed to his attention. His physical body and mind could then withstand insanity that was all around. He could even control himself.

****

HOPE

Ruth asked this question.

Is there any hope for the world of mankind? What is that hope?

James gave this response.

During the lifetime of Adamah he never called upon the Name of God. He never mentioned that idea. His children never heard that Name come out of their Father's mouth. So how could they know? Adamah had cut God from the minds of his children.

It was not until Enos (Seth's son-Genesis 4:26) was born that men began to call on the name of God as they knew it. But it was not God's true SAVING NAME. That Name was not revealed until it was delivered to man by God's only begotten son (after the Spirit).

Jesus came with mercy. It must be explained that even though sin has filled the beings of most, if not all, calling upon the Name of God attracts the power of the spirit to wash out the effects of sin before it destroys the mind and body.

Hebrews 4:15. We have not an high priest which cannot be touched with the feeling of our infirmities; but was in all points tempted like as we are, yet without sin.

Hebrews 4:16 LET US therefore COME BOLDLY unto the throne of grace, that we may obtain mercy, and find grace to help IN THE TIME OF NEED.

Instead of hiding behind the trees, man and woman could have come boldly to the Name of God (the Tree of Life) and received mercy, but instead they chose to disregard the mediator between God and man until they were filled with confusion. God caused them to become afraid of him because they would not CALL UPON HIS NAME. From that point they did not understand God or his reason, because they refused to use the formula God had so clearly placed in their 'beings' from the very beginning.

MANKIND STILL HAS HOPE, but only in the Name of God. Only then, by CALLING UPON AND HAVING FAITH IN IT. (Acts 4:12) Neither is there salvation in any other: for there is NONE OTHER NAME under heaven given among men, whereby we MUST BE SAVED.

God has brought confusion to all other people who have attempted to go to heaven by making a Name for themselves. (Genesis 11:4) God's Name only must be in the foreheads of the people. (Revelation 14:1)

****

Human sacrifice

Maxine asked this question.

What would you think if a voice said for you to offer your children as a burnt offering to God?

James gave this response.

It must first be understood that God had no intention of allowing Abraham to sacrifice his son as the heathen were doing. (Check Job 1:12) Abraham also understood this. Examine Gen. 22:5 And Abraham said unto his young men, Abide ye here with the ass; and ***I AND THE LAD*** will go yonder and WORSHIP, ***AND COME AGAIN TO YOU.***

Genesis 22:1 And it came to pass—that ***God did temp*** (test) Abraham, and said unto him, Abraham: and he said, Behold, here am I. (2) And he said, Take now thy son, thine only son Isaac, whom thou lovest, and get thee into the land of Moriah; AND OFFER HIM THERE FOR A BURNT OFFERING upon one of the mountains which I will tell thee of.

Abram's father, Terah, was an idol worshiper. This influenced Abram's thinking.

James 1:13 Let no man say when he is tempted, I am tempted of God: for ***God cannot be tempted with evil***, (how much more evil can killing your children be?) ***Neither tempteth he any man.***

Jeremiah 7:30 The children of Judah (31) have built the high places of Tophet, which is in the valley of the son of Hinnom, to BURN THEIR SONS AND THEIR DAUGHTERS in the fire; which ***I COMMANDED THEM NOT, NEITHER CAME IT INTO MY HEART.***

Genesis 22:11 And the ***Angel of the Lord*** (the good angel) called unto him (Abraham) out of heaven—. (12) And he said, Lay not thine hand upon the lad, neither do thou anything unto him—.

Compare this with the story of Jesus. Mark 1:13 And he was there in the wilderness, ***TEMPTED OF SATAN—.***

Matthew 4:11 Then the ***devil leaveth him***, (wrong thoughts) and, behold, ***angels came*** and ministered unto him.

2 Cor. 11:14 ***And no marvel; for Satan himself is transformed into an angel of light.***

(15) Therefore it is no great thing if his ministers also be transformed as the ministers of righteousness.

Galations 1:8—Though we, or ***AN ANGEL from heaven***, preach any other gospel unto you—let him be accursed.

The human mind knows how to create smooth, great sounding words to convince along any line of reasoning. After the commandments have been congealed for so many thousands of years (although they were not in force at the time of Abraham), shouldn't we be able to recognize the difference between the good voices and the evil ones even though they may be allowed by God? Or they may even say I am God.

Gen. 22:15 And the angel of the lord called unto Abraham out of heaven the second time, (16) And said, By myself have I sworn, saith the Lord, for because thou hast done this thing, and hast not withheld thy son, thine only son: (17) That in blessing I will bless thee—,

After reading the above, if we have trouble understanding this, we may do well to ask ourselves—,

If those same words were reiterated to our brain, would we attempt to carry them out, or sign ourselves into the nearest hospital, or call upon the Name of God and run to a church and receive spiritual help from God through the Holy Spirit?

When that holy spirit begins to flow out of the belly like rivers of living water (John 7:38) everything will become clear and all the voices in the world will be understood for what they are. Killing and violence will be washed away from the thoughts and the true God will shine with a brightness that has never been imagined in this world.

Ezekiel 18:32 For ***I have no pleasure in the death of him that dieth,*** saith the Lord GOD: wherefore turn yourselves, and live ye.

Above all things remember the commandment, Exodus 20:13, THOU SHALT NOT KILL. Do not do as Moses commanded regarding the penalties either before this commandment or after it. John 1:17 For the law was given by Moses, but GRACE and TRUTH came by Jesus Christ.

****

Imaginary?

aservant asked this question.

Known and loved Christian leader A W Tozer once said that all of our denominational differences are imaginary. Is it possible that all these labels and categories, even the offices held by many are purely of human invention and that God sees only one church? What does that do to all of our headquarters, synods, episcopates and "sees"? Do they mean anything at all? Could I go to the "head" of different "churches" and get different "answers" to the same theological question?

James gave this response.

NAMES

Consider the different names in religion.

There is only one name which designates the mediator between God and man.

God would not have changed the names of Abram and Sarai, (Gen. 17:5 & 15) to Abraham and Sarah, or Jacob to Israel, (Gen. 32:28) if names made no difference.

God confounded the language of the people because they wanted to make a ***NAME for themselves***. Gen. 11:4—They said, Go to, let us build us a city and a tower, whose top ***MAY REACH UNTO HEAVEN: and let us make a NAME—.***

God said, (Gen. 1:7) Go to, let us go down and there ***confound their language***, that they may not understand one another's speech.

Since the attempt to build the tower of Babel, confusion has spread throughout the world. People have always wanted to worship gods made of material objects because they cannot see or understand a God that is not visible to their natural eyes. Names have been given to most of their gods. Of course there was one god that they did not know. Acts 17:22—Paul stood in the midst of Mars hill, and said, Ye men of Athens, I perceive that in all things ye are too superstitious. (23) For as I passed by, and beheld your devotions, I found an altar with this inscription, TO THE UNKNOWN GOD. Whom therefore ye ignorantly worship, him declare I unto you. (24) God that made the world and all things therein, seeing that he is Lord of heaven and earth, dwelleth not in temples made with hands; (25) Neither is worshipped with men's hands, as though he needed anything, seeing he giveth to all life, and breath, and all things; (26) And hath made of one blood all nations of men for to dwell on all the face of the earth—. (27) That they should seek the Lord, if haply they might feel after him, and find him, though he be not far from every one of us: (28) For in him we live, and move, and have our being—. (29) Forasmuch then as we are the offspring of God, we ought not to think that the Godhead is like unto gold, or silver, or stone, graven by art and man's device.

ISAIAH WROTE OF NATURAL BABYLON.

(Babel is Babylon)

Isaiah 2:9—Here cometh a chariot of men, with a couple of horsemen. And he answered and said, Babylon is fallen, is fallen; and all the graven images of her gods he hath broken unto the ground.

JOHN WROTE OF THE SYMBOLIC BABYLON.

Revelation 14:8 And there followed another angel, saying, Babylon is fallen, is fallen, that GREAT CITY, because she made ALL NATIONS drink of the wine (doctrine) of the wrath of her fornication.

Babylon is symbolic of all the religious systems in the world that have said let us make a tower whose top MAY REACH UNTO HEAVEN. And let us make a NAME so that we may not be scattered abroad upon the face of the whole earth. We must be separated from others. We are the only ones going to heaven. The others will not be in the good graces of God because they do not understand our doctrine nor we theirs.

They are all deceived. We are the only ones that God has bestowed his special favors. After all, there is only one body of Christ and we are the only ones that belong to that body.

Herein lies the confusion. God has made it so. Why? Because they have refused to accept him as their God and believed in his only begotten son that he sent to the earth to show them the way. Jesus said I am the way, the truth and the life: no man cometh unto the father, but by me. (Not by any other name).

1 Tim. 2:1 I exhort therefore, that, first of all, supplications, prayers, intercessions, and giving of thanks be made for ALL MEN; (2) For kings, and for all that are in authority; that we may lead a quiet and peaceable life in all godliness and honesty. (3) For this is good and acceptable in the sight of GOD OUR SAVIOUR; (4) Who will have ALL MEN to be saved, and to come unto the knowledge of the truth. (5) For there is ONE GOD, and ONE MEDIATOR between God and men, the MAN CHRIST JESUS. (6) Who gave himself a ransom for ALL, to be testified in due time.

Paul said, 1 Cor. 8:4—There is none other God but ONE. (5) For though there be that are called gods, whether in heaven or in earth, (as there be gods many, and lords many,) (6) But to us there is but ONE GOD, the Father, of whom are all things, and we in him; and ONE LORD JESUS CHRIST, by whom are all things, and we by him.

Acts. 4:12 Neither is there salvation in any other: for there is none other NAME UNDER HEAVEN given among men, whereby we must be saved.

****

Immortality on Earth?

Quabal asked this question.

Yes, I am certainly a Christian and born again, imbued with the Holy Ghost as well. When Noah built the ark for 120 years there was nothing but mockery and laughter at his folly and his foolish preaching. Do you think they would mock him if they were not also living past 100 with the ability to do strenuous labor? I think they had lifetimes as long as his. If the sinners can have a long sinful life; why can't a Christian, who asks it for the glory of God, have a long righteous life as well? Also, God knows the appointed time of all men to die and who knows if he will look upon my request with favor?

James gave this response.

Christ—L Christus, Christ; Gr. Christos, Christ,

Jesus said, (John 14:6) I am the way, the truth, and the LIFE: no man cometh unto the Father, but by me.

Christ is the power and life of God. It is that light which was placed in the first human beings that were created and placed on the earth to live for ever. They were warned that in the day that they take into their mental system the knowledge of evil, (Gen. 2:9) it would drive out the power of God and ultimately cause their physical body to commence its deterioration.

The first human inhabitants failed miserably. With God a day is as a thousand years. (2 Pet. 3:8) Many of those people lived almost one of God's days. (Gen. 5:5—Adam 930 years, Gen. 9:29—Noah 950 years, Gen. 5:27—Methuselah 969 years). But during that time the majority patterned their lives after the actions of the other animals. Because of this they degenerated to the level of the wild beasts. The thoughts of their hearts were on evil continually. Gen. 6:5. They could not return to God by way of the Tree of Life (God's Name) because they could not stop sinning. The 'Thou shalt not' stipulation, which is the flaming sword, (Gen. 3:24) separated them from the power and presence of God. This weakened them to the point of no return. They were lost without the mediator.

The human body was designed to live eternally.

The body cells are continually dying and replaced entirely within each seven year period. The earth circles the sun each year and is short only a few seconds within a one hundred thousand year period. Men have been on the earth only four tenths of that time.

The ***immune system*** was designed to withstand any reasonable demands upon it. The bodies were structured to thrive well on fruits and vegetables (Gen. 1:29). The man was told to dress and keep the garden (Gen. 1:15) for the purpose of producing that sustenance required by his natural body.

The ***spiritual structure*** of the human body began to deteriorate because the first man refused to call upon the Name of God for strength to maintain the power of Christ within himself, and that caused him to fail from the very onset of his existence. In the beginning he was perfect in all his ways but iniquity (wickedness) was found in him because of his refusal to take hold of that Tree of Life.

Jesus was sent to the earth in the form of a natural man to determine what ingredient was needed for the health and survival of God's invention, that had been developed by Christ. Jesus discovered the infirmity in the human body because he was made of that same sinful flesh. The gene deterioration was also in his own body that was handed down from generation to generation all the way back to that first Adamah (man). Of course he did not sin (2 Cor. 5:21) as others had done before him. He was that last Adam, designed as a quickening spirit (life giving spirit, 1 Cor. 15:45) to retrieve that which was lost in the first man. (Matthew 18:11).

Jesus said, (John 14:16) I will pray the Father, and he shall give you another Comforter, (Holy Ghost) that he may abide with you FOR EVER. (17)—He dwelleth with you, and shall be in you. Before that time the Holy Ghost was not placed inside the man. (2 Pet. 1:21) Men spake as they were moved by the

Holy Ghost, but it had not yet been given them as a gift within themselves to become a part of their spiritual life and strength and guidance. (Acts 1:8 Power after, Acts 2:4 Filled with).

There were other gifts needed. Jesus said, (John 3:3) Except a man be born again, he cannot see the kingdom of God. This was referring to the ritual of water baptism and the killing of the Adamic spirit that was received from the natural father and replaced by a right spirit received from God, and the filling of the Holy Ghost. (John 3:5) Except a man be born of water and of the Spirit, he cannot enter into the kingdom of God. (6) That which is born of the flesh is flesh; and that which is born of the Spirit is spirit.

Paul wrote—Romans 6:6 Knowing this, that our OLD MAN (the spirit of the natural body that had been deteriorating since the beginning) is crucified with him, (Jesus) that the body of sin might be destroyed, that henceforth we should not serve sin. (7) For he that is dead is freed from sin.

John 3:16 God so loved the world, that he gave his only begotten Son, that whosoever believeth in him should not PERISH, but have EVERLASTING LIFE.

Psalms 51:10 Create in me a clean heart, O God; and renew a RIGHT SPIRIT within me. That degenerated spirit must be killed, taken out, and a right spirit installed in its place. This can only be accomplished through the operation of God and the willingness of each individual to want and ask for that change.

Ezek. 18:31 Cast away from you all your transgressions, whereby ye have transgressed; and MAKE you a NEW HEART and a NEW SPIRIT: for why will ye die—.

Life is still offered to mankind, but only through faith in, and calling upon the Name of God which has been delivered to the minds of men through his only begotten son, Jesus.

Acts 4:12 Neither is there salvation (saving a person from sin or danger) in any other: for there is none other NAME under heaven given among men, whereby we must be saved. (Saved from every conceivable destructive element in the world by the guidance of the Holy Ghost). (John 16:7 Comforter—Holy Ghost (John 16:13) will GUIDE you into all truth—.)

Quabal rated this answer:

Thanks for sharing your thoughts on this. Go with Christ my fellow laborer in Christ.

****

INCEST:

jdg asked this question.

After the beginning, when the first man and woman were created, is it true that the human race was increased by incest?

James gave this response.

It is evident that Cain went to the land of Nod (Gen. 4:16) with his sister. (17) And Cain knew his wife; and she conceived—.The only reason it would be called a sin, is that it was after the similitude of Adam's transgression.

(Romans 5:14)

Although it was later classed as a sin (by Moses. Lev. 18:9, 20:17) for them to come together as man and wife for the purpose of propagating, they were not charged with that sin because the law had not yet been accumulated, placed in a book, read to the people and confirmed by God.

Romans 5:13 (For until the law sin was in the world: but sin is not imputed (credited to or blamed on a person or cause) when there is no law.

Even Abram and Sarai, before the law, were related. They had the same father but not the same mother. (Gen. 20:12) And yet indeed she is my sister; she is the daughter of my father, but not the daughter of my mother; and she became my wife. Yet, Abraham, after his name was changed(Gen. 17:5) became the father of many nations. Gen. 17:3) And Abram fell on his face: and God talked with him, saying, (4) As for me, behold, my covenant is with thee, and thou shalt be a father of many nations.

(Gen. 12:3) And I will bless them that bless thee, and curse them that curseth thee: and in thee shall ALL THE FAMILIES OF THE EARTH BE BLESSED.

****

WITH OR WITHOUT THE LAW (Romans 6:1), Shall we continue in sin that grace may abound? (2) God forbid.

There would never have been sin in the world if men had left the process of propagation under the control of God's original plan. Nor would they have missed anything because they would never have known of the physical sensations associated with copulation. Those sensations have become an obsession and has caused uncontrollable sins.

****

Investing.

Edward asked this question.

Is it right to invest?

James gave this response.

Investing:

TALENT

It first should be understood that the word talent did not mean the same in Biblical times as it does now. Although it did use the words 'several (individual) ability, it was primarily referring to a piece of money, or gold, silver or lead.

A talent of Gold is listed in the Teachers addition of the Bible Dictionary—Wm. Smith, Copyright 1948 as being worth $26,280.00. This of course varies greatly as the economies fluctuate and monetary values change over the years.

Matthew 25:14-30 In this parable Jesus is comparing the spiritual with the natural, indicating that investing is not only allowed but desirable.

Matthew 25:27 ***THOU OUGHTEST*** therefore to have ***put my money to the exchangers (bankers), and then at my coming I should have received mine own with usury (interest).***

When a person has the ABILITY to invest wisely, or to save in a financial institution, he is not considered wicked, slothful, and unprofitable, and will not be found weeping and gnashing (grinding 'as teeth' together) because of poverty. Instead it will be said 'I will make you ruler over many things: enter thou into the JOY OF THE LORD.

We should remember that the Kingdom of God is being set up in people, on the earth. God and Jesus will dwell in that Kingdom with and in his people. They will be a prosperous congregation, both spiritually and naturally. God made the earth to be inhabited and enjoyed by his sons and daughters, those people that will call upon His Name as he had instructed the first man to do.

Romans 15:11—PRAISE THE LORD, ALL YE GENTILES; AND LAUD HIM, ALL YE PEOPLE.

With God there is no difference in people, whether they are white, black or anywhere in between. His only requirement is that they all call upon Him by HIS NAME always, without stopping.

The way is found in God's Name, along with truth, life and prosperity in spiritual and natural things.

Jesus said (John 14:6) I am the way, the truth, and the life—.

If we stay in the Name of God we will be guided by the spirit into all right thinking. From the beginning God intended that men be prosperous and be in health.

3 John 1:2 Beloved, I wish above all things that thou mayest prosper and be in health, even as thy soul prospereth.

Investing! Romans 14:22 Happy is he that condemneth not himself in that thing which he (God) alloweth.

****

Jabez, the Prayer of

bobbye274 asked this question.

Found in I Chronicles 4:10 tells us that " . . . God granted him that which he requested."

(1) Have you prayed this prayer? How long? Do you have an answered prayer(s) as a result of praying the "Prayer of Jabez?"

(2) Do you know his other name or title?

There was a poster that answered Jabez' prayer about 6 months ago. However, I would like actual "answers to the Jabez' prayer" if you should care to share—or any information you should like to share about this powerful Prayer. Thanks. Bobbye

James gave this response.

—or any information you should like to share—.

King James Version

JABEZ 1 Chronicles 4:10

Contained in the prayer of Jabez were the following words:

ME	5 times
MY	1
Thine	1
Thou	2

JESUS

Contained in the prayer of Jesus were the following words:

Matthew	6:9
OUR	4 times
THINE	1
THY	3
US	4
WE	1

Luke	11:2
OUR	3 times
THY	3
US	5
WE	1

This shows that Jesus was more caring for others. He was less self-centered and that he worked with the Father and with the people as their mediator (1 Tim 2:5). Although God answered Jabez's prayer, Jesus' prayer was more acceptable. Even God does not work alone, for he said (Gen. 1:26), LET US make man, in OUR image—.

Although Jabez was more honourable than his brethren

(1 Chron. 4:9), Job discovered a more pleasing prayer.

JOB 41:10—***The Lord turned the captivity of Job,***

WHEN HE PRAYED FOR HIS FRIENDS—.

Bobbye rated this answer:

Great analogies!

Thanks for sharing!

Bobbye

****

JAMES-son of Zebedee—

E Martin asked this question.

In the book “Jesus Freaks” by dc Talk and the Voice of the Martyrs, the reference is made that James, Son of Zebedee was beheaded along with the man who falsely accused him. In the book “More than a Carpenter” by Josh McDowell—It refers to James as having been killed by the sword. Which is correct? Thank you, Ellen Martin

James gave this response.

I have not read the reports you are referencing. I trust your report. Is it possible that both renditions are correct? Could it be that James was BEHEADED by the use of a SWORD?

I personally think that we should not continually relay the violence and ignorance of the past. But should look with anticipation to a better ‘thousand year’ day deficient of those past mistakes.

We can only know what others have said or written, coupled with our own thoughts. The world of people are designed to give and receive from one-another for the sake of humbleness.

The following is an excerpt from the book entitled, All the Men of the Bible. Herbert Lockyer.

James {Jamez}—supplanter

The son of Zebedee, and the elder brother of John, and one of the Twelve (Matt. 4:21; 10:2; 17;1; Mark 1:19, 29; 3:17; 5:37; 9:2; 10:35; 41; 13:3; l4:33; Luke 5:10; 6:14; 8:51; 9:28, 54; Acts 1:13; 12:2). From the foregoing references several facts emerge:

James’ father Zebedee, was a Galilean fisherman and prosperous, since he employed servants to assist in the management of his boats. Zebedee had a house in Jerusalem and was known as a friend of the High Priest, Caiaphas, and his household. This would mark Him as a man of social position.

His mother's name was Salome, whom tradition says was a sister of the Virgin Mary, which may help to throw light upon the relation of her sons to the Master. This would also make James a cousin to Jesus after the flesh.

(Insert debatable).

James worked in partnership with his father and brothers and was busy with his boats and nets when the call of Christ reached him. His name is coupled with his brother John in the lists of the apostles, which could mean that when they were sent forth two by two, James and John would be paired. Evidently they were men of like spirit and disposition and received from Jesus the title Sons of Thunder. He was on terms of special intimacy with Christ, although he never attained the distinction of his brother John.

HIS LIFE CAME TO AN UNTIMELY END when he was martyred by Herod Agrippa. The cup and the baptism of pain and death were his. Seventeen years passed between his call to service and his death. He was the second of the martyrs and the first of the apostles to give his life for Christ.

We have no word from his pen nor word he spoke unless Acts 4:24-30 be an exception, but James was content to be a disciple. He never sought fame, power, a great name. He had no ambition to be first.

E Martin rated this answer:

I agree with you, although sometimes as we study, it does help to know the facts. I appreciate your time and efforts in answering my question. Thank you, Ellen

****

Jehovah Witness?

Anonymous asked this question.

James, are you a Jehovah's Witness? Although I am not, I believe there is a lot of truth to their beliefs. I never understood why there is a resurrection if we are already in heaven or hell as soon as we die or shortly thereafter. Also the Trinity taught in Christianity seems far fetched to me. A mighty God or The mighty God coming to be on the cross. I have thought Jesus earned the right to be God's Son through obedience, not on the order of mortal sons and parents.

James gave this response.

No, I am not a Jehovah's Witness. There is some truth in all religions. They are all trying to reach God in their own way according to their respective understandings. We need them all to hold back the power of evil minds.

People in the various religions should not condemn others for their way of expressing themselves or even their doctrines. After all, there are also some wrong in all religions, primarily because they have not accepted the Name of God only. (Matt.17:8 Jesus only) They have all made a name for themselves. Herein lies confusion.

It is a greater fallacy when Christians fight Christians over various views. When they take the concordance and spend hours breaking down certain syllables and contending endlessly over miner differences. This debating does not save a person from sin or danger. Only Christ through unity by the Holy Ghost can do that.

Heaven has not yet been attained as it was intended by God in the beginning, but there is mercy extended to all those that walk with God.

Paul wrote, (Rom. 8:38) For I am persuaded, that neither death, nor life, nor angels, nor principalities, nor powers, nor things present, nor things to come, (39) Nor height, nor depth, nor any other creature, shall be able to separate us from the love of God, which is in Christ Jesus our Lord.

God's love for those that walk with him is the reason for the resurrection. Periodically there is a resurrection. Those that came out of their grave at the time of Jesus' resurrection did not come out with a physical body. (Matt. 27:52-53They could only be seen through visions) ***They were as the angels.*** (Matt. 22:30).

HEAVEN: Jesus said, (John 3:13)—No MAN hath ascended up to heaven, (This statement was made before the resurrection as stated above) but he that came down from heaven, even the Son of man which is in heaven. At that time Jesus was standing in the spiritual state of paradise. This is the same heaven the first man and woman were to enjoy forever. In that state there is no pain or sorrow, no fear and no death. Jesus' death was pre-arranged because he was the Son of God and was predestinated to come to the earth only to show men and women the way back to paradise. When his job was completed he returned to His Father. Even this could have been different if men had reverenced him, but they would not. Matt. 21:37

HELL:

Hell was created after the separation of man's mind from the presence of God. ***Men have created hell on earth***. It is not the work of God, nor is God to blame for the evils produced by the minds of men.

Other than hell on the earth created by the minds of men, is there also hell under the ground after death?

Eccl: 9:5—The living know that they shall die: but the dead know not anything, neither, have they any more a reward; for the memory of them is forgotten. (6) Also their love, and their hatred, and their envy, is now perished; neither have they any more a portion for ever in any thing that is done under the sun.

The only hope for those that had remained in the presence of the power of God during the time of the old testament was through a resurrection. At the time of that resurrection they became as the angels and joined the other created angels of God.

Heaven will be established on the earth at the appropriate time if/and/or when men collectively draw near God.

Revelation 21:2 And I John saw the holy city, new Jerusalem, coming down from God out of heaven, prepared as a bride adorned for her husband. (3) And I heard a great voice out of heaven saying, Behold, the ***tabernacle of God IS WITH MEN, and HE WILL DWELL WITH THEM, and*** they shall be his people, and GOD HIMSELF shall be with them, and be their God. (4) And God shall wipe away all tears from their eyes; and there shall be no more death, neither sorrow, nor crying, neither shall there be any more pain: for the former things are passed away. 1 THS. 5:21 Prove all things: hold fast that which is good.

****

Jericho:

Maxine asked this question.

Did God tell Joshua to kill everyone in the city of Jericho and then burn it?

James gave this response.

No!

The following are transcripts in part of what God told Joshua to do.

Joshua 1:7—Be thou strong and very courageous, that thou mayest OBSERVE TO DO ACCORDING TO ALL THE LAW, which my servant (Moses) commanded thee: TURN not from it to the right hand or to the left, that thou mayest prosper whithersoever thou goest.

Joshua 1:8 This book of the law shall NOT DEPART OUT OF THY MOUTH: but thou shalt meditate therein DAY AND NIGHT, that thou mayest OBSERVE TO DO ACCORDING TO ALL THAT IS WRITTEN therein: for then thou shalt make thy way prosperous, and then thou shalt have good success.

Joshua 6:2 And the Lord said unto Joshua, See, I have given into thine hand Jericho, and the king thereof, and the mighty men of valor.

3 And ye shall compass the city, all ye men of war (for an outward show of strength to affect the psychological balance of the King and the people of Jericho), and go round about the city once. Thus shalt thou do six days.

4 And seven priests shall bear before the ark seven trumpets of rams' horns: and the seventh day ye shall compass the city seven times, and the priests shall blow with the trumpets.

5 And it shall come to pass, that when they make a long blast with the ram's horn, and when ye hear the sound of trumpet, all the people shall shout with a great shout; and the wall of the city shall fall down flat, and the people shall ascend up every man straight before him.

The sound of the trumpets, the blast of the ram's horn, and the shouts of people do not normally kill. God is aware of the elements of the earth. He synchronizes his plans with those elements for the advancement of his Name. God knew the vibrations set up by the sound of the trumpets and voices of the people would be enough to trigger the earthquake. That earthquake caused the walls of Jericho to tumble.

God planned to develop fear in the minds of the inhabitants of Jericho, so that a take-over could be accomplished without violence.

The law stated 'THOU SHALT NOT KILL'. Exodus 20:13.But Joshua forgot to meditate in that law day and night so that he would not deviate from the precepts of that law.

God tried to help people all the way down through the ages, but every time he turned his back they forgot. Joshua forgot to conform to what he had been told. As a result he stood by as the people (Joshua 6:21) utterly destroyed ALL THAT WAS IN THE CITY, BOTH MAN AND WOMAN, YOUNG AND OLD, and ox, and sheep, and ass, with the EDGE OF THE SWORD. Except for Rahab (a prostitute) and her family, all the people were killed, and the city of Jericho was burned. (Joshua 6:23-24)

JESUS SAID, John 10:8 ALL THAT EVER came before me are thieves and robbers:

John 10:10 The thief cometh not, but for to steal, and to kill, and to destroy—.

****

Jesus—God ?

Maxine asked this question.

Is Jesus God and what is God's name?

James gave this response.

There are people in the world that believe in One God, Two Gods, Three Gods, and many gods. Many are confused about His Name.

1 Cor. 8:5—Though there be that are called gods, whether in heaven or in earth, (as there be gods many, and lords many,) (6) But to us there is but ONE GOD, the father, of whom are all things, and we in him; and ONE LORD JESUS CHRIST, by whom are all things, and we by him. (7) Howbeit there is not in every man that knowledge—.

1 Tim. 2:5 For there is ONE GOD, and one MEDIATOR between God and men, THE MAN, Christ Jesus.

The Jews said to Jesus—John 10:33 For a good work we stone thee not; but for blasphemy; and because that thou, being A MAN, MAKEST THYSELF GOD. (34) Jesus answered them, Is it not written in your law, I said, Ye are gods? (35) If he called them gods, unto whom the word of God came, and the scripture cannot be broken; (36) Say ye of him, whom the Father hath sanctified, and sent into the world, Thou blasphemest; because I said, I AM THE SON OF GOD?

WASN'T JESUS CALLED 'The mighty God, The everlasting Father?

No—His Name was!

Isa. 9:6—***His NAME shall be called*** Wonderful, Counselor, The mighty God, The everlasting Father, The Prince of Peace.

John 5:43—***I am come in My Father's Name,—.***

Wasn't Philip led to believe that Jesus was God.

No! It was God in Jesus who spoke with Philip. John 14:8 Philip saith unto him, Lord, show us the Father, and it sufficeth us. (9) (God through) Jesus saith unto him, Have I been so long time with you, and yet hast thou not known me, Philip? He that hath seen me hath seen the Father, and how sayest thou then, Show us the Father? (10)(Then Jesus said) Believest thou not that I am in the Father, and THE FATHER IN ME? The words that I speak unto you I speak not of myself: but the Father that dwelleth in me, he doeth the works.

(11) Believe me that I am in the Father, and the Father in me:—.

2 Cor. 5:19 To wit, that God was in Christ, reconciling the world unto himself—.

Isa. 43:10 Ye are my witnesses, saith the LORD, and my servant whom I have chosen: that ye may know and believe me, and understand that I AM HE: before me there was no God formed, NEITHER SHALL THERE BE AFTER ME. (11) I,EVEN I, AM THE LORD; and BESIDE ME THERE IS NO SAVIOUR.

Does Jesus (God) save? Yes, through his power, Christ, and the guidance of the Holy Ghost.

John 1:1 In the beginning was the WORD (God's Name), and the Word was with God, and the Word was God. (2) The same was in the beginning with God. (14) And the Word was made flesh, and dwelt among us.

His Name is also called the WORD of God—Rev. 19:13.

1 Cor. 15:234 Then cometh the end, when he shall have delivered up the kingdom to GOD, EVEN THE FATHER; when he shall have put down all rule and all authority and power. (25) For he (the Son) must reign, till he hath put all enemies under his feet—(28) And when all things shall be subdued unto him, then shall the Son ALSO HIMSELF BE SUBJECT unto him (God) that put all things under him (Jesus), that God may be ALL IN ALL.

Pro. 30:4 Who hath ascended up into heaven, or descended? Who hath gathered the wind in his fists? Who hath bound the waters in a garment? Who hath established all the ends of the earth? ***WHAT IS HIS NAME, AND WHAT IS HIS SON'S NAME,*** if thou canst tell?

Jesus said (John 3:13),—No man hath ascended up to heaven but he that came down from heaven, even the Son of Man which is in heaven. Men of the old testament died or was translated into death. Heb. 1:13 These all died.

****

Jesus, was he good?

n2fnlvn asked this question.

Why did Jesus indicate that he was not good?

James gave this response.

A person said to Jesus (Matthew 19:16) Good Master—and Jesus replied (17) Why callest thou me good? There is none good but one, that is, God:—.

Paul said, (Romans 7:18)—I know that in me (that is, in my flesh), dwelleth no good thing.

Jesus was aware of the fallen condition of his ancestors. Jesus was from the tribe of Juda. After Judah's wife died he enlisted the services of what he thought was a prostitute. This turned out to be his Daughter-in-law. Gen. 38:15-26 From that union Pharez was conceived. This was the genealogical line between Juda and David. Jesus was of the tribe of Juda. Jesus was called the Lion of the tribe of Juda, the root of David.—. Rev. 5:5. God was Jesus' Father after the spirit and it was stated that David was his father (after the flesh). (Luke 1:32).

David saw Bathsheba, Uriah's wife, when she was bathing, and had Uriah sent to the front lines where he knew Uriah would be killed. This happened.

(11 Samuel 11:1-17) Bathsheba conceived, but the first baby died. The second was named Solomon. Solomon had seven hundred wives and three hundred concubines (mistresses). (1 Kings 11:3) This was far from the original plan of God which consisted of one male with one female, a complete unit supplying the positive and the negative to support one life generating process by the flow of the power of God.

(Christ—John 1:9) (Genesis 2:24, Matthew 19:6) Jesus did no sin but his flesh was sinful. Rom. 8:3—God sent his own Son in the likeness of sinful flesh, and for sin, condemned sin in the flesh:

(2 Cor. 5:21) For he (God) hath made him (Jesus) to be sin for us, who knew no sin—.

Heb. 2:17—In all things it behoved him to be made like unto his brethren, that he might be a merciful and faithful high priest in things pertaining to God, to make reconciliation for the sins of the people. (18) For in that he himself hath suffered being tempted, is able to succour (help) them that are tempted. GOD WAS IN CHRIST—2 Cor. 5:29 God was in Christ, reconciling the world unto himself—.

IT WAS GOD IN JESUS THAT SPOKE WITH PHILIP

John 14:8 Philip saith unto him (Jesus), Lord, show us the Father, and it sufficeth us. John 14:9 Jesus saith unto him, Have I been so long time with you, and yet hast thou not known me, Philip? He that hath seen me hath seen the Father; and how sayest thou then, Show us the Father? (10) Believest thou not that I am in the Father, and the Father in me? The words that I speak unto you I speak not of myself: but the Father that dwelleth in me—.

God that was in Jesus was good, but the weakened genes that was in Jesus' natural body that had been handed down from generation to generation was not good.

Isaiah 53:2—he hath no form nor comeliness; and when we shall see him, there is no beauty that we should desire him. (3) He is despised and rejected of men; a man of sorrows, and acquainted with grief: and we hid as it were our faces from him; he was despised, and we esteemed him not. (4) Surely he hath born our griefs, and carried our sorrows: yet we did esteem him stricken, smitten of God, and afflicted. (5) But he was wounded for our transgressions, he was bruised for our iniquities: (wickedness).

****

Jesus Name Person—Hello to a

Levic asked this question.

James this is not a question, but to release an Acknowledgment from another person "called by the name of the Lord" JESUS. Your answers are precious indeed and food such as is rare in our time. Keep up the EXCELLENT work.

James gave this response.

Your response is very refreshing. The world of people need more faith in the Name of God. I have tried to direct people's attention to the 'handle of God' as presented by His Son Jesus for 40 years. My writings reflect what I am advocating and why I am still insisting that people call upon the Name of the Lord without ceasing.

Luke 18:8—when the Son of man cometh, shall he find faith on the earth?

****

Jesus—return?

Zenaide asked this question.

How did Jesus go away?

When did he return?

How will he return again?

James95204 gave this response.

How did Jesus go away?

Acts 1:9—While they (Apostles) beheld, he (Jesus) was taken up; and a cloud received him out of their sight.

Acts 1:10—And while they looked stedfastly toward heaven as he went up, behold, two men stood by them in white apparel; (11) Which also said, Ye men of Galilee, why stand ye gazing up into heaven? (Physical heaven) this same Jesus, which is taken up from you into heaven, shall so come in like manner as ye have seen him go into heaven.

When did Jesus return?

He returned with the Holy Ghost to the apostles and disciples (Acts 1:15) along with a total of 120 on the day of Pentecost. Jesus said (John 14:18) I will not leave you comfortless: ***I will come to you.*** (20) At that day ye shall know that I am in my Father, and ye in me, and I in you. (25) These things have I spoken unto you, being yet present with you. (26) But the Comforter, which is the Holy Ghost, whom the Father will send in my Name, he shall teach you all things—.

How will Jesus return again?

When Jesus was taken up into the physical heavens his body

had already been changed to a spiritual substance. From the time of his resurrection His body gradually changed from a natural to a spiritual substance. Toward the end of that forty days He could no longer be seen by the natural eyes. His body had been changed. He appeared for the forty days to people individually and collectively. Some did not immediately recognize who he was because their eyes didn't look at him while he was speaking with them, and others paid no attention how he came to them, only that he was there. On the day he was taken up into heaven, they saw Jesus ascending only in a collective vision form.

Acts 1:11—This same Jesus, which is taken up from you into heaven, shall SO COME IN LIKE MANNER as ye have seen him go into heaven. (In the form of visions).

To whom will he appear the second time?

Hebrews 9:28—***UNTO THEM THAT LOOK FOR HIM SHALL HE APPEAR THE SECOND TIME***—in the form of a vision.

Spiritual eyes allow a person to see real spiritual substance. That substance is just as material as the natural substance is to the natural eyes. There is no understanding of spiritual things without spiritual eyes and ears.

1 Cor. 2:14 The natural man receiveth not the things of the Spirit of God: for they are foolishness unto him: neither can he know them, because they are spiritually discerned.

As many as received him (Jesus-John 1:12), to them gave he power to become the sons of God, even to them that believe on his Name. Then and only then will people be able to see, hear and understand spiritual things.

****

Jesus

jdg asked this question.

How will Jesus return?

James gave this response.

How will/does Jesus return?

That is simple. ***We have already been told.***

This same Jesus, which is taken up from you (Apostles/ Disciples) into heaven (physical), shall so come in like manner as ye have seen him go into heaven. Acts 1:11.

Jesus' body had been changed from physical matter to a spiritual substance (which also is matter but cannot be seen with the sense of natural sight) within the time frame of forty days. The only way his spiritual body could be seen was and is through the process of visions.

The Apostles/disciples during the latter part of the forty days, saw him through individual and collective visions, including when he was returning to his Father God. At the appointed time every (spiritual) eye shall see him in this manner. Revelations 1:7 Behold, he cometh with clouds; (power of God) and EVERY EYE shall see him—even the Jews.

Matthew 24:26—If they say unto you, Behold, he is in the desert; GO NOT FORTH; behold, he is in the SECRET CHAMBERS (individual religions), BELIEVE IT NOT. (27) For as the lightning cometh out of the east, and shineth even unto the west; so shall also the coming of the Son (SUN Mal. 4:2) of man be.

The visions are seen individually and/or collectively by those that look for him.

Hebrews 9:28—UNTO THEM THAT LOOK FOR HIM SHALL HE APPEAR THE SECOND TIME—,

****

Jesus!

A curious researcher asked this question.

Could you please interpret Philip:2:6.

Does it mean Jesus is God or not?

Thank you so much for your time.

God bless you.

James gave this response.

Philip 2:6 Does not indicate that Jesus is God. Men can also become the sons of God through the rebirth of their spirit but that does not make them God.

God was in Christ reconciling the world unto himself. John 5:43.

JESUS/PHILIP

John 14:9 (God through) Jesus saith unto him, Have I been so long with you, and yet hast thou not known me, Philip? (Jesus said) He that hast seen me hath seen the Father; and how sayest thou then, Show me the Father?

Jesus said, (John 5:43) I am come in my Father's Name—.

1 John 4:9—God sent his only begotten SON into the world, that we might live through him. (Also John 3:16).

John said, (John 1:34) And I saw, and bare record that this is the Son of God

John 14:10 Believest thou not that I am in the Father, and the Father in me? The words that I speak unto you I speak not of myself: but the Father that dwelleth in me, he doeth the works. (11) Believe me that I am in the Father, and the Father in me—.

Let nobody impart to the mind that Jesus is God, but that Jesus is the mediator between God and man. Even Jesus himself said in answer to the Jews, (John 10:31-36) Say ye of him, whom the Father hath sanctified, and sent unto the world, Thou blasphemest; because I SAID I AM THE SON OF GOD?

Jesus came to replace that which was lost. Jesus tried to show people the way back to Paradise by faith in the Name of the Lord. That saving Name of the Lord that had always been in existence since the beginning, but had been lost to the minds of men. His Name was called the Word of God in (Rev.19:13) and (John 1:2) the same was in the beginning with God.

David said, (Proverbs 18:10) The Name of the Lord is a strong tower: the righteous (justified) runneth into it, and is safe.

Acts 2:21—It shall come to pass, that WHOSOEVER shall CALL on the NAME of the LORD shall be saved.

Did the early church know this?

Yes, but when the way got rough they forgot and began to doubt as Peter did when attempting to go to Jesus on the water. Matthew 14:31.

The church at Corinth.

1 Cor. 1:2 Unto the church of God which is at Corinth, to them that are sanctified in Christ Jesus, called to be saints, with

ALL THAT IN EVERY PLACE CALL UPON THE NAME OF JESUS CHRIST OUR LORD. (This was the name 'Jesus.' It was not one of the many names given in the Old Testament).

Believe in the Name of the Son of God.

John 3:18 He that believeth on him is not condemned: but he that believeth not is condemned already, because he hath not believed in the Name of the only begotten SON of God.

John 17:12 Jesus said, (John 17:12)—I kept them in thy Name: those that thou gavest me I have kept—. (26) I have declared unto them thy NAME, and will declare it—.

How will we know the name of the Father and the Son?

Proverb 30:4 Who hath ascended up into heaven, or descended? Who hath gathered the wind in his fists? Who hath bound the waters in a garment? Who hath established all the ends of the earth? What is HIS NAME, and WHAT IS HIS SON'S NAME, if thou canst tell?

The problems were partly caused by languages.

God caused to be written, (Zeph. 3:9) For then will I turn to the people a PURE LANGUAGE, that they may ALL CALL upon the NAME of the LORD, to serve him with one consent.

A quiet and peaceable life.

VIA—ONE GOD AND ONE MEDIATOR—HIS NAME

1 Tim. 2:3—This is good and acceptable in the sight of God our Savior; (4) Who will have all men to be saved, and to come unto the knowledge of the truth.

1 Tim 2:5 FOR THERE IS BUT ONE GOD, and ONE MEDIATOR between God and men, the MAN CHRIST JESUS.

1 Cor. 8:5 For though there be that are called gods, whether in heaven or in earth, (as there be gods many, and lords many,) (6) But to us there is but on God, the Father, of whom are all things, and we in him; and one Lord Jesus Christ, by whom are all things, and we by him.

****

Jesus—physical-spiritual body.

Anonymous asked this question on 7/22/2002:

I would like to see the answers to the seven questions that were deleted from the board.

James95204 gave this response.

1) On the resurrection morning, Jesus told Mary not to touch His body (tangible body?)

Time was required for the physical body of Jesus to be changed to spiritual substance. This was the reason it had been planned that his bones should not be broken. (John 19:36) In order to walk during that transformation he would need his legs. Right after his resurrection he told Mary Magdalene not to touch him because he had not yet ascended unto his father.

John 20:17 Jesus saith unto her, Touch me not; for I am not yet ascended to my Father: but go to my brethren, and say unto them, I ascend unto my Father, and your Father; and ***to my God, and your God.*** His ascension was not until 40 days later. Acts 1:9

John 20:27. Later in the day, Jesus told Doubting Thomas to touch His body (tangible body?)

(John 20:19) Then the same day at evening, being the first day of the week, 'when the doors were shut' (we must compare this with Luke 24:39) where the disciples were assembled for fear of the Jews, came Jesus and stood in the midst, and said unto them, Peace be unto you. (20) And when he had so said, he SHEWED unto them his hands and his side. Then were the disciples glad, when they SAW the Lord.

EIGHT DAYS LATER

John 20:26 And after eight days again his disciples were within, and Thomas with them: then came Jesus, 'the doors being shut,' and stood in the midst, and said, Peace be unto you. (27) Then saith he to Thomas, Reach hither thy finger, and behold (see or observe) my hands; and reach hither thy hand, and thrust it into my side: and be not faithless, but believing. John 20:28 And Thomas answered and said unto him, My Lord and my God. This passage did not state that Thomas actually touched Jesus. But it did reveal that Thomas recognized that God was in Jesus because he recognized them both.

Luke 24:39 Behold (see) my hands and my feet, that it is I myself: handle me, and see; for A SPIRIT HATH NOT FLESH AND BONES AS YE SEE ME HAVE. (40) And when he had thus spoken, he SHEWED them his hands and his feet. (Compare the above statement with the passages that state and 'when the doors were shut,' John 20:19, and 'the doors being shut,' John 20:26. It must be understood that natural, physical bodies do not pass through doors without opening them first. The people in the room did not observe when he came in, as in Luke 24:16 when the two Apostles did not recognize Jesus, because their eyes were holden that they should not know him. This same reasoning must also be applied when the word 'vanished out of their sight' is used. (Luke 24:31)

We are still coming out of the dark ages. Television and many ministers are not adding to logical thinking. Luke 24:40 And when he had thus spoken, he SHOWED them his hands and his feet. (This passage did not state that they touched him).

Jesus Christ in His(semi)glorified body asked for food and ate fish.

Jesus said, (Luke 24:41) Have ye here any meat? (42) And they gave him a piece of broiled fish, and of an honeycomb. (43) And he took it, and did eat before them.

Despite all the other confusing words like Luke 24:31 And he vanished out of their sight, and John 20: 19 when the doors were shut came Jesus and stood in the midst—, Jesus' body had not yet been totally changed from physical to spiritual. This complete change was not until the day of his ascension. Acts 1:9

The angel at the ascension states that this same Jesus will return in like manner to earth.

When Jesus ascended his body had been completely changed from natural to spiritual substance. Hebrews 9:28. Christ was once offered to bear the sins of many; and unto them THAT LOOK FOR HIM shall he appear the second time—. As he was seen in vision form when he ascended, so he will be seen in vision form when he returns ***to them that look for him.***

Revelation tells of the multitude wearing "robes". It takes a body to fill a robe, doesn't it?

Revelation is filled with symbolisms and this is one among many. White robes symbolizes God's righteousness (Rev. 19:8)which he gave to them that had been cruelly treated for the word of God, and for the testimony which they held. Rev.6:9-11.

When Christ returns to earth, all eyes will behold Him. With the human eye, can you see spirits?

A spiritual body cannot be seen with the natural eyes. His body was seen through the process of a group vision.

In Jesus' return it is in the same manner—through visions.

1 John 3:2 Beloved, now are we the sons of God, and it doth not yet appear what we shall be: but we know that, when he shall appear, we shall be like him; for we shall see him as he is.

Paul said, (2 Cor. 5:1) For we know that if our earthly house of this tabernacle were dissolved, we have a building of God, an house not made with hands, eternal in the heavens. (Remember that we are in the physical heaven where the first man and woman were supposed to remain eternally.) (2) For in this we groan, earnestly desiring to be clothed upon with our house which is from heaven.

1 Cor. 15:51 Behold, I show you a mystery; We shall not all sleep, but we shall all be changed. (52) In a moment, in the twinkling of an eye—This complete change in Jesus' body occurred at the time of his ascension. Acts 1:9. The change is necessary but the ascension was never planed for man.

7).The tree of life in Revelations is for food for the people. This is spiritual food.

Jesus came to the earth to show man the way back to the Garden of God, that spiritual place that was established for man and woman to live in on the earth forever. This is Paradise where the Tree of Life has always been. There is a natural body and there is a spiritual body. As the natural body requires natural food for sustenance, so the spiritual body needs spiritual food for its health. Man cannot live without both. This is what happened to the first man and woman. When they drifted away from God, their spiritual source, the Tree of Life, was out of their reach. This caused, first their spiritual life, and then their natural life to diminish continually until their demise.

FAITH

Jesus said, according to your faith so be it unto you. (Matt. 9:29. Why did God through Jesus heal all manner of diseases among the people (Matt. 4:23-24) if it was better that they die and go to heaven? The wages of sin is death.

Matthew 9:2 And, behold, they brought to him a man sick of the palsy, lying on a bed: and Jesus seeing their faith said unto the sick of the palsy; Son, be of good cheer; thy sins be forgiven thee.

Matthew 9:6—The Son of man (the Tree of Life) hath power on earth to forgive sins—, so that we may be healed and live.

1 Cor. 15:51 Behold, I show you a mystery; We shall not all sleep, (Die) but WE SHALL ALL BE CHANGED, (52) In a moment, in the twinkling of an eye, at the last trump: for the trumpet shall sound, and the dead shall be raised incorruptible, and we shall be CHANGED. (53) For this corruptible must PUT ON incorruption, and this mortal must PUT ON immortality. (54) So when this corruptible shall have put on incorruption, and this mortal shall have put on immortality, then shall be brought to pass the saying that is written, Death is swallowed up in victory.

Spiritual bodies are not affected by physical resistance. They can come and go at their own will. Although it takes time for their growth and movement, it can be figured in portions of a second whereas with the physical body it may require minutes, days, weeks, months or even years for their development and change.

In every case physical bodies do not dematerialize and reappear in another geographic location.

In resurrections, after the body has died and decayed, it does not come back in the same physical body. 1 Cor. 15:36-37—They are as the angels of God in heaven. Matthew 22:30.

A good example of a change in a physical body is in the development, growth, change and ascension of the Hawk Moth. In the beginning stages of the Hawk Moth it is a very small, horned caterpillar. It begins to eat the tomato leaves and develops in a few days into a very large, green caterpillar. At this time it burrows into the earth where it begins its change. After a few days it suddenly, in the twinkling of the eye, so to speak, appears as the winged Hawk Moth and makes its ascension.

What this shows is that physical bodies take time for growth and change. The actual change may seem to be sudden, but the preparation is always a prerequisite for that change.

****

JESUS, Thinking about

Maxine asked this question.

What do you think of Norman Vincent Peale's advice regarding 'Thinking about Jesus?'

James gave this response.

Dr. Norman Vincent Peal was one of the most popular preachers who ever lived. Dr. Peale had an effective technique that he used when counseling someone in distress.

First, he let the troubled person tell their story. Every little detail was hashed out. But after the person had explained their problem, then Dr. Peale asked the person to sit in silence for a full three minutes and think of nothing but Jesus. Just Jesus. This was the moment, Dr. Peale said, when they were to switch their focus from the problem to the power. No matter what your problem might be, said Dr. Peale, Jesus has the power to help you. He testified that USUALLY after these three minutes of thinking time, the person being counseled would have an answer to their problem—.

Doctor Peale came close to the mark but he missed it.

Thinking about Jesus for three minutes will never take the place of Calling upon the Name of the Lord all the time. Joel 2:32, Zech. 13:9 They shall call on my name, and I will hear them. Acts 2:21, Rom. 10:13.

When calling upon the Name of the Lord the Holy Ghost is summoned. God sends that gift and it resides within. The Holy Ghost then guides to the filling of the Holy Spirit and together the generation of the power of Christ begins. (the power of God). By this operation, God and Jesus takes up their abode within. (John 14:23)—We will come unto him and make our abode with him.

Out of his belly shall flow rivers of living water. John 7:38.

This flow, like water, washes out all the trash that has accumulated and gives the person's mind the freedom to do its job of keeping the body in perfect operating condition.

Without that water of life flowing from the belly, the trash remains and when the person being counseled leaves the preacher's office he or she ends up reiterating the same problems to friends, neighbors, relatives or psychiatrists over and over.

Without the power of God coming from within, there is no way for an individual to live in peace with themselves or anyone else in this worldly human environment.

The mind must be free to think and plan. Calling upon the Name of the Lord with the inner voice frees the conscious mind to do the work of planning and creating, and relieves the subconscious mind to effectively operate all the other functions of the body.

Luke 18:7—shall not God avenge his own elect, which cry DAY AND NIGHT unto him—(8) I TELL YOU THAT HE WILL AVENGE THEM SPEEDILY.

****

JESUS, will he cease to exist?

bjcole asked this question.

If God stops speaking will Jesus cease to exist?

James gave this response.

God will not stop speaking and Jesus will never cease!

Did God have a beginning?

It is certain that God did have a beginning!

IN THE ***BEGINNING*** WAS THE ***WORD***—AND THE ***WORD WAS GOD***. John 1:1

THE WORD WAS WITH GOD.

AND THE ***WORD WAS MADE FLESH***, AND DWELT AMONG US—.

John1:14.—thou shalt call his name JESUS.

Matt.1:21. ***God was in Christ*** 2 Cor. 5:19

HIS ***NAME*** IS CALLED THE ***WORD*** OF GOD. Rev. 19:13.

GOD said, ***I AM*** ALPHA—***the BEGINNING***—. Rev. 1:8.

Will there ever be an ending?

NO! And (Jesus, who came in His Father's Name) hath made us kings and priests unto God and His (Jesus') Father; to him (Jesus) be glory and dominion FOREVER AND EVER.

Rev 1:6.

Did Christ (the power of God) have a beginning?

YES!

CHRIST WAS THAT FIRST LIGHT GENERATED BY THE VIBRATIONS THAT FORMED THE SOUND OF GOD'S NAME.

So Christ having a beginning with God, will He ever have an ending?

No!

Jesus (the Name of God) Christ (the power and anointing of God) the same yesterday (this did not say Christ had no beginning) to day and FOREVER. Heb. 13:8.

Melchisedec, Melchizedek :

(Ref. All the men of the Bible by Herbert Lockyer. Page 235

Melchisedec was a man whose birth records, for what ever reason, were not available. Ezra 2:59-62. He had no record of father, mother, birth or death. Such silence is part of the divine plan to make him typify more strikingly the mystery of Jesus' birth and eternity of his priesthood. Melchisedec was a king and priest of Jerusalem, and like Jesus he was not of the Levitical tribe. (Ref. Bible Dictionary—Wm. Smith—Teacher's edition.

The earth abideth forever. Eccl. 1:4.

God and Jesus (God's Son and His Name) and His Christ

(God's power-anointing) will never cease. They will only become stronger and stronger as time continues. Since God and His Christ are in men (John 1:9), men too will finally move back into the Garden of God (Gen. 2:8)(Paradise Luke 23:43, 2 Cor. 12:4, Rev. 2:7) where God has always wanted them to live FOREVER.

John 14:23 Jesus said, If a man love me, he will keep my words and my Father will love him, and WE WILL COME UNTO HIM, AND MAKE OUR ABODE WITH HIM.

John 17:21 That they ALL may be one; as thou, Father, art in me, and I in thee, that they also be one in us: that the world may believe that thou hast sent me.

John 1:9 That (Christ) was the TRUE LIGHT, which lighteth EVERY MAN that cometh into the world. (not just one religion.)

****

JORDAN, CROSSING OF

How did this happen?

Josh. 3:15 And as they that bare the ark were come unto Jordan, and the feet of the priests that bare the ark were dipped in the brim of the water (for Jordan overfloweth all his banks all the time of harvest.)

(16) The waters which came down from above stood and rose up upon an heap VERY FAR FROM THE CITY OF ADAM, that is BESIDE ZARETAN: and those that came down toward the sea of the plain, even the salt sea, failed, and were cut off: and the people passed over right against Jericho.

During the harvest of each year the banks of the river Jordan are usually overflowing. It was during the time of

those torrential currents that its banks in the area of Zarethan gave-way to the undercutting of the swift currents and toppled over into the path of the river, cutting the water off long enough for Joshua, the priests and the children of Israel to pass over the river bed at Jericho thirty miles away.

WHERE IS THE MIRACLE? Due to the fact that in this region there are frequent earth quakes and tremors along with the yearly rain fall and flooding, this WOULD NOT BE CONSIDERED A MIRACLE had it not been for the fact that Joshua was informed by the Lord in advance of its happening.

THE MIRACLE IS THAT IT HAPPENED AT THE TIME IT WAS NEEDED and most remarkable that Joshua was INFORMED IN ADVANCE of its occurrence.

God is aware of all potential natural phenomena before it is developed and when it is beneficial or appropriate he guides people into such situations in order to advance HIS NAME in the minds of the people for their benefit not his own.

From the crossing to the City of Adam it is approximately 18 miles, and from Adam to Zaretan it is approximately 12 miles. This is a total of 30 miles from the crossing at Jericho to Zaretan.

****

Joseph, Mary and Jesus.

Edward asked this question.

On one occasion (Luke 2:48) Mary said to Jesus, "Thy father and I have sought thee sorrowing." Was Joseph Jesus' biological father or only a step-father? (Luke 1:35) When the

Holy Ghost came upon Mary, did he deliver the natural or spiritual seed?

James gave this response.

MARY, JOSEPH AND JESUS.

Matthew wrote: Now the birth of Jesus Christ was on this wise: When as his mother Mary was espoused (engaged)) to Joseph (Matthew 1:18), ***BEFORE THEY CAME TOGETHER,*** she was found with child of the Holy Ghost.

John recorded Jesus' words: ***If I bear witness of myself, MY WITNESS IS NOT TRUE***. (John 5:31).The Pharisees therefore said unto him (Jesus), Thou bearest record of thyself; thy record is not true. (John 8:13).

(Jesus said), It is also written in your law, that the testimony of two men is true. (John 8:17). (18) I am one that bear witness of myself, and the Father that sent me beareth witness of me.

GOD WAS JESUS' WITNESS TO US THROUGH MATTHEW. Matthew 3:17 And lo a voice from heaven, saying, 'This is my beloved Son, in whom I am well pleased.' Also Matt. 17:5. God also witnessed of Jesus through the writings of Mark and Luke. Mark 9:7, Luke 9:35, Mark 1:11, Luke 3:22, Matt. 18:16.

So in every case we need at least two witnesses to establish EVERY WORD, and this was lacking in the case of Matthew's words regarding Joseph and Mary. If God had been Matthew's second witness, he would have done so through some other witness or writer. Matthew was alone in his statement, 'BEFORE THEY CAME TOGETHER', therefore, his witness is not true.

With these facts in mind let us seriously examine the relationship between Joseph and Mary. Mary was not an hermaphrodite (Animal or plant having both male and female reproductive organs). She was constructed physically in accordance with the exact specifications set forth for the first woman.

A VIRGIN SHALL CONCEIVE

Isaiah 7:14 Therefore the Lord himself shall give you a sign; behold a virgin shall conceive, and bear a son, and shall call his name Immanuel.

JOSEPH WAS NOT AWARE OF WHAT HAD HAPPENED.

Matt.1:19 Then Joseph her HUSBAND, being a just man, and not willing to make her (Mary) a public example, was minded to put her away privily. (20) But while he thought on these things, behold, the angel of the Lord appeared unto him in a dream, saying, Joseph, thou SON OF DAVID, fear not to take unto thee Mary thy WIFE: for that which is conceived in her is of (by the direction of) the Holy Ghost. (21) And she shall bring forth a Son, and thou shalt call his name Jesus: for he shall save his people from their sins. (22) Now all this was done, that it might be fulfilled which was spoken of the Lord by the prophet, saying, (23) Behold, a virgin shall be with child, and shall bring forth a son, and they shall call his name Emmanuel, which being interpreted is, God with us. (2 Cor.5:19) (24) Then Joseph being raised from sleep did as the angel of the Lord had bidden him, and took unto him HIS WIFE: (25) and KNEW (not aware of her sexually) HER NOT TILL SHE HAD BROUGHT FORTH HER FIRSTBORN SON; and he called his name Jesus. (Firstborn indicates that Mary had more children after the birth of Jesus.)

Note that a female person is referred to as being a virgin until she has had her first full relationship with the opposite sex. At that time a virgin can conceive. Notice that Isaiah 7:14 did not stipulate there was no opposite sex involved; only that 'A virgin shall conceive, and bare a son.' Ideally, male and female of the human race are supposed to maintain their virginity, until they come together, and are joined by the power of God.

Neither Joseph nor Mary was aware of this operation, because IT WAS ACCOMPLISHED DURING THE TIME OF THEIR SLEEP, and was completely directed by the Holy Ghost. Joseph was informed of some facts in the dream so he would not separate from her.

It was too early in the development of mankind for the complete propagation process to be revealed to Joseph, John the baptizer, or any of the apostles, including Saul (Paul). They all saw through a glass darkly. 1 Cor. 13:12.

But now, at the beginning of the last thousand years of the sixth day, the complete story is being revealed, and 'that which is in part shall be done away.' (1 Cor. 13:10.

Luke 1:32 He (Jesus) shall be great, and shall be called the Son of the Highest: and the Lord God shall give unto him the throne of ***HIS FATHER DAVID.***

Luke 1:34 Then said Mary unto the angel, How shall this be, seeing I know not a man? (have not been aware of a man in a sexual way). (35) And the angel answered and said unto her, THE HOLY GHOST SHALL COME UPON THEE, AND THE POWER OF THE HIGHEST SHALL OVERSHADOW THEE: therefore ALSO that HOLY THING which shall be born of thee shall be called the ***SON OF GOD.***

JESUS' FATHER THROUGH THE SPIRIT IS GOD.

JESUS' NATURAL FATHER WAS JOSEPH.

Joseph and Mary were both from the lineage of David, therefor, Jesus was referred to as the ***Son of David in the natural***.

There is a natural body, and there is a spiritual body.

****

KEYS OF THE KINGDOM

LilBitOfHeaven asked this question.

Matthew 16:19

"I will give you the keys of the kingdom of heaven; whatever you bind on earth will be bound in heaven, and whatever you loose on earth will be loosed in heaven."

What does this mean?

Thank you

James gave this response.

Did Peter handle the case of ANANIAS AND SAPPHIRA the way Jesus would have?

Matthew 18:14—it is not the will of your Father which is in heaven, that one of these little ones should perish. (15) Moreover if thy brother shall trespass against thee, go and tell him his fault between thee and him alone: if he shall hear thee, thou hast gained thy brother. (16) But if he will not hear thee, then take with thee one or two more, that in the mouth of two or three witnesses every word may be established. (17) And if he shall neglect to hear them, tell it unto the church: but if he neglect to hear the church, let him be unto thee as an heathen man and a publican. (You still are not to kill him). (18) Verily I say unto you, Whatsoever ye shall bind on earth shall be bound in heaven: and whatsoever ye shall loose on earth shall be loosed in heaven. (Peter was given the power to bind or to loose, it was left up to him how he used that power).

PETER WANTED TO GET IT REAL CLEAR IN HIS MIND WHAT HIS ACTIONS SHOULD BE REGARDING FORGIVENESS.

Matthew 18:21 Then came Peter to him, and said, Lord, how oft shall my brother sin against me and I forgive him? till seven times? Matthew 18: 22 Jesus saith unto him, I say not unto thee, Until seven times: but, Until seventy times seven. (490 times)

PETER DENIED JESUS THREE TIMES. MATT. 26:34, JESUS FORGAVE HIM. Matthew 18:33 Shouldest not thou also have had compassion on thy fellowservant, even as I had pity on thee?

DID PETER CONFORM TO THE INSTRUCTIONS GIVEN BY JESUS REGARDING MERCY, WHEN HE DEALT WITH ANANIAS AND SAPPHIRA? LET US SEE.

Acts 5:1 But a certain man named Ananias, with Sapphira his wife, sold a possession. (2)And kept back part of the price, his wife also being privy to it, and brought a certain part, and laid it at the apostles feet. (Matthew 19:21)

Jesus said, go and sell that thou hast, and GIVE TO THE POOR,—AND COME AND FOLLOW ME. He did not say bring the proceeds to me and let me give it to the poor).Acts 5:3 But Peter said, Ananias, why hast Satan filled thine heart to lie to the Holy Ghost, and to keep back part of the price of the land? (4) Whiles it remained, was it not thine own? and after it was sold, was it not in thine own power? why hast thou conceived this thing in thine heart? thou hast not lied unto men, but unto God. (5) And Ananias HEARING THESE WORDS fell down, and gave up the ghost: (Ananias died of shock caused by fear and guilt) and GREAT FEAR CAME ON ALL THEM THAT HEARD THESE THINGS. (God is Love. 1 John 4:8, There is no fear in Love, but perfect love casteth out fear. 1 John 4:18, Keep yourselves in the Love of God. Jude 1:21.)

Acts 5:6 And the young men arose, wound him up, and carried him out, and buried him. (7) And it was about the space of three hours after, when his wife, not knowing what was done, came in. (8) And Peter answered unto her, Tell me whether ye sold the land for so much? And she said, Yea, for so much. (9) Then Peter said unto her How is it that ye have agreed together to tempt the Spirit of the Lord? behold the feet of them which have buried thy husband are at the door, and shall carry thee out. (10) Then fell she down straightway at his feet, and yielded up the ghost: (Sapphira died of shock caused by guilt and fear) and the young men came in, and found her dead, and carrying her forth, buried her by her husband. (11) And ***GREAT FEAR*** CAME UPON ALL THE CHURCH, AND UPON AS MANY AS HEARD THESE THINGS. (Fear is not of God).

Matthew 16:18 And I say also unto thee, That thou art Peter, and upon this rock I will build my church; and the gates of hell shall not prevail against it. (19) And I will give unto thee (Peter) the keys of the kingdom of heaven: AND WHATSOEVER THOU SHALT BIND ON EARTH SHALL BE BOUND IN HEAVEN: AND WHATSOEVER THOU SHALT LOOSE ON EARTH SHALL BE LOOSED IN HEAVEN.

Before Peter received the Holy Ghost he was a violent man. He was erratic and abrupt in his actions. Mark 14:47 And one of them (Peter) that stood by drew a sword, and smote a servant of the high priest, and cut off his (Luke 22:50—right) ear.

JESUS WAS NOT LIKE PETER.

Luke 22:51 And Jesus answered and said, Suffer ye thus far, and he touched his ear, and healed him. Before Peter received the Holy Ghost he used a natural sword. After he received the filling of the Spirit he used the 'SWORD OF THE SPIRIT', which was even more devastating.

WHY DID PETER DO THIS?

Because he still had his fallen human nature. (Gal. 5:17—The flesh and the Spirit are contrary the one to the other). ***He was given the power to 'bind' and he did not use this power in***

coordination with the instructions he had received from Jesus.

THINK IT THROUGH. Did he forgive Ananias and Sapphira four hundred and ninety times? Did he discuss with them and act in accordance with the instructions laid down by Jesus? Should there be fear in the church? Jesus, after his resurrection, gave the power to forgive sins to his disciples. John 20:21. Then said Jesus to them again, Peace be unto you: as my Father hath sent me, even so send I you.

John 20:23 Whose soever ***SINS YE REMIT*, *they are remitted unto them; and whose soever SINS YE RETAIN, they are retained.***

Romans 14:17—the kingdom of God is—righteousness and peace, and joy in the Holy Ghost. (Not fear!)Should Peter be judged for his actions?

1 Cor. 6:2 Do ye not know that the saints shall judge the world?

1 Cor. 6:3 Know ye not that we shall judge angels?

Isa. 12:2 BEHOLD, GOD IS MY SALVATION: I WILL TRUST, ***AND NOT BE AFRAID***.

****

KILL V MURDER

Ruth asked this question.

In some of the translations why have they changed the word 'KILL' to 'MURDER' in Exodus 20:13.

James gave this response.

Kill v Murder:

Exodus 20:13 THOU SHALT NOT KILL.

Deut. 32:35 To me belongeth vengeance, and recompense—.

Deut. 32:44 And Moses came and spake all the words of this song in the ears of the people.

In the original commandments there were no provisions given for Moses to enact penalties for the transgressions of those laws. Moses thought he was doing God service (Ref. John 16:2) when he gave instructions to take life for life, eye for eye, tooth for tooth, hand for hand, foot for foot, burning for burning, stripe for stripe—Exod. 21:23-25.

But Jesus said (Matt.5:38), Ye have heard that it hath been said, An eye for an eye, and a tooth for a tooth (39) But I say unto you, that ye (44) love your enemies—.

Jesus said (Matthew 19:18) Thou shalt do no murder. But Jesus did not deal with the penalty because he was aware that his Father was in charge of recompenses. (Deut. 32:33) God said—To me belongeth vengeance, and recompense; THEIR FOOT WILL SLIDE IN DUE TIME—.

The law 'Thou shalt not kill' was enacted because of what Cain had done unto his brother Able, but even then God did not want others to take vengeance against Cain. Gen. 4:14 Cain said, Everyone that findeth me shall slay me. And God said unto Cain (Gen. 4:15) Whosoever slayeth Cain, vengeance shall be taken on him sevenfold. (16) And the Lord set a mark upon Cain, lest any finding him should kill him.

God said (Ezek. 18: 32)—I have no pleasure in the death of him that dieth—.

The translators have not understood the ways of God, so they changed the word 'kill' to 'murder' so that it would conform to the instructions given by Moses.

The law was given by Moses, but GRACE and TRUTH came by Jesus Christ. (John 1:17)

People that will kill have the mentality of the animal, so they must be suppressed until they are changed from the base nature they have received from their fallen ancestors.

God said (Gen. 1:28)—replenish the earth, AND SUBDUE IT: and have DOMINION over—every living thing that moveth upon the earth.

God said (Deut 32:39) See now that I, even I, am he, and there is no god with me: I kill, and I make alive;—.

How does God kill? He lets evil destroy evil. He does not come to the rescue of those that will not CALL UPON HIS NAME, so that sickness, diseases, poverty, accidents, fear, hatred, etc., take hold and diminish the life from those that are not in the light of Christ. (The power of God).

Note: The following translations replaced the word Kill with Murder—WEB, YLT, NRS, TEV, NAS, NKJV.

The following translations left the word 'kill', DBY.

KJV STRONG, RHE, ASV.

Isa. 55:6 Seek ye the Lord while he may be found, CALL ye upon him while he is near: (7) Let the wicked forsake his way, and the unrighteous man his thoughts: and let him return unto the Lord, and he will have mercy upon him; and to our God, ***for he will abundantly pardon. (8) For my thoughts are not your thoughts, neither are your ways my ways, saith the Lord.***

God is a scientist. He is not concerned with the petty ideas of religious men. He only wants his invention to succeed, be kind to one another with compassion, and be prosperous and in health.

Moses deviated and the translators are confused.

Call upon the Name of God (Jesus) and he will give understanding, for Jesus is the way, the truth and the life. (John 14:6).

****

KILL, Does God ?

Maxine asked this question.

DOES GOD KILL?

Yes, where there is no mediator!

1 Tim. 2:5—there is one mediator between God and man, the man Christ Jesus.

How does he kill?

He allows evil to destroy evil.

Psalm 140:11—***evil shall hunt the violent man to overthrow him.***

Jer. 18:11 Thus saith the Lord; Behold, I FRAME EVIL against you, and devise a device against you: return ye now every one from his evil way, and make your ways and your doings good.

****

Kingdom of God-Jesus-John:

Zenaide asked this question.

WHY WAS JESUS IN THE KINGDOM OF GOD AND JOHN THE BAPTIST WAS NOT?

James gave this response.

Luke 7:28 For I say unto you, among those that are born of women there is not a greater prophet than John the Baptist: but he that is least IN THE KINGDOM OF GOD is greater than he.

Jesus received HIS SPIRIT FROM HIS FATHER GOD at the time of conception, by the overshadowing of the power of the Highest (God), and the direction of the Holy Ghost when it came upon Mary.

Luke 1:35 And the angel answered and said unto her (Mary), The Holy Ghost shall come upon thee, and the power of the Highest (God) shall overshadow thee; therefore ALSO that holy thing which shall be born of thee shall be called the Son of God.

John the Baptist was filled with the Holy Ghost from his mother's womb AFTER CONCEPTION, therefore, he received HIS SPIRIT from his father Zacharias.

Luke 1:15—and he shall be filled with the Holy Ghost, even from his mother's womb.

Luke 1:41 And it came to pass, that, when Elisabeth heard the salutation of Mary, the babe leaped in her womb; and Elisabeth was filled with the Holy Ghost. (At the time Elisabeth was filled with the Holy Ghost the statement made in Luke 1:15 was fulfilled, namely,—and he shall be filled with the Holy Ghost even from his mother's womb. THIS WAS AFTER CONCEPTION.

John the Baptist never RECEIVED THE RE-BIRTH OF HIS SPIRIT, therefore, HE WAS NOT IN THE KINGDOM OF GOD.

John 3:5 Jesus answered, Verily, verily, I say unto thee, EXCEPT A MAN BE BORN OF WATER AND of the SPIRIT he cannot enter into the Kingdom of God. (6) That which is born of the flesh is flesh: and that which is born of the Spirit is spirit.

In this setting Jesus was not speaking of the spirit of the Holy Ghost but of John's spirit, the spirit John received from his natural father. The Holy Ghost had already been received while John was still in his mother's womb.

****

Knowledge, Tree of

Charlene asked this question.

What was the Tree of Knowledge of Good and Evil?

James gave this response.

PEOPLE ARE CALLED TREES IN THE BIBLE.

Judges 9:8 The trees went forth on a time to anoint a king over them; and they said unto the olive tree, Reign thou over us.

Pharaoh and his people were considered as trees.

(Ezekiel 31).

John made reference to people when he said, Now also the ax is laid unto the root of the tree. (Matthew 3:10.

THE TREE OF KNOWLEDGE OF GOOD AND EVIL.

Genesis 2:9.

Genesis 3:3—God hath said, Ye shall not eat of it, neither shall ye touch it, lest ye die. Genesis 3:4 And the serpent (Adam) said unto the woman, Ye shall not surely die: Genesis 3:5 For God doth know that in the day ye eat thereof, then your eyes (of understanding) shall be opened, and ye shall be as gods, knowing good and evil. Genesis 3:6 And when the woman saw that the tree was good for food, and that it was pleasant to the eyes, and a tree to be desired to make one wise, she took of the fruit thereof, and did eat (partake of), and gave also unto her husband with her, and he did eat.

THE TREE WAS THE MAN AND THE WOMAN

The man and the woman were of ONE WHOLE UNIT. They were of one flesh. (Gen. 2:23-24) They were given a mind that could know good and also evil. The knowledge of evil would eventually cause them to die because the pressure on the mind would disrupt their immune system.

Genesis 3:7 And the eyes of them both were opened, and they knew that they were naked—.

Genesis 3:9 And the Lord God called unto Adam, and said unto him, Where art thou?

Genesis 3:10 And he said, I heard thy voice in the garden, and I was afraid, BECAUSE I WAS NAKED—.

Genesis 3: 11 And he said, who told thee that thou wast naked? Hast thou eaten of the tree, whereof I commanded thee that thou shouldest not eat?

Guilt flooded their minds because they knew they were not permitted to partake of the reproduction process as the other animals were openly engaged in. Before this occurrence they did not partake of the Tree of Life, therefore they did not have the strength to conform to the will of God regarding this matter.

****

Languages

Maxine asked this question.

Do you think there will ever be a UNIVERSAL LANGUAGE?

James gave this response.

A universal language is needed and very feasible. But, as long as there are different NAMES in religion there will be confusion.

THE TOWER OF BABEL

The people found a plain in the land of Shinar and said one to another, Go to, let us build a city and a tower, whose top MAY reach unto HEAVEN; and let us MAKE US A NAME—.

WHO CONFOUNDED THEIR LANGUAGE?

GOD!

Genesis 11:7 Go to, let us go down, and there confound their language, that they may not understand one another's speech.

HOW DID HE DO THIS?

God disturbed their concentration so that they could not focus on what they were being told by their fellow workers. Because of that confusion they were scattered by God and gradually separate groups began to develop their own sounds and gestures in communicating with one another. (Gen. 11:8)

If they had become one in God's Name there would have been nothing restrained from them, which they imagined to do, (Ref. Genesis 11:6) but instead, they wanted to make a name for themselves. (11:4)

When people begin focusing upon God's One Name, God will enlighten their understanding. It will be then that a UNIVERSAL

LANGUAGE can be prepared and accepted by all the educational systems in the world so that within four years from that starting point of the curriculum all students will be speaking and writing both their own native language and the UNIVERSAL LANGUAGE.

Morse code is already a kind of universal language but a better system is needed. With present technology it is simple to form that universal language.

****

Last Supper

Ronndonn asked this question.

And what is the explanation for the statement “my blood is poured out for many (mankind)” that took place at the last supper? Why wasn’t this said at the crucifixion since the statement is in the present tense “is”.

Thanks.

James gave this response.

Last Supper

The Prophet sees in fast motion.

Future prophetic moments for the advancement of mankind have already been in the plan of God from the beginning.

Revelation 13:8—the Lamb slain from the foundation of the world. This was a secondary or alternate plan in case man failed.

God knew man could fail because he gave him his freedom of choice, but it would have been unjust to say that man must or would fail.

Although man has his free will as an individual to disrupt God's plan, the plan will win in the long run.

The first Adam failed. The last Adam (1Cor. 15:45) did exactly what he was predetermined to do. The last Adam had more strength to withstand the evil in the world created by the minds of men. The first man Adam was made a living soul; the last Adam was made a guickening (life giving) spirit.

Jesus did not disrupt his father's plan, although he also could have done so, because he still had his free will. Jesus said (Matthew 26:39), not as I will, but as thou wilt. Jesus said (John 4:34), My meat is to do the will of him that sent me, and to finish his work.

A PROPHET SEES IN FAST MOTION THE WHOLE PICTURE AS IF IT HAS BEEN ALREADY ACCOMPLISHED.

JESUS WAS A PROPHET. HE SPOKE AS IF THE THING HAD ALREADY TRANSPIRED. (Matthew 13:57, 21:11, Mark 6:4, Luke 24:19, John 4:19, 4:45, 6:14, 7:40.)

If the plan is not carried out by one person it will eventually be performed by someone else, but always developed by the decision of the individual. The pattern has always been there from the beginning, but God will not force anyone to conform to it. Each person is given the two roads. Will he conform to God's plan or will he decide to go the other way? ronndonn rated this answer: thanks James

****

Law, Reproduction and Sin

Zenaide asked this question.

Explain law, reproduction and sin.

James gave this response.

I was shapen in iniquity: AND IN SIN DID MY MOTHER CONCEIVE ME. (Psalms 51:5)

What shall we say then? Shall we continue in sin that grace may abound? GOD FORBID. Romans 6:1

When man and woman lived in Paradise there was no need for law, for they automatically conformed to the plan of God.

They were FORBAD to take control of the process for the reproduction of life, and if they did, they would die. (Genesis 2:17)

Wasn't this a law?

Yes, it was a rule of law, but it was not a written law at first. They knew by God given understanding that they were not supposed to copy after the actions of the other animals around them. If they did the population of the world would increase more rapidly than the world could support.

The other animals were to live and die, but man and woman were to live forever, therefore, the reproduction of human life would have to conform to a very slow growth.

If they had called upon God's Name they would have been able to conform to that one rule. But since they didn't call upon God, they became too weak to resist the temptation to 'Touch the fruit' (Genesis 3:3). After touching they were propelled toward further action and ultimate death. (Spiritual and then natural).

The heaviness of guilt caused tremendous fear, and drove them from the presence of God. The power of Christ was driven out of them: traumatically at first, then gradually until the power of God had been dissipated to the point of no return, for their understanding had been darkened.

From the time of that first sin, they were unable to control their actions, which in turn caused the necessity for more laws to be enacted.

The laws were made by man, here a little and there a little. First by word of mouth, then as men became more knowledgeable, they began to use symbols and place them on what ever they had available.

Men still knew by God given instinct that they should not harm one another as the other animals were doing, for in doing so they sinned against the remaining power of God (Christ) that was in their fellows. (John 1:9) Christ is the light, which lighteth every man that cometh into the world.

But after those laws were enacted they found they could not conform to them by their own power and they had lost the true saving NAME of God.

It was man and woman's own guilt that brought fear and caused them to be driven from their Father, the merciful God, who would have given them life if they had not lost the knowledge of HIS TRUE SAVING NAME, THE TREE OF LIFE.

****

Lazarus John 11

AnaNicole asked this question.

Why is this event only in the Gospel of John and not in the others? I heard Peter dictated the remaining Gospels and that he was not there during Lazarus's resurrection. Still, how can any disciple forget an event of such magnitude?

James gave this response.

It seems you are basing your foundation thinking upon the fact that we must have at least two witnesses to establish every word. This principle is very true.

Although I used this principle in dealing with the making of wine, I had not even noticed that in John 11 and 12 there had been only one written witness regarding Lazarus until you brought it to my attention.

In looking for the truth it is necessary that we balance the information with two separate witnesses. After all, we must remember that even God did not work alone—He said, LET US make man in OUR image, after OUR likeness—Gen. 1:26.

After looking for a second witness in every subject the information may boil down to one central idea that there is one God and one mediator between God and man. (1 Tim 2:5) And that there is one central truth in everything. This truth, when it comes to the spirit, is found only by the direction of God, by the power of his name, and through the Holy Ghost. Natural eyes cannot see it.

There are various witnesses regarding resurrecting individuals from the dead, both in the old and new testament. Maybe it would be helpful for you to read a true story concerning the death of my father. He came back to life after he was pronounced dead in a hospital in Phoenix, Arizona, and lived for approximately six months.

Will you please explain the 'DEAD BEING RAISED?'

James gave this response.

After they did what men and women do, the man arose from the bed. He walked about fifteen feet, then collapsed and fell to the floor. He was having a heart attack. Immediately the ambulance was called. He was taken to the hospital.

The man could not be stabilized. Hours passed. The heart stopped. The doctors performed artificial respiration and cardiac pulmonary resuscitation. Even though the heart was not beating they continued messaging the heart for forty five minutes. The treatment was so severe that one of his ribs was broken in the process. There was no hope. The man was dead according to all the monitors. The tendons to his feet were cut so that his legs would not draw up from the contraction. They covered him with a sheet and moved him to another room.

The wife was called. She was asked to come to the hospital. There was no explanation as to why she should come. The wife, son and the daughter-in-law went to the hospital. The wife was asked to enter a room with the doctor. The son stood by listening.

"I'm sorry Mrs. Creed," the doctor said sympathetically, "But your husband passed away about an hour ago. We performed C.P.R., but could not revive him. Even if he had survived, he would be nothing but a vegetable. His mind would be gone. The flow of blood which carries oxygen was kept from his brain for too long."

The son walked to the hall. There was nothing else to do but call San Francisco.

"Hello, Charles?

"Jimmie, is that you? Where are you?"

"I am at the hospital in Phoenix, Arizona. Pop died of a heart attack. Will you call Jeanie in Portland, Oregon?"

The phone receiver was hung back on the wall. He stood pondering the situation. A nurse burst from the room where the father had been placed. She ran to the doctor. "That man is alive."

The doctors and nurses rushed back to the room. The tendons to his feet had to be re-connected. Time passed. He was taken from intensive care and placed in another room. Family members spoke with the man. His mind was clear. He could remember everything. Passed and present episodes were recalled when questioned.

If this could happen with all the technology in the twentieth century, what should we suppose could have happened in the first century. What about comatose patients, very shallow breathing, faint pulse, fibrillations? A body can appear to be dead when they are not.

A person can come back to life as long as the body has not decayed. When they are resurrected after the destruction of the physical body they are 'AS THE ANGELS'(Matt.22:30)possessing a spiritual body only.

John 11:1 Now a certain man was sick, named Lazarus, of Bethany, the town of Mary and his sister Martha. (4) When Jesus heard—he said, "This sickness is NOT UNTO DEATH, BUT FOR THE GLORY OF GOD, that the Son of God might be glorified thereby. (11)—After that he saith unto them, Our friend Lazarus sleepeth; but I go, that I may awake him out of sleep (coma). (12) Then said his disciples, Lord, if he sleep, he shall do well. (13) Howbeit Jesus spoke of his death: but they thought that he had spoken of taking of rest in sleep. (14) Then said Jesus unto them plainly, Lazarus is dead. (17) He had lain in the grave four days—. (39) Martha said, by this time he stinketh for he hath been dead four days.

John 11:40 Jesus saith unto Martha, if thou wouldest BELIEVE, thou shouldest see the glory of God. (43) (Jesus) cried with a loud voice, "Lazarus come forth."

Lazarus' body was in a comatose state (deep prolonged unconsciousness) and Jesus knew this. When this miracle is understood it ceases to be a miracle. This was all done so that the Name of God could be placed more vividly in the foreheads of people on the earth. The Name of God (Jesus) must be the center of human faith.

Eventually all truth will be understood by those that will call upon the Name of God without ceasing.

It should also be remembered that the Bible is true. It is a recording of what men have thought, said and done, even when it is in opposition to the will of God.

****

'Led by the Holy Spirit'

Ronndonn asked this question.

One person says "I was led by the Holy Spirit when I was reading my bible" and goes on to give the interpretation of a certain verse.

Another person hears this and looks up the verse and finds that the interpretation is very questionable since the verse has been taken out of context. Should the second person accept what the first has said since the first person is known to be very honest and is saying that they are led by the Holy Spirit?

James gave this response.

Through observance you will find that many of the ministers and laity alike use these tactics to lead the hearers into their way of thinking. It is only through wisdom, knowledge, understanding, and the guidance of the Holy Ghost, that we will be able to know the difference.

I am from way back to the 30s and 40s. People have been known to knock on the door and say the Lord told them to come, then they try to get anything they can by hook or crook. After all, it is a lot easier when the person is convinced that God sent them.

I have been told by at least one person that they could speak in tongues anytime they wanted to. Then they proved it. This was used to convince that what they were saying was the words of God. Dangerous business? Yes! But that is in the world.

People must wake up and ask God for spiritual eyes and ears, and the gift of the Holy Ghost for guidance, and then maintain the holy spirit within themselves in order to be saved from the tactics used by the sly ones.

How do we maintain the holy spirit within ourselves?

In the first place the holy spirit flows from God through the assembly of people gathered together in His Name. Matthew 18:20 For where two or three are gathered together in my NAME, there am I in the midst of them.

The holy spirit abides where God and his name is. John 14:23 Jesus said, If a man love me, he will keep my words: and my Father will love him, and WE will come unto him, and make our abode with him.

Wickedness (iniquity) drives out the holy spirit of God. Then the oil becomes deficient to keep the light of Christ burning, (John 1:9, 8:12, 9:5,12:46, Matt. 25:3) or the water of life flowing from the belly into continual life. (John 7:38) When this happens, the person drifts off into confusion and more weakness. (Darkness)

Ronndonn rated this answer:

This is an excellent answer you gave, and I mean really excellent. Your answer shows maturity and clearheadedness.

****

Life and destructive force.

Edward asked this question.

Explain destructive force and the holy spirit as it applies to the body, mind and spiritual well being of the human race.

James gave this response.

HUMAN DESTRUCTIVE FORCE COMES FROM WITHIN.

It takes the Holy Spirit flowing from the innermost being to render the destructive force inoperable and drive it out. Since men were created in the likeness of God (Gen. 1:26), he placed within them the mechanism for the creation of life similar to the life force that flows from himself. By this similarity men are called the sons of God.

It is the destructive power of the mind that cripples, and disrupts the effects of the holy spirit, and drives the man from the presence of God, and from the heavenly realms of Paradise. (Garden in Eden—Gen. 2:8, Paradise, 2 Cor. 12:4, Paradise and Tree of Life, Rev. 2:7, Gen. 2:9)

Heaven for man was originally upon the earth. It must return by man's knowledge of GOD'S NAME (The Tree of Life), and God's original purpose for the human race.

Isaiah 45:18 For thus saith the Lord that created the heavens; God himself that formed the earth and made it; he hath established it, he created it not in vain, he formed it to be INHABITED: I am the LORD; and there is none else.

Men can live long lives as they did in the beginning of their existence. And since the arrival of Christ (the anointing of God) men may even have life more abundantly. John 10:10.

Adam lived 930 years (Gen. 5:5)—Noah 950 years (Gen. 9:29)—Methuselah 969 years. (Gen 5:27). Oh yes, those years were essentially the same in length as ours. The earth still travels around the sun in one year.

Jesus said, I am come that they might have LIFE, and that they might have it more abundantly. MIGHT! It is up to each individual. Will they take hold of the Tree of Life and live?

****

Light, natural and spiritual.

Anonymous asked this question.

Will someone explain natural light and spiritual light?

James gave this response.

NATURAL LIGHT

In electricity light is caused by the flow of current through a wire small enough to cause resistance. The current when flowing through the wire (filament) causes the wire to heat to a white hot stage thereby emitting light. The current, back and forth motion, is caused by a generator.

In the U.S. electricity is created by the generator causing the current to flow from positive to negative, and back again sixty times per second. Electromotive force is force, due to differences of potential, that causes the electric current to seemingly flow. To find out how much power is created we must use the formula, P (power) = E (voltage). I (current).

SPIRITUAL LIGHT

The power of Christ is the light of the world. John 8:12 Jesus said, I am the light of the world: he that followeth me shall not walk in darkness, but shall have the light of life. John 1:9 That was the true light, which lighteth every man that cometh into the world. Darkness 'is' when there is no light. Darkness is NOT GENERATED BY ANYTHING. When light comes it is found that there is no darkness at all. Darkness cannot fight against light, because it is nothing, it is instantly destroyed by light.

People have always fought against any supposedly new thing, but they will not prevail this time. They are like water that flows in the direction of least resistance. They think God is not capable of injecting new understanding within the minds and spirits of men. Yet, until Revelations, the Bible has always increased in volume as the creation of God progresses toward maturity.

Let negativity continue, because without that force, the positive side cannot be revealed.

Everything God made is good and that true logical value will be revealed in time. The Light of Christ will prevail. Darkness will be gone in a flash.

****

LIVING FOREVER

Anonymous asked this question.

Genesis 3:22-24 God said He drove Adam and Eve out of the Garden and had angels guarding the tree of Life so Adam and Eve might not eat of the Tree and live forever. In Rev. 2:7 it says to him that overcometh will I give to eat of the tree of Life . . . . and the new testament says only God hath immortality.

James gave this response.

Only God hath immortality, But, God ***lives*** in the temple (body) so the temple lives. Acts. 17:28 For in him we live, and move and have our being. 1 Cor. 3:16 Know ye not that ye are the temple of God, and that the Spirit of God dwelleth in you?

Romans 2:7 To them who by patient continuance in well doing seek for glory and honor and immortality, eternal life.1 Cor. 15:53 For this corruptible must put on incorruption, and this mortal must put on immortality. (54) So when this corruptible shall have put on incorruption, and this mortal shall have put on immortality, then shall be brought to pass the saying that is written, Death is swallowed up in victory.

1 Tim. 6:14 That thou keep this commandment without spot, unrebukeable, until the appearing of our Lord Jesus Christ:

(15) Which in his times he shall show, who is the blessed and only Potentate,(God) the King of kings, and Lord of lords:

(16) Who only hath immortality, dwelling in the light which no man can approach unto; whom no man hath seen, nor can see: to whom be honor and power everlasting.

Jesus said, (John 3:13) No man hath ascended up to heaven, but he that came down from heaven, even the Son of man which is in heaven.

2 Tim. 1:10 But is now made manifest by the appearing of our Savior Jesus Christ, who hath abolished death, and hath brought life and immortality to light through the gospel.

There is something we must do!

Draw nigh to God, and he will draw nigh to you. James 4:8.

HOW DO WE DRAW NEAR GOD?

Jesus said (John 14:6)—I am the way, the truth, and the life: NO MAN cometh unto the Father, but by me.

WE MUST CALL UPON THE NAME OF GOD.

Acts 2:21 And it shall come to pass, that WHOSOEVER shall CALL ON THE NAME OF THE LORD shall be saved. (Also Romans 10:13, Joel 2:32). Rom. 10:14 How then shall they call on him in whom they have not believed? And how shall they believe in him of whom they have not heard?

THE TREE OF LIFE

Jesus, said, I am the vine, and my Father is the husbandman. Every branch in me that beareth not fruit he taketh away; and every branch that beareth fruit, he purgeth it, that it may bring forth more fruit. John 15:1-2.

Oh taste and see that the LORD is good. Psalm 34:8.

How do we bear the fruit of the spirit.

James 4:8 Cleanse your hands, ye sinners; and purify your hearts ye double minded. (10) Humble yourselves in the sight of the Lord and he shall lift you up.

We cannot change our ways by our own power, but when we call upon the Name of God sincerely and relentlessly, God will direct us to the Holy Ghost, which will in turn, guide us into all truth and give us the power to conform to his will and make us worthy of the fruit of life. Rev. 2:7 To him that overcometh will I give to eat of the Tree of Life, which is in the midst of the Paradise of God. (This is the same spiritual place in which God established the first man and woman).

We may pray as David did—Psalm 51:10 Create in me a clean heart, O God; and renew a right spirit within me. (11) Cast me not away from thy presence; and take not thy holy spirit from me.

BUT GOD MAY SAY,

Ezek. 18:31 Cast away from you all your transgressions, whereby ye have transgressed: and make you a new heart and a new spirit, for why will ye die—. (32) For I have no pleasure in the death of him that dieth, saith the Lord God: wherefore TURN YOURSELVES, and live ye.

God designed the human body so that it could live physically upon the earth, renewing itself as time continues, but when guilt suppresses the mind it weakens the immune system and the body deteriorates, allowing sickness and all manner of disease to take over and lead to death.

Call upon the Name of God (Jesus), so that we will receive strength to turn ourselves and have right to the fruit of that tree which will give us life and that more abundantly.

John 10:10. Jesus said,—I am come that they might have life, and that they might have it more abundantly.

The wages of sin is death; but the gift of God is eternal life through Jesus Christ our Lord. Rom. 6:23.

Can a person sin their way to heaven? If death is the way to heaven, why did God through Jesus heal so many people of all their sickness and disease? (Matt. 4:23) Why didn't he just let them die so that they could be with God and Jesus in heaven?

No! God and Jesus' desire is to be in us here on the earth and generate more power within ourselves as time continues. This has been their desire since the beginning, but sin and the resulting guilt got in the way.

Rev. 1:18 I am he that liveth, and was dead; and, behold, I am alive for evermore, Amen; and have the keys of hell and of death.

Luke 9:56—The Son of man is not come to destroy men's lives, but to save them.

Jesus said, (John 11:25) I am the resurrection, and the life—in this setting he was not speaking of some future time. He was speaking of raising Lazarus from his sleep—at that moment—(26) And whosoever liveth and believeth in me shall never die, Believest thou this?

1 Cor. 15:55 O death, where is thy sting? Of grave, where is thy victory? (56) ***The sting of death is sin***—.

****

Longevity:

Maxine asked this question.

When men were first created did they really live longer lives than now?

James gave this response.

The first men were saturated with the strength they received from God, and with their clean environment, SOME of them lived long lives, even though they had been influenced by the violent actions of the animals around them. It took almost a thousand years before their own minds subdued themselves, and by the influence of guilt and violence they were finally drawn into death.

YES, THEIR YEARS WERE ESSENTIALLY THE SAME AS OURS.

On a Jewish Religious Basis: (Ref. Bible Dictionary—William Smith-Teacher's edition).

From the time of the institution of the Mosiac law downward the month was a lunar one. The cycle of religious feasts commencing with the passover depended not simply on the month, but on the moon; the 14th of Abib was coincident with the full moon; and the new moons themselves were the occasions of regular festivals. Num. 10:10; 28:11-14. The commencement of the month was generally decided by observation of the new moon. The usual number of months in a year was twelve, as implied in 1 Kings 4:7; 1 Chron. 27: 1-15; but since twelve lunar months would make but 354 1/2 days, the years would be short twelve days of the true year, and therefore it follows as a matter of course that an additional month must have been inserted about every third year, which would bring the number up to thirteen. No notice, however, is taken of this month in the Bible. In the modern Jewish calendar the INTERCALARY month is introduced seven times in every nineteen years.

During Noah's time the month was considered 30 days. Consider Gen. 8:3. 150 days divided by 30 = 5 months. They were on the ark one year and ten days.

DID ADAM, NOAH AND MATHUSALA LIVE LONG LIVES?

Yes! Men did live long lives. Their years were essentially the same then as now.

Adam did live nine hundred and thirty years. Gen. 5:5 And all the days that Adam lived were nine hundred and thirty years; and he died.

Noah lived nine hundred and fifty years. Gen 9:29 And all the days of Noah were nine hundred and fifty years: and he died.

Methuselah lived nine hundred sixty and nine years: Gen. 5:27 And all the days of Methuselah were nine hundred sixty and nine years : and he died. Mehhuselah died the year of the flood. He did not go on the ark.

HAS IT ALWAYS TAKEN A YEAR FOR THE EARTH TO CIRCLE THE SUN?

The following information was taken from The Funk & Wagnalls New Encyclopedia of Science, Vol 20, and Page 1714.

The modern calendar is based on sidereal time. A sidereal day lasts 23 hours, 56 minutes, and 4 seconds. The time it takes the earth to complete an orbit around the sun is called the sidereal year. The sidereal year lasts 365 days, 6 hours, 9 minutes, and 9.54 seconds. Sidereal time is more accurate than solar time. The earth is slowing down but no more than 3.53 1/3 minutes in the last 40,000 years. This should be researched further to determine its veracity.

As it took Adam nine hundred and thirty years to fall from the strength he had with God, it may take some time for men and women to retrieve what was lost, and then only by calling upon the Name of the Lord. It is faith in God's Name that will make the difference.

God wants people to live in his garden (spiritual state) and he also wants them to enjoy all the things he has made, otherwise he would not have made them.

****

Man and Beast:

Rachelle asked this question.

MAN AND BEAST—HOW OLD ARE THEY?

James gave this response.

It is easy to speak and write of millions of years since the beginning of the creation of animal life, but there is no proof of its existence more than forty eight thousand years ago. Even the carbon-dating process is not always accurate. (i.e. man and beast, not fish and foul)

The fact is, the soil of the earth is teaming with life or potential life, and at the proper time that life comes forth as rapidly as in the spring time of each year.

The recorded history of man is only six thousand years, so it is conceivable that during an eight thousand year period prior to forty thousand years, and the fifth day consisting of 49,000 years, many experimentations were accomplished in the field of biology, i.e. the science of living beings and life processes.

God did not create man without first experimenting with many other forms of life. In fact, at the end of the forty eight thousand years of the sixth day, it has been 293,000 years since God said, "Let there be light". During all that time the earth was being conditioned to support a higher form of intelligence. It was called Homo Sapien, whose advanced cranium would contain God's Greatest invention, the Brain of man.

God knew of the benefits of freedom of thought and of the side effects. He knew that man would be susceptible to suggestion portrayed to his brain by the things he saw and thought. That was why God revealed to man his own Name so that he would have something physical to hang on to, and have faith in. In that manner he would not be drawn down by the destructive elements of the earth.

But man was young. He had little experience. He did not understand the consequences of his actions. He quickly succumbed to violence and was corrupt (Gen. 6:11) to the point that God would not help him when the rains started and the water overflowed the then known world.

God's first thought was to destroy man off the face of the earth

(Gen. 6:7), but then understood that men were young and said, “I will not again curse the ground any more for man’s sake; for the imagination of man’s heart is evil from his youth.”

WAS MAN PERFECT IN THE BEGINNING?

Yes, when he was very young. But he would not call upon the Name of God for strength to conform to the logical plan for man’s gradual growth into a perfect reflection of God himself. Man could not understand that he must be guided by the spirit of God to conform to God’s ways. As a result, man was not given the Holy Ghost as a gift to assist him in right thinking. The Holy Ghost was not given as a gift until after John the baptizer was filled with the Holy Ghost even from his mother’s womb. (Luke I:15) And Jesus was conceived by the direction of the Holy Ghost. (Matthew 1:18). Jesus prayed to God that he give the Holy Ghost to his disciples (John 14:16 and 26) After that the Holy Ghost spread throughout the world.

****

MAN, In The Image Of . . .

Jsargent asked this question.

Gen 1:27 says “So God created man in His own image, . . ”

John 1:1 says “In the beginning was the Word, and the Word was with God, and the Word was God.”Would it be valid to say that man was created in the image of THE WORD? What is your opinion? How would this viewpoint affect how we live our lives and our viewpoint of various theologies?

James gave this response.

God is a spirit (John 4:24). He is an individual. His body is made of spiritual substance. It cannot be seen by the natural eyes of man. It can be seen through the form of visions. God can come to man, speak with, through, and walk in him, if the man's physical, mental and spiritual body is conditioned to accept the power that emanates from a being of such magnitude.

Acts 17:28 For in him we live, and move, and have our being.

John 1:1 In the beginning was the Word, and the Word was with God, and the Word was God.

This merely is bringing to the forefront the importance of GOD'S NAME. His Name was JESUS. That NAME was the NAME of GOD. It was with God, it was the 'Handle' of God, and God sent an angel through a dream to Joseph (Matthew 1:20-21) advising him to call the new born's NAME 'JESUS.'

That name was revealed so that all that believe in him and call upon his Name SHALL BE SAVED FROM THE EFFECTS OF THEIR SINS. Faith in that NAME activates the flow of Christ, the Power of God, and washes away the guilt that is produced by sins and gives the person the power to overcome the acts of sin in the future.

Joel 2:32 And it shall come to pass, that WHOSOEVER shall CALL on the NAME of the LORD shall be delivered—.

Acts 2:21 And it shall come to pass, that WHOSOEVER shall CALL on the NAME of the LORD shall be saved. (Also Rom. 10:13).

Here are three witnesses to show that faith in and calling upon the Name of God is all that is necessary to reach God and his power to overcome all that is in the world. For in calling upon the Name of God, it will attract all the spiritual gifts necessary to do the job complete.

This is what God told Adamah to do in the beginning, but he forgot. The true saving Name of God was lost to the knowledge of men. God replaced it through HIS SON, JESUS for placement in the foreheads of men (Rev. 14:1), for their protection and safety in this otherwise violent environment.

People are animals. They have the temperament of the wild, but they have been given the power to become the sons of God.

John 1:12—as many as received him, to them gave he power to become the SONS of GOD, even to them that believe on HIS NAME.

We must have something to hang on to, to have faith in. Grab that NAME. CALL UPON IT. Make it your raft in the vast boisterous, tempest (violent storms) of life. It is quiet there. It is a calm place. The NAME of the LORD is a strong tower—. (Proverbs 18:10). Run into it—it is safe.

Jsargent rated this answer:

Amen! For there is no other name given AMONG men whereby you MUST be saved. May God richly bless you.

****

MAN SHOULD ENJOY

Socurious asked this question.

I would like for someone to enlighten me further on the scripture Ecclesiastes 2:24. I think there is a bigger message than I am reading.

Thank you . . . always . . . Socurious

James gave this response.

God designed the world and everything in it for the sole purpose of supporting the physical life of his natural son. God then placed Adamah in a spiritual state of Paradise (Rev. 2:7) here on the earth designed after the ecstasies of the natural heavens where the spiritual beings reside.

If the man and woman would have called upon God through the mediator (God's name) from the rising of the sun unto the going down of the same, (Psalm 113:3, From the rising of the sun unto the going down of the same the Lord's name is to be praised, Psalm. 119:55 I have remembered thy Name, O LORD in the night, and have kept thy law.) they would have been able to conform to God's will in every respect.

When man and woman (as one unit) would not continue drawing near God through His Name with their whole mind and spirit, they became too weak to conform to the will of God.

This one rule was not for God's benefit but for the stabilization of the man and woman's natural and spiritual equilibrium.

If they had remained in that spiritual state of the garden they would have ***enjoyed all the physical benefits*** that God had in store for them forever.

Eccl 2:24 There is nothing better for a man, than that he should eat and drink, and that he should make his soul enjoy good in his labor. (Dress and keep the garden Gen. 2:15). This also I saw, that it was from the hand of God.—(25) For God giveth to a man that is good in his sight wisdom, and knowledge, and joy: but to the sinner he giveth travail,—. KJV

****

MAN, THE CREATION OF

Ruth . . . asked this question.

Did the ancestor of man come from the ocean?

James gave this response.

God had experimented with seeds, herbs and fruit trees since the beginning of the third day. On the fifth day he developed the birds, fish and whales. Then on the sixth day he spent eight thousand years creating the beasts and cattle of the earth. This was a total span of two hundred and fifty three thousand years since the beginning of the creation. God's creative day is 49,000 years. 6 x 49,000= 294,000-1,000=293,000. 1000 years left before the end of the 6th day.

Eight thousand years into the sixth day Adamah was formed of the dust of the ground,

NOT OF THE SAND AND SEAWEED OF THE OCEAN.

Gen. 2:7 And the Lord God formed man of the DUST OF THE GROUND.

Over the years decaying wood mixed with the hard earth, and volcanic ash formed chemicals of the right consistency to make life of a higher intelligence feasible.

The two part seed of microscopic size, at first, was constructed by God and his son, and placed in the earth at the right time of year for germination and development. Exactly the right temperature was needed, so the place was selected very carefully: A locality where many trees, and vegetation had grown for long enough to produce a good loam. As more leaves fell to the ground, they became compacted and the chemical reaction caused an even warmth of the right temperature for the germination of the seed. Even though some nights were normally too cold for the embryo (living being in its earliest stages), and later the fetus (vertebrate not yet born), the chemical action kept the ground surrounding the new life at an even temperature.

There were ample nutrients in the ground, such as vitamins and minerals, for the sustenance of the unborn life. Those nutrients were drawn by the new life from the earth through the umbilical cord and placenta.

Later the design of the 'belly button' in the female was caused by the cloning effect in budding. (i.e. the umbilical cord was not used for the sustenance of the woman (she received her sustenance from the man by budding from the side), but the design was transferred to the female from the male for future use in their offspring.

It took nine months and four days for Adamah (man) to be born; the same time it later took for the birth of the last Adam. (Jesus)

1 Cor. 15:45 And so it is written, The first man Adam was made a living soul; the last Adam was made a quickening spirit. The last Adam was born in a manger, but he was more fortunate than the first man, because he had a mother of the same species (a class of individuals having some common characteristics or qualities): whereas, the first man had to be nursed by a Chimpanzee that was currently living in the area. This is why some have mistakenly thought that man developed from the Chimpanzee.

The mother Chimpanzee was confused, but did not have the intelligence enough to know exactly what was happening. She did know there was a baby that appeared something like her own, so she raised it without undue (excessive) concern.

In God's many experiments he found that there were only a couple different genes needed in the creation of man as was used in the development of the Chimpanzee.

****

Marriage:

Zenaide asked this question.

There are many advocates that believe it is better to be alone; that the union between male and female actually interferes with the ability to reach God. Paul seems to condone this kind of thinking. (1 Cor. 7:33-35, 1 Cor 7:8)What is your opinion?

James gave this response.

It should be impressed upon the minds of individuals (male and female) that it is NOT GOOD TO BE ALONE.

Genesis 2:18 And the Lord God said, It is not good that the man should be alone; I will make him an help meet for him.

Is there any scientific proof that positive can function properly without the accompanying benefits of the negative?

While it is true Paul said (1 Cor. 7:32), He that is unmarried careth for the things that belong to the Lord, how he may please the Lord: (33) But he that is married careth for the things that are of the world, how he may please his wife.

I Cor. 7:34 There is difference also between a wife and a virgin. The unmarried woman careth for the things of the Lord, that she may be holy both in body and in spirit: but she that is married careth for the things of the world, how she may please her husband.

Paul stated in I Cor. 7:40, that these above statements concerning this subject were after his own judgment. It is very important that his other words be considered, namely these:

I Cor. 13:9 For WE KNOW IN PART, and we prophesy in part. (10) But when that which is perfect in come, then that which is in part shall be DONE AWAY.

Matthew 19:4 Jesus said, Have ye not read, that he which made them at the beginning made them male and female. (5) For this cause shall a man leave father and mother, and shall cleave to his wife: and they twain shall be one flesh?

****

Mary, did she have other children beside Jesus ?

Anonymous asked this question.

> Hi,
>
> I wanted to know, did Saint Mary remain a virgin all her life? Or did she have children who were brothers and sisters to Jesus? Is James Jesus' brother? Thanks
>
> James gave this response.
>
> Galatians 1:19 (James, the Lord's brother)
>
> On one occasion (Luke 2:48) Mary said to Jesus, "Thy father and I have sought thee sorrowing."
>
> Was Joseph Jesus' biological father or only a step-father? (Luke 1:35) When the Holy Ghost came upon Mary, did he deliver the natural or spiritual seed?
>
> Insertion: Matthew 13:55 Is not this the carpenter's son? is not his mother called Mary? and his brethren, James, and Joses' and Simon, and Judas? (56) And his sisters, are they not all with us?

John 19:25. John wrote that Mary had a sister by the name of Mary. Why is it that in no other place in the bible is this statement corroborated? Don't we need at least two witnesses?

End of insert.

MARY, JOSEPH AND JESUS.

Matthew wrote: Now the birth of Jesus Christ was on this wise: When as his mother Mary was espoused (engaged) to Joseph (Matthew 1:18), BEFORE THEY CAME TOGETHER, she was found with child of the Holy Ghost.

John recorded Jesus' words: "If I bear witness of myself, MY ***WITNESS IS NOT TRUE***". (John 5:31). The Pharisees therefore said unto him (Jesus), Thou bearest record of thyself; thy record is not true. (John 8:13).

(Jesus said), It is also written in your law, that the testimony of two men is true. (John 8:17). (18) I am one that bear witness of myself, and the Father that sent me beareth witness of me.

GOD WAS JESUS' WITNESS TO US THROUGH MATTHEW.

Matthew 3:17 And lo a voice from heaven, saying, 'This is my beloved Son, in whom I am well pleased.' Also Matt. 17:5. God also witnessed of Jesus through the writings of Mark and Luke. Mark 9:7, Luke 9:35, Mark 1:11, Luke 3:22,Matt. 18:16.

So in every case we need at least two witnesses to establish EVERY WORD, and this was lacking in the case of Matthew's words regarding Joseph and Mary. If God had been Matthew's second witness, he would have done so through some other witness or writer. Matthew was alone in his statement, 'BEFORE THEY CAME TOGETHER', therefore, his witness is not true.

With these facts in mind let us seriously examine the relationship between Joseph and Mary. Mary was not a hermaphrodite (Animal or plant having both male and female reproductive organs). She was constructed physically in accordance with the exact specifications set forth for the first woman.

A VIRGIN SHALL CONCEIVE

Isaiah 7:14 Therefore the Lord himself shall give you a sign; behold a virgin shall conceive, and bear a son, and shall call his name Immanuel.

JOSEPH WAS NOT AWARE OF WHAT HAD HAPPENED.

Matt.1:19 Then Joseph ***her HUSBAND***, being a just man, and not willing to make her (Mary) a public example, was minded to put her away privily. (20) But while he thought on these things, behold, the angel of the Lord appeared unto him in a dream, saying, Joseph, thou ***SON OF DAVID***, fear not to take unto thee Mary thy WIFE: (This indicated they were more than just engaged) for that which is conceived in her is of (by the direction of) the Holy Ghost. (21) And she shall bring forth a Son, and thou shalt call his name Jesus: for he shall save his people from their sins. (22) Now all this was done, that it might be fulfilled which was spoken of the Lord by the prophet, saying, (23) Behold, a virgin shall be with child, and shall bring forth a son, and they shall call his name Emmanuel, which being interpreted is, God with us. (24) Then Joseph being raised from sleep did as the angel of the Lord had bidden him, and took unto him ***HIS WIFE***: (25) and KNEW (not aware of her sexually) HER NOT TILL SHE HAD BROUGHT FORTH HER ***FIRSTBORN*** SON; and he called his name Jesus. (Firstborn, indicates that there were more children after the first). (Joseph refrained from having conscious intimate sexual relations with Mary until after the baby was born).

Note that a female person is referred to as being a virgin until she has had her first full relationship with the opposite sex. At that time a virgin can conceive. Notice that Isaiah 7:14 did not stipulate there was no opposite sex involved; only that 'A virgin shall conceive, and bare a son.'

Ideally, male and female of the human race are supposed to maintain their virginity, until they come together, and are joined by the power of God.

Neither Joseph nor Mary was aware of this operation, because IT WAS ACCOMPLISHED DURING THE TIME OF THEIR SLEEP, and was completely directed by the Holy Ghost. Joseph was informed of some facts in the dream so he would not separate from her.

It was too early in the development of mankind for the complete propagation process to be revealed to Joseph, John the baptizer, or any of the apostles, including Saul (Paul). They all saw through a glass darkly. 1 Cor. 13:12.

But now, at the beginning of the last thousand years of the sixth day, the complete story is being revealed, and 'that which is in part shall be done away.' (1 Cor. 13:10.)

Luke 1:32 He (Jesus) shall be great, and shall be called the Son of the Highest: and the Lord God shall give unto him the throne of HIS FATHER DAVID.

Luke 1:34 Then said Mary unto the angel, How shall this be, seeing I know not a man? (have not been aware of a man in a sexual way). (35) And the angel answered and said unto her, THE HOLY GHOST SHALL COME UPON THEE, AND THE POWER OF THE HIGHEST SHALL OVERSHADOW THEE: therefore ALSO that HOLY THING which shall be born of thee shall be called the ***SON OF GOD***.

JESUS' FATHER THROUGH THE SPIRIT IS GOD.

JESUS' NATURAL FATHER WAS JOSEPH.

Joseph and Mary were both from the lineage of David, therefor, Jesus was referred to as the ***Son of David*** in the natural.

If Jesus was Mary's only child why was it recorded in Luke that Jesus was her ***FIRSTBORN***? Luke 2:7 And she brought forth her firstborn son—.

Jesus was called her 'FIRST-BORN,' a term implying that other children followed after the order of natural generation (Luke 2:7). Herbert Lockyer—All the Women of the Bible. Page 92.

Mary was of the tribe of Judah, and the line of David. In the royal genealogy of Matthew and the human genealogy of Luke, ***Mary is only mentioned in the former, but her immediate forebears are not mentioned.*** She became the wife of ***Joseph, the son of Heli*** (legal father—Luke 3:23). (Note that Matthan and Matthat are one and the same person). Jacob and Heli were brothers, sons of Matthan/Matthat.

Matthew 1:16 And JACOB begat Joseph the husband of Mary, of whom was born Jesus, who is called Christ.

Note that Matthew stated that ***Jacob begat Joseph*** and Luke stated that ***Joseph was the son of Heli***. So how can this be?

Deut. 25:5 If brethren dwell together, and one of them die and have no child, the wife of the dead shall not marry without unto a stranger: her husband's brother shall go in unto her, and take her to him to wife, and perform the duty of an husband's brother unto her. (6) And it shall be, that the firstborn which she beareth shall succeed in the Name of his brother which is dead, that his name be not put out of Israel.

John 6:42 And they said, is not this Jesus, the son of Joseph, whose father and mother we know?

Psalms 69:8 I am become a stranger unto my brethren, and an alien unto my mother's children.

****

Masturbation

Epucks asked this question.

What does the bible say about masturbation?

James gave this response.

The bible does not deal much with this subject. Something close to it is listed in Gen. 38:9 concerning Onan and his brother's wife.

Sexual gratification in any form.

First, it should be understood that there was no feeling of condemnation in the mind until the first man and woman transferred the sensual sensations in connection with propagation from their sub-conscious to the conscious part of their brain. The man was put into a deep sleep (Gen. 2:21, while God created man's counter-part. This 'sleep process' was intended to be continued in the reproduction of all new human life. This process was not necessary among the other animals because they were not designed to live eternally.

Genesis 3:3 But of the fruit of the tree (Tree = man and woman = one unit) which is in the midst of the garden, God hath said, Ye shall not eat (partake) of it, neither shall ye touch it, lest ye die.

This was the only rule of law imposed upon the man and the woman. When this rule was broken it caused condemnation in the minds of of the couple, which in turn drove out the Christ of God. (Christ was the light that lighteth every man that cometh into the world. (John 1:9). They were driven out of the presence of God from that day forward. Thy died spiritually and later physically.

They could not return to Paradise (Gen. 2:8, Rev. 2:7) because they became confused and had no power to effectively control the newly developed desires in their mind caused by the uncontrollable sensations running rampant throughout their bodies.

Since they had lost their only spiritual guidance, they became weaker as time continued, until the earth was corrupt and filled with violence. (Gen. 6:11) And the sons of God (Gen. 6:2) (through Seth—Adam, the Grandfather was the son of God, therefore Seth was also the son of God) took wives of the daughters of men (Cain's lineage after he had been severed from God).

Such deviations from the way of God led to continued condemnation, promiscuity (not restricted to one sexual partner), and more violence.

Men were aware of the difference between right and wrong. They voiced their opinion to one another. At first the words were delivered by word of mouth and carried down from one generation to the next. Then various documents were prepared in piece-meal fashion and eventually came into the hands of Moses.

When the cloud stood still (Num. 9:22) Moses began to bring at least ten of the documents together and place them in a book, which he read to the people. (Exodus 24:7) Exodus 24:12 Moses went into the mountain where he chiseled in stone the primary rules which had been accumulated since the beginning of the history of man.

It followed, of course, that even he could not conform to those rules. Because of his disgust when he came down the mountain he gave instructions that the men should go in and out from gate to gate throughout the camp, and slay every man his brother, his companion and his neighbor. (Exodus 32:27) This was in direct violation of the commandment 'Thou shalt not kill'. (Exodus 20:13)

(Remember that the voices sound the same, it is what they say that makes the difference—2 Cor. 1:14 No marvel; for Satan himself is transformed into an angel of light. God will not confirm 'Thou shalt not kill,' then turn around and give a commandment that killing is permissible under some circumstances.

Any deviation from the original plan of God for the reproduction of human life brings condemnation to the mind and spirit of the man and woman, WHETHER ALONE, with someone of the opposite, or same sex. God understands that through the hereditary process men have become weak and the imaginations of his heart (and mind) is evil from his youth. (Gen. 8:21). It has taken time for man and woman to become weak and it will take AGE and the guidance of the Holy Ghost to enable men and women to OVERCOME the weakness that is in their bodies.

Revelation 2:7 He that hath an ear, let him hear what the Spirit saith unto the churches; To him that OVERCOMETH will I give to EAT of the TREE OF LIFE, which is in the midst of the PARADISE OF GOD.

The tree of life was in the Garden in Eden (Gen. 2:9), therefore, the garden in Eden and Paradise is one and the same. It is a spiritual state. The Name of God is the Tree of Life. The fruit of that tree brings life.

Jesus said, I am come in my Father's name . . . (John 5:43) I am come that they might have life and have more of it. John 10:10.

****

Matthias as the replacement apostle

Cherub_ asked this question.

In Acts, Chapter 1, Peter leads the delegation into a selection of a replacement apostle for Judas. The ultimate decision was made by casting lots, and the lot fell on Matthias.

Yet, the Lord selected Paul as an apostle, so, several questions . . .

1. Are there only 12 apostles? Revelation cites that there were 12 foundations in heaven, one for each apostle.

2. Was Matthias a true apostle? What is the criteria for apostleship? Peter cites, "one of the men who have been with us the whole time", yet the Apostle Paul was not with them from the beginning.

3. I am reading that the system of casting lots as described in the selection of Matthias is a basis for the "democratic" voting within a church, and that the Bible supports a voting system of government for the church. Is it appropriate to tell God what the choices are, and tell Him to pick the right choice? Does "voting" support the idea of God being omnipotent and omniscient?

4. What passages do support the government or organization of a church?

What say ye? ~cherub~

James gave this response.

First it must be understood how a person became an apostle.

Explanation taken from the Bible Dictionary—William Smith LLD—Teacher's addition—Copyright 1948.

Their office.—(1) The original qualification of an apostle, as stated by St. Peter on the occasion of electing a successor to the traitor Judas, was that he should have been personally acquainted with the whole ministerial course of our Lord, from his baptism by John till the day when he was taken up into heaven.

(2) They were chosen by CHRIST HIMSELF.

(3) They had the power of working miracles.

(4) They were inspired. John 16:13.

(5) Their work seems to have been pre-eminently that of founding the churches and upholding them by supernatural power specially bestowed for that purpose.

(6) THE OFFICE CEASED, AS A MATTER OF COURSE, WITH ITS FIRST HOLDERS; ALL CONTINUATION OF IT, FROM THE VERY CONDITIONS OF ITS EXISTENCE (cf.1 Cor.9:1) BEING IMPOSSIBLE. also see 2 Cor. 12:11 Paul in defense.

Did God, Jesus, Holy Ghost or the Apostles appoint Saul as an apostle?

NO!

Who did?

SAUL PUT HIMSELF IN THAT POSITION.

It has been stated that 'Send' as in Acts 13:3-4 means the same as 'Apostle'. But consider that Jesus could have named Saul as an apostle the same as he did with the other twelve + Matthias—Acts 1:23-26, but he didn't.

LUKE 6:13 AND WHEN IT WAS DAY, HE (JESUS) CALLED UNTO HIM HIS DISCIPLES: AND OF THEM HE CHOSE TWELVE, WHOM ALSO HE NAMED APOSTLES;—.

LATER WHAT DID HE SAY TO SAUL?

Acts 9:4 And he (Saul) fell to the earth, and heard a voice saying unto him, SAUL, SAUL, why persecutest thou me?

5 And he said, Who art thou, Lord? And the Lord said, I am Jesus whom thou persecutest.

6 And he trembling and astonished said, Lord, what wilt thou have me to do? and the Lord said unto him, Arise, and go into the city, and it shall be told thee what thou must do.

THIS IS ALL JESUS SAID TO SAUL. HE DID NOT CHANGE HIS NAME NOR MAKE HIM AN APOSTLE.

JESUS THEN CAME TO ANANIAS AT DAMASCUS IN A VISION.

Acts 9:11 And the Lord said unto him, Arise, and go into the street which is called Straight, and inquire in the house of Judas for one called SAUL, of Tarsus: for, behold, he prayeth, (12) And hath seen in a vision a man named Ananias coming in, and putting his hand on him, that he might receive his sight.—15 ***Go thy way: for he is a chosen vessel unto me, to BEAR MY NAME before the Gentiles, and kings, and the children of Israel: (16) For I will show him how great things he must suffer for my NAME'S sake.***

THIS IS ALL JESUS SAID TO ANANIAS.

Saul's way consisted of a three way mixture.

1. ***The way of Christ***

2. ***The way of the Pharisees***

3. ***The way of Saul.***

SAUL ON OCCASION DID IT HIS WAY.

Peter said (John 6:68)—to whom shall we go? THOU HAST THE WORDS OF ETERNAL LIFE.

Jesus said (John 14:25) These things have I spoken unto you, BEING YET PRESENT WITH YOU.

John 6:26 But the Comforter, which is the Holy Ghost, whom the Father will send in my Name, he shall teach you all things, and bring ALL THINGS TO YOUR REMEMBRANCE, WHATSOEVER I HAVE SAID UNTO YOU.

John 16:13 Howbeit when he, the Spirit of truth is come, he will guide you into all truth: for HE SHALL NOT SPEAK OF HIMSELF (on his own accord) but whatsoever he shall hear, that shall he speak:—. (14)—he shall receive of mine, and shall show it unto you.

John 17:8—Jesus said, I have given unto ***them*** the WORDS WHICH THOU GAVEST ME—. John 17:20 Neither pray I for these alone (twelve apostles), but for them also which shall believe on me THROUGH THEIR WORD—. (21) That they all may be one; as thou, Father, art in me, and I in thee, that they also may be ONE in US.

Saul preferred not to hear THEIR WORDS. (the words that came from God through Jesus to the Apostles and then out to the world).

SAUL WAS ARROGANT.

He wrote (Gal. 1:11), But I certify you, brethren, that the gospel which was preached of me is NOT AFTER MAN, neither was I taught it, but by the REVELATION OF JESUS CHRIST. (15) But when it pleased God, who separated me from my mother's womb, and called me by his grace, (16) To reveal his Son in me, that I might preach him among the heathen; immediately I CONFERRED NOT WITH FLESH AND BLOOD—(17) Neither went I up to Jerusalem to them which were apostles before me; but went into Arabia, and returned again unto Damascus. (18) Then after three years I went up to Jerusalem to see Peter, and abode with him FIFTEEN DAYS. (19) But other of the apostles saw I none, save James the Lord's brother. (21) Afterwards I came into the regions of Syria and Cilicia; Gal. 2:1 Then FOURTEEN YEARS AFTER, I went up again to Jerusalem with Barnabas, and took Titus with me also. (20) And I went up by revelation, and communicated unto them that gospel which I preach among the Gentiles—.

IF REVELATIONS ALONE COULD HAVE SAVED HUMANITY, THEN IT WAS UNNECESSARY FOR JESUS TO COME INTO SUCH A VIOLENT AND CONFUSED WORLD.

THERE ARE MANY VOICES IN THE WORLD, HEREIN LIES CONFUSION. JESUS ONLY MUST BE HEARD.

Paul wrote (1 Cor. 13:9) For we know in part, and we prophesy in part. (10) But when that which is perfect is come THEN THAT WHICH IS IN PART SHALL BE DONE AWAY.

Saul was brought up at the feet of a PHARISEE named Gamaliel (Acts 5:34), and taught according to the perfect manner of the law of the fathers (Acts 22:3).

Phlp. 3:8-9 Paul said, after reiterating accomplishments in his religious up-bringing, 'I count it as loss, and do count them but dung'. But he, like any educated individual, drew here and there upon his knowledge gained from the teachings of the Pharisee's religion. This is unavoidable.

BEWARE OF THE LEAVEN.

Jesus said to his disciples (Matt. 16:6), Take heed and beware of the leaven of the Pharisees and of the Sadducees.—.

Matt. 16:12—the disciples understood he was referring to the ***doctrines*** of those religious movements.

Ref: Cruden's Concordance. Jesus denounced the Pharisees for their hypocrisy, which was shown by their care for the minutest formalities imposed by the traditions of the elders, but not for the MIND AND HEART which should correspond. They were AMBITIOUS, ARROGANT, AND PROUDLY SELF-RIGHTEOUS, of which qualities were contrary to the teachings of Jesus.

Cherub_ rated this answer:

Interesting.

Matthias was appoint by Peter, Paul was appoint by God.

And you tell me that only Jesus must be heard. Jesus called Paul to the apostleship. Jesus didn't call Matthias.

God qualifies people, not Peter.

James gave this follow-up answer.

God was going to deliver Saul/Paul to the Gentiles one way or another. It would have been easier if Paul was not so arrogant and self willed.

Acts 21:11 And when he (Agabus) was come unto us, he took Paul's girdle, and bound his own hands and feet, and said, Thus saith the Holy Ghost, So shall the Jews at Jerusalem bind the man that owneth this girdle, and shall deliver him into the hands of the Gentiles.

(12) And when we heard these things, both we, and they of that place, besought him not to go up to Jerusalem.

Paul said with arrogance, and pride coupled with bragging—(13) I am ready not to be bound only, but also to die at Jerusalem for the name of the Lord Jesus. (14) And when he would not be persuaded, we ceased, saying, The will of the Lord be done. (God's will was going to be done in spite of Saul's attitude).

Paul argued with the Lord.

While Paul was speaking before the people at the castle in Jerusalem (Acts 21:40) he told of a trance he had undergone at Jerusalem after he returned from Damascus.

Acts 22:17 And it came to pass, that, when I was come again to Jerusalem, even while I prayed in the temple, I was in a trance; (18) And saw him ***(Jesus) saying unto me, Make haste and get thee quickly out of Jerusalem; for they will not receive thy testimony concerning me.***

(19) And I said, Lord, they know that I imprisoned and beat in every synagogue them that believed on thee:

(20) And when the blood of thy martyr Stephen was shed, I also was standing by, and consenting unto his death, and kept the raiment of them that slew him.

(21) And he said unto me, Depart: FOR I WILL SEND THEE FAR HENCE UNTO THE GENTILES.

Acts 22:22 And they gave him audience unto this word, and then lifted up their voices, and said, Away with such a fellow from the earth.

Saul's/ Paul's own pride, arrogance and self willed nature caused most of his problems. God through the Holy Ghost along with God's son, Jesus, were all trying to guide him toward the Gentiles, but he, in his rebellion caused himself to undergo beatings that he would not have had to endure if he had been more sensitive to the guidance of the spirit.

Proverbs 16:7 ***When a man's ways please the LORD, he maketh even his enemies to be at peace with him.***

If all of Saul/Paul's ways pleased the LORD he would have been guided by the Holy Ghost and presented before the Gentiles, kings, and the children of Israel at the appropriate time, and in a manner that would have been more of a glory to the Name of Jesus.

Jesus said, (Matthew 23:15) Woe unto you, scribes and Pharisees, hypocrites! For ye compass sea and land to make one proselyte—. ***The scribes and Pharisees were guilty of this, but who else was doing the same thing, that also was raised a Pharisee? Saul/Paul.!***

Paul said, Romans 8:1—walk not after the flesh, but after the Spirit. If Paul had practiced his own instructions he would have by-passed all destructive forces that prevailed around him. God had the power to save back then the same as he has during this present time, when a person is calling upon the Name of the Lord.

Saul even had authority from the chief priests to bind all that were calling on the name of Jesus. (Acts 9:14)

Yes, he converted after that, but still had his nature to contend with. Paul wrote, (Rom. 7:22) I delight in the law of God after the inward man: (23) But I see another law in my members, warring against the law of my mind, and bringing me into captivity to the law of sin which is in my members.

When a person is not calling upon the Name of the Lord as the saints were doing in all places during the time of the early church they may be susceptible to sights and sounds that are not conducive to a stable and protected life. When letting the eyes stray from Jesus, the mediator between God and man, they may cause the brain to be filled with all kinds of destructive forces.

What the mind thinks the body will follow. What a man thinketh, so is he. (Proverbs 23:7)

What a person sees in another person, thing, or deity, either alive or dead, as in idols, is reflected back into himself. If it is an inanimate object, it causes the mind and spirit to become lethargic. This, in turn, weakens the body.

If a person believes in two Gods, his mind becomes divided, and his eyes see double. In this level of understanding the person becomes unstable. Matthew 6:22—if the eye is single, the whole body shall be full of light. (Of course Matthew was writing about serving God and natural treasures) But this statement can be applied to anything that causes the person to drift from the presence of God. Peter became distracted by the waves of the sea and took his eyes off Jesus, the mediator for man, and the only one that can save all men from the destructive elements in this world.

Cherub_ asked this follow-up question.

Just explain this passage:

Acts 6:6

So he [Paul],trembling and astonished, said, “Lord, what do You want me to do?”

and verse 15, 16

> “But the Lord said to him, “Go, for he is a chosen vessel of Mine to bear My name before Gentiles, kings, and the children of Israel. For I will show him how many things he must suffer for My name’s sake.”

James gave this response.

Yes, you are referring to Acts 9:6, 15-16 as I stated above. It still didn’t call him an apostle. In verse 15 Jesus was speaking with Ananias. Also, Saul was not going by the name of Paul at that time, nor did Jesus address him as Paul. Saul started using the name of Paul just after he became acquainted with Sergius Paulus Acts 13:7,9. Saul/ Paul would have been bearing the Lord’s name to the Gentiles by working in close coordination with the Apostles, but this too he refused to do.

Cherub_ asked this follow-up question.:

> James,
>
> The twelve foundations of Heaven which are numbered twelve for the apostles, whose names will be borne on each foundation?
>
> Judas, a man chosen of Christ
>
> Matthias, the man received by vote
>
> Paul, the man chosen by Jesus Christ.
>
> ~cherub‘

James gave this follow-up answer.

MATTHIAS!

Acts 1:23 And they appointed two, Joseph called Barsabas, who was surnamed Justus, and Matthias. (24) And they prayed, and said, Thou, Lord, which knowest the hearts of all men, show whether of these two THOU HAST CHOSEN, (25) That he may take part of this MINISTRY AND APOSTLESHIP, from which Judas by transgression fell, that he might go to his own place. (26) And they gave forth their lots; and the lot fell upon Matthias; AND HE WAS NUMBERED WITH THE ELEVEN APOSTLES.

If it had not been for Paul/Saul's forcefulness, the world would have known less about God and the name of His Son Jesus. Through Paul we also can see more of the shortcomings in the nature of us all.

****

Mental Health 'Stark Scenario for'

Lonnie asked this question.

Hello,

Despite impressive medical advances in many aspects of health care, notes an article published in Synergy, a newsletter of the Canadian Society for International Health, we face a stark global scenario for mental health. One report concluded that 1 out of 4 people worldwide suffers from mental, emotional, or behavioral disorders.

Another study indicated that 1 out of 3 patients seeing a health worker does so because of suffering from depression or anxiety problems. And those numbers, say researchers, are increasing.

Why? A study conducted by Harvard University's Department of Social Medicine notes that such illnesses as clinical depression, schizophrenia, and dementia are multiplying because more people live to the age of risk. However, living longer is not the only reason. Economic problems are also to blame, as is the increased stress of modern living.

How can this gloomy picture be changed? Does the Bible hold out hope for those who suffer from Mental illness? What care has God placed for these ones? Can we as humans change the way these ones are cared for, or is God the only one that can change their outlook in life?

Peace be with you, Judona :0)

James gave this response.

Saint Louis 1960

Great floods of fear came over Jim as another pang took hold of his brain. They won't get me; my coat. I must run, quickly, my coat. I have to leave here.

Where will you go? Ruby asked.

Jim ran to the closet, yanked the coat from the hanger and turned for the door. With the coat halfway on, he grabbed at the knob, but with that movement came the realization that he had no place else to run. Not knowing where to go he felt like a trapped animal; the wall the wall. He jumped for the top of the door facing. He couldn't reach it. He must climb the wall. The hurt, the fear, he could not rid himself of it. Another pang of fear made a jab at his brain. He grabbed his hair with both hands. He must get it out; all of it. He pulled and tugged. It made his brain feel better. Twisting his hands from side to side, why won't it come out?

Tears were streaming down Ruby's face. A voice spoke with her. GO CAST THE DEVIL OUT OF HIM.

I can't. I don't know how, she said. But what else was there to do? How else would the end come to this?

Ruby was standing beside him. She said, DEVIL, COME OUT OF THIS MAN THROUGH THE NAME OF JESUS.

Jim's body fell to the floor. It lay limp and motionless. He looked at his hands. There were strands of hair between each finger. He felt his head. All of his hair had not been taken.

Fear was gone for a while. He walked over to the bed, relaxed upon his back. Just like the undulations of the ocean waves, another one was coming. He wouldn't dare stop calling upon the Name of the Lord. It was his only chance to live, and be free of himself.

Jim knew he could not continue that way. Help was needed. Ruby said to her brother, Eldon, He says he needs help.

Do you want to go to the hospital? Eldon said.

No, I want to go to a church. NOW! Jim said urgently.

Eldon was parked along side the church when the minister unlocked the door. He explained the problem to the preacher, and by the time everyone was inside the church, about six saints had arrived. The preacher stood in the middle of the group and said,

The Lord tells me this man is to go all the way.

The saints had gathered around Jim, and as the minister laid hands on his head, the same vehicle took hold of his body that Jim thought was epilepsy before. He was thrown to the floor, right in the middle of the church. He began to squirm, calling upon Jesus. All of a sudden the words were spoken direct to his mind.

HERE IS THE HOLY GHOST, THE TONGUES WILL COME LATER.

The preacher stood up again and said,

THIS MAN NEEDS WATER BAPTISM.

Old clothes were available for baptismal services. They were borrowed, and the whole group paraded down the steps to the basement where the baptistry was located. Eldon and Ruby (Ruth) decided to be baptized along with Jim (James). They each held their breath as they were submerged backwards in the Name of Jesus.

Arizona 1961:

James stood in the aisle at the end of the benches. It was during the time of praise. His tongue began to form words which he did not understand. He listened. He didn't know what he was saying. He had no control over his tongue. He did try to have control. He wanted to be sure that it was the tongues. He remembered the words that were spoken with him while in the floor of the church in Saint Louis. 'HERE IS THE HOLY GHOST THE TONGUES WILL COME LATER.'

Time continued to another day: The service progressed. People's minds and voices began to blend together. Lightness of spirit prevailed. It was the afternoon service. They spoke with tongues, others interpreted. A man's voice rang loud and clear, which said, IF YOU DON'T RECEIVE THE FILLING OF THE SPIRIT YOU WILL FALL.

About three hundred people moved forward. Ruth and James were there. Each was instructed to touch the person in front of them, on the shoulder or back. James had had the lamp all along, but he like the foolish virgins found himself short of oil. He was now in the store house of them that had to sell. It was like a large pitcher tipping to spill into his lamp, until the pitcher was emptied and James was full. His eyes then could see on both sides of the fence. Evil was not the only thing directed to his attention. His physical body and mind could then withstand insanity that was all around. He could even control himself.

Mental problems are corrected by the gifts of the spirit. Those spiritual gifts are necessary for people to move back into Paradise (second heaven state), where man had originally been placed.

Physical defects caused by accidents or the malfunction of the physical body caused by generations of degraded humanity may need the assistance of medical science. Without gene manipulation a second leg or additional sets of teeth will not be replaced.

God does not mind if we know and understand.

****

Mind control:

Charlene asked this question.

Does God control the mind when all the spiritual gifts are received by an individual?

James gave this response.

No!

Humanity will always have their own free will to think and do anything they want to do. When they do wrong, their conscience is affected, which disrupts the physical operation of the body.

If they do right their mind is free and light, allowing it to perform its natural duties of maintaining the bodily functions.

The spiritual gifts help the mind and gives strength to control the thinking, if the individual wants it controlled.

Even with the spiritual gifts, if a person continues to think of doing certain things, they will be doing them in time. If they are wrong acts, the perpetrator, after the commission of the deed, may say, I don't know what made me do it.

It was the previous thoughts that became part of the subconscious force that compelled the doing of the act.

It was NOT AN INDIVIDUAL DEVIL. It was the product of the thoughts.

So we should not dwell on anything wrong, whether they are vices (immoral habits, depravity) or any other criminal acts. For in doing so we invite the doing of the thing imagined.

Stop the mind from thinking about such things, and the subconscious area of the brain will guide our lives by the flow of the spirit and the guidance of the Holy Ghost.

Without the Holy Ghost, and the holy spirit of God, it requires a continuous striving by the person to control the thoughts. There is no let up. With the help of the spirit we can, but it is something we have to do. The right way is not forced upon us. God made no robots.

This is the price of having freedom of choice. God was aware of this potential weakness in the mental structure. That is the reason for the formula—Call upon the Name of God—and place God's name in the mind instead of destructive thoughts. This is the road back to Paradise.

****

Minds of men.

Anonymous asked this question.

WHY HAVE THE MINDS OF MEN BECOME WEAK?

In the beginning the operation of the human mind was comparable to the quickness of the spirit. But over the process of time the mind has become weakened.

Men have refused to call upon the Name of the Lord. When Adam's Grandson, Enos, was born, then men began to call upon the Name of the Lord. (Gen. 4:26) Enos lived 905 years. Others, down through time have advocated it, but when the waves of life became turbulent they have always forgotten, primarily because of doubt and lack of faith. (Matthew 14:31).

Faith is increased when calling upon the Name of the Lord. Because of this refusal to adhere to the name of God, the minds have become weakened and those infirmities have been transferred to the offspring through the genetic process.

Since the first man and woman would not call upon the name of the Lord for strength to conform to the will of God, they began to be weakened by the physical actions they saw in the other animals around them. Since their minds originally were tuned in to the spirit, they knew by that God given instinct that they, being the son and daughter of God, should not perform as the other animals did for the purpose of propagating the world with human life.

Because of the guilt advanced by their actions, the power of God was driven out of their spiritual system, and the depression, which took its place, caused their bodies to be drawn toward their ultimate demise. A part of that death process was the usage of various drugs to nullify their deep feelings of despair.

To drive out guilt, men and women must be filled with the holy spirit of God. Without that spirit, their beings become filled with many other weaknesses they observe around them.

Eph. 5:28—Be not drunk with wine, wherein is excess; but be filled with the Spirit.

Luke 1:15 For he (John) shall be great in the sight of the Lord, and shall drink neither wine nor strong drink; and he shall be filled with the Holy Ghost, even from his mother's womb.

Acts 2:4—They were all filled with the Holy Ghost—.

But even then, every time God has turned his back, men have forgotten. Men should remember always to call upon the Name of God to maintain sufficient faith and strength to conform to the will of God even when it seems that God as an individual is nowhere to be felt.

Why did Jesus drink wine? Jesus came to the earth to experience all the weaknesses in the human body so that he could prescribe the remedy for the retrieval of all mankind. Isaiah 52:14—His visage was so marred more than any man, and his form more than the sons of men.

Hebrews 4:15 (Jesus) was in ALL POINTS TEMPTED like as we are, yet without sin.

After determining that the human body needed the water of life (holy spirit) flowing from his inner being (out of his belly—John 7:38-39) he said, (John 14:16)—I will pray the Father, and he shall give you another Comforter, (Holy Ghost) that he may abide with you for ever—.

God is not a tyrant to stand above his victims and punish evil for evil as Moses did. The human race is God's invention. His fondest desire is that they prosper and be in health, physically, mentally and spiritually. He wants people to come into the knowledge of His Name and live peacefully among themselves, and with a sound mind.

When people are out of focus with God, their own minds lead them into destruction.

****

Money—Conscience

Zenaide asked this question.

BY GIVING MONEY can our conscience be relieved?

James gave this response.

NO! The power of God (Christ) through God's Name (Jesus)is the only thing that can relieve the mind of past sins, and we cannot buy that power with money. Matthew 9:6—That ye may know that the Son of man hath power on earth to forgive sins.

Acts 8:18 (closely related incident) When Simon saw through laying on of the apostles hands the Holy Ghost was given, he offered them money, (19) Saying, Give me also this power, that on whomsoever I lay hands, he may receive the Holy Ghost. (20) But Peter said unto him, Thy money perish with thee, because thou hast thought that the gift of God may be purchased with money.

Should we 'WILL' our property to a church for the WORK of God?

NO! (John 6:29) Jesus answered and said unto them THIS IS THE WORK OF GOD, that ye believe on him (Jesus) whom he (God) hath sent.

Jesus also did not say sell your property and bring the proceeds to me. Instead, he said, (Matthew 19:21 If thou wilt be perfect, go and sell that thou hast, ***and give to the poor***, and thou shalt have treasure in heaven: ***and come and follow me.*** Also Mark 10:21.

Anybody that states or implies (expresses indirectly) that we will have a better place in heaven if we 'WILL' or give them anything of a monetary (relating to money) nature, do not understand what heaven is. In the first place they have forgotten that originally Heaven (Paradise) was here on the earth and that is where it must be established again.

The church, however large or small, represents people coming together to interchange the power of God between themselves for more spiritual and ultimately physical and mental strength.

Pooling money for the purchase and upkeep of a meeting house is understandable and desirable, although this was not true in the beginning of the church. They met primarily in homes. Jesus repeatedly taught in the Synagogues and healed the servant of a centurion who had built a synagogue for the people. It was primarily because of the centurion's faith that Jesus healed his servant. Luke 7:2-10

But the times of fleecing the people of millions of dollars for use on the whims of greedy men have come to a halt.

The people's understanding is being enlightened.

****

MORONI

Aservant asked this question.

Is the angel Moroni ever mentioned in literature besides that of Joseph smith? why should I believe he appeared to joseph if there were no witnesses? And if what he said is in contradiction to the new testament, even if he WERE an angel from heaven, must I believe him?

Now, saints, the important question: Do you know of any such contradictions?—even one? Just one sentence from Mormonism that is in direct contradiction to the apostles of Jesus? let's be sure we have a reason for the things we most surely believe.

James gave this response.

The minister stood behind the bible stand with the book open before him. Words came forth from his lips as the eyes followed the lines of print.

This is my beloved Son, in whom I am well pleased, HEAR YE HIM.

Ears heard those words. They were young ears belonging to a man in the congregation. He also later read those passages along with many others from a book just like the minister used. (The Bible)

One day this young man had a fever. He tried to climb over a fence, at which time he could hardly make it because of his sickness. He fell to the ground. Through his hot feverish mind and eyes he saw two personages. The one pointed toward the other and said, This is my beloved Son, in whom I am well pleased, HEAR YE HIM.

What caused the vision?

The words that had been heard and read!

Was this God speaking about his only begotten Son?

Yes!

Some time later the same boy saw an angel. This angel told him of a book that was under a rock. The boy was instructed by the angel not to look at the book for a year. As young as he was he could not comprehend all that was transpiring around him, so he conferred with his natural father.

"Father," he asked, "Is this vision of the angel from God?"

The father answered, "Yes son, it is of God."

The boy had been told implicitly (complete and unquestioning) who to hear but he listened to his natural father instead.

All religions do some good and have truth in varying degrees. We need all the churches and we should be kind to one another in our trek toward the full understanding of the truth. That truth lives with God's only begotten son, NO ONE ELSE.

Jesus came to the earth bearing HIS FATHER'S NAME for placement in the foreheads (Rev. 7:3) of human inhabitants on the earth.

Christ is the light which lighteth every man that cometh into the world. (John 1:9) Call upon the Name of God, Jesus(Joel 2:32, Zeph 3:9, Zech 13:9, Acts 2:21, Rom. 10:13), and let the light overflow from the innermost parts of the belly. (John 7:38 as water)

Jesus said, (John 17:12) While I was with them in the world, I kept them in THY NAME—, I pray not that thou shouldest take them out of the world, but that thou shouldest keep them from the evil—(John 17:15).

The only way to avoid falsehoods is to stay in God's Name continually. When drifting away from the handle of God the destructive elements take over and lead into all manner of imaginations.

The book was seen by only one person then the angel took it away.

Jesus said, (John 5:31) If I bear witness of myself, my witness is not true.

Jesus said, (John 8:17) It is also written in your law, that the testimony of two men is true.

Aservant rated this answer:

I'm sure you meant to say God's WORD, not God's NAME. Of course, that name is JESUS. But it is HIS WORD that sets us apart.

James gave this follow-up answer.

Revelation 19:13 And he was clothed with a vesture dipped in blood:

AND HIS NAME IS CALLED THE WORD OF GOD.

What has been written remains.

In the beginning was the Word—and the Word was God.

The WORD WAS HIS NAME, not the Bible. There was no Bible at that time.

****

Moses and Muslim Bible

a servant asked this question.

I am in full agreement with those trying to spare innocent Muslims from our normal way of "racial profiling" in America. God help us to love every created being of God. Nevertheless, it is my understanding that the Muslim Bible does indeed contain directives for Muslims that involve the destruction—militarily, in the flesh—of all enemies. Could someone point me to those quotations, or a source that I could check for them? I happen to be a fundamentalist in things Christian. I believe that every single word from God is normative for every believer. I know that mine is a minority view, and I live with that. majorities don't bother me any more.

And though the Muslims who attempt to destroy us are in the minority, are they not in the "normative" position of Islam? I mean, are they not simply obeying their "good book" ? Please supply me with quotes in either direction or direct me to the proper source. (This is one of those questions I really desire an answer to, not trying to start an online war!)

Locust eaters gave this response.

(Surah 9:5,29,41) Slay the infidels wherever ye find them, and take them, and besiege them, and prepare for them each ambush . . . . Fight against such of those who have been given the Scripture as believe not in Allah nor the last day . . . Go forth, light-armed and heavy-armed, and strive with your wealth and your lives in the way of Allah!

James gave this response.

WHAT ABOUT US?

When Moses came down the mountain with the commandments, of which one of those passages stated '***Thou shalt not kill***,' he was very disturbed when he understood that the people were worshiping a golden calf. (Exod. 32:3) MOSES THOUGHT HE WAS DOING GOD SERVICE. (Exo.32:10, John 16:2-3) (He did not understand that vengeance belongs to God and that God would take care of it in time.) Deut. 32:35, Psalm 94:1, Heb. 10:30,

He threw the commandments down (Exo. 32:19)and remembering what God had said he was going to do,(10) gave his own instructions. He said, (27)—Put every man his sword by his side, and go in an out from gate to gate throughout the camp, and slay every man his brother, and every man his companion, and every man his neighbor. (28) And the children of Levi did according to the WORD of MOSES: and there fell of the people that day about three thousand men.

Moses wrote: Exodus 21:24 Eye for eye, tooth for tooth hand for hand, foot for foot. (25) Burning for burning, wound for wound, stripe for stripe.

God had confirmed the commandments but Moses compiled the penalties. John 1:17.

Jesus said, (Matt. 5:38) Ye have heard that it hath been said an eye for an eye, and a tooth for a tooth. (43) Ye have heard that it hath been said, Thou shalt love thy neighbor, and hate thine enemy. (44) But I say unto you, Love your enemies—.

Jesus said, (John 10:8) ALL THAT EVER came before me are thieves and robbers,—(10) The thief cometh not, but for to steal, and to kill, and to destroy: I am come that they might have life—.

There is only one true God. And under that one deity many religions have developed. They have all been influenced by the minds of men that have been confused ever since the confounding of the languages at the time of the tower of Babel. (Gen. 11:9) Why did they become confused? They wanted to make a name for themselves.

(Gen. 11:4) God wants all nationalities and religions to know his Name and the Name of His son.

Proverbs 30:4 Who hath ascended up into heaven, or descended? (John 3:13) Who hath gathered the wind in his fist? Who hath bound the waters in a garment? Who hath established all the ends of the earth? What is HIS NAME, and what is HIS SON'S NAME, if thou canst tell.

As there are many colors in the rain bow and in the flowers, so men have become many nationalities and shades of color. Take a look at them. Everyone is beautiful. The black and the white and every shade in between. They are all trying to reach God in the only way they have individually understood.

When they find out what God's true saving name is they will call upon it and be saved from the destructive elements of the earth and the negative thoughts of men.

Zeph. 3:9 For then will I (God) turn to the people a pure language, that they may ALL CALL UPON THE NAME OF THE LORD, to serve him with one consent.

The name of God was delivered to the world by His Son. He said, I am come in my Father's Name—(John 5:43).

Acts 4:12 Neither is there salvation in any other: for there is none other NAME under heaven given among men, whereby we must be saved. 1 Tim. 2:5—There is ONE GOD, and one mediator between God and men—. What is that mediator's Name if thou canst tell.

If it is known—call upon it for It shall come to pass that, that WHOSOEVER, shall call on the Name of the Lord shall be saved. (Acts 2:21, Rom. 10:13).

****

Moses a terrorist ?

aservant asked this question.

Maybe I shouldn't keep following board folks down these rabbit trails, but i was a bit amazed to find a response to my query in which a writer actually compared the terrorism of fundamentalist muslims to the persons in the Bible who came against accursed nations and disobedient Jews. They say Moses should not have slain the calf-worshipers at Sinai, David and the rest should not have come against the canaanite nations etc. Is this your thought too? Is there not a TRUE GOD who issues TRUE commands to judge TRUE sin? Shall not that same God judge the world with fire that will make the 11th seem like a Scouting trip campfire? Should we not see Jesus' GREAT MERCY with a backdrop of this truly JUDGING and HOLY GOD? Have we not been SPARED HIS WRATH if we know Jesus? Has God not always been a HOLY WRATHFUL person and have we not always deserved his judgment? Did the New Testament reveal a different God or one who desperately wanted to FORGIVE us? and for goodness' sake, is there ANY way that all of this compares to Tuesday, when the directions were supposedly given by a 7th century moon god?

James gave this response.

The LORD said to Moses,

Exodus 32:10 (The LORD said) ***Now therefore let me alone, that my wrath may wax hot against them,*** and that I may consume them—.

Exo. 32:11-14 Moses talked God out of consuming the people.

Then the LORD repented of the evil which he thought to do unto his people. (clue: Num. 23:19)

Who's anger waxed hot?

Then (Exo. 32:19) ***MOSES' ANGER WAXED HOT***, and he cast the tables out of his hands, and brake them beneath the mount. (Moses literally broke the tables of stone, then he broke the commandment as it was written, namely, Thou shalt not Kill. (Exo. 20:13.)

Moses did not wait for God's judgment. He dispensed judgment himself. He thought he was doing God service. (Check John 16:2 These were also following Moses as an example)—the time cometh, that whosoever killeth you ***will think that he doeth God service.***

Deut 32:35 To Me (GOD) belongeth vengeance, and recompense; ***their foot shall slide in due time—.***

Rom. 12:19 Avenge not yourselves, but rather give place unto wrath—.

I pray that God will open the eyes of the people so that they will be able to understand these simple facts and stop all this violence. What a person sees in someone else or a deity, is reflected back into themselves. It should be plain to see that the compassion that was in Jesus was a reflection of His Father God that was in him. That loving God was in the process of reconciling the world unto himself by his love, kindness and forgiveness that he extended to them through His Son.

Luke 22:66 The elders, the chief priests and the scribes asked Jesus (67) Art thou the Christ? Tell us. And Jesus said unto them, If I tell you, ye will not believe.

Jesus said, (John 3:12) If I have told you of earthly things, and ye believe not, how shall ye believe, if I tell you of heavenly things.

Jesus said to Peter, (Matthew 26:52) Put up again thy sword into his place: ***for ALL they that take the sword shall perish with the sword.***

Jesus said, (Matthew 5:38) Ye have heard that it hath been said, an eye for an eye, and a tooth for a tooth. (39) But I say unto you, That ye resist not evil—. (43) Ye have heard that it hath been said, Thou shalt love thy neighbor, and hate thine enemy. (44) But I say unto you, Love your enemies—.

These statements and many more that conformed to the commandments were made by Jesus approximately two thousand years ago.

HAS ANYONE HEARD HIM YET?

John 1:17 The law was given by Moses, but GRACE (unmerited divine assistance) and TRUTH came by Jesus Christ.

Acts 15:21 For Moses of old time hath in every city them that preach him, being read in the synagogues every sabbath day.

(***This continues even in the Christian churches***).

Matthew 17:4 Peter said to Jesus, Let us make here three tabernacles; one for thee, and ***one for Moses***, and one for Elias.

(5) A voice said, This is my beloved Son,—hear ye him. Then they saw no man, save ***JESUS ONLY***. (9) This was a vision.

Words alone cannot change the heart of men. It takes a re-birth of the spirit. This Jesus also said. John 3:3 Except a man be born again he cannot see the Kingdom of God.

Proverbs 21:2 Every way of a (natural) man is right in his own eyes: but the Lord pondereth the hearts.

1 Cor. 2:14 The natural man receiveth not the things of the Spirit of God: for they are foolishness unto him: neither can he know them, because they are spiritually discerned.

What must we do to be SAVED from the violence in the world and the devastation caused by the minds of men?

Acts 2:21 It shall come to pass, that WHOSOEVER shall call on the Name of the Lord shall be SAVED.

That is all we can do—the spiritual changes will be done by God.

****

Moses', original words?

Question answered by James.

jdg31743 asked this question.

What were the original words brought together by Moses and inspired by God.

James gave this response.

(Job 32:8—there is a spirit in man: and the inspiration of the Almighty giveth them understanding.

2 Tim 3:16 All scripture is given by inspiration of God—).

GOD SPEAKS FIRST

Exodus 20:4 Thou shalt not make unto thee any GRAVEN image OR ANY LIKENESS OF ANYTHING THAT IS IN THE HEAVEN ABOVE, OR THAT IS IN THE EARTH BENEATH, OR THAT IS IN THE WATER UNDER THE EARTH.

What is the difference between the molten calf made of gold, which was the LIKENESS OF SOMETHING THAT IS IN THE EARTH—AND THE CHERUBIMS THAT WAS THE

LIKENESS OF SOMETHING IN HEAVEN? Was it only because it was graven? No! Because here again the word 'OR' was used. OR ANY LIKENESS OF ANYTHING.

The Cherubims were first mentioned in the Garden of Eden which can be likened unto Paradise, or second heaven as described by Paul—(2 Cor. 12:2-4). It depicted the SPIRITUAL STATE where Adamah and woman had been placed at the time of their creation. (2 Cor. 12:2 Up TO third heaven, not INTO. 2 Cor. 12:4 INTO Paradise (a second heaven spiritual place where Adamah and woman were placed.). The third heaven is where God and the angels reside. Paul did not go into the third heaven because no man, in his physical body can live there. He was in the second heaven state and he only heard things that were not lawful for man to utter at that time.

But Adam did not call upon God. He and his wife together began to eat of the tree of knowledge of evil. Their conscience began to hurt, and they became weakened.

Gen 3:24 So he drove out the man; and he placed at the east of the garden of Eden Cherubims, and a flaming sword which turned every way, to KEEP THE WAY OF THE TREE OF LIFE.

The flaming sword was the 'WORD' that stated, 'Thou shalt not. If you do, your conscience will drive you from that heavenly state.

The Cherubims were the angels placed in second heaven expressly for guarding, protecting and ensuring continuous life for those that chose to live in that spiritual state.

IT WAS NEVER INTENDED THAT THESE ANGELS (Cherubims) be reduced to images of beaten gold created by the hands of a man.

Well, why did God tell Moses to make those cherubims? (God

knew they didn't need it but they wanted it so he gave it to them)

Exo. 25:18 And thou shalt make two cherubims of Gold, of beaten work shalt thou make them—. (22) And there I will meet with thee, and I will commune with thee from above the mercy seat,—.

God has always tried to help man. On many occasions he had to stoop very low. In this case he had to meet man between two idols, of which thing he hates. Even lower did he stoop when he sent his beloved son into such a drunken violent world.

Doesn't it seem unusual that Jesus never spoke of the Cherubims? Isn't it even more unusual that none of the Apostles wrote of them? Neither Jesus, the Apostles, the Holy Ghost of God said anything about the cherubims in the New Testament. Only on one occasion Saul mentioned them. (not one of the men Jesus named Apostles even hinted of their existence. Luke 6:13).

(Saul-Paul wrote) Heb. 9:5. And over it the Cherubims of glory shadowing the mercy seat; of which we cannot now speak particularly.

So then how important was the cherubims as constructed by Moses? If they were important to God, why don't we have them yet today? What happened to them?

Ref. Dic. Bible, Wm. Smith Teacher's edition.

(The Ark of the Covenant)—was probably taken captive or destroyed by Nebuchadnezzar, so there was no ark in the second temple.

Ref: The New English Bible with Apocrypha.

Esdras 10:22—the Ark of our covenant has been taken spoil;—

Ref: 1 Sam. 4:11 And the ark of God was taken.

CAN MAN STEAL FROM GOD? OR CAN MAN DESTROY GOD'S SPIRITUAL WORK?

****

Mountain and Fig Tree:

Maxine asked this question.

By faith do fig trees die and mountains tumble into the sea?

James gave this response.

NO, SYMBOLIC MOUNTAINS CRUMBLE AND DISINTEGRATE INTO NOTHING.

God through Jesus and his disciples healed the sick. (Matthew 8:13, 8:16, 14:14, Mark 1:34)

Matthew 4:23 And Jesus went about all Galilee, teaching in their synagogues, and preaching the gospel of the kingdom, AND HEALING ALL MANNER OF SICKNESS AND ALL MANNER OF DISEASES among the people.

But the power of God does not work without the faith and belief of the people. In Jesus' own country (Mark 6:5) he could there do no mighty work, save that he laid his hands upon a few sick folk and healed them. (6) And he marvelled because of their unbelief.—.

Matthew 17:16 A man brought his Lunatic son to Jesus and said "I brought him to thy disciples and they could not cure him?

JESUS HEALED HIM

Matthew 17:19 Then came the disciples to Jesus apart, and said, Why could not we cast him out?" (20) And Jesus said unto them, Because of your UNBELIEF: for verily I say unto you, If ye have FAITH as a grain of mustard seed, ye shall say unto THIS MOUNTAIN, Remove hence to yonder place; and it shall remove—.

FAITH OF THE PEOPLE

Matthew 9:20-22 Jesus said to the woman that had the blood disease, "Daughter, be of good comfort; THY FAITH hath made thee whole.

Matthew 9:27 Two blind men came to Jesus. Jesus said unto them, "Believe ye that I am able to do this? They said unto him, Yea, Lord. (29) Then touched he their eyes, saying, "According to YOUR FAITH be it unto you."

The disciples observed the wilting leaves of the Fig Tree. Matthew 21:20 And when the disciples saw it, they marveled, saying, How soon is the fig tree withered away! (21) Jesus answered and said unto them, Verily I say unto you, If ye have faith, and doubt not, ye shall not only do this which is done to the fig tree, but also if ye shall say unto this mountain, Be thou removed and be thou cast into the sea; it shall be done.

THE FIG TREE DIED, BUT THE MOUNTAINS STILL STAND. THEY ARE THE MOUNTAINS OF DISEASES THAT ARE BEING DESTROYED BY FAITH IN GOD AND SCIENCE. The word faith is used only twice in the Old Testament, but in the New Testament there are many witnesses other than Matthew that emphasize its importance.

Jesus sometimes used parables and without a parable spake he not unto them (the multitude). Matthew 21:21.

PARABLE: Simple story illustrating a moral truth.

When we were in Jerusalem in 1985 I looked around to make sure nobody was looking, then I said to the Fig tree, (Matt.21:19, Mark 1;14) Let no fruit grow on thee henceforward for ever, but I didn't go back the next day to see if the leaves had withered.

****

Musical Instruments

Why do some churches disallow musical instruments in their meetings?

James gave this response.

Jubal was the descendant of Cain through Lamech. This entire unrighteous line became extinct with the advent of the flood. All of Cain's offspring was lost during that time.

Jubal was the inventor of music, organ, and harp.

This was the primary reason Jesus, along with all of the apostles did not use or mention the playing of instruments during the time of their assemblages. They did sing hymns. Matthew 26:30, And when they had sung an hymn, they went out into the mount of Olives. Second witness: Mark 14:26.

Music affects the emotions through the ear drums which are connected directly to the brain. There is no connection with the holy spirit of God. It cannot attract nor repel the operation of God's spirit. The same as closing of the eyes and chanting with forced concentration cannot summon God's spiritual forces. These physical acts only excite the imagination.

Music alone can do little in producing either good or evil thoughts. The words along with the music, when understood, can produce thoughts which may lead to the acts of destruction or the building up of a serene emotional superstructure (mental foundation).

1 John 3:4 Sin is the transgression of the law.

John 8:34 Jesus (said),—I say unto you, whosoever committeth sin is the servant of sin.

What law is broken by playing or listening to music? But if the lyrics (words of a song) lead to the act of sin, then it becomes a transgression.

Romans 14:22—Happy is he that condemneth not himself in that thing which he alloweth. Romans 14: 23 Whatsoever is not of faith is sin.

Bread may be produced by atheists, or individuals of an unrighteous heritage, but it is no sin to eat bread. Jesus said, (Matthew 6:11) Give us this day our daily bread. This can be applied to both spiritual and physical bread.

Men were given dominion over all the earth (Gen. 1:26). They are the sons of God. As God creates so men have the ability to create. They are allowed to enjoy the products of their creations. Freedom is achieved by faith and is enjoyed by those that are filled with the holy spirit of God and his power of Christ.

Romans 8:14 For as many as are led by the Spirit of God, they are the sons of God. (15) For ye have not received the spirit of BONDAGE again to fear; but ye have received the Spirit of adoption, whereby we cry, Abba, Father.

There is freedom in Christ to do anything and everything as long as it does not incur harm to one's own self or to any other person.

The words of natural men subject the mind to bondage and condemnation. These things ought not so to be.

If you want music, go ahead, based upon many instances in the Old Testament, but music was not used in the New among the apostles or Jesus. We still read the Psalms, but generally music is not added as David did.

A person usually knows what they want to believe before they do the research. All the churches, except one, we have attended use musical instruments in their meetings.

If a person wants to prove to their satisfaction that musical instruments are condoned by the New Testament all they need to do is consider the word psalms. Then stretch their imagination.

Strong's Concordance under the definition of the original Greek word:

psallo 5567 To rub or touch the surface, to twitch or twang, i.e. to play on a stringed instrument. Celebrate the divine worship with music. Twang, i.e. to play on a stringed instrument.

5568: psalmos. From 5567, . . . music, i.e. accompanied with harp or other instrument.

New Testament

The following three passages are by Paul who was influenced by the Pharisees religion.

1Cor 14.26: 'psalm' 5568. (hath a psalm)

Eph 5.19: 'psalms'5568, 'melody'5567. (Singing)

Col 3.16: 'psalms'5568. (singing)

Jas 5.13: 'psalms' 5567. (sing)

Is any among you afflicted? let him pray. Is any merry? let him SING psalms.

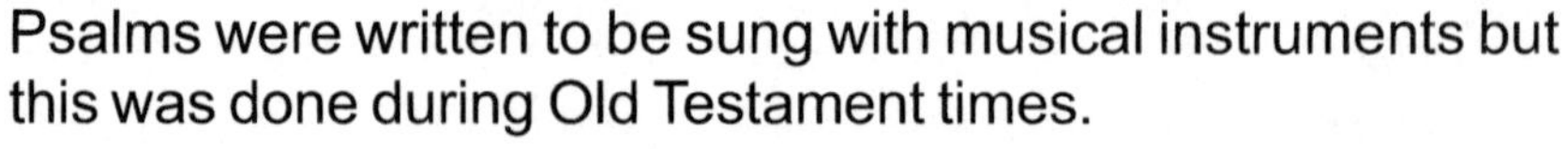

Psalms were written to be sung with musical instruments but this was done during Old Testament times.

****

It should be made very clear that I do not condone or reject music during the time of assembly, it is immaterial.

If the Son therefore shall make you free, ye shall be free indeed.

John 8:36.Stand fast therefore in the liberty wherewith Christ hath made us free, and be not entangled again with the yoke of bondage. Galatians 5:1.

****

Name of God, Faith in the

Edward asked this question.

WHAT CAN FAITH IN JESUS AS THE NAME OF GOD, DO?

James gave this response.

Matthew 9:28 (two blind men)—Jesus said, Believe ye that I am able to do this? They said unto him, yes, Lord. (29) Then touched he their eyes, saying, ACCORDING TO YOUR FAITH BE IT UNTO YOU, (30) And their eyes were opened—.

Luke 17:19 (one of the ten lepers) And he said unto him, arise, go thy way: THY FAITH HATH MADE THEE WHOLE.

Matthew 9:22 (The woman with the issue of blood for twelve years) But Jesus turned him about, and when he saw her he said, Daughter, be of good comfort—THY FAITH HATH MADE THEE WHOLE.

Luke 7:50 (A sinful woman in the city washed Jesus' feet) And he (Jesus) said to the woman, THY FAITH HATH SAVED THEE—.

Luke 18:42 (a blind man at Jericho) And Jesus said unto him, Receive thy sight: THY FAITH HATH SAVED THEE.

Eph. 3:17 That Christ may dwell in your hearts BY FAITH,—(20) unto him that is able to do exceeding abundantly above all that we ask or think—.

Mark 9:23 Jesus said unto him (one of the multitude regarding his son) If thou canst believe, all things are possible to him that believeth. (24) And straightway the father of the child cried out, and said with tears, Lord, I believe; HELP THOU MINE UNBELIEF.

Matthew 15:28—O Woman, GREAT IS THY FAITH: be it unto thee even as thou wilt. And her daughter was made whole from that very hour.

ALL OF THOSE AND MANY OTHER 'WORKS OF APPARENT MIRACLES' WERE CAUSED BY FAITH IN JESUS—FAITH IN ANYTHING ELSE DOES NOT HAVE A LASTING EFFECT. THERE IS ONLY ONE MEDIATOR BETWEEN GOD AND MEN.

1 Tim. 2:5 For there is ONE GOD and ONE MEDIATOR between GOD AND MEN, the MAN CHRIST JESUS, WHO GAVE HIMSELF A RANSOM FOR ALL TO BE TESTIFIED IN DUE TIME.

****

Name of God—Wrong way?

Edward asked this question.

Is there a wrong way to call upon the Name of the Lord?

James gave this response.

PEVELY MISSOURI

The man went into the bath room and filled his hands with water. He washed his face. The water felt good. The towel was in his hands. He dried. A voice came to his ears. It spoke clearly—.

“YES, I HAVE SPOKEN WITH YOU, BUT THE DEVIL (the man’s own thoughts) HAS TALKED WITH YOU TOO. FROM NOW ON YOU WILL HAVE WISDOM ENOUGH TO KNOW THE DIFFERENCE. YES, THAT IS WHAT I TOLD ADAM TO DO IN THE BEGINNING, BUT NOT THE WAY YOU ARE TRYING TO DO IT. IT HAS BEEN HYPNOTIZING YOU.”

“Well I’ll be,” James said to himself, “so that’s it. I have been doing it wrong.” Until that moment he had been imagining a streak of light going up from above his left eye into his brain, then a streak going up from over his right eye back into his brain, in rhythmic motion that happened, each time he said Jesus with his inner voice. He had been hypnotizing himself.

December l960

It was the last time God had spoken with James. Other than God, previously, all the other voices came from his own mind. It could have been either right or wrong, depending on the truthfulness of the knowledge stored in his brain. The information came from what Jim had heard, thought, said, done and read. James had not been taken over by the spirit of John or Peter or anyone else. He was only being hypnotized to what he had read in the Bible.

God seldom speaks with men. Most voices heard are derived from weakened minds. That weakness can be the product of the lack of minerals and vitamins, drug use, diseases of many kinds, and hereditary gene malfunctions.

THIS STILL REMAINS!

Luke 18:7 And shall not God avenge his own elect, which cry day and night unto him, though he bear long with them? (8) I tell you that he will avenge them speedily.

Psalms 113:3 From the rising of the sun unto the going down of the same the Lord's Name is to be praised. (4) The Lord is high above all Nations.

Acts 2:21 And it shall come to pass, that WHOSOEVER shall call on the Name of the Lord shall be saved. DO IT THE RIGHT WAY! And be saved from the destructive elements of the world and minds.

****

Name, Early Church calling on :

jdg asked this question.

WERE THE PEOPLE OF THE EARLY CHURCH AWARE OF THE NEED FOR CALLING UPON THE NAME OF THE LORD?

James gave this response.

YES! Joel 2:32 And it shall come to pass, that WHOSOEVER shall call on the Name of the Lord shall be delivered.

This passage was referred to in—Acts 2:21 And it shall come to pass, that WHOSOEVER shall call on the Name of the Lord shall be saved.

And again Saul (Paul) referred to it in—Romans 10:13

For whosoever shall call upon the Name of the Lord shall be saved.

THE PEOPLE BEGAN TO HEAR THIS PREACHING, and they exercised that privilege of Calling Upon the Name of the Lord at Jerusalem, Damascus, Corinth, and in every place. (1 Cor. 1:2)

Acts 9:14 And here he (Saul) hath authority from the chief priests (at Jerusalem) to bind all that CALL ON THY NAME. (He was going to use that authority in Damascus).

1 Cor. 1:2 Unto the church of God which is at Corinth, to them that are sanctified in Christ Jesus, called to be saints, with ALL THAT IN EVERY PLACE CALL UPON THE NAME OF JESUS CHRIST OUR LORD—.

Isa. 12:3 Therefore with joy shall ye draw water out of the wells of salvation. (salvation: Saving of a person from sin or danger).Isa. 12:4 And in that day shall ye say, praise the Lord, CALL UPON HIS NAME, MAKE MENTION THAT HIS NAME IS GREAT

****

Name—The

James gave this response.

GOD SAVES THROUGH FAITH IN JESUS, HIS NAME, AND THE NAME OF HIS SON. God was in Christ, reconciling the world unto himself. 2 Cor. 5:19.

Isa. 45:22 Look unto me, and be ye saved, all the ends of the earth: for I am God, and there is none else. (23) I have sworn by myself, the word is gone out of my mouth in righteousness, and shall not return, That unto me every knee shall bow, every tongue shall swear. (24) Surely, shall one say, in the LORD have I righteousness and strength: even to him shall men come: and all that are incensed against him shall be ashamed.

Romans 14:11 For it is written, As I live, saith the Lord, (Jesus) every knee shall bow to ME, and every tongue shall confess to GOD. (Jesus' Father)

Phlp. 2:10 That at the NAME OF JESUS every knee should bow, of things in heaven, and things in earth, and things under the earth: (11) And that every tongue should confess that Jesus Christ is Lord, to the glory of God the Father.

By these passages Jesus was referring to the Name JESUS.

Matthew 1:20—Behold, the angel of the Lord appeared unto him in a dream, saying Joseph, thou son of David, fear not to take unto thee Mary they wife: for that which is conceived in her is of the Holy Ghost. (21) And she shall bring forth a son and thou shalt call HIS NAME JESUS: for he shall save his people from their sins.

Matt. 1:22 Now all this was done, that it might be fulfilled which was spoken of the LORD by the prophet, saying, (23) Behold, a virgin shall be with child, and shall bring forth a son, and they shall call his name Emmanuel, which being interpreted is ***God with us.*** (25)—And he (Joseph) called HIS NAME JESUS.

The answer to the question lies wholly within the passage made in Phlp. 2:10, that AT THE NAME OF JESUS EVERY KNEE SHOULD BOW—.

2 Cor. 5:19—God was in Christ, reconciling the world unto himself—.

1 Tim. 2:5 For there is ONE GOD, AND ONE MEDIATOR between God and men, the MAN Christ Jesus.

John 5:43 (Jesus said), I am come in my FATHER'S NAME.

It is the name God gave the angel to show to Joseph in the dream.

Proverbs 30:4—What is HIS NAME, and what is HIS SON'S NAME, if thou canst tell?

Put it this way:

My Father's name is James.

I came in my father's name

My name is also James.

Of all the names listed in the Old Testament as being the name of God, the Name Jesus stands above them all. It is the name of God (that was lost to the knowledge of men) which God selected for the mediator between himself and man. Faith in that name will guide the inhabitants of the earth back into the Garden of God.

1 Cor 8:6—To us there is but ONE GOD, the Father, of whom are all things, and we in him; and ONE LORD JESUS CHRIST, by whom are all things, and we by him. (7) Howbeit, (at this point) there is not in every man that knowledge—.

Acts 17:28 For in him we live, and move, and have our being.

****

Names:

Edward asked this question.

Names—Do they make a difference?

James gave this response.

The light of the new day is approaching, and along with it is coming the understanding of the Name of God.

What is in the Name? Does it make a difference?

If it did not make a difference in the environment of humanity, then God would not have changed the names of so many people when trying to help them.

Yes, our Name does make a difference in the direction of our natural and spiritual lives.

ABRAM'S NAME WAS CHANGED. Gen 17:5 Neither shall thy name any more be called Abram, but thy name shall be Abraham—.

SARAI'S NAME WAS CHANGED. Gen. 17:15. And God said unto Abraham, as for Sarai thy wife, thou shalt not call her name Sarai, but Sarah shall her name be. (Note: God did not tell Sarai this but only told her husband).

JACOB'S NAME WAS CHANGED. Gen. 32:28 And he (God) said,

> Thy name shall be called no more Jacob, but Israel–.

There are other instances where names have been changed, but two or three witnesses are enough to establish the truth of this matter.

Sometimes the environment and spiritual conditions change so drastically over a period of time, it becomes necessary to change the names, as in the case of God himself who changed his Name eight times in his relationship with men. This primarily was because of the different languages that started with the tower of Babel. (Gen. 1:9)

But since his True saving Name has been revealed, there will be no more change. His Name (word) was in the beginning with God, it was God, and it became flesh and dwelt among the people on the earth. John 1:1.

Hebrews 13:8 JESUS Christ the same yesterday, and to day, and forever. God's Name has always been the same from the beginning, but it was lost from the minds of humanity, so God has by steps been drawing men back to himself through various names, until he finally placed his True Saving Name in the earth through his only begotten Son.

Grab hold of that Name. Hold to it. Have faith in it, call upon it with the assurance that it is the only real weapon that can bring power and protection from every destructive element in the world.

Psalms 20:6 Now know I that the LORD saveth his anointed; he will hear him from his holy heaven with the ***saving strength*** of his right hand.

Psalms 20:7 Some trust in chariots, and some in horses: but we will remember the NAME OF THE LORD OUR GOD.

Joel 2:32—It shall come to pass, that whosoever shall CALL on the NAME of the LORD shall be delivered.

Zeph. 3:9 For then will I turn to the people a pure language, that they may all call upon the Name of th LORD, to serve him with one consent.

Acts 2:21 And it shall come to pass, that WHOSOEVER shall CALL on the NAME of the Lord (Jesus) shall be SAVED. (also Rom. 10:13)

SAVED: 1) RESCUED FROM DANGER

2) GUARDED FROM DESTRUCTION

3) REDEEMED FROM SIN.

Mark 10:52 Jesus said unto him, (the blind man) Go thy way; thy FAITH hath made thee whole.

Acts 3:16 Peter said to the people, His (Jesus') Name through f***aith in His Name*** hath made this (lame) man strong. Yea, the faith which is BY HIM hath given him this perfect soundness in the presence of you all.

****

NOTHING, WITHOUT ME YE CAN DO

jdg asked this question.

I understand that God was in Christ reconciling the world unto himself. (2 Cor. 5:19). Please explain more clearly the statement God made through Jesus when he stated (John 15:5) 'Without Me ye can do nothing?'

James gave this response on 5/15/2000:

At what time we think WE can do great things the arrogance (showing an offensive sense of superiority)drives out the power of God (Christ) and we can do nothing.

//

The filling station was all lit up, but there wasn't much activity. The attendant was sitting at the desk inside the office. James walked to the door. He opened it and went in.

"Good evening," the attendant said, "May I help you."

"No," James replied, "I am just walking around, getting some fresh air."

“It sure is cold out,” said the attendant.

“At least it stopped snowing,” James answered.

When James glanced outside at the pumps a voice spoke directly to his mind. “I'M GOING TO FILL THIS PLACE UP.”

Immediately James heard the screeching of tires on the concrete along side the gas pumps. Someone had suddenly decided they needed gas. Before they had completely stopped at the pumps, another car pulled in on the other side. Then another one from the other direction. The last space was filled before the attendant served the first customer. (This was before self service stations).When the attendant came running into the office to ring up one of the sales, he said, “I'm busier now than I've been all evening.”

“I know,” James said.

James walked quietly and confidently from the station. He stood on the corner and thought. Look what power I have. Everywhere I go, prosperity will come to everyone. I will go across the street and bring business to them. There are two men over there doing nothing. This power I have will put me in a position of great demand.

When James entered the station he felt awkward.

“Good evening,” James said.

“Hi,” the attendants replied.

There was nothing else for James to say. He could not sound like he did on the other side of the street. He stood there and gazed up and down the street from the attendant's office. Nothing happened. No words came to him. What was wrong? Did they think James was here to rob? Why didn't they ask him what he wanted, so he could say, ‘I am just out for a bit of fresh air.’

Humiliated, he walked from the station. He could feel their eyes as they followed him. He crossed North Florrisant. He noticed the attendant from the first station. He was standing out by the pumps, just looking at James. James wished he knew what the man was thinking. Had a voice also conversed with him?

James was learning. He realized at this point, that Jim's spirit had been killed and taken out, but his brain cells and desires of his body remained. This was something James must deal with. Did he have enough strength to do the job? Could he fight the world and the nature of Jim Creed? Could he stay above the waves of the sea? Time would tell.

Enough fresh air had filled the lungs. He was tired of learning. He trudged slowly through the ice and snow toward the apartment. He ascended the stairs and flopped onto the bed right along side Ruth.

****

Oil—Praying for sick?

Maxine asked this question.

Should we anoint with oil when praying for the sick?

James gave this response.

If you want to. It is immaterial. (not relevant)

ANOINTING WITH OIL WHEN PRAYING FOR THE SICK.

NAZARETH

Mark 6:5 And he (Jesus) could there do no mighty work, save that he laid his hands upon a few sick folk, and healed them. (6) And he marveled because of their unbelief.

Note that Jesus even in this low ebb of faith and unbelief of the people did NOT USE OIL when he laid hands on the sick.

Mark 6:7 (Then Jesus) called unto him the twelve, and began to send them forth by two and two; and gave them power over unclean spirits (over those people that were mentally disturbed); (8) And commanded them that they should take NOTHING for their journey, save a staff only; no scrip (provision bag), no bread, no money in their purse: (9) But be shod with sandals; and not put on two coats.

Note: JESUS DID NOT TELL THEM TO TAKE OIL!

But then notice the change from what Jesus told them to do.

Mark 6:13 And they cast out many devils, and ANOINTED WITH OIL many that were sick, and healed them.

James carried on this practice of ANOINTING WITH OIL, and instructed others to do so, but remember this was not a doctrine of Christ.

James 5:14 Is any sick among you? Let him call for the elders of the church; and let them pray over him, ANOINTING HIM WITH OIL in the Name of the Lord: (15) And the prayer of faith shall save the sick, and the Lord shall raise him up; and if he have committed sins, they shall be forgiven him.

Remember, those works were performed in Jesus's own country (Mark 6:1 and 6) among the villages in Galilee after he and his disciples left Nazareth.

Jesus had said (Mark 6:4), A prophet is not without honor, but in his own country, and among his own kin, and in his own house.

Though the disciples did cast out many devils (relieved their minds of the pressures of past sins), and healed many that were sick by the healing virtue that flowed from them to the people, they felt that the flow could be enhanced by making a better contact by the use of oil. This was a fallacy—Jesus did not advocate or use it.

Jesus did use spittle, but it was not for contact purposes. (John 9:6—he (Jesus) spat on the ground, and made clay of the spittle, and he anointed the eyes of the blind man (he had been blind from his birth) with the clay. (7) And said unto him, Go, wash in the pool of Siloam. He went his way therefore, and washed, and came seeing. ***This act was to show humbleness and obedience***.

Other eyes were opened without using this process.

Matthew 20:29 And as they departed from Jericho, a great multitude followed him (Jesus). (30) And, behold, two blind men sitting by the way side, when they heard that Jesus passed by, cried out, saying, Have mercy on us, O Lord, thou son of David. (32)—Jesus stood still, and called them, and said, What will ye that I shall do unto you? (33) They say unto him, Lord, that our eyes be opened. (34) So Jesus had compassion on them, and TOUCHED THEIR EYES: AND IMMEDIATELY THEIR EYES RECEIVED SIGHT—.

The anointing oil was used in a ritual during old testament times to anoint the kings and priests, (Leviticus 8:12) And he poured of the anointing oil upon Aaron's head, and anointed him, to sanctify him.

This was why Jesus said to Simon, the Pharisee, Luke 7:36 & 46,—My head with oil thou didst not anoint—. Jesus was not considered a priest, for he was not of the Levitical priesthood. Nor did they consider Jesus as a king.

Heb. 7:11 If therefore perfection were by the Levitical priesthood, (for under it the people received the law,) what further need was there that another priest should rise after the order of Melchisedec, and not be called after the order of Aaron?

Although the disciples were not primarily religious, as the Pharisees and Sadducees, etc., but they, being Jews, were familiar with the anointing oil of the Old Testament times.

This 'Holy ointment' was made of olive oil (Exodus 30:24). (25)—thou shalt make it an oil of holy ointment, an ointment compound after the art of the apothecary (druggist): it shall be an holy anointing oil.

The law of Moses was a natural shadow of spiritual things to come. Jesus did away with the old and brought in the new. He did not advocate the use of oil in the new testament either for healing or for anointing Apostles to the ministry.

It was the disciples' knowledge of the old testament, and of the rituals in the synagogues of their time that influenced them to use oil in the process of praying for the sick.

****

Organizational names.

Edward asked this question.

Why are there so many organizational names and variations in beliefs among the Christian people?

James gave this response.

Isaiah 4:1—Seven women (churches) shall take hold of one man, (Religious body) saying, We will eat our own bread (rather than to accept Jesus, and his teachings as the Bread of Life), and wear our own apparel: (Denominational names) only let us be called by thy name (Jesus) to take away our reproach.

Jesus said, (John 5:43) I am come in my Father's Name, and ye receive me not: if another (man) shall come in his own name, him ye will receive.

Since the tower of Babel, people have always wanted to build a tower, (Church) whose top may reach unto heaven, and affix a name to that tower. (Gen. 11:4) But God has confounded them so that they may not understand one another's speech. (Gen. 11:7). This is the reason for the slow progress of those that call themselves Christians. Incidentally, the word Christian was not coined during the time Jesus was physically on the earth. (Acts 11:26, 28, 1 Peter 4:16.)

Observe the statistics

Nine percent of the world's population speak English. Ninety percent of the world's Christians come from the nine percent who speak English. Ninety four percent of the ordained ministers in the world serves the nine percent who speak English.

Jesus said, (John 10:36) I am the Son of God—. (38) The Father is in me, and I in him. (John 17:11) Holy Father, keep through thine OWN NAME those whom thou hast given me, that THEY MAY BE ONE, AS WE ARE.

Isaiah 4:2 In that day shall the branch of the Lord be beautiful and glorious, and the fruit of the earth shall be excellent and comely for them that are escaped of Israel. (Those that have emerged from natural Jewish religion and come into the spiritual level of the New Jerusalem).

Revelations 3:12 Him that overcometh will I make a pillar in the temple of my God, and he shall go no more out: and I will write upon him the NAME of my God, and the name of the city of my God, which is NEW JERUSALEM, which cometh down from heaven from my God: and I will write upon him my NEW NAME—JESUS.

WHY HAS PROGRESS BEEN IMPEDED?

Jesus said, (John 15:5) I am the vine, ye are the branches: He that abideth in me, and I in him, the same bringeth forth much fruit: for without me ye can do NOTHING. (6) If a man abide not in me, he is cast forth as a branch, and is withered—.

Peter did not understand. He wanted to build three churches and give them names after each respective founder. Only one name was accepted by God.

Matthew 17:4 Then answered Peter, and said unto Jesus, Lord, it is good for us to be here: if thou wilt, let us make here three tabernacles; one for thee, and one for Moses, and one for Elias. (Elijah) (5) God said, This is my beloved Son, in whom I am well pleased; HEAR YE HIM. (8) And when they (Peter, James and John) had lifted up their eyes, they saw no man, save JESUS ONLY.

There are many advisors in the world. Voices abound, stemming from every conceivable brain. It is what the voices say that make a difference. Without the 'O'(as in ONE) they become vices.

Acts 4:11 This is the stone which was set at nought of you BUILDERS, (religious leaders) which is become the head of the corner. (12) Neither is there salvation in any other: for there is NONE other NAME under heaven given among men, whereby we MUST be SAVED.

Matthew 16:18 And I say also unto thee, That thou art Peter, and upon this rock I will build my church; and the gates of hell (the religious systems of the world) shall not prevail against it. (Acts 1:15 Peter was the spokesman, (1 Cor. 10:4, Rom. 9:33 1 Pet. 2:8) But Christ is that rock.

His (Jesus') Name is called the Word of God. (Rev. 19:13)

There is no other name that can ever take president over that name. There were many churches that branched out from that original foundation established on the day of Pentecost. They were located in homes in Jerusalem, in Asia and other surrounding areas. They were designated by their location but no other names were given.

Rev. 1:4—The Seven Churches of Asia. Unto Ephesus, Smyrna, Pergamos, Thyatira, Sardis, Philadelphia, Laodicea. These are not the names of the churches, only their locations. A house. (Rom.16:5) A church is formed when people come together for the purpose of worshiping God.

The church of God designates the church God set up through His Son Jesus, otherwise known as The Christ. There should be no other name given to a church. Names do make a difference. When any other name is inserted between man and God, it causes division, discord, strife and dissent, even above that which is inherent in the fallen nature of man.

The Body of Christ in the bible was not the name of a church. (Romans 7:4, Rom 12?5, 1 Cor 10:16, 12:12, 27. Eph. 5:23—Christ is the head of the church: and is the Saviour of the Body. (30) For we are members of His Body,—.

Col. 3:15—Let the peace of God rule in your hearts, to the which also ye are called in ONE BODY; and be ye thankful (16) Let the WORD of Christ, (his teachings) dwell in you richly in all wisdom—. (17) And whatsoever ye do in word or deed, do ALL IN THE NAME OF THE LORD JESUS, giving thanks to God and the Father by HIM.

The temple of God was designating the name of a place in Jerusalem, not the name of a church.

1 Cor. 3:16 Know ye not that ye are the temple of God, and that the Spirit of God dwelleth in you?

This is God's church through his son, Jesus—: People that are filled with the holy spirit of God, and assemble together in the Name of God's only Son that he sent to the earth for saving people from the devastation of their own guilt; by the washing of the spiritual rivers of living water, that proceed from their belly in the continual life giving process. (John 7:38)

****

PARADISE

Chrisewarner asked this question.

Why did Jesus tell the man on the cross this day you shall be with me in paradise, yet later said I have not yet ascended to my father?

James gave this response.

There are three places in the Bible that mention Paradise.

1) Luke 23:43 And Jesus said unto him, verily (it is true) I say unto thee, To day shalt thou be with me in Paradise. A PLACE WHERE PAIN IS NON-EXISTENT.

2) 2 Cor. 12:4 How that he was caught up into Paradise, and heard unspeakable words, which it is not (at that time) lawful for a man to utter.

   Paul was speaking of himself who had been (in vision form) caught into Paradise. It was the same spiritual state where God had placed the first man and woman. And the same spiritual level where the Tree of Life resided. And the place people are in at the time they receive the Holy Ghost.

3) The Tree of life was originally in the Garden of Eden. Revelations 2:7 prove that Paradise and the Garden of Eden is the same place. The garden of Eden was the

natural place where the man and woman were placed, and Paradise was the spiritual state they were in. Revelation 2:7 He that hath an ear, let him hear what the Spirit saith unto the churches; To him that overcometh will I give to eat of the TREE OF LIFE, which is in the midst of the PARADISE of God.

Jesus explained that NO MAN had ascended out there where God and the angels reside. (God and Jesus dwells in you via the Holy Ghost).John 3:12 And NO MAN hath ascended up to heaven, but he that came down from heaven, even the son of man which is in heaven. (Paradise)

Jesus came from God to experience all of the weaknesses and temptations that man is confronted with. Heb. 4:14—(JESUS) was in all points tempted like as we are, yet without sin.

John 8:42—I proceeded forth and came from God; neither came I of myself, but he that sent me. Ref: John 10:36, 13:1.

John 16:28 I came forth from the Father, and am come into the world: again, I leave the world, and go to the Father.

From the time Jesus' ministry started until he returned to His Father he was in Paradise. He was raised into that spiritual place the day he received the gift of the Holy Ghost at the time of his water baptism by John.

Luke 3:21—Jesus also being baptized, and praying, the heaven was opened. (22) And the Holy Ghost descended in a bodily shape like a dove upon him,—(23)Jesus was 30 years old) Luke 4:1 And Jesus being full of the Holy Ghost returned from Jordan—.

TOUCH ME NOT

John 20:17 Jesus saith unto her (Mary Magdalene), Touch me not; for I am not yet ascended to my Father: At that time Jesus' body was in a transition phase from a physical substance to a spiritual substance. But during that same day (John 20:19), in the evening, he appeared to the disciples. At that time they did not touch him.

Eight days later Jesus said to Thomas (John 20:26-27), Reach hither thy finger, and behold my hands; and reach hither thy hand, and thrust it into my side: It was not stated that Thomas actually touched Jesus, but only that the invitation was given. (John 20:28) It only states that Thomas answered and said unto him, My Lord and my God. He recognized that God was in Jesus, so he acknowledged them both.

Jesus did not ascend unto his Father until the forty days had expired. (Acts 1:2-3) He was with his Apostles on the mount called Olivet when he was taken up into heaven. (In the form of a vision).

Acts 1:9—He was taken up; and a cloud received him out of their sight. (10) And while they looked steadfastly toward heaven as he went up, behold, two men stood by them in white apparel; (11) Which also said, Ye men of Galilee, why stand ye gazing up into heaven? This same Jesus, which is taken up from you into heaven, shall so come in like manner as ye have seen him go into heaven.

Jesus' complete transition from a physical body to a spiritual body was completed within forty days. He then returned to His Father and Our Father.

When we ALL get to heaven (Paradise—The Garden of God—Eden) What a day of rejoicing that will be. When we ALL SEE JESUS—.

Revelations 21:4 And God shall wipe away all tears from their eyes; and there shall be no more death, neither sorrow, nor crying, neither shall there be any more ***pain***.

****

Philip snatched away:

Ruth asked this question.

Did Philip's body dematerialize and materialize in

Azotus?

James gave this response.

The New American Bible states: Acts 8:29 The Spirit said to Philip, Go and catch up with that carriage. (30) PHILIP RAN AHEAD. (39) The Spirit of the Lord SNATCHED PHILIP AWAY. (40) Philip found himself at Azotus next.

KJV: Acts 8:39—the Spirit of the Lord caught away Philip—(40)—Philip was found at Azotus—.

Both the new American and the King James version is misleading for people that do not choose to think logically.

If the spirit could make Philip disappear and reappear at another place, why did the angel say, arise and go toward the south? And why did Philip have to Run at all?

I submit to you that he WALKED from City to City, including from Gaza to Azotus. (There does not seem to be a road from the desert to Ashdod (Azotus) except through Gaza—Staying on the road was safer.

Acts 8:26 And the angel of the Lord spake unto Philip, saying, arise, and go toward the south unto the way that goeth down from Jerusalem unto Gaza, which is desert. (27) And he arose and went. (29) Then the Spirit said unto Philip, go near, (30) And Philip RAN thither to him.

The physical body of man does not, in any case, appear and disappear. If it seems to be that way, it is because of the usage of improper wording, or a trick of the mind.

Even Jesus had to walk or ride a donkey. (Burro, Jackass).Matthew 21:7, John 12:14-15, Luke 13:33, John 7:1

Luke 13:32-33 I must walk to day, and to morrow, and the day following—. Only when Jesus' body was perfected and changed from physical to spiritual substance could he go from place to place without riding or walking.

The earth was formed to be inhabited (Isa. 45:18) by man and beast. They have physical bodies. They were not intended to live in the physical realms of heaven away from the earth until they learn to go there by physical means. Jesus said (John 3:13)—No man hath ascended up to heaven, but he that came down from heaven, even the Son of man which is in heaven. (Paradise on the earth).

Bodies of the earth (Terra, Terra firma-solid earth) are physical. They cannot appear and disappear.

A baby grows slowly from the embryo to full maturity of man or woman. There is no other way for physical bodies to develop, even the first woman also developed slowly from the side of man. If there was a better way, God would have known it and he would not have expended so much effort in the creation of the cells for the construction of physical bodies.

1 Cor. 15:40 There are also celestial bodies, and bodies terrestrial: (Terra). (44) There is a natural body and there is a spiritual body. Philip had a physical body. Jesus' body was changed over a period of forty days from a physical to a spiritual substance.

God, His Son and the Angels as individual beings, are not bound to the earth, but the spirit of God, Christ, is with those that are calling upon the Name of God, for guidance through the power and direction of the Holy Ghost.

In fact when people receive the Holy Ghost, God dwells within them through the Holy Ghost. 2 Cor. 6:16 Ye are the temple of the living God; as God hath said, I will dwell in them, and walk in them; and I will be their God.

Acts 17:28 For in Him we live, and move, and have our being.

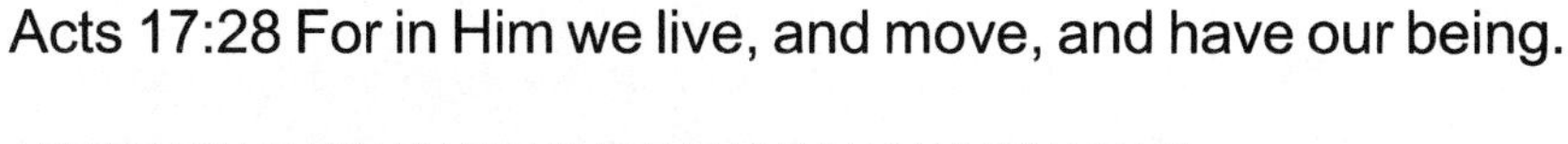

“James, don’t you think that with God all things are possible?” Ruth asked. (Matt. 19:26). “What about the crossing of the Red Sea, the Jordan River and the calming of the wind over the Lake of Gennesaret?”

James gave this response.

God is a scientist. All things are possible with God, but he has developed a scientific process for each and every project he has ever attempted in this world and all others.

All those occurrences would have happened even if there had not been anyone around. Those miracles were accomplished by the Spirit of God through the Holy Ghost delivering the people to the proper place at the exact time for their deliverance.

God delivered the Israelites to the finger of the Red Sea in advance of the strong east wind. (Exo.14:21).

‘YES, GOD DID IT BY A STRONG EAST WIND ALL THAT NIGHT.’

And then the Lord said unto Moses (Exo.14:26), Stretch out thine hand over the sea, that the waters may come again—.

This was done in advance of the change in the course of the wind, and return of the water to advance God’s Name in the minds of men.

THE JORDAN RIVER.

The people crossed Jordan at Jericho when the water had been cut off by a land slide into the river caused by the water undercutting the hills. This occurred 'very far from the City of Adam,' (Josh.3:16)that is, beside Zaretan: and those (waters) that came down toward the sea of the plain, even the salt sea, failed and were cut off.

THE SEA OF GENNESARET (Galilee)

Matt. 8:24—there arose a great tempest in the sea—. (Ref: Smith Bible Dic.—Teacher's addition. Page 204-Line 35). The scenery is bleak and monotonous, being surrounded by a high and almost unbroken wall of hills, on account of which IT IS EXPOSED TO FREQUENT, SUDDEN AND VIOLENT STORMS. (Note: Those storms sometimes leave as suddenly as they arrive.) God is aware of all this.

Matt. 8:26—Then he (Jesus) arose, and rebuked the winds and the sea; and there was a great calm.—What manner of man is this, that even the winds and the sea obey him!

Here again God coordinated Jesus' actions with the course of the winds. All those apparent miracles have been staged with one purpose in God's mind. That is to increase men's faith in His Name.

Proverbs 18:10 THE NAME OF THE LORD IS A STRONG TOWER:

THE RIGHTEOUS RUNNETH INTO IT, AND IS SAFE.

There is safety in God's Name. When we call upon him we are guided by the Holy Ghost into righteousness (in accordance with God's time) and into all safe places in advance of destructive occurrences, whether they are of a natural phenomenon or by the hands of violent men.

****

Pray for persecutors.

Maxine asked this question.

How do we pray for those that persecute us?

James gave this response.

According to Matthew 5:44 Jesus said Pray for them which despitefully use you and persecute (to harass, or torment) you.

HOW DO WE PRAY FOR SUCH PEOPLE?

Pray that God will CAUSE THEM TO SUCCEED ACCORDING TO HIS WILL.

Love your enemies (Matthew 5:44). We should NEVER pray for their destruction, for in doing so we may create pitfalls for ourselves. (Esth.7:9)

God can save from every conceivable destructive force in the world. It may be when we pray for the success of our enemies according to God's will, they will become entangled in the devise (invent-plot) they have set for our entrapment.

****

PRAYER

Charlene asked this question.

To whom do we pray? Do we pray to Jesus or God?

James gave this response.

When Jesus was physically on the earth he said, Matthew 11:28

Come unto me, all ye that labor and are heavy laden, and I will give you rest. This was God speaking through Jesus. Remember that God was in Christ, reconciling the world unto himself. 2 Cor. 5:19.

Pray to God through the name of HIS SON, JESUS.

(John 16:22) Jesus said, I will see you again, and (John 16:26) At that day ye shall ASK IN MY NAME: and I say not unto you, that I will pray the Father for you: (27) For the Father himself loveth you, because ye have loved me—. He was showing that we must love one another, then God will love us because Christ is in every man that cometh into the world. (John 1:9)

Before Jesus' departure he said, (John 14:16) I will pray the Father, and he shall give you another Comforter, (Holy Ghost) that he may abide with you forever—. Jesus came with the Holy Ghost (Comforter) on the day of Pentecost. Acts 2:4 This Spirit (Holy Ghost) also helpeth our infirmities: for we know not what we should pray for as we ought: but the Spirit itself maketh intercession for us with groanings which cannot be uttered. (27) And he that searcheth the hearts knoweth what is the mind of the Spirit, because he maketh intercession for the saints ACCORDING TO THE WILL OF GOD.

AFTER THE HOLY GHOST HAS BEEN GIVEN

John 16:23—In that day ye shall ask me nothing,—Whatsoever ye shall ask the Father IN MY NAME, he will give it you. (24) Hitherto have ye asked nothing in MY NAME: ask, and ye shall receive—.

How then should we pray?

(The following is an example of how we should pray)

When you pray, say, Our Father which art in heaven, Hollowed be thy name, Thy kingdom come. Thy WILL be done, as in heaven, so in earth. Matthew 6:9

We must pray according to God's will.

Jesus prayed, O my Father, if it be possible, let this cup pass from me; nevertheless not as I will, but as thou wilt. Matthew 26:39. (42) thy will be done.

Jesus said, (John 14:13)—Whatsoever ye shall ask in MY NAME, (of course, according to God's will) that will I do, that the Father may be glorified in the Son. (14) If ye shall ask anything in MY NAME, I will do it.

Then why are prayers not answered?

James 4:3 Ye ask, and receive not, because ye ask amiss, that ye may consume it upon your lusts.

A person should not expect to receive assistance from God, for things that are against the commandments, even though the prayers may be made through the name of Jesus.

John 9:12-38. The Pharisees determined that both Jesus and the man that had been healed by God through his son Jesus, were both sinners primarily because the work was done on the Sabbath, and that the man or his parents must be sinners, otherwise he would not have been born blind.

They did not believe that Jesus was the Son of God, and that God was working through him. They said to the man that was born blind, and that had been healed of that blindness, (31) Now we know that God heareth not sinners: but if any man be a worshipper of God, and doeth his will, him he heareth. They were right about God not hearing sinners but wrong about Jesus and the man, or his parents being sinners. (3)Jesus said, Neither hath this man sinned, nor his parents: but that the WORKS OF GOD should be made manifest in him. The defect in this man had come from weaknesses which had developed in previous generations.

****

Prayer.

Zenaide asked this question.

To whom do we pray?

James gave this response.

TO WHOM DO WE PRAY?

GOD, THROUGH HIS NAME, JESUS!

Jesus said,—Pray to thy Father—. Matt.6:6 After this manner therefore pray ye: Our Father which art in heaven, Hallowed (declared sacred) be thy Name.

I—pray to my Father—. Matt. 26:53.

I said, I am the Son of God—. John 10:36.

I ascend unto my Father, and YOUR FATHER; and to my GOD, and your GOD. John 20:17.

John 16:26 At that day ye shall ask in my Name, and I say not unto you, that I will pray the Father for you: (27) For the Father himself loveth you, because ye have loved me, and have believed that I came out from God.

1 Timothy 2:5 For there is one God, and one mediator between God and men, the man Christ Jesus.

We do not pray to Jesus. We pray to God through the name of Jesus, his only begotten son.

We do not pray to a woman that has lived on the earth and passed on.

We do not pray to angels.

We do not pray to saints.

We do not pray to any other god, either made of animated (having life), or inanimate (destitute of life) material objects or substances.

Blessed material objects do nothing. No, they do not protect anybody from evil. It is only a psychological feeling produced by superstition.

There are no spooks, evil spirits, or goblins; only minds deficient of the power of Christ, which gives all men their strength, power and understanding.

There is no other way to God except by calling upon him by His Name continuously. And prayers do not need to be re-iterated. God is not deaf.

Matthew 6:7 But when ye pray, use not vain repetitions, as the heathen do: for they think that they shall be heard for their much speaking. (8) Be not ye therefore like unto them: for your Father knoweth what things ye have need of, before ye ask him.

Does this admonition also apply to calling upon the Name of the Lord?(Gen. 4:26, Joel 2:32, Acts 2:21, Rom. 10:13).

No! Calling upon the Name of God is not for the benefit of God, but it stabilizes the man and woman mentally, spiritually and ultimately physically. It increases faith in God and attracts and generates his power (Christ)for protection and guidance by the Holy Ghost in an otherwise violent world. This was the formula devised by God in the beginning and should have been used in the beginning again. (This beginning again may be used at the beginning of the recorded history, approximately six thousand years ago, during Noah's time, and 70 a.d.)

No matter if the man or woman, boy or girl is too weak at the time to keep from sinning, the Name of the Lord must be called upon anyway. In time, and with age, faith in that Name will cause the person to be raised to a stronger level of life in all areas.

*** ***Prayers:***

Edward asked this question.

WHEN PRAYERS ARE MADE, WHERE DO THEY GO?

James gave this response.

Christ (the power of God) is the light which lighteth every man that cometh into the world. John 1:9.

God is not millions of miles away.

Acts 17:27—seek the Lord—feel after him and find him—he is not far from EVERY ONE OF US.

God and his power (Christ) dwells within every man until man drives it out through forceful acts that sear the conscience. 1 Tim. 4:2.

Prayers that are made toward God, go to God that lives within and then the power of God flows to the person being prayed for. It is then disseminated by God through his power to the brain of the person being prayed for. The brain then uses those messages to decide what action to take. Then it sends out signals to the muscles and other organs of the body for its healing. The extent of healing depend on the level of pressure on the brain caused by either unbelief, guilt or other weaknesses or deformities inherited by a long line of fallen generations. (This degenerate condition is not God's fault).

Jesus said (John 14:23) If a man love me, he will keep my words: and ***MY FATHER will love him, and WE will come unto him, and make OUR abode with him.***

Where is God?

God lives in his kingdom!

Luke 17:21 Neither shall they say, Lo here! Or, lo there! For, behold, the KINGDOM OF GOD is WITHIN YOU. (God's Temple)

****

Preacher's prayers.

Jdg asked this question.

Do ministers always have success in their prayers.

James gave this response.

DO MINISTERS ALWAYS HAVE SUCCESS IN THEIR PRAYERS?

The day was not a good one. The sun had not shown. Clouds hung low. Air which contained a misty spray was all around. Cold chilled the spine. All the leaves had fallen. The voice of crying split the air. Daddy, I can't breathe. Mommy, I can't breathe.

"What are we going to do?" Ruth questioned James.

Eldon arrived. He would not speak with James or Ruth. He continued through the house to the other rooms.

"I do not know what we are going to do, Ruth," James said. " We could pray for her, but in the past we have had no results."

Hattie went to the phone. She dialed. "Hello, is the minister there?" she questioned. " When will he be back? Oh! Okay. Will you ask him to come over as soon as possible? Charlene is having an asthma attack. Thank you."

The minister and his wife finally arrived. They shook hands with Eldon. They looked at Ruth and James, then turned to Charlene. She was breathing hard. The minister laid hands on her head. He spoke. " In the Name of Jesus, asthma, release this child in the Name of Jesus." Charlene looked at the preacher then at his wife, expecting something to happen. It did not come. Fear seized her mind. It was even harder to breathe.

Eldon whispered to Hattie. Ruby and Jim should leave the room. They have the devil in them. That is why he can't do anything for her. James and Ruth were told to leave the room.

"In the Name of Jesus, the preacher demanded," while placing his one hand on the small of her back and the other on her abdomen.

James and Ruth were observing through the open door.

"Come out of this child in the Name of Jesus."

With eyes red and tears rolling down her face, Charlene cried out, "I can't breathe."

"Get a sheet," the preacher instructed his wife.

"Hattie, do you have a sheet and a vaporizer?" She asked as she came from the living room to the bedroom.

"Yes I do," Hattie said, as she went directly to the chest of drawers for the sheet and then to the kitchen for the vaporizer.

Everyone stood looking on. Charlene had had asthma ever since she was six months old. This would not help. James had sat up with her half the night on occasions, giving her medicines of various kinds. Sometimes they put her in the car and drove around. For some reason that seemed to help.

The tent was erected. The vaporizer was plugged in. Steam filled the tent. Charlene wheezed. She cried.

"Roland, that will not work," James stated.

"It is not working," Roland agreed.

"I know what to do, but I do not have the money now," James said.

"What is that?" Roland asked with interest.

"I have not said anything because she broke her atomizer. It will cost for that beside the Asthma Niferine."

"Lets go to the drug store and get it if you know what to get. That girl should not suffer like that," he said, as he picked up his coat and they both went out the back door to the car.

Roland drove. James thought. Why was his back healed?

Why was Charlene not healed? Jesus said, You will say Physician heal thyself. Luke 4:23. The widow, there was only one helped. Luke 4:26. There was only one Leper helped by the name of Naaman. Luke 4:27. Jesus only helped one man at the pool of Bethesda. John 5:5. While Jesus was among his own people, he could do no mighty work, save that he laid his hands upon a few sick folk, and healed them. Mark 6:5.

Roland stayed in the car. James went into the drug store. "Asthma Niferine and an atomizer," James said to the druggist. James handed him the money which Roland had given him and returned to the car. Roland drove home.

Ruth took the atomizer, filled it with Niferine and handed it to Charlene. She took four deep breaths while squeezing the bulb and was relieved. The preacher, his wife and Eldon left.

God is a scientist. He expects his sons and daughters to follow in his foot steps. Until men and women's immune systems become as strong as they were in the beginning they sometimes need medical assistance along the way.

Weaknesses have been handed down from generation to generation. It took Adam nine hundred and thirty years (Gen. 5:5) to drive all traces of the power of God (Christ) out of his system and lower his immune system. It may take a long time to retrieve that which was lost.

****

Pre-existence ?? A Mormon's

Gray Eagle asked this question.

Everyone's pre-existence??

Because of Joseph Smith's background in the occult and Masonry he made a new religion which synthesized the marriage of the occult with elements of Christianity. Shrouded in secret known to only a few were the real meanings of Smith's teachings. What is known and taught today is what Smith taught; that Lucifer and Christ were spirit brothers, Lucifer who wanted his plan of salvation to be used was rejected and thrown out of heaven. Mormons teach the pre-existence of gods and each brother presented a plan to them to win the ability to offer salvation. They claim it is Jesus who came forth with the better plan. But in practice it is Lucifer's doctrine they use; that one can become like God. It became his plan that Adam and Eve accepted that made them fall, and it is his plan the Mormon uses as model for their progression to exaltation yet they claim it is Christ's plan that was accepted.

God the eternal father did of his own will ordain and established the plan of salvation whereby Christ and all his spirit children might have power to advance and progress and become like him. (Promised Messiah B. McKonkie P.48)

The appointment of Jesus to be the Savior of the world was contested by one of the other sons of God. He was called Lucifer. . . . this spirit-brother of Jesus desperately tried to become the Savior of mankind, (The Gospel Through The Ages, M. R. Hunter p. 15).

In the Discourses of Brigham Young, pp.53-54 Lucifer is called the second son, the one known as Son of the Morning. Who will redeem the earth, who will go forth and make the sacrifice for the earth and all things it contains? The Eldest Son said: Here am I; and then he added, Send me. But the second one, which was Lucifer, Son of the Morning, said, Lord, here am I, send me, I will redeem every son and daughter of Adam and Eve that lives on the earth, or that ever goes on the earth.

A momentous contest took place between two brothers, Jehovah and Lucifer, sons of Elohim (Spencer W. Kimball, Conference Report, April 1964, p.95)

Long before you were born a program was developed by your creators . . . The principal personalities in this great drama were a Father Elohim, perfect in wisdom, judgment, and person, and two sons, Lucifer and Jehovah. (Teachings of Spencer W. Kimball, pp. 32-33).

Thus when the Father presented his own plan in the pre-existent council, he asked for volunteers from whom he could choose a Redeemer to be born into mortality as the Son of God. Lucifer offered to become the Son of God on condition that the terms of the Father's plan were modified to deny men their agency and to heap inordinate reward upon the one working out the redemption. Christ, on the other hand, accepted the Father's plan in full, saying, Father, thy will be done, and the glory be thine forever. (Moses 4:1-4; Abraham 3:22-28.)

Apostle Bruce R. McConkie wrote in Mormon Doctrine, The first spirit to be born in heaven was Jesus, p. 129, and That Lucifer, the son of the morning, is our elder brother and the brother of Jesus Christ (Bruce R. McConkie, Mormon Doctrine, p.163-164). So Jesus is the Devils older brother, but we too are in the same family as McConkie also explains, Since all men are the personal spirit children of the Father, and since Christ was the firstborn spirit offspring, it follows that he is the Elder Brother of all men (Mormon Doctrine, p.214).McConkie also said of Christ, He is the Firstborn of the Father. By obedience and devotion to the truth he attained that pinnacle of intelligence which ranked Him as a God, as the Lord Omnipotent while yet in His preexistent state' (Mormon Doctrine, p. 129).

So he is God's first spirit child from heaven and then we are born afterwards. So the Father is his daddy and yours? President Young said Adam was Michael, the Archangel and he was the Father of Jesus Christ and is our God and that Joseph taught this principle. (Wilford Woodruff Journal, Dec. 16, 1867). So in Mormon teaching from its inception we find Adam was actually Michael who is actually God. The enigma of where we came from is solved from Smith's revelation to Brigham Young to others. An angel who is God and listened to the other angel who offered the gospel and was rejected by the Gods, and this they call Christianity.

The Encyclopedia of Mormonism Vol.4, Appendix 4 states, Jesus Christ is not the Father of the spirits who have taken or yet shall take bodies upon this earth, for He is one of them. He is The Son, as they are sons and daughters of Elohim.

The spirit brother of Jesus desperately tried to become the savior of mankind. (Gospel through the Ages, p.15)

The Bible teaches God did not want Adam or Eve to sin, Lucifer came and said God was keeping from them their Godhood. To a Mormon this was a good thing to learn of this so they could be exalted on another planet as all other God's who came before them. So although Jesus won the bid for salvation it was Lucifer who really taught them the truth (according to Mormonism). So he actually becomes their (disguised) savior because they are following what he said more than what the real Jesus said in the Bible! No Mormon believes what Jesus said of himself in the Bible: about who He is nor about his death on the cross being the ONLY way to have your sins forgiven.

So how does this spiritual fantasy work? More importantly, how does anyone who has ever heard of the Bible actually believe this? We were begotten by our Father in Heaven; the person of our Father in Heaven was begotten on a previous heavenly world by His Father; and again, He was begotten by a still more ancient Father; and so on, from generation to generation, . . . we wonder in our minds, how far back the genealogy extends, and how the first world was formed, and the first father was begotten (The Seer, p.132).

Heber C. Kimball, who was a member of the First Presidency, made these similar comments: . . . then we shall go back to our Father and God, who is connected with one who is still farther back; and this Father is connected with one still further back, and so on . . . (Journal of Discourses, vol. 5, p.19). So we have a lot of Grandfathers and Grandmas according to Mormonism.

James gave this response.

THE ANSWER IS VERY SIMPLE. It may be too simple for the wise and learned to see it.

///

The minister stood behind the bible stand with the book open before him. Words came forth from his lips as the eyes followed the lines of print.

This is my beloved Son, in whom I am well pleased, HEAR YE HIM.

Ears heard those words. They were young ears belonging to a man in the congregation. He also later read those passages along with many others from a book just like the minister used. (The Bible)

One day this young man had a fever. He tried to climb over a fence, at which time he could hardly make it because of his sickness. He fell to the ground. Through his hot feverish mind and eyes he saw two personages. The one pointed toward the other and said, This is my beloved Son, in whom I am well pleased,

HEAR YE HIM.

What caused the vision?

The words that had been heard and read!

Was this God speaking about his only begotten Son?

Yes!

Some time later the same boy saw an angel. This angel told him of a book that was under a rock. The boy was instructed by the angel not to look at the book for a year. As young as he was he could not comprehend all that was transpiring around him, so he conferred with his natural father.

"Father," he asked, "is this vision of the angel from God?"

The father answered, "Yes son, it is of God."

The boy had been told implicitly (complete and unquestioning) ***who to hear but he listened to his natural father and a supposed angel instead.***

All religions do some good and have truth in varying degrees. We need all the churches and we should be kind to one another in our trek toward the full understanding of the truth. ***That truth lives with God's only begotten son, NO ONE ELSE***.

Jesus came to the earth bearing HIS FATHER'S NAME for placement in the foreheads (Rev. 7:3) of human inhabitants on the earth.

Christ is the light which lighteth ***every man*** that cometh into the world. (John 1:9)

Call upon the Name of God, ***Jesus***(Joel 2:32, Zeph 3:9, Zech 13:9, Acts 2:21, Rom. 10:13), and let the water that sustains life overflow from the innermost parts of the belly. (John 7:38)

Jesus said, (John 14:6) I am the Way, the Truth, and the life: no man cometh unto the Father, but by me. (Truth=Light, water=the holy spirit of God-Christ)

Jesus said, (John 17:12) While I was with them in the world, I kept them in THY NAME—, I pray not that thou shouldest take them out of the world, but that thou shouldest ***keep them from the evil***—(John 17:15).

The only way to avoid falsehoods is to stay in God's Name continually. When drifting away from the 'handle of God' the destructive elements take over and lead into all manner of imaginations.

1 Timothy 2:5 For there is one God, and one mediator between God and men, the man Christ Jesus; (6) Who gave himself a ransom for ***ALL***, to be testified in due time.

Although there have been occasions when the names of angels have been revealed, this should not have happened, because it takes away from keeping the eyes focused toward the One True Saving God through His Christ.

Gen. 32:29 And Jacob asked him, and said, Tell me, I pray thee, THY NAME, And he said, Wherefore is it that thou dost ask after MY NAME. And he blessed him there.

NOTE: ***He did not reveal his name.***

Acts 4:12 Neither is there salvation in any other: for there is none other NAME under heaven given among men, whereby we must be saved.

All other names lead to darkness.

Grayeagle rated this answer:

Well, history documents where Old Joe Smith's visions came from . . . A bottle of whiskey! The churches must work as a whole body is correct, but.When one claims to have a whole new gospel, well.

Gal 1:8 But though we, or an angel from heaven, preach any other gospel unto you than that which we have preached unto you, let him be accursed.

Gal 1:9 As we said before, so say I now again, If any [man] preach any other gospel unto you than that ye have received, let him be accursed.

James gave this follow-up answer.

In order to conform to the passage 'Love thy neighbor as thyself, (Lev. 19:18, Matthew 19:19, 5:43)we must eliminate placing curses on one another.

Accursed: (1) Being under a curse. (2) damnable.

And we should not cut a man's ear off, thinking we are doing God service. (Matthew 26:51, John 16:2).

Well yes, the Bible is true. ***It is a recording of the actions of men versus the will of God.*** The writers were inspired by God to convey the truth even though it might be against the person doing the writing.

Whether the young man was under the influence at the time of his vision of the two personages or not, it still remains that ***God was instructing him to hear His Son rather than any other voice.*** This he failed to do. His excessive drinking, if this was the case, may have been a result of his deviation from the Name of God as given to His Son Jesus, and his adherence to the other voices.

We should not condemn a person for using alcohol since it is a known fact that Jesus did consume alcoholic beverages and did no sin. (2 Cor. 5:21, Heb. 4:15). Even Paul advocated the drinking of wine, (1 Tim. 5:23) And thanked God and took courage when he saw the three taverns. (Acts 28:15)

But Jesus came to take away the sin of the world. (John 1:29) The excessive use of alcohol can lead to many sins.

The drinking of wine was discontinued, as far as Jesus was concerned, at the time of the Last Supper (Passover), (Matthew 26:29) and was to be replaced by the New Wine (spiritual) on the day of the Harvest Feast. (Acts 2:13-15)

Let it be known that we do not drink alcoholic beverages at all.

Paul said, (Eph. 5:18) Be not drunk with wine wherein is excess; but be filled with the Spirit. This happened on the day of Pentecost. (Acts 2:4)

****

Propagation.

Maxine asked this question.

Why was it necessary for God to control reproduction of human life as opposed to the other animals?

James gave this response.

GUILT caused the man and woman to hide behind the trees.

Why did they feel guilty?

They observed the processes for reproduction as performed by the other animals and it became a part of their lives.

Didn't God say, Be fruitful, and multiply?

HE SAID THIS TO THE SUBCONSCIOUS MIND!

The sleep process as was used in the creation of Eve was supposed to continue in the reproduction of all human life. Of course, not from the side, but according to the plan devised by God for the conception, growth and birth. This would have eliminated the pain in child birth, and the overpopulation of the world as time continued.

Overpopulation was not the only problem. It was relatively easy for the mind to be swayed. Without a continual focus upon one goal, or vision, or thing, the mind could be drawn toward destructive thoughts as portrayed by the other animals, and ultimately be drawn toward violence, killing and destruction.

So God figured out a formula to correct this problem. The answer resided in His Own Name. He told man to call upon His Name with his inner voice without ceasing. From the rising of the sun unto the going down of the same the Lord's Name is to be praised. (Psalm 113:3) I have remembered thy Name, O Lord, in the night, and HAVE KEPT THY LAW.

If man and woman had conformed to that one formula they would have had strength to conform to the one rule God had set forth in the beginning.

DON'T EVEN TOUGH IT LEST YE DIE!

When they took control of the life making processes against God's will, they ***immediately knew they were naked.*** At that point their conscience filled their beings with guilt, and fear of God caused them to hide behind the trees.

The man and the woman were not aware of the sexual sensations in their bodies until after they deliberately experienced the sexual acts as they had observed in the other animals.

God did not want to keep some good thing from man and woman, but to develop a human family on the earth that would maintain eternal life, God must regulate propagation. If this was not done, then death would be necessary, as in the case of the other animals, to eliminate overpopulation. Men and women were the sons and daughters of God, the other animals were not.

****

PROPAGATION, FUTURE

Zenaide asked this question.

Within the confines of a thousand years will human life continue to be reproduced?

James gave this response.

Yes, If men and women continue to develop according to the original plan of God.

The results of prophesies can only materialize when the mind produces the results. There is no iron clad force that propels men against their own will, except the force of repulsion for the protection of those, two by two, that CALL upon GOD'S NAME.

In the perfect plan of God, how will propagation be initiated? Conception will be automatically guided by the subconscious mind during the sleeping hours of the male and female human animal. For those automatic movements to transpire, both the man and the woman must be living in Paradise, the second heaven spiritual state. During that time sin and death will be abolished and reproduction will be greatly reduced so the earth will not become overpopulated.

This is the ultimate plan of God, but it will never work until men and women decide to conform to God's perfect plan for His sons and daughters on the earth.

The plan of God is concrete. There is no forced time for complete fulfilment. It could have been from the beginning. It can be now or a thousand years from now, or never. Freedom has been completely turned over to men and women. What will they do with that freedom?

****

Prophesy, why not fulfilled?

Maxine asked this question.

Why was the complete prophesy as recorded in Matthew24:21 not fulfilled?

James95204 gave this response.

For then shall be great tribulation, (70 a.d.) such as was not since the beginning of the world to this time,

NO, NOR EVER SHALL BE.

When Titus and his army carried on the siege of Jerusalem on September 8, 70 A.D., as was foreseen by Jesus, the loss of lives was minuscule when compared to the Holocaust. Why was this prophesy, '***No, nor ever shall be,' not fulfilled?***

Jesus came to deliver the ***Name of God to his own people***; to his own nationality, but they rejected it. Because of that rejection, the destruction of the temple and the devastation of that nation was proclaimed by Jesus. He was not being vindictive, but because men cannot be saved except by calling upon the Name of God. The Name 'Jesus' as being the name of God, was not accepted by them.

The offspring of those people have had many chances to accept the Name of God. Jesus said (John 5:43), ***I am come in my Father's name, and ye receive me not—***.

When Jesus was on the earth they (of the Jewish religious system) did not call upon that name because they did not believe in Jesus. And during the Holocaust their offspring did not call upon the saving name of God because they had been mislead by their ancestors.

Psalms 113:2 Blessed be the Name of the LORD from this time forth and for evermore.

God will SAVE if humanity will Call upon him by His Name. It doesn't matter what nationality or color, or religion they may be. People of most religions believe there is a God, only some are confused about the exact nature of His Name, and what faith in it can do.

Jesus spoke with the leaders in Jerusalem (Matthew 23:39) ***I say unto you, ye shall not see me henceforth, till ye shall say, Blessed is he that cometh in the Name of the Lord.*** (This was a quote from Psalms 118:26).

God put it this way through Moses. Deut 30:15 See, I have set before thee this day life and good, death and evil; (16) In that I command thee this day to love the Lord thy God, to walk in his ways, and to keep his commandments—. (17), but if thine heart turn away, so that thou wilt not hear,—. (18) I denounce unto you this day, that ye shall surely perish,—.

So it is left to humanity to draw near God (James 4:8), and there is no way to draw near God except by calling upon His Name.

It was recorded in Acts 4:12 ***Neither is there salvation (saving of a person from sin or danger) in any other: for there is none other Name under heaven given among men, whereby we must be saved.***

Joel 2:32 And it shall come to pass, that ***WHOSOEVER*** shall Call on the Name of the Lord shall be delivered—.

So when God makes promises, or prophesies, either good or bad, evidently those promises, or judgments are contingent upon the actions of the people (Refer to the story of Jonah—Jonah 1:1).

Psalms 86:17 ***In the day of my trouble I will CALL UPON THEE: FOR THOU WILT ANSWER ME.***

Zephaniah 3:9 ***For then will I turn to the people a pure language, that they may ALL CALL upon the NAME OF THE LORD to serve him with one consent.***

****

Psychiatrists and Books:

Maxine asked this question.

Can books and psychiatrists help?

James gave this response.

CAN PSYCHIATRISTS HELP?

Yes, if that psychiatric practitioner has had his/her spirit killed, taken out, and a right spirit installed in its place: If spiritual eyes and ears have been received: If they have received the gift of the Holy Ghost: If their heart (center of their being) has been filled with the holy spirit from God.

DO BOOKS HELP?

Without those aforementioned spiritual gifts nobody can, through any amount of education as expressed through books or by any other means, thoroughly understand the operation of the mind, spirit, and body of anyone.

1 Corinthians 2:14—The natural man receiveth not the things of the Spirit of God: for they are foolishness unto him: NEITHER CAN HE KNOW THEM, because they are spiritually discerned.

Is God concerned with the natural body? God made both. He is equally concerned with the welfare of both the physical and the spiritual. 1 Corinthians 15:44 There is a natural body, and there is a spiritual body—. But, especially, the spiritual body cannot be understood by a natural person without the spirit.

The majority of the people with mental problems need spiritual help, and they cannot receive that help from a natural man that does not understand spiritual things. This does not only apply to psychiatrists, but to anyone that works in that capacity, including preachers that have not been born again of the spirit.

A properly functioning brain can cause the body to live, but with a depressed mind because of guilt, or any other reason such as hereditary gene defects, the body malfunctions. This is why an individual needs the water of life flowing freely within his/her being.

John 7:38 He that believeth on me (Jesus) as the scripture hath said, out of his belly shall flow rivers of living water.

This spiritual water is needed to continuously wash out the effects of guilt before it has a chance to destroy the mind and body of the individual. A permanent cure cannot be effected by words of natural men, ***OR ANY DRUG***.

DOES NATURAL WATER BAPTISM WASH AWAY SINS?

NO! THE WATER OF LIFE DOES. John 4:14—***the water that I shall give him shall be in him a well of water springing up into everlasting life.***

Ananias said to Saul—Acts 22:16 Be baptized, AND WASH AWAY THY SINS, ***CALLING ON THE NAME OF THE LORD.***

BAPTISM IN WATER IS A RITUAL TO OUTWARDLY SHOW THAT A PERSON HAS DECIDED TO TURN FROM HIS SINFUL WAYS AND START LIVING A BETTER LIFE. The attitude of the Pharisees and Sadducees when they came to John the baptizer was not based on their desire to change. So John said, Matthew 3:7 O generation of vipers, who hath warned you to flee from the wrath to come? (8) Bring forth therefore fruits (attitude) meet for repentance. (Mark 1:4) John was preaching the baptism of repentance for the remission of sins, but water alone could not remit (pardon) those sins. It took faith in and calling upon the Name of God to do that.

The effects of sin drives out the holy spirit of God: but it cannot destroy the Gift of the Spirit: That gift remains forever. John 14:16 (Jesus said), And I will pray the Father (ask earnestly), and he shall give you another Comforter, that he may abide with you FOREVER. (Holy Ghost).

****

RAPTURE

James gave this response.

Matthew 24:34. I tell you the truth, this generation will certainly not pass away until all these things have happened.

Note: This generation (at that present time) shall not pass UNTIL ALL THESE THINGS BE FULFILLED. Jesus was prophesying of a. d. 70.

And 'NO' the word rapture is not in the Bible.

For a better understanding we should go back to the beginning.

Genesis 2:9 Out of the ground made the Lord God to grow every tree that is pleasant to the sight, and good for food; (This was the natural trees for food) the TREE OF LIFE also in the midst of the garden, and the TREE OF KNOWLEDGE OF GOOD AND EVIL. The tree of life is the Name of God that we are to call upon and have faith in, and the tree of knowledge deals with the conscience. Knowledge of evil weakens the immune system and causes death.

Gen. 2:16 And the Lord God commanded the man, saying, Of EVERY TREE of the garden thou mayest FREELY EAT:(Gen. 3:2) (17) BUT OF THE TREE OF THE KNOWLEDGE OF GOOD AND EVIL, thou shalt not eat of it: for in the day (a day with the Lord is a thousand years—(2 Pet 3:8) that thou eatest thereof thou shalt surely die.

God intended that man and woman live in the Garden of Eden (Paradise Rev. 2:7) by eating of the Tree of Life in Paradise. In the day they took into their mental system, the knowledge of evil, it caused destruction to come to their spiritual body and ultimately during that day (1000 YEARS)their physical being.

John 17:15 ***I pray not that thou shouldest take them out of the world, but that thou shouldest keep them from the evil.***

God still wants man and woman to prosper and be in health in this world as the soul prospers. (3 John 1:2) If God had wanted them to live in the physical heavens other than on the earth, he would have created them there as he did the angels. Jesus said (John 3:13) ***NO MAN hath ascended UP TO HEAVEN,*** but he (Jesus) that came down from heaven, even the Son of man which is in heaven. (Jesus was in Paradise (Spiritual state) here on the earth when he made that statement).

We should also understand that the earth is a part of the physical heavens. Six months from now the earth will be on the other side of the sun—(93 million miles X 2). Will we be better off then?

Mark 14:62—ye shall see the Son of man sitting on the right hand of power, and coming in the clouds of heaven. (These are not physical clouds, but are the clouds of glory produced by the power of God as people call upon the Name of the Mediator—Jesus (1 Tim 2:5).

Matthew 26:64 Jesus said—Hereafter shall ye see the Son of man sitting on the right hand of power, and coming in the clouds of heaven.

Mark 13:26 And then shall they see the Son of man coming in the clouds with great power and glory. 1 Thes. 4:17—we—shall be caught up together with them in the clouds, to meet the Lord in the air: (Air extends only about 600 miles) and so shall we ever be with the Lord.

How far out do the clouds extend?

Even much less than the atmosphere!

Rev. 21:3 And I heard a great voice out of heaven saying, Behold, the tabernacle of God is WITH MEN, and he will DWELL with them, and they shall be his people, and God ***himself*** shall be with them, and be their God.

Man and woman were to live forever on the earth, but was warned that in the day they took into their mental and physical system, the knowledge of evil, they would die. Gen. 2:17 for in the day that thou eatest thereof thou shalt surely die.

But the mediator came to save us from death. 1 Cor. 15:24 Then cometh the end, when he shall have delivered up the kingdom of God, even the Father; when he shall have put down all rule and all authority and power. (25) For he MUST reign, (No matter how long it takes) till he hath put all enemies under his feet. (26) The last enemy that shall be destroyed is death.

Zech. 10:1 Ask ye of the Lord rain in the time of the latter rain; so the Lord shall make BRIGHT CLOUDS,(glory and power of God) and give them showers of rain, to every one grass in the field.

John 5:39 ***Search the scriptures; for in them ye think ye have eternal life: and they (the scriptures) are they which testify of me.***

John 5:40 And ye will not come to me (Jesus), that ye might have life.

Regarding the Old Testament

Did anybody during the Old Testament times go out there into other parts of the heavens?

No! These all died.

Heb. 11:13 ***These ALL DIED in faith, not having received the promises—.***

---

1 Cor. 2:14 But the natural man receiveth not the things of the Spirit of God: for they are foolishness unto him: neither can he know them, because they are spiritually discerned.

A person must have been born again of his/her spirit,(John 3:3) receive the Holy Ghost Acts 2:4, and be filled with the holy spirit. They must be given spiritual eyes and ears before they can understand spiritual things.

****

Red Sea, Crossing the

Ruth asked this question.

How did the Lord cause the water to go back when Moses stretched out his hand over the sea?

James gave this response.

CROSSING OF THE RED SEA

Numbers 33:6 And they departed from Succoth and pitched in Etham, which is in the edge of the wilderness.

Numbers 33:7 And they removed from Etham, and TURNED

AGAIN unto Pihahiroth which is before Baalzephon: and they pitched before Migdol.

Exodus 14:21 And Moses stretched out his hand over the sea; and the Lord caused the sea to go back BY A STRONG EAST WIND ALL THAT NIGHT, and made the sea dry land, and the waters were divided.

God is aware of the intensity of the impending winds: when they will arrive and when they will subside.

Eccl. 1:6 The wind goeth toward the south, and turneth about unto the north; it whirleth about continually, and the wind returneth again according to his circuits.

He understands the crushing power of the continental plates: the building pressures beneath the earth's surface is not hidden from the knowledge of God. ***According to his purpose he guides men into perfect coordination with those elements for the advancement of his Name.***

Elijah prayed (James 5:17-18) before the beginning of the three years and six months drought, and then he prayed again for the rain to return. God created rain but the rain always comes in seasons (Deut. 11:14). Moses stretched out his hand at the time the winds were due. (Matthew 8:26) Jesus rebuked the winds and the sea; and there was a great calm. God was with Moses, Elijah, and Jesus and many others strewn across the pages of history. Without the timely direction of God those men could have done nothing, and the Name of God would not have been known.

Jesus said, (John 5:19) The Son can do nothing of himself, but what he seeth the Father do—. (20)—The Father loveth the Son, and showeth him all things that himself doeth—.

Dic. Wm. Smith BAALZEPHON: A place in Egypt near where the Israelites crossed the Red Sea (Sea of Reeds).

Baalzephon is placed on the western shore of the Gulf of Suez, a little below its head, which at that time was about 30 or 40 miles northward of the present head. The country, is now a desert of gravelly sand, with wide patches about the old sea bottom, of rank marsh land, now called the Bitter Lakes.

THAT AREA WAS NOT A DEEP PART
OF THE RED SEA.

That was why the ***VERY STRONG EAST WIND ALL THAT NIGHT*** could have driven back the water so that the Israelites could pass. Then the wind changed its course and the waters returned. (Exodus 14:26)

Exodus 14:22 The waters were a WALL unto them on their right hand and on their left.

Stand on the sea shore. Look out over the sea toward the horizon. At that distance the water seems to go upward as a wall. This is what they saw on both sides.

****

RELATIONSHIPS, SAME SEX

Kathy asked this question.

In my thoughts God made both sexes for a reason. I don't think two people of the same sex should be together; what is your thoughts on this, was God against it?

James gave this response.

What do you think about same sex marriages?

Luke 17:34 I (Jesus) tell you, that night there shall be><><><><>***TWO MEN IN ONE BED***;<><><><><> the one shall be taken, and the other left.

Although this prophecy was rightly applied to the destruction that came upon Jerusalem in the year Anno Domini 70, it can be equally applied to any approaching end of an era. (This condition also existed before the flood).

There is no doubt about the original plan of God. Nature and science bear out that positive and negative must operate together for progress in the production of life.—not negative with negative or positive with positive. There is no argument in this matter: No, it can't even happen during the couple's sleeping hours as was intended for the male and female from the beginning.

If any person, whether of the negative set or the positive set decides to Call upon the Name of God with every heart beat forever, he or she will be eventually TAKEN toward perfection. They will be guided to, and given all the spiritual gifts necessary to effect a change in their animalistic nature.

The person or persons that believes calling upon the Name of God is foolishness, and refuses to occupy him or herself in such supposed nonsense, will be left to wallow around in their weaknesses and misguided confusion. There will be no hope for them, because there is no other way for man or woman to be saved from destruction, except through faith in, and calling upon the Name of God. This formula for the strength, guidance, and protection of human life was devised when the first seed for the creation of man was placed in the earth.

Jesus came to sever ties.

Matthew 10:34 Think not that I am come to send peace on earth: I come not to send peace, BUT A SWORD. (spiritual)

The sword (not natural sword) is used to divide the believer from the unbeliever; to rearrange associations, whether they are among a person's own family or improper physical or spiritual connections.

Some Bible references—Sodom Gen. 13:13, 18:20, Gen. 19:4-11

Men of the city—Sodom and Gomorrah-brimstone Gen. 19:24.

****

Resurrection

Zenaide asked this question.

Did the saints that arose, after Jesus's resurrection, have physical bodies?

James gave this response.

DID THE SAINTS THAT AROSE AFTER JESUS' RESURRECTION HAVE PHYSICAL BODIES?

Matthew. 27:52 And the graves were opened; and many bodies of the saints which slept arose. (53) And came out of the graves after his resurrection, and went into the holy city, and APPEARED unto many.

NO! After the physical body has decayed that same body is not retrieved.

Mat. 22:29—ye do err, not knowing the scriptures, nor the power of God. FOR IN THE RESURRECTION THEY NEITHER MARRY, NOR ARE GIVEN IN MARRIAGE, BUT ARE LIKE THE ANGELS IN HEAVEN.

Luke 20:35 But they which shall be accounted worthy to obtain that world, and the resurrection from the dead, (36) NEITHER CAN THEY DIE ANY MORE: FOR THEY ARE EQUAL UNTO THE ANGELS—.

Well then, were the five hundred brethren that saw Jesus at once the same men that were resurrected?

NO! They were men that were still alive at that time.

1 Cor. 15:5 And that he was seen of Cephas, then of the twelve. (6) After that, he was seen of above five hundred brethren at once; of whom the greater part remain unto this present, BUT SOME ARE FALLEN ASLEEP. (died)

NO! THEY ARE NOT RESURRECTED WITH A PHYSICAL BODY. THEY ARE AS THE ANGELS AND THEY CANNOT DIE ANY MORE.

1 Cor. 15:35 But some man will say, How are the dead raised up? and with what body do they come? (36) THOU FOOL, THAT WHICH THOU SOWEST IS NOT QUICKENED EXCEPT IT DIE: (37) and that which thou sowest, THOU SOWEST NOT THAT BODY THAT SHALL BE. (44) It is sown a NATURAL BODY: it is raised a SPIRITUAL BODY.

****

RESURRECTION, ANGELS AND MEN.

Writings of the bible are directed to many groups of people. The following is just a small example of three of those groups.

FIRST: Those that die and have hope of a resurrection.

John 11:25 Jesus said unto her (Martha), I am (at the present time) the resurrection, and the life: he that believeth in me, though he were dead, yet shall he live.

SECOND: Those that are resurrected after death and decay, will become as the angels reigning (sovereign's authority or rule) from the spiritual side of God's creation.

Matthew 22:30 In the resurrection they neither marry, nor are given in marriage, but ARE AS THE ANGELS OF GOD IN HEAVEN.

THIRD: Those that become stronger to live and reign with Christ here on the earth. They are natural people fulfilling what Jesus referred to when he said, (John 11:26) And whosoever ***liveth and believeth in me*** shall never die. Believest thou this?

> 1 Cor. 15:52—the dead (spiritually dead—Matt. 8:22, Luke 9:60) shall be raised incorruptible—.
>
> 1 Cor. 15:51 Behold, I show you a mystery; We shall not all sleep, but we shall ALL be changed.
>
> 1 Cor. 15:53—this corruptible must put on incorruption.
>
> 1 Cor. 15:53 This mortal must put on immortality . . . .
>
> 1 Cor. 15:54 So when this corruptible shall have put on incorruption, and this mortal shall have put on immortality, then shall be brought to pass the saying that is written, ***Death is swallowed up in victory.***
>
> 1 Cor. 15:55 ***O death, where is thy sting? O grave, where is thy victory?***
>
> 1 Cor 15:57—***thanks be to God, which giveth us the victory through our Lord Jesus Christ.***

This is the ultimate plan of God, that men should live on the earth eternally—.

It has been two thousand years since Jesus came to the earth with the message of life. ***How long will it take?***

For the unbeliever it will never happen. It depends upon the willingness of men, women, boys and girls to draw near God by calling upon him by His Name.

Strength is coming to the family of man upon the earth.

The angels, seen and unseen, are ready to help those that will call upon the Name of the Lord. There is no end to the success of mankind when they understand and call upon the Name of God, and ***stop making names, and having faith in those names.***

Gen. 11:4 LET US MAKE US A NAME.

NO! Don't make another name, and dissolve the names in religion that you have. For the world to come into a peaceful state, and all the peoples become one in purpose, they all must call upon the Name of God. That Name is One. It was in the beginning with God: It was God. (John 1:1) It was the Name given to God's only begotten son (after the spirit).

IT WAS JESUS.

IT IS JESUS,

AND IT ALWAYS WILL BE JESUS.

Hebrews 13:8 ***Jesus Christ the same yesterday, and to day, and for ever.***

Look around. Observe the vast number of people 'Calling upon the Name of the Lord. In coordination with that fact, are people not living longer on the earth?

CHRIST IS RETURNING

Jer. 31:34—they all shall know me, from the least of them unto the greatest of them, SAITH THE LORD—.

Did not the darkness of ignorance begin to roll back as the church emerged from the wilderness by the people's faith in the Name of God? Were not they calling upon the Name of God similar to the way the early church did? This work must continue. Gal. 3:3 (for a phrase only) having begun in the Spirit, are ye now made perfect by the flesh?

NO! Unless God does it, it will not be done, and God will not do it, unless people continue calling upon HIS NAME so that they may not be unduly influenced by words. Words are spirit. It takes the spirit of Christ to offset their influence.

Sagan, Carl

Soluod asked this question.

Anybody hear what Carl Sagan said the first moment after he died?

"Ooops!"

James gave this response.

HE SAID NOTHING!

The wages of sin is death. (Romans 6:23) The only hope for a person that dies is through a resurrection, and that is not moments later. (Matthew 27:53)

Eccl. 9:5 For the living know that they shall die: but the dead know not anything, neither have they any more a reward; for the memory of them is forgotten.

Eccl. 9:6 Also their love, and their hatred, and their envy, is now perished; neither have they any more a portion for ever in anything that is done under the sun.

Proverbs 30:4 Who hath ascended up into heaven, or

descended? who hath gathered the wind in his fists? who hath bound the waters in a garment? who hath established all the ends of the earth? WHAT IS HIS NAME, AND WHAT IS HIS SONS NAME, if thou canst tell?

JESUS IS HIS SON'S NAME!

Jesus said, (John 5:43) I am come in my Father's name.

Jesus said, (John 3:13)—No man hath ascended up to heaven, but he that came down from heaven, even the Son of man which is in heaven. (When Jesus made the above statement he was standing in Paradise. The same spiritual state the first man and woman had been placed—the garden in Eden). Gen. 2:8.

Rev. 2:7 He that hath an ear, let him hear what the Spirit saith unto the churches; To him that overcometh will I give to eat of the TREE OF LIFE, which is in the midst of the paradise of God.

John 3:14 And as Moses lifted up the serpent in the wilderness, even so must the Son of man be lifted up: (15) That WHOSOEVER believeth in him should NOT PERISH, but have ETERNAL LIFE.

This is the same eternal life that was offered to the first man and woman, but they would not call upon the name of God, therefore, they became too weak to conform to the one requirement that God placed before them, and that was to leave the automatic life making process under the control of God, so that overpopulation would not occur and create the necessity for death.

Don't even touch it lest ye die. Gen. 3:3.

Jesus came to the earth to show man/woman the way back into that Paradise of God: heaven on earth the same as God intended from the beginning.

John 14:6 Jesus said, I AM THE WAY, THE TRUTH, AND THE LIFE: NO MAN COMETH UNTO THE FATHER, BUT BY ME.

Call upon the Name of the Lord, and he will show the way through the guidance of the Holy Ghost. Joel 2:32, Acts 2:21, Rom. 10:13.

soluod rated this answer:

'T'was a joke, man.

James gave this follow-up answer.

I KNOW!

****

Saints Identified?

Edward asked this question.

DID THE RESURRECTED SAINTS IDENTIFY THEMSELVES BY NAME WHEN THEY APPEARED UNTO MANY AT JERUSALEM?

James gave this response.

Matthew 27:52—The graves were opened; and many bodies of the saints which slept arose, (53) And came out of the graves after his resurrection, and went into the holy city, and appeared unto many. (Matthew 22:30) In the resurrection they—***are as the angels of God in heaven.***

Angels are seen only in vision form. When the body decays It does not come back to life as a natural body.

NO, the angels did not identify themselves. It is a detriment to the spiritual well being of people when any other NAME separates them from the NAME OF GOD.

Acts 4:12 Neither is there salvation in any other: for there is none other ***NAME*** under heaven given among men, whereby we must be saved.

Luke 4:8—Thou shalt worship the Lord thy God, and ***him only*** shalt thou serve.

THERE ARE TWO ANGELS IDENTIFIED BY NAME IN THE BIBLE, namely, Michael and Gabriel. Their names were originated in Daniel's vision.

(Michael—meaning 'Who is like God).

(Gabriel—meaning 'Man of God'.)

Daniel 8:16 And I heard a man's voice between the banks of Ulai, which called, and said, Gabriel, make this man to understand the vision.

Daniel 12:1 And at that time shall Michael stand up, the great prince which standeth for the children of thy people: (compare Jude 9—Michael—archangel).

Gabriel appeared to Zacharias BY NAME in vision form. He did not appear BY NAME to Joseph in his dream or to Mary in her vision.

(Luke said it was Gabriel but the angel did not divulge his name to Mary. (Luke 1:26).

Luke 1:19 And the Angel answering said unto him (Zacharias in a vision) I am Gabriel, that stand in the presence of God: and am sent to speak unto thee. (regarding John).

Matt. 1:20—the angel of the Lord appeared unto him in a dream, saying, Joseph, thou son of David, fear not to take unto thee Mary ***thy wife***: for that which is conceived in her is of the Holy Ghost. (The angel did not identify himself). Luke 1:28 And the angel came in unto her, (without introducing himself) and said, Hail, thou that art highly favored, the Lord is with thee:

JACOB ASKED THE MAN'S NAME BUT RECEIVED NO REPLY.

Gen. 32:29 And Jacob asked him (the 'man' that wrestled with him) And said, tell me, I pray thee thy name. And he said, wherefore is it that thou dost ask after my NAME? And he blessed him there. (He ignored the request). (30) And Jacob called the name of the place Peniel; (Penuel) Meaning 'face of God.' or 'face of El': for I have seen Elohim face to face.

Exodus 33:20 And he (God) said, Thou canst not see my face: for there shall NO MAN SEE ME. AND LIVE. (23)—thou shalt see my back parts: but my face shall not be seen.

THE ANGEL OF THE LORD FOUND HAGAR BUT HE DID NOT DIVULGE HIS NAME.

Gen. 16:13 And she (Hagar) called the name of the Lord that spake unto her, 'Thou God seest me': for she said, Have I also here looked after him that seest me? (No answer was given). (14) Wherefore the well was called Beerlahairoi, meaning a well of the living—or living spring.

It is important to remember that God wants His Name (Jesus)in the foreheads of the people for ***their own single spiritual focus***. (Rev. 14:1)

****

SALVATION

(saving a person from sin or danger)

Anonymous asked this question.

Ok, I am a born again Christian. I use to be in to devil worshiping, Now what do I do?

James gave this response.

Satan, Devil, Serpent, and Great Dragon.

Revelations 12:8-9. The great dragon—that old serpent called the Devil, and Satan—***is one and the same***. It describes the fallen nature of man caused by the separation of the human mind from the mind of God.

The first woman did not call upon the Name of the Lord, nor did her husband with her. (Gen. 4:26) Because of this they became weakened and sensual. Feelings and ideas came into their conscious mind that God did not intend from the beginning.

Their thoughts wondered. The husband reasoned with his wife. He (man) was more subtle than any beast of the field which the Lord God had made. Gen. 3:1

The man questioned the woman. Did God say you shall not eat of every tree of the garden?

Gen. 3:2 The woman replied to the serpent, (her husband) We may eat of the (natural) fruit of the trees of the garden : but of the ((((symbolic tree—man and woman—People are called trees in the Bible. (Judges 9:8, Ezekiel 31, Matthew 3:10)))) tree which is in the midst of the garden, God said you shall not eat (partake)of it, neither shall you touch it, lest you die. Gen. 3:4 Her husband, the symbolic serpent, said unto her, You shall not surely die (5) For God knows that when we partake of the delicacies of this tree, our eyes will be opened to the truth and we will be as God to know both good and evil.

Gen 3:6 When the woman was convinced by her husband's interpretation that God really didn't mean what he had said, she willingly submitted to the desires of her husband. They placed within their control the production of new life. It was at this point that they realized they were naked and they became afraid because of their condemnation. Gen. 2:25, 3:7,10-11.

When God spoke with the woman and asked what she had done, she said the serpent (her husband) beguiled me, and I did eat. (Partake of). Then God said to the woman (Gen 3:16) I will greatly multiply thy sorrow and thy conception; in sorrow thou shalt bring forth children—.

SATAN

Peter's reasoning was not right, so Jesus said unto him, Get thee behind me, SATAN: YOU are an offence unto me: for you savor not the things that be of God, but those that be of men. Matthew 16:23.

JESUS WAS TEMPTED OF SATAN.

Matthew 4—Jesus was hungry because he had done without food for forty days, so it came into his mind, if I am the son of God I should be able to command these stones that they become bread. But then he remembered a passage that stated that 'man shall not live by bread alone, but by every word that proceeds out of the mouth of God.'

Then his mind led him to the pinnacle of the temple, and

reasoned that if he were the son of God (Matthew 4:5) he should be protected by the angels if he should leap from the wall to the ground. But Jesus remembered another passage that stated 'Thou shalt not temp the Lord thy God.'

Then Jesus was led to a mountain site. As he gazed over the city, he reasoned that he could have all the kingdoms and glory of the world if he would only worship the material things rather than God. Then Jesus came to his senses and said, Get away from me, SATAN: for it is written, Thou shalt worship the Lord thy God, and him only shalt thou serve. It was then that the DEVIL left him, and angels came and ministered unto him. Matthew 4:11. (here again Satan and Devil is the same).

Romans 8:6—To be carnally minded is death, but to be spiritually minded is life and peace. (7) Because the carnal mind (sensual) is enmity (Hatred) against God: for it is not subject to the law of God, neither indeed can be. (8) So then they that are in the flesh cannot please God.

Rev. 12:9 And the great dragon was cast out, that old serpent, called the Devil, and Satan, which deceiveth the whole world: he was cast out into the earth, and his angels were cast out with him. (10) And I heard a loud voice saying in heaven, Now is come salvation, and strength, and the kingdom of our God, and the power of his Christ:

The thoughts and interpretations of men have deceived the whole world, but(John 14:6) Jesus said I am the way, the truth, and the life: no man cometh unto the Father, but by me. Call upon His Name and be saved from the destructive elements of the earth and the minds of men. Joel 2:32, Acts 2:21, Rom. 10:13.

Since paraphrasing was used here for clarity, it is suggested that the readers go to the concordance and select all the passages dealing with the words, Devil, Satan, Serpent and Dragon. 1 Thes. 5:21 Prove all things: hold fast that which is good.

Anonymous asked this follow-up question.

But this didn't answer the question. I already know who Satan is, remember I worshiped him! The question was what do I do now?

James gave this response.

When we listen to the advisors we find ourselves going around in circles.

To become stabilized we must remain associated with the right kind of people; the persons that are calling upon God's Name.

Paul said (Heb. 10:25) ***Not forsaking the assembling of ourselves together, as the manner of some is; but exhorting one another—***.

The church consists of people coming together in the Name of God, as in the first church. (There are scriptures in my other writings to designate where those passages are found).

According to Matthew 18:20, Jesus said,—Where two or three are gathered together in My Name (Jesus), there am I in the midst of them.

From two or three as in the home, comes the expansion into larger numbers as to the neighbors, to a church building, to the county, state, nation and the world.

All this starts in the home. Two people calling upon the Name of the Lord. This, they were doing in the early church.

Acts 2:21 And it shall come to pass, that WHOSOEVER shall call on the NAME of the LORD, shall be saved.

This, do without ceasing, and all the spiritual gifts will be given so that you will make it all the way.

****

Saul to Paul

Edward asked this question.

Did Jesus change Saul's name to Paul?

NO! Jesus referred to him as Saul.

Acts 9:4 And he (Saul) fell to the earth, and heard a voice saying unto him SAUL, SAUL, why persecutest thou me?

Paul's Jewish name was Saul, given at birth after his father or some near kin, or even after the famous Old Testament King Saul, who like Paul was from the tribe of Benjamin.

Paulos was Paul's official Roman name but he did not go by that name as recorded in the New Testament until he met ***Sergius Paulus***. (small or little).

Saul—a grander name than that of Paul. (asked for or demanded).

Did the Holy Ghost refer to Saul as Paul?

NO! ***The Holy Ghost referred to him as Saul.*** Acts 13:2 As they ministered to the Lord, and fasted, the Holy Ghost said, Separate me Barnabus and SAUL, for the work whereunto I have called them.

Acts 26:16 Jesus said, But rise, and stand upon thy feet: for I have appeared unto thee for this purpose,—to make thee a minister and a witness. (Not an apostle—Saul wrote this himself. Rom. 1:1)

When Jesus spoke with Ananias what did he call Saul?

Acts 9:11—Arise, and go into the street which is called straight, and inquire in the house of Judas for ***one called SAUL***, of Tarsus:

How did Ananias address Saul?

Acts. 9:17 And Ananias went his way, and entered into the house; and putting his hands on him said, ***BROTHER SAUL,—.***

THE NAME PAUL APPEARED FOR THE FIRST TIME JUST AFTER SAUL BECAME ACQUAINTED WITH Sergius PAULus.

Acts 13:7 Which was with the deputy of the country, Sergius Paulus, a prudent man; who called for Barnabas and SAUL, and desired to hear the word of God. (8) But Elymas the sorcerer (for so is his name by interpretation) withstood them, seeking to turn away the deputy from the faith.

Acts 13:9 Then SAUL, (WHO ALSO IS CALLED PAUL),—.

Notice how close the name PAUL is to the name PAULus and how quickly Saul began using the name Paul (His Roman Name) after their meeting.

****

SAUL (Paul) an Apostle?

Charlene asked this question.

DID JESUS DESIGNATE SAUL (Paul) AS AN APOSTLE?

James gave this response.

First it must be understood how a person became an apostle.

Explanation taken from the Bible Dictionary—William Smith LLD—Teacher's addition—Copyright 1948.

Their office.—(1) The original qualification of an apostle, as stated by St. Peter on the occasion of electing a successor to the traitor Judas, was that he should have been personally acquainted with the whole ministerial course of our Lord, from his baptism by John till the day when he was taken up into heaven.

(2) They were chosen by CHRIST HIMSELF.

(3) They had the power of working miracles.

(4) They were inspired. John 16:13.

(5) Their work seems to have been pre-eminently that of founding the churches and upholding them by supernatural power specially bestowed for that purpose.

(6) THE OFFICE CEASED, AS A MATTER OF COURSE, WITH ITS FIRST HOLDERS; ALL CONTINUATION OF IT, FROM THE VERY CONDITIONS OF ITS EXISTENCE (cf.1 Cor.9:1) BEING IMPOSSIBLE.

Paul in defense.

2 Cor. 12:11 I am become a fool in glorying; YE HAVE COMPELLED ME: FOR I OUGHT TO HAVE BEEN COMMENDED OF YOU: for in nothing am I behind the very chiefest apostles-

Did God, Jesus, Holy Ghost or the Apostles appoint Saul as an Apostle?

NO!

Who did?

SAUL PUT HIMSELF IN THAT POSITION.

It has been stated that 'Send' as in Acts 13:3-4 means the same as 'Apostle'. But consider that Jesus could have named

Saul as an apostle the same as he did with the other twelve. Matthias was made an Apostle because he conformed to all the requirements necessary to become an apostle.—Acts 1:23-26.

LUKE 6:13 AND WHEN IT WAS DAY, HE (JESUS) CALLED UNTO HIM HIS DISCIPLES: AND OF THEM HE CHOSE TWELVE, WHOM ALSO HE NAMED APOSTLES;—.

LATER WHAT DID JESUS SAY TO SAUL?

Acts 9:4 And he (Saul) fell to the earth, and heard a voice saying unto him, SAUL, SAUL, why persecutest thou me?

5 And he said, Who art thou, Lord? And the Lord said, I am Jesus whom thou persecutest.

6 And he trembling and astonished said, Lord, what wilt thou have me to do? and the Lord said unto him, Arise, and go into the city, and it shall be told thee what thou must do.

THIS IS ALL JESUS SAID TO SAUL. HE DID NOT CHANGE HIS NAME NOR MAKE HIM AN APOSTLE.

JESUS THEN CAME TO ANANIAS AT DAMASCUS IN A VISION.

Acts 9:11 And the Lord said unto him, Arise, and go into the street which is called Straight, and inquire in the house of Judas for one called SAUL, of Tarsus: for, behold, he prayeth, (12) And hath seen in a vision a man named Ananias coming in, and putting his hand on him, that he might receive his sight.—15 Go thy way: for he is a chosen vessel unto me, to BEAR MY NAME before the Gentiles, and kings, and the children of Israel: (16) For I will show him how great things he must suffer for my NAME'S sake.

THIS IS ALL JESUS SAID TO ANANIAS. Saul's way consisted of a three way mixture.

1. The way of Christ

2. The way of the Pharisees

3. The way of Saul.

SAUL DID IT HIS WAY.

Peter said (John 6:68)—to whom shall we go? THOU HAST THE WORDS OF ETERNAL LIFE.

Jesus said (John 14:25) These things have I spoken unto you, BEING YET PRESENT WITH YOU.

John 6:26 But the Comforter, which is the Holy Ghost, whom the Father will send in my Name, he shall teach you all things, and bring ALL THINGS TO YOUR REMEMBRANCE, WHATSOEVER I HAVE SAID UNTO YOU.

John 16:13 Howbeit when he, the Spirit of truth is come, he will guide you into all truth: for HE SHALL NOT SPEAK OF HIMSELF (on his own accord) but whatsoever he shall hear, that shall he speak:—. (14)—he shall receive of mine, and shall show it unto you.

John 17:8—Jesus said, I have given unto them the WORDS WHICH THOU GAVEST ME—.

John 17:20 Neither pray I for these alone (twelve apostles), but for them also which shall believe on me THROUGH THEIR WORD—. (21) That they all may be one; as thou, Father, art in me, and I in thee, that they also may be ONE in US.

Saul preferred not to hear THEIR WORDS. (the words that came from God through Jesus to the Apostles and then out to the world).

SAUL WAS ARROGANT.

He wrote (Gal. 1:11), But I certify you, brethren, that the gospel which was preached of me is NOT AFTER MAN, neither was I taught it, but by the REVELATION OF JESUS CHRIST. (15) But when It pleased God, who separated me from my mother's womb, and called me by his grace, (16) to reveal his Son in me, that I might preach him among the heathen; immediately I CONFERRED NOT WITH FLESH AND BLOOD—(17) Neither went I up to Jerusalem to them which were apostles before me; but went into Arabia, and returned again unto Damascus. (18) Then after three years I went up to Jerusalem to see Peter, and abode with him FIFTEEN DAYS. (19) But other of the apostles saw I none, save James the Lord's brother. (21) Afterwards I came into the regions of Syria and Cilicia; Gal. 2:1 Then FOURTEEN YEARS AFTER, I went up again to Jerusalem with Barnabas, and took Titus with me also. (20) And I went up by revelation, and communicated unto them that gospel which I preach among the Gentiles—.

IF REVELATIONS ALONE COULD HAVE SAVED HUMANITY, THEN IT WAS UNNECESSARY FOR JESUS TO COME INTO SUCH A VIOLENT AND CONFUSED WORLD.

THERE ARE MANY VOICES IN THE WORLD, HEREIN LIES CONFUSION. JESUS ONLY MUST BE HEARD.

Paul wrote (1 Cor. 13:9) For we know in part, and we prophesy in part. (10) But when that which is perfect is come THEN THAT WHICH IS IN PART SHALL BE DONE AWAY.

Saul was brought up at the feet of a PHARISEE named Gamaliel (Acts 5:34), and taught according to the perfect manner of the law of the fathers (Acts 22:3).

Phlp. 3:8-9 Paul said, after reiterating accomplishments in his religious up-bringing, 'I count it as loss, and do count them but dung'. But he, like any educated individual, drew here and there upon his knowledge gained from the teachings of the Pharisee's religion. ***This is unavoidable.***

BEWARE OF THE LEAVEN.

Jesus said to his disciples (Matt. 16:6), Take heed and beware of the leaven of the Pharisees and of the Sadducees.—.

Matt. 16:12—the disciples understood he was referring to the ***doctrines*** of those religious movements.

Ref: Cruden's Concordance. Jesus denounced the Pharisees for their hypocrisy, which was shown by their care for the minutest formalities imposed by the traditions of the elders, but not for the MIND AND HEART which should correspond. They were AMBITIOUS, ARROGANT, AND PROUDLY SELF-RIGHTEOUS, of which qualities were contrary to the teachings of Jesus.

****

Saved and seeking

Ronndonn asked this question.

If the theology convinces a person "I am saved since I have met all the requirements of being saved" . . . is that a good thing?

Is it a good thing for a person to think they are saved and that sometime in the future they are going to be given a spiritual body simply because they believed a Certain thing and jumped through all the hoops they were told about? Is that a good thing if a person becomes convinced that they have been saved??

I ask this question since the instruction I have read is this . . . "Seek Ye first the Kingdom of God . . . " I ask the question because if a person is convinced that they are saved, what will motivate them to seek anything?? If they think they are saved, then they may think, Oh, the seeking is over now, and all I need to do is save others . . . so they go about trying to convince others that they need to believe this or that and confess this or that and then they too are saved.

So where is the seeking in all this? What about the treasure hidden in a field? What about the pearl that is still there in the ocean. Have they been convinced that they already have it when in fact they don't.

So the question is . . . is convincing someone that they are saved . . . is that a good thing when it comes to seeking the kingdom of God?? (I am looking at this whole thing as Jesus spoke about it of course)

James gave this response.

There is more to being saved than has been preached!

Acts 2:21—It shall come to pass, that WHOSOEVER shall CALL on the NAME of the LORD shall be SAVED. Also Romans 10:13 and Joel 2:32 (delivered). Here are three witnesses that establish these words.

Faith without ***works*** is dead. James 2: 17—Faith, if it hath not works, is dead, being alone. (18)—show me thy faith without thy works, and I will show thee my faith by my works.

It is work to Call upon the Name of the Lord. Heb. 7:19—The law made nothing perfect, but the bringing in of a BETTER HOPE did; by the which we draw nigh unto God. (25)—He (Jesus) is able also to SAVE them to the uttermost that come unto God by him, seeing he ever liveth to make intercession for them,—.

Acts 4:12 Neither is there salvation (saving from sin or danger) in ANY OTHER: for there is none OTHER NAME under heaven given among men, whereby we MUST BE SAVED.

James 4:8 Draw nigh to God, and he will draw nigh to you.

Then what must be done? Cleanse your hands, ye sinners, and purify your hearts ye DOUBLE minded. (Look to God through Jesus only—no one else).

It is not within our strength to overcome anything. When we draw near God by calling upon His Name we are led by the spirit to all the spiritual gifts necessary to overcome the weaknesses in our bodies that we received as a result of our fallen ancestors all the way back to the first man and woman. THEY DID NOT CALL UPON THE NAME OF THE LORD, (proof-Gen. 4:26) and that is why they became too weak to conform to the will of God.

Adamah and woman were put here on the earth to live in that spiritual state of heaven forever, always increasing in strength as the years continued, but they did not see a need for calling upon God by His Name in order to keep HIS POWER flowing from their belly into everlasting life. John 7:38-39).

Being saved is more than shaking hands with the preacher and confessing that you believe in Jesus. It is a continual work of drawing near God by Calling upon His Name.

When a person (whosoever) is calling upon the Name of the Lord, God will kill that old adamic spirit that was received from the weakened father and place a RIGHT SPIRIT within. Psalm 51:10 Create in me a clean heart, O God; and renew a right spirit within me. (11) Cast me not away from thy presence; and take not thy holy spirit from me. (12) Restore unto me the joy of thy salvation; (saved from sin or danger) and uphold me with thy FREE spirit. (It is a free gift of God not to be bought with money. Acts 8:18-19).

When a person continues Calling upon the Name of the Lord, God will perform an operation on the eyes and ears to make them see and hear spiritual things.

If a person continues Calling upon the Name of the Lord, God will lead them by the spirit to the Gift of the Holy Ghost and the filling of the Holy spirit. This spirit must be continually maintained by increased faith and calling upon the Name of the Lord. Of course, it is an inside work, not outwardly. God wants us to be intelligent and always in our right mind, (Mark 5:15) ever becoming stronger and stronger as the years continue, always abounding until time will be no more, because death is abolished.

1 Cor. 15:55 O death, where is thy sting? O grave, where is thy victory? Romans 7:24 O wretched man that I am! Who shall deliver me from the body of this death?

Romans 7:25 I thank God through Jesus Christ our Lord.

Ronndonn rated this answer:

Lots of nice quotes. Thanks James. This thing about good works is interesting since drawing closer to God gives REST and rest means that we can be more dynamic in activity. So that relationship does make common sense too.

James gave this follow-up answer.

When I was thirty one and literally coming to the end of my life, I needed to grab hold of something. I began to look through the Bible for some kind of hope. I found the Name of Jesus.

I asked God to create within me a clean heart and a right spirit. Psalm 51:10.

Calling upon the Name of the Lord was advocated in Joel 2:32, Zeph. 3:9, 13:9, Rom. 10:3, and Acts 2:21—It shall come to pass, that WHOSOEVER shall Call on the Name of the Lord shall be saved. Acts 9:14, 1 Cor 1:2—with all that in every place Call upon the NAME of JESUS Christ our Lord.

I NEEDED TO BE SAVED

Then I saw in Genesis 4:26 when men began to Call upon the Name of the Lord. Psalm 113:3 From the rising of the sun unto the going down of the same the Lord"s Name is to be praised. Psalm 119:55 I have remembered thy Name, O Lord, in the Night, and have kept thy law.

I had not kept the law. I didn't have strength enough to do that, but I needed to be saved from all the weaknesses in my body and mind. So I prayed this prayer: God give me strength to say Jesus just one more time forever. I knew that as long as I had strength I would do just that. I had to be relieved of all that wretched condemnation I felt within my brain and spirit. Since 1960 I have called upon the Name of the Lord with every heart beat, with every breath. There have been oppositions from most ministers and some of the family alike, but since I made a vow, I am obligated for conscience sake to keep that promise, if for no other reason. I have never quit, in spite of all the words of the advisors.

It came as quite a surprise that I was not the first to know, when I found a book that had a section in it called JAPAM. This story is about a Russian Peasant—It is listed among one of my answers under Japam in my book titled "They Built a Flying Saucer.".

Have I done everything right since I started calling on the Name of the Lord? No! But I found that we still have grace extended to us until we become strong enough to overcome the weaknesses that have been handed down from our ancestors. (Our spirit may be changed but our nature remains. This is what we have to overcome—it is easier with age. Gen. 8:21 The imagination of man's heart is evil from his youth.)

Matthew 12:31—I say unto you, ALL manner of Sin and blasphemy shall be forgiven unto men: but the blasphemy against the Holy Ghost shall not be forgiven unto men.

Romans 3:23 For all have sinned, and come short of the glory of God. (24) Being justified freely by his grace through the redemption that is in Christ Jesus.

Hebrews 7:25 Wherefore he is able also to save them to the uttermost that come unto God by him, (Jesus) seeing he ever liveth to make intercession for them.

Romans 6:1 What shall we say then? Shall we continue in sin, that grace may abound? (2) God forbid—.

But by faith in and Calling upon the Name of the Lord we can overcome! (If I had not returned to reality after 1960, I would never have known that our nature is a very strong influence that forces our actions. This is what must be overcome in time).

And (Rev. 2:7) To him that overcometh will I give to eat of the Tree of Life, which is in the midst of the Paradise of God.

At the age of 73 I found that it is easier to refrain from sinning. This comes from age, time and experience. God is waiting—He has long patience. James 5:7

Ronndonn asked this follow-up question.

Japam, yes I think I know what you are talking about. You may have come across something spontaneously that others learn from spritual teachers and that is good. Sounds wonderful to me. The body should become the temple and finding God within is certainly biblical.

Proof is in the pudding so if it has helped you then you know you have the proof so you know more than the others who want to discourage you. Its wonderful that your walk has been so spontaneous. Being guided from within is best. Sounds like you are on a wonderful path. Wishing you Great speed in your journey.

****

Saved? "Who Then Can Be." ?

a servant asked this question.

Per Innocent III of Romanism and Bruce McConkie of Mormonism (1966 "Mormon Doctrine", Salt Lake City) there is no salvation outside those two groups. Yea, according to McConkie, without Joseph Smith there would be no salvation period. (p.670). (Since Innocent was a Pope speaking ex cathedra I'm assuming that his words are eternally significant. I don't know McConkie, but this exhaustive book of doctrine must have some weight too.)

Now I ask you to give me a Biblical response to the phenomenon of exclusive statements like this. Who will be included in the final roll call of the saints? Is it a particular group or philosophy? Is it a series of doctrines that make us worthy? submission to a particular leader? ***What must modern folks do to be saved***. Romanism and Mormonism were both absent from the early equations. Have either of them changed the script?

James gave this response.

Acts 2:21 And it shall come to pass, that WHOSOEVER shall call on the Name of the Lord SHALL BE SAVED.

Romans 10:13 For WHOSOEVER shall CALL UPON THE NAME OF THE LORD SHALL BE SAVED.

Joel 2:32 And it shall come to pass, that WHOSOEVER shall call on the Name of the Lord shall be delivered—.

Two or three witnesses are all that is needed to establish every word. So then the name of the Lord, Jesus, is the way to God. There is no other way. Jesus is the mediator between God and man.

1 Tim. 2:5 For there is one God, and one mediator between God and men, the man Christ Jesus. (No one else)

John 3:18 He that believeth on him is not condemned: but he that believeth not is condemned already, because he hath not believed in the NAME of the only begotten Son of God.

Acts 4:12 Neither is there salvation in any other: for there is none other Name under heaven given among men, whereby we must be saved.

All other names must be dissolved. God himself has caused the confusion in religion because of their desire to make a name for themselves instead of accepting Jesus only.

Each religion has said as in Gen. 11:4—Go to, let us build us a city and a tower, whose TOP MAY REACH UNTO HEAVEN; and let us MAKE A NAME, lest we be scattered abroad upon the face of the whole earth. (7) (And the Lord said) Go to, let us go down, and there confound their language, that they may not understand one another's speech.

Do they understand one another?

No!

Matthew 17:8 And when they (Peter, James and John) had lifted up their eyes, they saw NO MAN, save JESUS ONLY.

I know you know all these passages and many more, but sometimes they get lost among so many voices in the world of religion. Who can reach the masses? I have tried and found I have not been able to do it. Maybe you can.

****

Scornful men?

Ruth asked this question.

WHO WERE THE SCORNFUL MEN AT JERUSALEM?

James gave this response.

Isa. 28:14 Wherefore hear the word of the Lord, ye scornful men, that rule this people which is in Jerusalem.

The religious leaders that were jealous of Jesus, and were afraid they would lose their position.

John 11:48 If we let him thus alone, all men will believe on him: and the Romans shall come and take away both our place and nation.

WHY COULDN'T MEN of the established churches (Synagogues) be taught?

THREE REASONS—PLUS.

1} They were older and had been indoctrinated for their entire lives in their respective religious faiths.

2} The minds were addled (confused) by the use of too much alcohol. This activity was carried down from their forefathers of the Old Testament time.

Isa. 28:7 But they also have ***erred through wine***, and through strong drink are out of the way; the priest and the prophet have erred through strong drink, they are swallowed up of wine, they are out of the way through strong drink; they err in vision, they stumble in judgment.

Isa. 28:8 For all tables are full of vomit and filthiness, so that there is no place clean.

3) They were afraid of losing their position.

GOD THROUGH JESUS HAD TO TURN TO THE YOUNG.

Isa. 28:9 Who shall he teach knowledge? And whom shall he make to understand doctrine? Them that are weaned from the milk, and drawn from the breasts. (This analogy can be used both figuratively or literally).

The religionists of Jesus' time would not humble themselves and conscientiously consider what Jesus had to say. They would not start again and examine what must be, precept upon precept, precept upon precept, line upon line, line upon line; here a little, and there a little: a laborious task which at their age were not willing to tackle. (Isa. 28:10)

The stammering lips came from what they considered 'unlearned and ignorant men'. Isaiah 32:4 The heart also of the rash shall understand knowledge, and the tongue of the STAMMERERS shall be ready to speak plainly.

Acts 4:13 Now when they saw the boldness of Peter and John, and perceived that they were UNLEARNED AND IGNORANT men, they marveled and they took knowledge of them, that they had been with Jesus.

They were YOUNG MEN that were relatively ignorant of the doctrines of the religious systems of their time. They were young and eager to receive every word that came from Jesus' mouth. They, unlike the religionists, had in them little conflicting thoughts regarding the rituals and traditions in religion.

Jesus said (Matt. 9:17), Neither do men put new wine (doctrine) into old bottles: else the bottles break, and the wine runneth out, and the bottles perish, but they put new wine (doctrine) into new bottles (young men and women), and both are preserved.

Jesus said to his students, (Mark 4:11) Unto you it is given to know the mystery of the kingdom of God: but unto them that are without, all these things are done in parables. (Simple story 'illustrating a moral—concerned with right and wrong—truth).

Mark 4:12 They seeing they may see, and not perceive; and hearing they may hear, and not understand—.

Ministers are generally sincere. They work hard at their profession. They have searched the scriptures and in them they have been led to believe they have eternal life. But those scriptures were written prophetically concerning Jesus; and they have not accepted the idea of calling upon that NAME so they can be born again and receive everlasting life.

John 5:39 Search the scriptures; for in them ye think ye have eternal life: and they are they which testify of me. (40) And ye will not come to me, that ye might have life.

John 5:43 I am come in MY FATHER'S NAME, and ye receive me not—.

IT'S DIFFERENT THIS TIME!

****

Scripture: Memorizing

Zenaide asked this question.

Can we reach God by memorizing scripture?

James gave this response.

Maybe there is another way. Maybe through memorizing the scriptures he could get away from so much condemnation. That couldn't be the answer either for he had tried that from time to time most his life. He remembered back to the four years with the Northwestern National Bank of Saint Louis. He put the figures into the savings bookkeeping machine, struck the motor bar, and began quoting scripture silently to the rhythm of the clunkity, clunkity, clunk and return of the carrier. He quoted the first nine chapters of Revelation word for word without looking at the Bible while on a bus ride from Saint Louis to Hannibal, but when it came time to stand and speak in the Hannibal church he lost his words. He just stood frozen, looking at the audience. Finally he took his seat flushed with embarrassment for the rest of the service.

NO! Memorizing the scriptures didn't seem to be the way, for even while at Thrift Homes, Inc., he was doing plenty of that, but it made things no better. The prominent factor in his life was discontent. What was he going to do? This time he was broken. He could run no further from himself. Things were no different in Saint Louis than they had been in Tombstone, Yuma, San Diego, Los Angeles, San Francisco, or Phoenix. It was time to meet himself, but how could he do that? He hated himself. He was afraid. He was afraid of what the world might think if it knew him the way he did. It was the horrible picture that made him run. But at that point he was with himself.

On occasion when the office work was caught up, the office manager gave his car keys to Jim with instructions to pick up material here and there for the business of constructing prefabricated homes. One day the field was a little short handed. One of the workers was attempting to install a large picture window all by himself. Jim was more than happy to be his assistant, for it would give him most of the day out of the office.

It was about an hour's drive to the northwest of Saint Louis. Jim's mind had always been stimulated more while driving, and that day more than usual. The words of Dudley Fraze (a preacher in a St Louis church) came vividly back to his mind. And His Name shall be in their forehead. And His NAME shall be in their FOREHEAD.

I wonder, he thought, could it mean you should keep His Name in your mind rather than other destructive thoughts? Other scripture then started to fall in place with it. WORDS ARE SPIRIT. If groups of words are spirit, then maybe just one word is spirit, if you know what the word means; like HATE, LOVE or FEAR. They all affect a different emotion if said with thought.

His NAME is called the WORD OF GOD. That WORD was with God and was God in the beginning, and that same WORD BECAME FLESH. EAT MY FLESH, AND DRINK MY BLOOD. Did all these sayings have anything to do with one central idea? That WHOSOEVER SHALL CALL UPON THE NAME OF THE LORD SHALL BE SAVED.

The saints at Jerusalem were calling on the NAME OF JESUS, and even Saul had his SINS WASHED AWAY BY CALLING ON JESUS. Maybe that's what Jesus meant when he said to Thomas, You know the way. But Thomas didn't know—.

Call upon Jesus—O, taste and see that the Lord is good. Eat my flesh, the bread of life, water, Christ springing up out of your belly into everlasting life. Call on the Name to be saved. Look to Jesus the author and finisher of our faith. If anyone needed to be saved, Jim did. Saved from the devil—himself. Saved from all his helpers. Those little spirit beings of Hate and Fear working hand in had to tear down and destroy by manipulating his emotions.

God is a God of knowledge. It is alright and admirable to memorize scripture, but it is not the way to God.

James 4:8 Draw nigh to God, and he will draw nigh to you—.

Call upon the Name of God without ceasing. Have faith in that name. Acts 2:21 And it shall come to pass, that WHOSOEVER shall CALL on the NAME of the LORD shall be saved.

1 Tim. 2:3 This is good and acceptable in the sight of GOD our SAVIOR; (4) Who will have ALL MEN to be SAVED, and to come unto the knowledge of the truth.

****

Scripture: Portions of

Edward asked this question.

Why are portions of scripture used instead of whole passages?

James gave this response.

There are times when many subjects are suggested in one sentence, paragraph or chapter. Portions of scripture are referred to, not for the purpose of 'TAKING AWAY', as referred to in Revelation 22:19 And if any man shall take away from the words of the book of this prophecy, God shall take away his part out of the book of life—, but for the purpose of a clearer understanding with respect to one particular subject at a time as the scripture referred to in . . . .

Isaiah 28:10 For precept must be upon precept, precept upon precept; line upon line, line upon line: ***here a little, and there a little:***

Eventually, all the pieces of the puzzle will fit together perfectly.

The spirit comes and goes quickly. To be instant in season, out of season (2 Tim. 4:2) the mind must be flexible to the operation of the spirit. When the spirit leaves, the human mind draws from accumulated knowledge, no matter how fallacious (false ideas) that knowledge might be based on. The only way a person will be able to live constantly in the spirit, is to permanently move into Paradise, the spiritual state of second heaven here on the earth.

Each individual moves into Paradise at the moment the Holy Ghost is received, but at this early stage, they move quickly back out. When the second heaven is permanently set up on the earth, people will remain in that spiritual state and rule with Christ for the next thousand years and beyond. (Rev. 20:6—)

****

Serpents:

Edward asked this question.

Did a serpent actually talk with the woman?

James gave this response.

YES, THE SERPENT DID TALK WITH THE WOMAN!

PEOPLE ARE CALLED SERPENTS—VIPERS.

Matthew 23:33 Ye serpents, ye generation of vipers, how can ye escape the damnation of hell?

Matthew 12:34 O generation of vipers, how can ye being evil, speak good things? For out of the abundance of the heart the mouth speaketh.

Matthew 3:7 But when he (John the baptizer) saw many of the Pharisees and Sadducees (Men) come to his baptism, he said unto them, O generation of vipers, who hath warned you to flee from the wrath to come?

THE SERPENT WAS THE SUBTLETY IN MAN. (Hardly noticeable, clever way of getting what he wants).

Genesis 3:1 Now the serpent (mind of Adamah-man) was more subtle than any beast of the field (he was the most intelligent of all the animals) which the Lord God had made. And he (Adam) said unto the woman (he wanted to bring up the subject) Yea, hath God said, Ye shall not eat of every tree of the garden?

Genesis 3:2 And the woman said unto the serpent (Adam), We may eat of the fruit of the trees of the garden (Natural fruit of the natural trees):

Genesis 3:3 But of the fruit of the tree which is in the midst of the garden, (man and woman as one unit or one tree that had been placed in the midst of the garden.) God hath said, Ye shall not eat of it, neither shall ye touch it, lest ye die.

Natural snakes do not talk. They have never talked and will never talk.

****

SERVICE TO OTHERS, Person who represents

Trumpeta1 asked this question.

Hello!

I had a quick question. I've been thinking over this question lately. Who is the person in the Bible who best represents service to God and others in the Bible? Besides Jesus of course. I was thinking maybe Joseph or Moses. But I would like others in put.

Please give me a reason or scripture for your opinions.

Thanks a bunch! :o)

Tara

James gave this response.

Other than Jesus, there are none good, no not one. Even Jesus, knowing of the weakness in his physical body, caused by generations of fallen ancestors, said, Why callest thou me good, there is none good but one, that is God. Matthew 19:17. Jesus was a man, tempted in all points like as we are, yet without sin. Hebrews 4:15.

God is good. He was in Jesus, reconciling the world unto himself—. 2 Corinthians 5:19. Jesus was not God! He was and is the mediator between God and men—. 1 Timothy 2:5 For there is ONE GOD, and one mediator between God and men, the Man Christ Jesus. Jesus said, he that sent me is with me: the Father hath not left me alone; for I do always those things that PLEASE HIM.

Jesus said, ***ALL that ever*** came before me are thieves and robbers—. John 10:8 The thief cometh not, but for to steal, and to kill, and to destroy—. John 10:10.

MOSES AND ELIJAH

God denounced Moses and Elijah when Peter wanted to make three tabernacles, one for Jesus, and one for Moses, and one for Elias. Matthew 17:4. God Said, This is my beloved Son, in whom I am well pleased; HEAR YE HIM. And when they lifted up their eyes, they saw NO MAN, save JESUS ONLY.

Moses threw down the tables of stone—Exodus 24: 12, wherein was written 'Thou shalt not kill'—Exodus 20:13, and gave commandment saying, put every man his ***sword*** by his side, and go in and out from gate to gate throughout the camp, and slay every man his brother, and every man his companion, and every man his neighbor. Exodus 32:27.

Matthew 26:52 Then said Jesus unto him, (Peter) put up again thy sword into his place: for ***all*** they that ***take the sword shall perish with the sword.***

Ezekiel 18:32—I have no pleasure in the death of him that dieth, saith the Lord God; wherefore turn yourselves, and live ye.

ABRAM

Abram, before his name was changed to Abraham, and before the laws were accumulated and placed in a book, armed three hundred and eighteen of his trained servants and SLAUGHTERED Chedorlaomer and the kings that were with him at the valley of Shaveh. Genesis 14:14-17.

Sin was in the world even before the law. Romans 5:17. It does not matter for what reason a person kills, it has always been against the will of God. God was not pleased when Cain slew his brother Able. Genesis 4:8-16.

JOSHUA

Joshua killed under the guidance of Moses. Exodus 17:9-13 And later after Moses's example. God was going to use fear to drive out the inhabitants of Jericho but Joshua—Joshua 6:21—utterly destroyed all that was in the city, both man and woman, young and old—, and then burnt the city with fire. Joshua 6:24. He saved only the prostitute, Rahab and her family. 6:25

It is time for the world to spiritually awaken and see the truth that is recorded in the Bible. Tens of thousands of people have been killed because of the ignorance of violent men. God is not like they have imagined him to be. Men have heard voices. Most of the time the sounds come from their own minds. They have not had wisdom enough to know the difference. The ten commandments are pure and good. When any voice speaks contrary to those commandments, that voice is not coming from God, even if it states I am god. Well, yes, the Bible is true, but that does not mean every thing written is right. It is a recording of the thoughts and actions of men versus the will of God. The book is filled with the ways of God, but it also shows the deviations of fallen men.

Jesus came to show men and woman the way back to Paradise, the garden of God, by faith in God's Name, but greedy jealous men said "come let us kill him." Matthew 21:38.

****

Sex before you're married.

csaatasu asked this question.

Where in the bible does it say sex before you are married is wrong. In the ten commandments it says you should not commit adultery. The definition of adultery is not having sex with someone that is married unless you are the spouse. I have searched the bible and I can not find that sex is wrong if you are both unmarried.

PS: I do not feel like I committed a sin having sex with my girlfriend.

James gave this response.

Sex between two unmarried (not joined by God) individuals is called ***fornication.***

Acts 15:20 & 29,—Abstain from fornication—.

Acts 21:25 Gentiles keep themselves from fornication.

Romans 1:29 filled with fornication.

1 Cor. 5:1 Fornication—that one should have his father's wife. (It would be fornication on the part of the son, but Adultery on the part of the father's wife, unless the father was dead, and Of course it is not made clear whether the father's wife was also the son's biological ken. In the old testament it was common that a man should have multiple wives.

1 Cor. 6:13 The body is not for fornication.

1 Cor 6:18 Flee fornication, Every sin that a man doeth is without the body; but he that committeth fornication sinneth against his own body.

1 Cor. 7:2 To avoid fornication, let every man have his own wife, and let every woman have her own husband.

1 Cor 10:8 Neither let us commit fornication, as some of them committed, and fell in one day three and twenty thousand.

Galations 5:19 The works of the flesh are manifest, which are fornication, etc.

Col. 3:5 Mortify therefore your members which are upon the earth; fornication, etc.

1 Ths. 4:3 This is the will of God,—that ye should abstain from fornication.

Jude 1:7 Even as Sodom and Gomorrah, and the cities about them in like manner, giving themselves over to fornication, The first man and woman were joined together by God. There was no license/certificate of marriage issued. The required license was initiated by man partly for enforcement purposes to ensure that the couple would take the responsibility of caring for their offspring.

When the male and the female are joined together by God, the power/current initiated by God begins to flow between the two. When either become associated with another outside of that union it becomes a sin against the power of God—(that power that was designed by God). It disrupts the natural flow of current between the male/negative and the female/positive of that union.

BILL OF DIVORCEMENT

Mark 10:2—The Pharisees came to him, (Jesus) and asked, Is it lawful for a man to put away his wife? (3) Jesus answered, What did Moses command you? (4) And they said, Moses suffered to write a bill of divorcement, and to put her away. (5) Jesus said, For the hardness of your heart he wrote you this precept (6) But from the beginning of the creation God made them male and female. (7) For this cause shall a man leave his father and mother, and cleave to his wife; (8) And they twain shall be one flesh: so then they are no more twain, but one flesh. (9) What therefore God hath joined together, let not man put asunder. (11) Whosoever shall put away his wife and marry another, committeth adultery against her. (12) And if a woman shall put away her husband, and be married to another, she committeth adultery.

The first man and woman were joined together by God. After that time the human race has become weaker and weaker. Their connection with God has been severed and the only way they can come back to that perfect order God had in mind from the beginning is to be born again of their spirit. After that they must be united with their proper mate by the direction of God. When that occurs their spirit becomes one, inseparable except by their own forceful will. Individuals that have not been born again of their spirit and joined together by God are considered ungodly and are (Psalms 1:4) like the chaff which the wind driveth away. (5) Therefore the ungodly shall not stand in the judgment—.

Ye must be born again John 3:3-7

How can a person become born again? Jesus said, I am the way, the truth and the life: no man cometh unto the Father, but by me. (John 14:6) Call upon His Name and God will hear and make your life complete.

It is not good for a man to be alone, (Gen. 2:18) this also applies to the woman.

Heb. 13:4 Marriage is honorable in all, and the bed undefiled: but whore mongers and adulterers God will judge.

Joel 2:32—It shall come to pass, that WHOSOEVER shall call on the NAME of the LORD shall be delivered—(from all the destructive elements and confusion in the world).

****

SICKNESS does not necessarily constitute Sin ? ? ?

Jsargent asked this question.

Heb 4:15 says "For we have not an high priest which cannot be touched with the feeling of our infirmities; but was in all points tempted like as[we are, yet] without sin."

The above scripture is speaking about physical weakness and/or sickness, and says that the Lord Jesus was tempted in ALL points like as we are, yet without sin.

According to the above scripture do you believe that the Lord Jesus also suffered sickness? If He did suffer sickness then we must conclude that sickness, in and of its self, does not constitute sin, neither is it an indication of unbelief. Shouldn't this one scripture be enough to cause many "Health and Well being" preachers to re-examine their theology? The very same scripture that shows that the Lord Jesus is our healer, also shows that sickness does not constitute sin, otherwise you have to throw out the "without sin" part of the above verse, and then the entire basis for the sinless sacrifice and atonement of Jesus Christ is made void, together with salvation. Some doctrines undo themselves by not taking into counsel the "whole" counsel of God.

May God richly bless you.

James gave this response.

John 9:1 And as Jesus passed by, he saw a man which was blind from his birth. (2) And his disciples asked him, saying, Master, WHO DID SIN, this man, or his parents, that he was born blind? (3) Jesus answered, Neither hath this man sinned, nor his parents: but that the works of God should be made manifest in him.

Even the sickness of Lazarus was not because of his sin, but for the intent that the people's faith might be increased.

Jesus said, (John 1:4) This sickness is not unto death, but for the glory of God, that the Son of God might be glorified thereby.

John 11:15 I am glad for your sakes that I was not there, to the intent ye may believe—. And to show that the power of his resurrection was for all present times and not only for some future date.

John 11:23 Jesus saith unto her (Martha), Thy brother shall rise again. (24) Martha saith unto him, I know that he shall rise again in the resurrection at the last day. (25) Jesus said unto her, I AM THE RESURRECTION, and the LIFE: he that believeth in me, though he were dead, yet shall he live:(26) And whosoever liveth and believeth in me shall never die. Believest thou this?

The following is clearly not a declaration of Jesus' sickness but only a statement that the people of his own hometown and among his own people would not readily believe the stories they were hearing of his works in other places.

Luke 4:23 And He said unto them, Ye will surely say unto me this proverb, Physician, heal thyself: whatsoever we have heard done in Capernaum, do also here in thy country. (24) And he said, Verily I say unto you, No prophet is accepted in his own country.

They were saying physician heal your reputation here in your own country. We hear of the things you supposedly are doing in other parts of the country, but we don't believe it. Heal yourself. Prove it here before us.

JESUS' KIN SAID UNTO HIM.

John 7:4—There is no man that doeth anything in secret, and he himself seeketh to be known openly. If thou do these things, show thyself to the world. (5) For neither did his brethren believe in him.

THE PROPHESY (prediction) OF ISAIAH.

Isa. 52:14 Many were astonied at thee; his visage (face) was so marred more than any man, and his form more than the sons of men:

Jesus lived in a genetically weakened body because of the degeneration of his forefathers, but sickness never overtook his immune system. Even if it had, it would not have been because of his sin, for he knew no sin. (2 Cor. 5:21) Jesus said, (John 8:29) I do always those things that please him. (the Father). Therefore, even though his appearance was not desirable, his physical system was never weakened because of the pressure of his own guilt, nor by the absence of proper nutrients. God supplied all his needs.

Sickness can be caused by a person's own sin, or weaknesses of their ancestors from many previous generations, not necessarily because of their immediate parents.

It was because of Jesus' sinless life that he was able to heal those that had sinned or was made weak because of their fallen ancestors.

Jesus said, (Matthew 9:5) For whether is easier, to say, thy sins be forgiven thee; or to say, Arise, and walk? (6) But that ye may know that the Son of man hath power on earth to forgive sins, (then saith he to the sick of the palsy,) Arise, take up they bed, and go unto thine house.

****

SIN PROOF

Zenaide asked this question.

Why didn't God make men sin proof?

James gave this response.

MEN WERE SIN PROOF-IF!

(Good and Evil before ALL)

Freedom of Choice-Free to think and do.

Deuteronomy 30:15 See, I have set before thee this day life and good, and death and evil; (16) In that I command thee this day to LOVE the LORD thy God,—.

But if thine heart turn away, so that thou wilt not hear, but shalt be drawn away, and worship other gods—. (Anything that diverts the mind and spirit from the only ONE GOD). (18) I denounce unto you this day, that ye shall surely perish,—.

//

It was necessary for Jesus to be born into the world the same as all other men to experience their temptations, disappointments, sadness and relations. To be tempted in all points like as we are. (Hebrews 4:15).

Jesus was God's only begotten son after the spirit. He had to be placed in the world WITHOUT THE HOLY GHOST (Ref. Mark 1:10, Luke 4:1) as a comforter to experience what it was like to live among men who had not received the benefit of such a gift, TO DO OTHERWISE WOULD HAVE GIVEN JESUS AN UNFAIR ADVANTAGE.

Jesus had to know 'first hand' so he could perform the final adjustments to the creation of the perfect man.

Ephesians 3:9 God—created all things by Jesus Christ.

Colossians 1:16 For by him were all things created, that are in heaven, and that are in earth, visible and invisible, whether they be thrones, or dominions, or principalities, or powers: all things were created by and for him. (17) And he is before all things, and by him all things consist.

BUT JESUS CAME AS A MAN WEAKENED BY GENERATIONS OF FALLEN ANCESTORS.

Jesus' spiritual body was conceived through the overshadowing of the Holy Ghost at conception, (Luke 1:35) And the angel answered and said unto her (Mary), The Holy Ghost shall come upon thee, and the power of the Highest shall overshadow thee: therefore ALSO (not only will he be called the Son of David, but ALSO the Son of God), that holy thing which shall be born of thee shall be CALLED THE SON OF GOD.

But his natural body with all its defective genes, which had been weakened from generation to generation since the creation of man, was received from his natural father and mother at the time of that same conception.

Jesus had no advantage over men regarding his natural mind and body. Hebrews 2:16 For verily he took not on him the NATURE OF ANGELS; but he took on him the seed of Abraham. Joseph and Mary were the offspring of Abraham and David through Jacob.

Hebrews 2:17 Wherefore in all things it behooved him (Jesus) to be made like unto his brethren, that he might be a merciful and faithful high priest in things pertaining to God, to make reconciliation for the sins of the people. (18) For in that he himself hath suffered being tempted (not of God, but because of his own cravings in his body and mind), he is able to succor (help) them that are tempted.

Jesus did not sin (2 Cor. 5:21, Heb. 4:15) but in his body he did not consider himself to be good.

Matthew 19:17—Why callest thou me good? There is none good but one, that is, God: If he had not felt that weakness within himself he would not have been able to have mercy on others.

Jesus learned obedience by the things which he suffered. (Hebrews 5:8 Though he were a Son, yet learned he obedience by the things which he suffered.

****

SIN that does not lead to death

Wes asked this question.

What is the sin that does not lead to death? (1 Jn 5:16)

James gave this response.

All sin leads to death if not forgiven, starting with the original sin.

The sin that does not lead to death is that sin that has been forgiven. Until Jesus came on the scene there was no way made for remission of those sins. Pertaining to the conscience the sacrifices as prescribed by Moses had little or no effect. (Heb. 9:9, Heb. 10:5-10, Heb 10:18)

God had said 'In the day you eat (the knowledge of Evil) ye shall surely die. (Gen. 2:17). And now lest he put forth his hand, and take also of the tree of life and eat, and live forever—(Gen. 3:22) He and his wife were driven from that spiritual state of Paradise by the power of their own conscience, and could not return because of the (flaming sword) 'thou shalt not.' (Gen. 3:24) Once they started sinning they could not, by their own power, stop. Without spiritual help they were condemned to death. They could not come boldly to the throne of grace. Heb. 4:16.

The first Adam's head was bruised and 'thou' the last Adam (1 Cor. 15:45) was required to bruise his heel. (Gen. 3:15.)

Ezekiel 18:32 I have no pleasure in the death of him that dieth, saith he Lord God—

So God sent His Son into the world—.

John 3:17 God sent not his Son into the world to condemn the world; but that the world through him might be saved.

John 3:16 For God so loved the world, that he gave his only begotten Son, that whosoever believeth in him should not perish, but have everlasting life.

There is only one sin that MAY not be forgiven!—Blasphemy against the Holy Ghost.

(Exception: Suicide, because forgiveness must be asked for before death.)

Please read—Blasphemy, Eternally judged and Suicide.

****

SIN WILFULLY

Jerry Wayne asked this question.

Can Christians sin, knowing what they are doing, and God just look over it?

James gave this response.

SIN WILFULLY?

Hebrew 10:26—If we SIN WILFULLY after that we have received the knowledge of the truth, there remaineth no more sacrifice for sins. (27) But a certain fearful looking for of judgment and fiery indignation, which shall devour the adversaries.

Saul (Paul), YOU SAW THROUGH A GLASS DARKLY. 1 Cor. 13:12.

Matthew 18:21 Then came Peter to him (Jesus), and said, Lord, how oft shall my brother sin against me, and I forgive him? Till seven times? (22) Jesus saith—Until 490 times!

Why would Jesus make this statement if God was not willing to forgive at least that many times, plus?

There is only one sin that God will not forgive and that is blasphemy against the Holy Ghost. Matthew 12:31 Wherefore I say unto you, ALL MANNER of SIN and blasphemy shall be forgiven unto men: but the blasphemy against the Holy Ghost shall not be forgiven unto men. (32) And whosoever speaketh a word against the Son of man, it shall be forgiven him: but whosoever speaketh against the Holy Ghost, it shall not be forgiven him, neither in this world (that era), neither in the world (era) to come.

WE ARE STILL UNDER GRACE. (Grace—Unmerited divine assistance).

Jesus was full of Grace and truth. John 1:14 The law was given by Moses (the Thou shalt not's), but grace and truth came by Jesus Christ. John 1:17. Being justified by His grace through the redemption that is in Christ Jesus. Rom. 3:24.

Romans 5:20—The law entered, that the offence might abound. But where sin aboundeth, GRACE DID MUCH MORE

ABOUND.—ETC., ETC . . . Romans 6:15 What then? Shall we sin, because we are not under the law, but under grace? GOD FORBID.

MAN IS YOUNG

God said (Gen. 8:21), I will not again curse the ground any more for man's sake; for the imagination of man's heart is evil from HIS YOUTH; neither will I again smite any more every thing living, as I have done.

MEN AND WOMEN HAVE BECOME WEAKENED because of the deeds of their/our ancestors. The sins that were committed before the flood are still being committed, and even on a larger scale. But God extends grace. God said (Ezekiel 18:32), I have no pleasure in the death of him that dieth—.

Romans 6:1 What shall we say then? Shall we continue in sin, that grace may abound? (2) GOD FORBID.

Through ignorance people have become addicted to many things. Without faith in the Name of God it is almost impossible to overcome those additions. A person may know they are committing the sin of destroying the temple of God (their body—1 Cor. 3:16) but are unable to turn themselves around. We are like the dog that is turned to his own vomit again; and the sow that was washed to her wallowing in the mire. 2 Peter 2:22.

Thanks to Jesus, His Son, God understands this, and still is willing to show extended grace until we become knowledgeable of the strength that is available through faith in calling upon the Name of God.

Heb. 10:26 For if we sin wilfully after that we have received the knowledge of the truth,—. THIS IS TRUE, BUT THE WHOLE TRUTH HAS NOT YET BEEN REVEALED.

GOD IS NOT LIKE THEY HAVE IMAGINED HIM TO BE. AFTER ALL, MAN IS GOD AND HIS SON'S INVENTION. GOD IS STANDING BY WITH ANTICIPATION THAT MAN WILL AT LAST BE ABLE TO USE HIS FREEDOM OF CHOICE WISELY, AND UNDERSTAND BY CALLING UPON GOD'S NAME, HE WILL BECOME STRONG ENOUGH IN TIME, TO OVERCOME ALL THE WEAKNESSES THAT HAVE BEEN HANDED DOWN FROM HIS FALLEN ANCESTORS.

This knowledge is not for just one religion, but for all mankind, for CHRIST IS THE TRUE LIGHT WHICH LIGHTETH EVERY MAN THAT COMETH INTO THE WORLD. John 1:9

Jerry Wayne rated this answer:

That's the way to go! Jerry

****

SIN, The CARDINAL

aservant asked this question.

Imagine yourself a part of the coming one-world government, meaning also a part of the coming one-world church. In your mind (as a new-ager) what is the very WORST sin? (I have an answer in mind, but there is no right or wrong on this, since it is not revealed in Scripture. It seems to be getting rather obvious, though, and we've seen it on this board)

James gave this response.

THE CARDINAL SIN

(of basic importance)

I know nothing of the new-ager, but if you will tolerate my observation I would like to pass it on.

1 John 5:16 There is a sin unto death: I do not say that he shall pray for it. (17) All unrighteousness is sin: and there is a sin unto death.

Matthew 12:31—All manner of sin and blasphemy shall be forgiven unto men: but the blasphemy against the Holy Ghost shall not be forgiven unto men. (32—whosoever speaketh against the Holy Ghost, it shall not be forgiven him, neither in this world (age), neither in the world (age) to come.

Mark 3:29—he that shall blaspheme against the Holy Ghost hath never forgiveness, but is in danger of eternal damnation. (He said this) 30 ***Because they said, He hath an unclean spirit.***

But it should be remembered that through Jesus, the mediator, God, His Father, is a very merciful God. In the past statements have been made out of ignorance, and the Son of God said, Father forgive them; for they know not what they do. Luke 23:34. Jesus honored his Father even though, he as the Son of God also had power to forgive sins. (Matthew 9:6)

****

SUICIDE

Unforgivable sin

Kathy asked this question.

I was always told the only unforgivable sin was suicide. Is this true or untrue? And can you elaborate.

James gave this response.

SUICIDE: ACT OF KILLING ONESELF PURPOSELY.

The only reason a person cannot be forgiven for suicide is that they must ask for forgiveness and this cannot be accomplished after death.

Other than suicide, there is only one sin that MAY not be forgiven!

ETERNAL JUDGMENT

Judged forever without hope of forgiveness.

Matthew 12:31 Matthew quoted Jesus as saying, Wherefore I say unto you, ALL MANNER OF SIN AND BLASPHEMY SHALL BE FORGIVEN UNTO MEN; BUT THE BLASPHEMY AGAINST THE HOLY GHOST SHALL NOT BE FORGIVEN UNTO MEN.

See elaboration at the bottom of this writing.

Matthew 12:32 And whosoever speaketh a word against the Son of man, it shall be forgiven him but: whosoever speaketh against the Holy Ghost, it shall NOT BE FORGIVEN HIM, neither in this world, neither in the world to come. (During Jesus' era or the next era after him).

So it is clear, other than suicide, blasphemy against the Holy Ghost is the ONLY way a person can be eternally judged.

HOW DOES A PERSON BLASPHEME AGAINST THE HOLY GHOST?

When an individual states that someone has an "Unclean Spirit, an Evil Spirit, or it is of the Devil, or Beelzebub, or Satan, when it is in fact the Holy Ghost.

Mark 3:22 And the scribes which came down from Jerusalem said, He hath Beelzebub, and by the prince of the devils casteth he out devils.

Mark 3:29 But he that shall blaspheme against the Holy Ghost hath NEVER forgiveness, but is in danger of ETERNAL DAMNATION. (3) BECAUSE THEY SAID, HE HATH AN UNCLEAN SPIRIT.

1 John 5:16 There is a sin unto death: I do not say that he shall pray for it. (Suicide also falls into this catagory)

SATAN

The word Devil was never mentioned in the Old Testament. This word was first used in Matthew 4:1. In Revelations the words Dragon, serpent, devil, and Satan are all proven to be one and the same.

Revelations 12:9—The great dragon was cast out, that old serpent, called the devil, and Satan, which deceiveth the whole world: and his angels were cast out with him.

In the Bible there have been many symbolisms, (representation of meanings with symbols), metaphors (use of a word denoting one kind of object or idea in place of another to suggest a likeness between them), and parables (simple story illustrating a moral truth.)

Jesus extensively used parables. Matthew 1:34 Without a parable spake he not unto them. (the multitude).

The old serpent is the same that talked with the woman. It was the mind of man with his cunning way of convincing the woman to perform with him the acts which eventually led to their death. (original sin). They were both in heaven (Paradise). Paul referred to this place as being the second heaven. 2 Cor. 12:4 (caught up TO third heaven, not into third heaven, but in Paradise which implies second heaven or the Holy Place as designated in the tabernacle).

Will God forgive the Devil?

Yes, Peter was forgiven! Matthew 16:23 (Jesus) turned, and said unto Peter, get behind me, SATAN: thou art an offense unto me: for thou (Peter—not anyone else) savourest not the things that be of God, but those that be of men. (Peter was not yet given the Holy Ghost.)

Yes, even all the devils, satan, dragons, and false prophets can be forgiven and saved from the destructive elements of the earth and the power of deranged minds of men if they will take hold of that Tree of Life, the Name of God. Call upon it and have faith in it.

Joel 2:32—It shall come to pass, that WHOSOEVER shall CALL on the NAME of the LORD shall be delivered—.

Acts 2:21—It shall come to pass, that WHOSOEVER shall call on the NAME of the LORD shall be saved. Also Rom.10:13.

The perfect state of man has not yet arrived. Men have seen through the glass darkly. (1 Cor 13:12) They have not seen clearly. Many things have been said through ignorance but God is still in the business of forgiving those that come boldly unto the throne of grace (Heb. 4:16), instead of running behind the trees to hide. (Gen. 3:8).

Jesus said to the Jews(John 8:44), Ye are of your father the DEVIL, and the lusts of your father ye will do. He (man-Adamah) was a murderer from the beginning, and abode not in the truth.

Jesus came in his Father's NAME for placement in the foreheads (Rev. 14:1) of men (John 17:12) so that they could be healed and return to heaven (Paradise) where the first man had been placed before his mind alienated himself from God.

Hebrews 7:25—He (Jesus) is able also to save them to the uttermost that come unto God by him, seeing he ever liveth to make intercession for them.

If Jesus advocated forgiving 490 times (Matthew 18:21-22), why wouldn't God through the power of his name forgive men that have been influenced by the power of their own mind and the minds of other weakened men. God wants (His, and His Son's) invention to prosper and be in health (3 John 1:2). (Gen. 1:16, God said let US make man in our image and likeness).

Ezek.18:32—I (God) have no pleasure in the death of him that dieth—wherefore turn yourselves, and live. (31) Cast away from you ALL your transgressions, whereby ye have transgressed; and make you a new heart and a new spirit: for why will ye die.

OF COURSE, NOW, (to deal with your question)

1 Cor. 6:19 What? know ye not that your body is the temple of the Holy Ghost which is in you, which ye have of God—?

The false witnesses said of Jesus (Mark 14:58), We heard him say, I WILL DESTROY THIS TEMPLE that is made with hands, and within three days I will build another made without hands.

BUT, John 2:19 Jesus answered and said unto THEM, DESTROY THIS TEMPLE, and in three days I will raise it up. (He was speaking of his body. He was saying 'If YOU destroy this body.')

God dwells in the Temple of our bodies (1 Cor. 3:17) by way of the Holy Ghost. If a person destroys God's temple they would be eternally judged.

Why? Because even though God would forgive the act of suicide, in order to receive forgiveness a person must ask for forgiveness, and there is no forgiveness in the grave.

Eccl 9:5 For the living know that they shall die: but the dead know not anything, neither have they any more a reward—.

Eccl. 9:10 Whatsoever thy hand findeth to do, do it with thy might; for there is no work, nor device, nor knowledge, nor wisdom, in the grave—.

1 Cor. 15:19 If in this life only we have hope in Christ, we are of all men most miserable.

There is hope beyond that vail between the Holy Place (second heaven where we are supposed to be living) and the Holy of Holies (where God and all the angels reside), but only for those that CAll upon the NAME of GOD TO BE SAVED.

John 5:24 Verily, verily, I say unto you, He that heareth my (Jesus') word, and believeth on him (God) that sent me, HATH EVERLASTING LIFE, and shall not come into condemnation; but is PASSED FROM DEATH TO LIFE. When a person passes from death to life in the resurrection they are as the angels. Matthew 22:30.

****

SUICIDE

BIBLICAL INJUCTIONS AGAINST SUICIDE

rbrtptrck asked this question.

Where, if anywhere, in the Bible is suicide forbidden?

James gave this response.

Judas killed himself. Although he could be forgiven the sin of betrayal, (Matthew 27:3) because at that time he was yet alive, but after he was dead, because it could not be called suicide until after he was dead, he could not be forgiven because it was impossible to repent and ask God for that forgiveness.

THOU SHALT NOT KILL IS CORRECT! Exodus 20:13

The translators have not known how to correlate all the violence of the Bible with the ways of God, expressed by his only begotten Son, Jesus. So they have used the word murder in the place of kill so that they may be able to conform to the penalties established by Moses. The law came by the direction of God through Moses, but the penalties came by Moses' own reasoning.

John 1:17 For the law was given by Moses, (inspired by God, of course) but ***grace*** and ***truth*** came by Jesus Christ.

Moses, at that time, did not understand God's ways.

Deut. 32:35 To ***me*** belongeth vengeance, and recompense; their foot shall slide in due time.

Heb. 10:30 For we know him that said Vengeance belongeth unto me, I will recompense, saith the Lord.

The tools of recompense are readily available, and are used against the person that will not draw near God by calling upon His Name. Those tools consist of poverty, starvation, sickness caused by diseases of many kind, good emotions such as fear, hate, love, jealousy, etc., that have become unbalanced due to the lack of the mind being centralized upon one object, namely, the Name of God.

It is God's desire to eradicate the word 'kill' and 'murder' from the thoughts and actions of mankind.

Ezek. 18:32 For I have no pleasure in the death of him that dieth, saith the Lord God: wherefore TURN YOURSELVES, and live ye.

We cannot turn ourselves by our own power, but God will turn us if we Call upon Him by His Name without forgetting.

Matthew 7:21 Not every one that saith unto me, Lord, Lord, shall enter into the kingdom of heaven; but he that doeth the will of my Father which is in heaven.

Herein lies the Flaming sword. The 'Thou shalt not's. We cannot break the commandments and expect to live a serene life just because we call upon the Name of the Lord. The conscience, even with a person that does not acknowledge the reality of God, still condemns when any of the commandments are disregarded. This condemnation that depresses the mind is the automatic force that causes retribution. Guilt and condemnation is the major force that drives people to excessive drugs and ultimately to suicide.

John 3:18 He that believeth on him is not condemned: but he that believeth not is condemned already, because he hath not believed in the Name of the only begotten Son of God.

1 Cor. 3:16 Know ye not that ye are the temple of God, and that the Spirit of God dwelleth in you? (17) If any man defile (much less kill) the temple of God, him shall God destroy; for the temple of God is holy, which temple ye are.

SUICIDE

If anybody is being tormented by those kind of thoughts they should consider these writings and turn to God with all their mind. Matthew 22:37

rbrtptrck rated this answer:

Thank you very much for your response. it is most helpful. Just to set your mind at ease, I am not thinking of suicide. I am just writing a poem and needed, if possible, a Biblical injunction against suicide. Again, thanks.

****

Sinner's Prayer:

Maxine asked this question.

Why do you say God does not hear a sinner's prayer? How then can a sinner reach God? All have sinned. Does this mean we have no hope?

James gave this response.

The Jews, Pharisees, said to the man that had received his sight (John 9:31), Now we know that God hearth not sinners: but if any man be a worshipper of God, and doeth his will, him he heareth.

This statement was made by the Pharisees. They were trying to destroy the credibility of Jesus by saying he was a sinner. Part of this phrase was true. 'If any man be a worshipper of God, and doeth his will, him he heareth.

When a person is sinning those wrongful acts develop the feelings of guilt in the mind, and in turn, it drives out the power of God. (Water of Life).

John 14:23 Jesus said, If a man love me, he will keep my words: and my Father will love him, and WE will come unto him, and make OUR ABODE with him.

The thoughts of sin drives the power of God out and reduces his name to nothing more than a word. But (1John 1:9) If we confess our sins (to God), he is faithful and just to forgive us our sins, and to cleanse us from all unrighteousness.

So God does not hear a sinner's prayer while we are yet sinning, but if we turn to God with our (Matt. 22:37) whole heart, soul, mind, and ask forgiveness, God will wash away the effects of those sins the same as he did for Saul.

ANANIAS SAID TO SAUL

Acts 22:16—Wash away thy sins,

CALLING ON THE NAME OF THE LORD.

****

SINNERS, COMPANY WITH

(Not to be disclosed) asked this question.

Hello, can you please tell me what you think this means?

1 Corinthians 5:11

“But now I have written unto you not to keep company with anyone named a brother who is sexually immoral or covetous or . . . not even eat with such a person.”

Does this mean that we must stay away from gays, thieves, liars, etc,. that are in our community or church or etc., but it is alright if we keep company with gays, thieves, liars, etc. if they are outside our community?

ps If you would like, read the surrounding scriptures. I just gave you verse 11 because it is the main one, I believe.

James95204 gave this response.

1 Corinthians 5:9

I wrote unto you in an epistle not to company with fornicators: (10) Yet not altogether with the fornicators of this world, or with the covetous, or extortioners, or with idolaters; for THEN MUST YE NEEDS GO OUT OF THE WORLD.

(11) But now I have written unto you not to keep company, if any man that is CALLED ***A BROTHER*** be a fornicator, or covetous, or an idolater, or a railer, or a drunkard, or an extortioner; with such an one no not to eat.

Luke 16:9 And I say unto you, ***Make to yourselves friends of the mammon of unrighteousness;*** that, when ye fail, they may receive you into everlasting habitations.

Let me write from observation. The accumulated references are too voluminous for this discourse. (Vengeance and recompense belongs to God, not man,(Deut. 32:35, Heb. 10:30) also people do not socialize for long with others that are not like themselves. This produces a natural repulsion. It needs no other action).

Jesus came to save that which was lost. (Matthew 18:11) (12) How think ye? If a man have an hundred sheep, and one of them be gone astray, doeth he not leave the ninety and nine, and goeth into the mountains, and seeketh that which is gone astray? (14) It is not the will of your Father which is in heaven, that ONE OF THESE (***a brother***) little ones should perish.

Jesus associated with publicans and sinners. This kind of thinking and behavior received opposition from the Scribes and Pharisees which were a self righteous bunch that wanted complete control over the people. They were afraid that if Jesus and the apostles continued having success they themselves would lose their position.

The men God chose through Jesus were not saints, nor did they have an elaborate religious background. Some of them (1 Pet. 4:3) in time past of their lives—walked in lasciviousness, lusts, excess of wine, revellings, banquetings, and abominable idolatries.

Paul, on the other hand, (Acts 26:5) was educated after the most straightest sect at the feet of Gamaliel, and taught according to the perfect manner of the law of the fathers,—and he lived a Pharisee. His educational background influenced his thinking. When he could not receive commandment from the Lord, (1 Cor. 7:25) he used his own judgment. He drew upon his reservoir of doctrines received from his Pharisee teacher. As a result, at times, he became more judgmental and harsh, a trait not at all like Jesus.

Some time after Saul was blinded, because he was attempting to bind all those that were calling upon the Name of the Lord, and saw the vision of Jesus and became aware that he was being called to preach the good news to the Gentiles, he began using his Roman name, Paul (Acts 13:7-9) instead of his Jewish birth name Saul. He also dubbed himself as an apostle which was not accepted by the Corinthians. (11 Cor. 12:11). Paul could not conform to the requirements met by the original apostles, including Matthias. (Acts 1:21-22)

In Paul's zeal he compassed sea and land to convert proselytes (Matt. 23:15) into the Christian religion seasoned both by the doctrines of Christ and those of the Pharisees. As a result we still have that mixture in the Christian movement. This is the problem.

What the Christian churches need to do is to remember the vision on the mountain when Peter said, (Matt.17:40) It is good for us to be here: if thou wilt, let us make here three tabernacles; one for thee, and one for Moses, and one for Elias. (5)—A voice out of the cloud said, This is my beloved Son, in whom I am well pleased; HEAR YE HIM.

Matthew 17:8 And when they had lifted up their eyes, (Peter, James and John) they saw NO MAN SAVE JESUS ONLY.

Jesus is the only begotten Son of God—hear him.

****

Spirit Right—Clean Heart?

Edward asked this question.

DOES GOD CREATE IN YOU A RIGHT SPIRIT AND A CLEAN HEART?

James gave this response.

Yes, God has answered David's prayer. Psalm 51:10 Create in me a clean heart, O God; and renew a right spirit within me.

BUT IT IS FOR US TO START THE PROCESS.

David said, Ps. 78:8—A stubborn and rebellious generation: a generation that SET NOT THEIR HEART ARIGHT, AND WHOSE SPIRIT WAS NOT STEADFAST(faithful or determined) WITH GOD.

Ezek. 18:30 God said to Israel—REPENT, and TURN YOURSELVES from all your transgressions; so iniquity shall not be your ruin. (31) CAST AWAY from you all your TRANSGRESSIONS, whereby ye have transgressed; and MAKE YOU A NEW HEART AND A NEW SPIRIT: for why will ye die?—. (32) For I have no pleasure in the death of him that dieth, saith the Lord God: wherefore TURN YOURSELVES and live ye.

SO THEN, it is the responsibility of mankind to draw nigh God.

James 4:8 Draw nigh to God, and HE WILL DRAW NIGH TO YOU. CLEANSE your hands, ye sinners; and purify your hearts, ye double minded.

Then God will begin drawing you to himself through his Son. Jesus. John 6:44 No man can come to me, except the Father which hath sent me draw him.

IT IS THROUGH FAITH IN JESUS (THE NAME OF GOD) THAT THE PROCESS BEGINS.

Heb. 7:19 For the law made nothing perfect, but the bringing in of a better hope did: by the which WE DRAW NIGH UNTO GOD.

THE ONLY HOPE IS IN JESUS.

****

Socialize:

Maxine asked this question.

Should we socialize with people in the world the way Jesus did?

James gave this response.

SHOULD WE SOCIALIZE WITH PEOPLE OF THE WORLD IN ORDER TO HELP THEM AS JESUS DID?

YES, we may be able to. But when we do, we must be sure we have as much of the power of God in our system as Jesus had.

If we act as though we are above them, they will be alienated from us. If we partake of the vices they are involved in, we may become entangled in those vices.

If while socializing with the world their vices should overtake us, amazingly ***those friends will disappear***. Seldom do they visit when you are in the hospital with a destroyed liver, or in a facility for the insane because the brain has been destroyed, or the body is lying with aides, or any one of the many diseases which can be contracted when the immune system is low.

No, we are living in a different time period now. The grace period is concluding for the world. In Jesus' time he instructed those servants to go out into the highways and hedges, and compel them to come in (Luke 14:23). But during this age and two thousand years later they have already heard (or if they haven't, they will hear shortly), of the Name of God. Now they must go to God by calling upon His Name. They do not need a middle man, nor do they need to PAY for the services of a mediator, because Jesus, the MEDIATOR is the only way to God.

Jer. 31;34 They shall teach no more every man his neighbor, and every man his brother, saying, Know the LORD: for they shall all know me, from the least of them unto the greatest of them, saith the LORD.

IT IS NOT NECESSARY for us to worship God in Samaria or Jerusalem (John 4:21), or out in the desert, or in the secret chambers (Matt. 24:26) of any religion. The church starts in the home, two by two, and then it meanders throughout the world.

John 4:24 God is a Spirit: and they that worship him must worship him in spirit and in truth.

Psalms 22:3 God inhabits praises. Psalms 135:3 Sing praises unto His Name; for it is pleasant. Psalm 47:6 Sing praises to God, sing praises: sing praises unto our King of all the earth; sing ye praises with understanding.

****

Stones made into bread:

Charlene asked this question.

Why didn't Jesus command that the stones be made bread?

James gave this response.

Matthew 4:2—When he (Jesus) had fasted forty days and forty nights, he was afterward an hungered. (3) And when the tempter came to him, he said, ***IF THOU BE THE SON OF GOD, COMMAND THAT THESE STONES BE MADE BREAD.*** (Luke 4:3 stone).

Matthew 4:1—***Jesus (had been) led up of the Spirit into the wilderness TO BE TEMPTED OF THE DEVIL.***

Jesus knew this was the power of his own thoughts

questioning his relationship with God. ***He also was aware that, although the roots of plants do extract minerals from stones and other nutrients from soil, it is not done instantaneously. It must take time in the process of growth for all plant and animal life to develop.***

If there had been an easier way, God would not have placed the first Adamah (man) in the garden to dress and keep it. Gen. 2:15. ***Why bother with cultivating and planting seeds of corn, wheat, barley, etc., if there was an easier, less labor intensive way?***

In order to make bread, barley (or some other grain) must be planted, watered, cultivated, crushed, kneaded and baked. Jesus was fully aware of this.

Jesus recognized that bread was not instantaneously made from stones. That process was not according to the laws of nature and the laws of God. On that basis, when the thought filtered into his mind, he did not listen to such nonsense to satisfy his own hunger, ***nor would he do this later for anyone else. (all things are possible with God, but not in this manner.) (***Matthew 14:19, 15:34, Mark 6:38-43, John 6:11, Matthew 16:9, Mark 8:18-19, Luke 18:26-27)

Remember that the apostles attempted to write later from memory about the way they saw things while Jesus was with them. While Jesus was with them they did not have the Holy Ghost as a gift within themselves. Jesus did not write anything except on one occasion when he wrote on the ground. John 8:6.

We have no original manuscripts and there are clerical and translation errors in what we have. The translation errors many times are caused by the understanding of the translators. So we must rely on common sense and the guidance of the Holy Ghost in search of all truth.

****

Charlene asked this question.

Please explain how the multiplying of the fishes and loaves were accomplished. (Five and four thousand people being fed.—Matthew 14:21, Matthew 16:10, Mark 8:20).

James gave this response.

After Jesus left his own country he was teaching round about the villages. (Mark 6:1-6) Then he came to Tiberias. The disciples were following him and by that time many people had begun to follow.

Mark 6:31 And he (Jesus) said unto them (Disciples), Come ye yourselves apart into a desert place, and rest a while: for there were many coming and going, and they had no leisure so much as to eat. 32 And they departed into a desert place by ship privately. 33 And the people saw them departing, and many knew him, and RAN AFOOT thither out of all cities, and OUTWENT THEM, and came together unto him.

They went on foot and by boat to the outskirts of Tiberias.

Mark 6:34 And Jesus, when he came out, saw much people, and was moved with compassion toward them, because they were sheep not having a shepherd and he began to teach them many things.

Ref: John 6:32—God was giving them the true BREAD from heaven through Jesus.

Matt. 14:15 And when it was evening, his disciples came to him, saying, This is a desert place, and the time is now past; send the multitude away, that they may go into the villages, and buy (they had money) themselves victuals. (16) But Jesus said unto them—They need not depart; give ye them to eat. (17) And they said unto him, We have here but five loaves, and two fishes. (Sometimes the writer leaves certain points out.

For instance, where did the loaves and fishes come from?) John 6:9 There is a LAD here, which hath five barley loaves, and two small fishes: but what are they among so many?

Note that the people had followed Jesus to Tiberias, then the people of Tiberias along with the people that had come from other villages went on foot to the out-skirts of Tiberias to where Jesus docked. The people on foot was even there at the bank of the lake before Jesus arrived. It was not far from Tiberias.

Why did the lad have more food than he needed? It was intended for sale, but the children of that day were taught to share.

The feeding of the 5000 occurred at the outskirts of Tiberias. Matt. 14:18 He said Bring them hither to me. (19) And he commanded the multitude to sit down on the grass, and took the five loaves, and the two fishes, and looking up to heaven, he blessed, and break, and gave the loaves to his disciples, and the disciples to the multitude. (20)And they did all eat, and were filled: and they took up of the fragments that remained twelve baskets full. (21)And they that had eaten were about five thousand men, besides WOMEN AND CHILDREN.

What percentage of women would walk into the desert with their children without assuring they had enough food?

During the time of Jesus the people used a SCRIP when they traveled. The scrip of the Galilean peasants was of leather, used especially to carry their food on a journey, and slung over their shoulders. Matt. 10:10; Mark 6:8;Luke 9:3; 22:35.

This day when the people left Tiberias and other cities on foot to follow Jesus, many of them took their 'scrip' full of food. The lad that had five fishes and two barley loaves, had more food than he needed. He had this food for selling, the same as young boys do even to this day in parts of Israel. But the people during that time were taught to give freely and that is what this lad did along with many others that had more than they needed.

PAUL PUT IT THIS WAY.

2 Cor. 8:14 ***But by an equality, that now at this time your abundance may be a supply for their want, that their abundance also may be a supply for your want: that there may be equality:***

2 Cor. 8:15 ***As it is written, He that had gathered much had nothing over; and he that had gathered little had no lack.***

If you have trouble with this analogy, go back to the time when Jesus was coming off of a forty day fast. When he hungered, the ***TEMPTER-DEVIL said (It came into his mind) If thou be the Son of God turn this stone into bread.***

Matt. 4:2 And when he had fasted forty days and forty nights, he was afterward an hungered. (3) And when the temper came to him, he said, If thou be the Son of God, command that these stones be made bread. (4) But he answered and said, It is written, Man shall not live by bread alone, but by every word that proceedeth out of the mouth of God.

Luke 4:2 Being forty days ***tempted of the devil***. And in those days he did eat nothing: and when they were ended, he afterward hungered. (3) And the devil said unto him, If thou be the Son of God, command THIS STONE (not stones as Matthew stated) that it be made bread. (4) And Jesus answered him, saying, It is written, That man shall not live by bread alone, but by every word of God.

If Jesus recognized that this was not according to the laws of nature and the laws of God, and on this basis, he did not listen to such nonsense, to satisfy his own hunger after forty days, why would he capitulate to such thoughts and

tactics for anyone else that had only done without eating for one to three days?

It should be remembered that the apostles attempted to write later from memory about the way they saw things while Jesus was with them. Jesus did not write anything except on one occasion when he wrote on the ground. John 8:6.

Remember too, that the apostles, although they were given the power to cast out devils (heal the minds) and heal the sick (by the power of God through the faith of the people), they did not have the gift of the Holy Ghost. This was not given until the day of Pentecost. The Holy Ghost when it came was to ***guide into all truth***. At the time of the various writings, they had not come together for comparison. Each wrote their own story in their own way from memory of the various events. If they had made a comparison the Holy Ghost would have guided them into the whole truth of all those matters.

Also, we have no original manuscripts and there are clerical and translation errors in what we have. So we must rely on COMMON SENSE and the guidance of the Holy Ghost in search for all truth.

Ref: John 16:23 Howbeit when he, the Spirit of truth is come, he will guide you into ALL TRUTH.

Acts 2:4 And they were all filled with the Holy Ghost—.

****

SWORD, SELF DEFENSE

kindj asked this question on 8/2/2001:

I am having trouble understanding Luke 22:36—

"Then he (Jesus) said unto them, "But now, he that hath a purse, let him take it, and likewise his scrip: and he that hath no sword, let him sell his garment, and buy one."

I don't quite understand what he is telling us. When we travel, especially with valuables, are we to be armed for our own defense? How does this fit in with the contextual verses? Maybe I'm reading it wrong, or am thinking about it too much, but it doesn't seem to fit with what he was talking about before and after.

Thanks,

Dennis

James gave this response.

GOD HAS THE POWER TO SAVE

Even during the Old Testament time the natural sword was not necessary, if only they had remembered to call upon the Name of the Lord without forgetting. God would have extensively used ***Hornets, fear, dread, sickness, poverty,*** etc., to control and drive back those that were the enemies of God and his people. Of course his people should have always remembered that vengeance belongs to God. Deut. 32:35 To me (God) belongeth vengeance, and recompense; their foot shall slide in due time—.

Psalm 34:7 (KJV) The angel of the Lord encampeth round about them that fear him, and delivers them. (Fear = honor—Today's English version.)

Psalm 34:8 (NAB) Taste and see how good the Lord is; happy (is) the man who takes refuge in him.

Proverbs 18:10 (KJV) The NAME of the Lord is a strong tower: the righteous runneth into it, and is safe.

The Tree of Life was in the midst of the garden in Eden (Paradise) Gen. 2:9, Rev 2:7)

The Name of the Lord was symbolically called the Tree of Life. The man and the woman should have eaten of that tree. If they had, they would never have become too weak to be enticed into taking into their mental and spiritual system the knowledge of evil which eventually destroyed them. They never, in their life time, called upon the Name of the Lord. It was not until the birth of Adam's Grandson that men began to call upon the Name of the LORD. Gen. 4:26. Even then men had the tendency to forget. They called upon God only spasmodically. When the symbolic waves of the sea became boisterous they began to doubt and take matters into their own hands instead of calling upon the Name of God and placing all their trust in him. Matthew 14:31.

As has already been explained, Jesus said He that hath no sword—buy one (Luke 22:26). (37) ***because This that is written must yet be accomplished in me. And he was reckoned among the transgressors. (Isa. 53:12)*** But Peter misunderstood. Jesus had no intention of Peter using the sword to cut off the servant's right ear. Luke 22;50 Jesus put the ear back on and healed it. Mark 14:47, Luke 26:51, John 18:26.

Matthew 26:52 Jesus said—***Put up your sword for all that take the sword shall perish with the sword. In fact Jesus even told the soldiers to do violence to no man. (Luke 3:14)***

****

SUSTENANCE

MINISTERS OF GOD WILL RECEIVE SUSTENANCE FROM THE PEOPLE.

Sustenance—

(1) nourishment

(2) something that sustains or supports.

Jesus instructed that the disciples (12-Mark 6:7-10, Luke 10:4-8) should take nothing with them except staff, sandals (no (extra?)shoes) and only one coat. And what house they enter they should remain until they depart from that city. The people of that house would supply their every need. (7) And in the same house remain, eating and drinking such things as they give: for the laborer is worthy of his hire. Jesus was only showing that God would furnish their necessities through the people they came in contact with.

WHATEVER WE DO OR SAY

And whatsoever ye do in word or deed, do all in the NAME OF THE Lord Jesus, giving thanks to God and the Father by him. Col. 3:17.

He shall CALL upon ME, and I will answer him: I will be with him in trouble; I will deliver him,—. Joel 2:32 And it shall come to pass, that whosoever shall CALL on the NAME of the LORD shall be delivered—.

Acts 2:21 And it shall come to pass, that WHOSOEVER shall call on the NAME of the LORD shall be saved. Also Rom. 10:13.

1 Cor. 1:2—to them that are sanctified in Christ Jesus, called to be saints, with all that in every place CALL upon the NAME of Jesus Christ our Lord,—.

For those calling upon the Name of the Lord, there is no need to despair. God will save them to the uttermost. Heb. 7:25 He (God) is able also to save them to the uttermost that come unto God by him (Jesus), seeing he ever liveth to make intercession for them.

In our language the Name of the Lord is Jesus as represented by many passages in the Bible. This contention will be dissolved when God turns to the people a pure language, that they may all CALL UPON THE NAME OF THE LORD, to serve him with one consent. At that time all will understand that God can still save as was explained in Psalms 91.

TALKING INAPPROPRIATELY

Saying or talking in an inappropriate manner

Blackheaven asked this question.

Is saying dammit a sin? Not only dammit if not other kind of expressions. Or any kind of other words that "WE" humans recall as bad. Or is it the meaning that came from our heart maybe on depression or loneliness whatever the case.

In other words, can't we express ourselves of what we feel, by the words that are most appropriate for "x" situation?

Regards for all of ya. Javier

James gave this response.

IDEAS RUN RAMPANT

God speaks first then the human mind takes over. This is one of the reasons we have so many religions in the world. Only one of the reasons, I say. The main reason is that, as at the time of the Tower of Babel, (Gen. 11:4) the people said,' let us make a name.' This accounts for various languages and the many religious names presently in force.

But, Acts 2:21—It shall come to pass, that WHOSOEVER shall call on the NAME of the Lord shall be saved. (Joel 2:32, Rom. 10:13)

Other than that—

Matthew 5:37—***Let your communication be Yes, yes; no, no: for whatsoever is more than these COMETH OF EVIL.***

Definitions

SWEAR: Use profane language.

PROFANE: Treat with irreverence.

DAMN:

1) Condemn to hell

2) Curse

OATH:

1) Profane utterance, Or

2) solemn appeal to God as a pledge of sincerity.

FORSWEAR:

1) Renounce under oath

2) perjure

PERJURE: Voluntary violation of an oath to tell the truth.

Matthew 5:33—Ye have heard that it hath been said by them of old time, Thou shalt not forswear thyself, but shalt perform unto the Lord thine oaths: (34) But I say unto you, ***SWEAR not at all***: neither by heaven; for it is God's throne: (35) Nor by the earth; for it is his footstool: neither by Jerusalem; for it is the city of the great king. (36) Neither shalt thou swear by thy head, because thou canst not make one hair white or black.

PETER CURSED: Matthew 26:74, Mark 14:71. He also lied—

He was wrong, Matthew 26:74 Then began he (Peter) to curse and to swear, saying, I know not the man—. (Jesus)

Mark 14:71 But he (Peter) began to curse and to swear, saying, I know not this man (Jesus) of whom ye speak.

Mark was the only writer that stated the following regarding the words of Jesus.

Mark 11:21 And Peter calling to remembrance saith unto him, Master, behold, the fig tree which thou (Jesus) ***cursedst*** is withered away.

Matthew did not call it a curse. Matt. 21:19. And when he (Jesus) saw a fig tree in the way, he came to it, and found nothing thereon, but leaves only, and said unto it, Let no fruit grow on thee henceforward for ever.

But Mark11:14 ***also did not call it a curse***.

And Jesus answered and said unto it, No man eat fruit of thee hereafter for ever. Mark in 11:21 said that Peter used the word 'cursedst'.

So we have two witnesses that designate this as Jesus speaking with the fig tree and only one witness that merely relates what Peter supposedly said regarding the word 'cursedst'.

TONGUE FULL OF DEADLY POISON

James 3:8 But the ***tongue can no man tame; it is an unruly evil, full of deadly poison***. (9) Therewith bless we God, even the Father; and therewith ***curse we men***, which are made after the similitude of God. (10) Out of the ***same mouth proceedeth blessing and cursing. My brethren, these things ought not so to be.*** (11) Doth the fountain send forth at the same place sweet water and bitter? (13) Who is a wise man and endued with knowledge among you? Let him show out of a good conversation his works with meekness and wisdom.

This may not be accomplished unless the being is filled with the Holy Ghost and God's holy spirit.

****

Testimony, Give Your

Locust_eaters asked this question.

Everyone,

I would be very interested to know how you came to know the Lord Jesus Christ. Please share some details of the circumstances that brought you to Jesus.

Peace (not as the world giveth)

Locust_eaters' dad

James gave this response.

I was born in 1929. I remember the tent meetings at a very young age, but my spiritual experiences started in 1960. They consisted of too many happenings to post them all here. They are all posted in my answers on this board.

Please read.

FILLING OF THE HOLY SPIRIT

GOD, CALLING ON THE NAME OF?

GOD, DOES HE CAUSE PAIN IN CHILDBEARING?

GOD, HOW CAN WE REACH HIM?

GOD, HOW DID HE APPEAR?

GOD, IS HE AN AUTOMOBILE MECHANIC?

HEALING LINES

HEALING, WIFE

HOLY GHOST AND WATER

HOLY SPIRIT, FILLING OF THE

MULTIPLIED? IF NOT FOR THE FALL HOW WOULD THEY

ORIGINAL SIN. SECOND WITNESS

ORDINATION

OUT OF BODY EXPERIENCE

PREACHER'S PRAYERS

PROPAGATION

TONGUES

James gave this follow-up answer.

After the kitchen chores were completed the children came to the bedroom one by one, until they had all assembled without being told, in line from east to west. What power caused this coordination in their family without words? Jim looked at each as he spoke.

"Children, I have resigned from my job today, for I have been called to do a spiritual work. It means we won't have money coming in regularly as we have been accustomed, but we will not go hungry any length of time."

"God will care for us, if—we continue calling upon HIS NAME all the time. We will need your help more now than before. Just SAY JESUS, JESUS, JESUS INSIDE YOURSELVES WITH YOUR INNER VOICE," then without thought, Jim said, ***"GOD IS HERE."***

In vision Jim saw the form of a man dressed in a blue suit descending through the ceiling, and came even with the floor, just in front of him. His head and hands were not visible. Jim turned toward the north, and as the form of God stepped back into Jim's body He began to speak through Jim's vocal organs—, "THIS IS WHAT I TOLD ADAM TO DO IN THE BEGINNING."

"ALL THE WAY DOWN THROUGH THE AGES, I HAVE TRIED TO HELP MAN, BUT EVERY TIME I TURN MY BACK, MAN FORGETS."

"THREE ANGELS SAW THESE WORDS COMING UP, SO THEY CAME DOWN TO SEE WHO WAS CAUSING THEM. AFTER THEY SAW WHAT WAS HAPPENING, THEY CAME BACK UP AND TOLD ALL THE OTHER ANGELS, 'THERE'S A MAN DOWN THERE THAT HAS FOUND THE FORMULA.'

"ALL THE ANGELS ARE JUST SO TICKLED. IT HAS NEVER HAPPENED BEFORE. WE WENT TO THE BOOKS, AND FOUND THAT HIS NAME WAS JIM CREED, AND THAT HE HAD BEEN MARRIED TWICE."

"IT WAS RECORDED THAT JIM CREED WAS NOT A GOOD MAN, SO WE KILLED HIM. YOU SHOULD GO BY THE NAME OF JAMES."

"I WILL BLESS ALL FIVE OF YOUR CHILDREN," he said, as he moved to the end of the line, stooping to speak with Maxine and Terrence. "SAY JESUS ALL THE TIME, AND TELL ALL THE OTHER LITTLE CHILDREN TO SAY JESUS. WE NEED

EVERYONE. I WILL GIVE EACH ONE OF YOU A PLANET TO PLAY WITH."

Then placing His hand with James' on the top of their heads, first Maxine, then Terrence, Zenaide, then Charlene. The last was the abdomen of Ruby.

"YES, I MADE EVE THE WAY IT WAS DESCRIBED, BUT SHE WASN'T AS OBESE AS YOU ARE."

"THEY NAMED YOU WRONG, YOUR NAME SHOULD HAVE BEEN RUTH."

"WELL, YES THE BIBLE IS TRUE."

"NO, THEY WILL NOT REACH THE OTHER PLANETS THE WAY THEY ARE TRYING TO DO IT. THEY WON'T LAST THAT LONG." (not satellite) (space machines must use a different fuel (than they were using in 1960), and travel faster in order for the astronauts to survive the length of time necessary to complete the trip to other planets).

"YES, I UNDERSTAND ALL LANGUAGES.

"YES, I HAVE A SOUL. IT IS A LITTLE DIFFERENT THAN YOURS, BUT I HAVE ONE."

"I AM A SCIENTIST. I AM NOT LIKE THEY HAVE IMAGINED ME TO BE."

"YOU MAY HAVE A GLASS OF WATER IF YOU WANT IT."

They both walked together to the kitchen, picked up a glass, filled it with water, and drank it together. As God and James stood there drinking the water, James wondered why God, that had created everything, should spend so much time with him. Why?

Upon sitting the glass down in the sink they returned to the bedroom where everyone still waited in perfect line.

“THEY CAN’T EVEN COME TO YOU UNLESS I WANT TO HELP THEM.”

“ YOU WILL THINK YOU ARE DOING THINGS IN YOUR OWN SELF, BUT YOU WON’T BE, I WILL BE WORKING THROUGH YOU.”

“ALTHOUGH YOU HAVE BEEN MARRIED TWICE, WE WILL DO ALL WE CAN FOR YOU ANYWAY, BECAUSE YOU HAVE FOUND THE FORMULA.”

“JIM CREED DID A LOT OF READING, BUT HE DIDN’T UNDERSTAND.”

“YOU WILL BECOME DISCOURAGED BUT WE WILL HELP YOU ANYWAY BECAUSE OF THE FORMULA.”

Sitting down within James on the side of the bed, GOD looked at each one as He asked, “ARE THERE ANY QUESTIONS?”

Everyone stood calmly, and without a word. He sat there for a few moments, then went upward to—James wished he had asked Him where.

Locust_eaters rated this answer:

I regret that I have not had time to read all that you have submitted as your testimony.

I will try to make time to read all of it.

****

Tests & Trials

Anonymous asked this question.

Can anyone explain to me why there has to be tests in life? Obviously there is a purpose. From Adam in the garden to Job to Jesus in the garden there were tests. Take Adam & Eve in the garden there must have been a purpose that they were presented a choice of obeying or not.

Thanks

James gave this response.

Some have said that the word Temp should have been 'Test'.

If this is the case then the scripture that states, (1 Cor. 10:13) There hath no temptation (test) taken you but such as is common to man: but God is faithful, who will not suffer you to be tempted (tested) above that ye are able; but will with the temptation (testing) also make a way to escape, that ye may be able to bear it.

Heb. 2:18 For in that he himself hath suffered being tempted,(tested) he is able to succor (help) them that are tempted (tested).

James 1:13 Let no man say when he is tempted,(tested) I am tempted (tested))of God: for God cannot be tempted (tested) with evil, neither tempteth (testeth) he any man.

James gave this response.

Death reigned from Adam to Moses, even over them that had not sinned after the similitude of Adam's transgression.

It is first necessary for us to understand God's original purpose for man and woman on the earth.

What was Adam's transgression?

(Adamah—man and woman together as one unit, one flesh. Gen. 2:24)

The man and the woman took the life making process and placed it under their own conscious control. This was the only thing God had asked them not to do, because God knew once they had experienced the physical sensations associated with that process they would not be able to stop its proliferation. This would overpopulate the world and cause death in order to balance the 'NEED WITH SUPPLY.'

Even those that partly understood the original sin and tried to make themselves celibate or separate themselves from the opposite gender could not change the inborn degeneration received from their ancestors. Death has still reigned.

But God has had mercy—looking forward to the time when men will grow out of their foolish years, for the imagination of man's heart is evil from his YOUTH. (Gen. 8:21).

But eventually all sin will be washed out of our systems as we partake of that TREE OF LIFE (the name of God), and the washing of the living water that flows out of our belly—(John 7:38) into eternal life. (John 3:15)

Natural will-power plays little part in this process. Any physical attempt to correct the problem caused by the inherited genes will only cause separations. Two by two, male and female, went into the ark (Gen. 6:19). The Holy Ghost will guide (John 16:13) and the holy spirit of God must flow from within—then time and understanding along with the power of God will raise the foundation of human life.

There were trees in the garden of Eden to be sure, but eating of the fruit of a natural tree was not the sin. Eve said unto the serpent, (Adam) We may eat of the fruit of the trees of the garden. Gen. 3:2. These were the natural trees of the garden: but of the fruit of the tree which is in the midst of the garden, (man and woman) God hath said, Ye shall not eat of it, neither shall ye touch it, lest ye die.

People are called trees in the garden. The man and the woman represented one unit, one tree, the tree that had the ability to know good as well as evil. If the knowledge of evil entered their system it would drive out the spirit of God. The spiritual water would not flow from their belly into eternal life. John 7:38, Titus 1:2.

GUILT caused the man and woman to hide behind the (physical) trees.

Why did they feel guilty?

They observed the processes for reproduction as performed by the other animals and it became a part of their lives.

Didn't God say, Be fruitful, and multiply?

HE SAID THIS TO THE SUBCONSCIOUS MIND!

The sleep process as used in the creation of Eve was supposed to continue in the reproduction of all human life. This would have eliminated overpopulation of the world as time continued.

Overpopulation was not the only problem. It was relatively easy for the mind to be swayed. Without a continual focus upon one goal, or vision, or thing, the mind could be drawn toward destructive thoughts as portrayed by the other animals, and ultimately be drawn toward violence, killing and destruction.

So God figured out a formula to correct this problem. The answer resided in His Own Name. He told man to call upon His Name with his inner voice without ceasing. From the rising of the sun unto the going down of the same the Lord's Name is to be praised. (Psalm 113:3) I have remembered thy Name, O Lord, in the night, and HAVE KEPT THY LAW.

If man and woman had conformed to that one formula they would have had strength to conform to the one rule God had set forth in the beginning. DON'T EVEN TOUCH IT LEST YE DIE!

When they took control of the life making processes against God's will, they ***immediately knew they were naked***. At that point their conscience filled their beings with ***guilt, and fear of God caused them to hide behind the trees.***

The man and the woman were not aware of the sexual sensations in their bodies until after they deliberately experienced the sexual acts as they had observed in the other animals.

God did not want to keep some good thing from man and woman, but to develop a human family on the earth that would maintain eternal life, God must regulate propagation. If this was not done, then death would be necessary, as in the case of the other animals, to eliminate overpopulation. Men and women were the sons and daughters of God, the other animals were not.

Whether the word is testing or tempting, it doesn't matter. Jesus said, (Matthew 11:29) Take my yoke upon you, and learn of me; for I am meek and lowly in heart: and ye shall find REST unto your souls.

Just call upon His Name, that's all. With ease the Holy Ghost will guide into all truth.

****

THREE QUESTIONS

Yeremias asked,

1) How vital is faith to salvation?

2) Does faith maintain your salvation or is something else required to be saved, and

3) What one thing should a Christian remember above all else?

Thank you in advance for all of your answers,

Yeremias.

James gave this response.

1) How vital is faith to salvation

   What is faith?

   Heb. 11:1—Faith is the substance of things hoped for, the evidence of things not seen.

   Faith is mentioned only twice in the Old Testament. Deut.32:20 and Hab. 2:4.

   Hebrews 11:6 Without faith it is impossible to please him: for he that cometh to God must believe that he is, and that he is a rewarder of them that diligently seek him.

   Matthew 17:20 If ye have faith as a grain of mustard seed, ye shall say unto this mountain, Remove hence to yonder place; and it shall remove; and nothing shall be impossible unto you.

   It may be preferable to think in terms of mountains of sickness, poverty, and depressions, many of which were caused by alcoholic beverages. There were no recordings of physical mountains being removed, other than a few earth quakes here and there, but there were many healing accomplishments taking place by the faith of the people in Jesus and in the apostles.

   Matthew 9:28—The blind men came to him: and Jesus saith unto them, Believe ye that I am able to do this? They said unto him, Yea, Lord. (29) Then touched he their eyes saying, ACCORDING TO YOUR FAITH BE IT UNTO YOU.

Matthew 9:2 And, behold they brought to him a man sick of the palsy, lying on a bed: and Jesus seeing THEIR FAITH said unto the sick of the palsy; Son, be of good cheer; thy sins be forgiven thee—. (Saved or receiving Salvation means being saved from Sin or danger. In theological use, deliverance from the power and penalty of sin; redemption).

Matthew 9:20—A woman, which was diseased with an issue of blood twelve years, came behind him, and touched the hem of his garment: (21) For she said within herself, If I may but touch his garment, I shall be whole. (22) Jesus said, Daughter, be of good comfort; thy FAITH hath made thee whole. And the woman was made whole from that hour.

Matthew 15:22 (A woman of Canaan) Said, my daughter is grievously vexed with a devil. (28) Jesus said, GREAT IS THY FAITH: be it unto thee even as thou wilt. And her daughter was made whole from that very hour.

Acts 3: 2-16 A man at the beautiful gate which had been lame from his birth was healed by God through Peter. Then Peter said to the people, "Jesus' name, through FAITH IN HIS NAME, hath made this man strong. The faith which is by him hath given him this perfect soundness in the presence of you all.

2) Does faith maintain your salvation or is something else required to be SAVED.

Joel 2:32—It shall come to pass, that WHOSOEVER shall CALL on the NAME of the LORD shall be delivered.

Acts 2:21—It shall come to pass, that WHOSOEVER shall CALL ON THE name OF THE Lord shall be SAVED.

Romans 10:13 For whosoever shall CALL upon the NAME of the Lord shall be saved.

3) and What one thing should a Christian remember above all else?

Eph. 2:8—By grace are ye SAVED through FAITH; and that not of yourselves: it is the gift of God: (9) Not of works, (of the law) lest any man should boast. (Calling upon the Name of the Lord is not the kind of works Paul was writing about. He was speaking about the works of the law.) Paul was not nullifying all the other passages throughout the Bible regarding the necessity of calling upon the Name of the Lord.

Luke 18:8—When the Son of man cometh, shall he find faith on the earth?

Yeremias rated this answer:

Thank you very much for your answer. I appreciate it and will study all of your passages fully.

May God Bless You Fully,

Yeremias

****

TITHING

Charlene asked this question.

Explain where the idea of Tithing came from.

James gave this response.

Tithing

The first root of tithing.

After Abram and his servants SLAUGHTERED Chedorlaomer, and the Kings that were with him,(Gen 14:17) Melchizedek said to Abram,

Genesis 14:20—Blessed be the most high God, which hath delivered thine enemies into thy hand, AND HE (ABRAM) GAVE HIM (MELCHIZEDEK) TITHES OF ALL.

The second root of tithing.

Genesis 28:20 And Jacob vowed a vow, saying, If God will be with me, and will keep me in this way that I go, and will give me bread to eat, and raiment to put on, (21) So that I come again to my father's house in peace; THEN shall the Lord be my God; (22) And this stone, which I have set for a pillar, shall be God's house; and of ALL that thou shalt give me I will surely give the TENTH unto thee.

Genesis 29:1 Then Jacob went on his journey, and came into the land of the people of the east, (Mesopotamia)

(Check Gen 28:15 God did not ask for a vow)

Did Jacob give a tenth of all that God gave him to God's house?

NO!—He gave at least ten percent to his brother Esau so that he would not follow through on his threat to kill him. (Gen. 32:17-20. The exact percentage was not given). (Gen. 33:11 Esau took the presents).

Gen. 27:41 And Esau hated Jacob because of the blessing wherewith his father blessed him: and Esau said in his heart, The days of mourning for my father are at hand; then will I slay by brother Jacob.

So the FIRST ROOT OF TITHING was based on KILLING and the SECOND ROOT was based on FEAR.

God has need of nothing from man except his heart and his adherence. He does not need man's money.

Psalms 50:11 I know all the fowls of the mountains: and the wild beasts of the field are mine. IF I WERE HUNGRY, I would not tell thee: for the world is mine—.

TITHE—FIRST ENACTMENT

The first enactment of the law with respect to TITHING is the declaration that the tenth of all produce, as well as of flocks and cattle, belongs to Jehovah, and must be offered to him. Lev. 27:30-33. This tenth is ordered to be assigned to the Levites as the reward for their service.

This clearly shows that they did not understand God and what he wanted. Refer to: Cruden's Complete Concordance.

TITHE:—***In the New Testament, neither our Saviour, nor his apostles have commanded anything in this affair of TITHES.***

It was recorded in Luke that Jesus said, Luke 11:42 But woe unto you, Pharisees! For ye tithe MINT and RUE and all manner of HERBS, and pass over judgment and the love of God: these OUGHT YE TO HAVE DONE, and NOT TO LEAVE THE OTHER UNDONE.

Matthew wrote that Jesus said, Matt. 23:23 Woe unto you, scribes and Pharisees, hypocrites! For ye pay tithe of mint and anise and cummin, and have omitted the weightier matters of the law, judgment, mercy, and faith: THESE OUGHT YE TO HAVE DONE, AND NOT TO LEAVE THE OTHER UNDONE.

In a way we have two witnesses here regarding what Jesus said, although it is indirect and not a command. The fact remains that if Jesus believed in Tithing he would have instructed his disciples, especially his apostles, as to that fact.

Jesus gave his all—He was a great advocate of giving to the poor. In fact he said, (Matthew 19:21)—If thou (a young man) wilt be perfect, go and sell that thou hast, and GIVE TO THE POOR, and thou shalt have treasure in heaven: AND ***COME AND FOLLOW ME.***

Note: ***JESUS DID NOT TELL HIM TO BRING THE MONEY AND LAY IT AT HIS FEET.*** (Jesus is still the best person to follow than even the Apostles.)

Mark 10:21—one thing thou lackest; go thy way, sell whatsoever thou hast, and ***GIVE TO THE POOR, and thou shalt have treasure in heaven: and come take up the cross, AND FOLLOW ME.***

WHAT IS THE ANSWER?

Change the tithe to free will offerings.

2 Cor 9:7 Every man according as he purposeth in his heart, so LET HIM GIVE, NOT GRUDGINGLY, OR OF NECESSITY: FOR GOD LOVETH A CHEERFUL GIVER.

Jesus was impressed because a certain centurion had built a synagogue for the people, so Jesus healed the centurion's servant. (Luke 7:5)

There is nothing wrong with building structures for religious services and supporting the ministers and their families, as Moses did for the Levites, or giving money to any charitable cause we desire. It is our money to do with as we wish. But it should be remembered that ***Moses represented the Government and the church through the Levits*** for the Israelites after they left Egypt. The church presently is separated from the state and does not generally perform the duties of the Government.

Yes, Mal. 3:8 was taken into consideration when researching the practice of tithing. Jesus didn't even believe he was obligated to pay the temple tax. In fact he told Peter to pay the tax for them both with a coin he was to find in the mouth of a fish. (Matthew 17:24-27).

****

Tomb of Jesus outside the walls of (Old) Jerusalem

Cherub asked this question.

In 333, a pilgrim from Bordeaux, France wrote, As you pass through the gate of Neapolis [the present Damascus gate] . . . on your left is the hillock Golgotha where the Lord was crucified, and about a stone's throw from it to the vault where they laid his body and he rose again on the third day." (Egeria's Travels)

This is a reference to the garden tomb where it is presumed that the body of Christ was laid. It has a rolling stone closure.

And then, we have the "Holy Sepulchre of Christ" Including the five million dollar dome over the venerated tomb where tradition says Jesus was buried and resurrected. (no stone here)

So, where is the burial tomb of the Risen Lord?

(Remember, only four rolling stone tombs were in existence in first century Jerusalem)

James gave this response.

Cherub: I agree with hwood74, but my wife and I visited both tombs in 1985 and we feel sure that the Garden Tomb conforms more to the description given in the bible. In fact I drew a picture of the tomb and asked permission to put it in my book and was told if I used it they would have me in court. So needless to say I took it out. In that same year we spent 5 days in Jerusalem and the rest of 14 days touring Israel. No, we are not experts but we were there and saw things first hand. We feel that this trip should be a part of every person's experience that are trying to do a spiritual work.

Cherub rated this answer:

And, James, my day is coming soon to see also.

Thanks for the comments.

~cherub~

James gave this follow-up answer.

Conditions are much worse now than they were in l985. After the 14 day tour in Israel we went to Paris where they thought our video camera was a machine gun. Then we went to Germany and Switzerland. We have determined that we are better off at home.

I still think that a speaker has more weight if the places he/she speaks of have been visited by him/her. Although I found that most people are not concerned or interested about home videos or where you have been.

****

TONGUE, FORKED

"Forked Tongue" christians and faith healers!!!

(Not to be disclosed) asked this question.

Christians are so blessed. Jesus has blessed them with jobs, wealth, money, cars, homes, and everything they have has been blessed on them by either GOD or Jesus. Well you dopes—here is reality. Jesus not once when He was on this earth blessed anyone with finances, jobs, homes, cars or really anything you forked tongue Christians and so called Jesus

Followers screech & cry to others about. Hell dum butts read the BIBLE every now and then. Every miracle was of "psychical healing" yet over & over on these boards—in the church pews—on the air waves—we hear these TOTAL NIN COM POOTS telling & yelling to us how JESUS has blessed them from every thing from the cars they have to the homes they live. Then we even have the worst of the lot telling us how they were blessed by Jesus and gave up everything from SEX to DOPE. If Jesus did not bless anyone with the crap you lay on his doorstep when here walking & talking & making the disciples live in poverty & humility—WHY WOULD ANY MAN OR WOMAN POSSIBLY BELIEVE OR ACTUALLY YELL TO THE WORLD—"we are blessed in this way or that by JESUS". Well hope you nin com poots get a GREAT BLESSING FROM THIS—you are a joke & bringing this nation into the wrath of the entire world with what you are doing to everyone here and across these great oceans.

James gave this response.

X_xxxxxx_X is not signed up as an Expert in any categories

First of all, you are correct in some of the things you are saying. But—

There is positive and negative in everything. You are seeing the negative in everything around you. There is a balance needed here, but you will never be able to strike that balance unless you receive the Holy Ghost, the filling of the holy spirit, receive spiritual eyes and ears, have your spirit that you received from your natural father killed, taken out, and a right spirit installed in its place. (Psalms 51:10, John 3:3) After that you must maintain the holy spirit within yourself by associating with people that are in contact with God through the mediator, God's only begotten son, that came to the earth with His Father's Name to be placed in the foreheads of all people on the earth.

The only way the process can start is for you to call upon the Name of God without ceasing.

Luke 18:7—Shall not God avenge his own elect, which cry day and night unto him, though he bear long with them? (8) I tell you that he will avenge them speedily.

I Ths. 5:17 Pray without ceasing. (18) In everything give thanks: for this is the will of God in Christ Jesus concerning you.

Joel 2:32 And it shall come to pass, that WHOSOEVER (this includes you) shall CALL on the NAME of the LORD, shall be delivered—.

Zeph. 3:9 For then will I turn to the people a pure language, that they may ALL CALL upon the NAME of the LORD, to serve them with one consent.

Zech. 13:9—they shall call on my name, and I will hear them—.

Acts 2:21 And it shall come to pass, that WHOSOEVER shall CALL on the NAME of the Lord shall be saved.

Rom. 10:13 For whosoever shall CALL upon the NAME of the Lord shall be saved. (Also Prov. 18:10)

What are we saved from? Primarily from our own selves. From our destructive thoughts and hatred that we feel for everything around us. Without being saved from this evil that permeates our being we cannot see good in anybody or anything around us. But as we call upon God by His Name, the mediator, God's holy spirit fills our being and begins to be generated from our belly (John 7:38) into eternal life. This flow like rivers of living water washes out all the destructive forces within us that will otherwise disrupt the spiritual and natural process of life.

Peter began to say unto him,(Jesus, Mark 10:28) Lo, we have left all, and have followed thee. (Mark 10:28) (29) And Jesus answered and said, Verily I say unto you, There is no man that hath left house, or brethren, or sisters, or father, or mother, or wife, or children, or lands, for my sake, and the gospel's, (30) But he shall ***receive an***

hundredfold now in this time, HOUSES, and brethren, and sisters, and mothers, and children, and LANDS—.

Sometimes separations from the unbelievers are necessary.

2 Cor. 6:14 Be ye not unequally yoked together with unbelievers: for what fellowship hath righteousness with unrighteousness? And what communion hath light with darkness? (15) And what concord hath Christ with Belial? Or what part hath he that believeth with an infidel? (16) And what agreement hath the temple of God with idols? For ye are the temple of the living God; as God hath said, ***I will dwell in them, and walk in them;*** and I will be their God, and they shall be my people. (17) Therefore come out from among them, and be ye separate, saith the Lord—.

(Not to be disclosed) rated this answer:

You are so confused—pray to god and get a life fatso!!!!!!!

****

Tongues: Another & Other

Ruth asked this question.

When Isaiah wrote (Isa. 28:11) For with stammering lips and ANOTHER tongue will he speak to this people: was he predicting OTHER TONGUES as was operating on the day of the feast of Pentecost? (Christian feast on the 7th Sunday after Easter)

James gave this response.

Peter did not mention Isaiah. He said (Acts 2:16), This is that which was spoken by the prophet Joel—Joel 2:28.

Acts 2:17 And it shall come to pass in the last days, saith God, I will pour out of my Spirit upon all flesh; and your sons and your daughters shall prophesy, and your young men shall see visions, and your old men shall dream dreams;

Acts 2:18 And on my servants and on my handmaidens I will pour out in those days of my Spirit; and they shall prophesy:

Acts 2:21 And it shall come to pass, that whosoever shall call on the name of the Lord shall be saved.

During the feast of Pentecost the Holy Ghost was not stammering, but was speaking good clear words through the men of Galilee, to the people of many different countries and languages.

Acts 2:1 And when the day of Pentecost was fully come, they were all with one accord in one place.

Acts 2:2 And suddenly there came a sound from heaven as of a rushing mighty wind, and it filled all the house where they were SITTING.

Acts 2:3 And there appeared unto them cloven tongues like as of fire, and it sat upon each of them.

Acts 2:4 And they were all filled with the Holy Ghost, and began to speak with OTHER tongues (not another, as meaning only one), as the Spirit gave them utterance.

Isa. 28:11, Ps 68:18—Thou hast ascended on high—thou hast received gifts for men—John 16:7 If I go not away, the comforter will not come unto you—.

Acts 2:5 And there were dwelling at Jerusalem Jews, devout men, out of EVERY NATION UNDER HEAVEN.

Acts 2:6 Now when this was noised abroad, the multitude came together, and were confounded, because that every man heard them speak in his own language. (7) And they were all amazed and marveled, saying one to another, Behold are not all these which speak Galilaeans? (8) And how hear we every man in our own tongue, wherein we were born?

GOD UNDERSTANDS ALL THE LANGUAGES.

Listed here are the languages the Spirit of God spoke through the Holy Ghost, showing his mighty power in the earth when people were calling upon His Name.

Acts 2:9 Parthians, and Medes, and Elamites, and the dwellers in Mesopotamia, and in Judaea, and Cappadocia, in Pontus, and Asia. (10) Phrygia, and Pamphylia, in Egypt, and in the parts of Libya about Cyrene, and strangers of Rome, Jews and proselytes, (11) Cretes and Arabians, we do hear them speak in our tongues the wonderful works of God.

Paul stated (1Cor. 14:21) In the law it is written, with men of OTHER tongues and other lips will I speak unto this people;—
.

COMPARE Isa. 28:11 For with stammering lips and ANOTHER tongue (Greek—because Isaiah's Bible was written in Hebrew, but at the time this prophesy was to be fulfilled the bible will have been translated into Greek (another tongue).

****

TONGUES? JESUS

*j*dg asked this question.

DID JESUS SPEAK WITH TONGUES, AND WHAT BIBLE DID HE READ?

James gave this response.

What Bible did Jesus read?

The Bible of Jesus's time was the Septuagint (seventy),a Greek version of the Old Testament, including the Pentateuch (the first five books of the Bible), which was translated from Hebrew to Greek at Alexandria, Egypt about 380 B.C.

DID JESUS SPEAK WITH TONGUES?

Yes, Jesus spoke Hebrew, Aramaic and Greek, all by his own knowledge.

DID JESUS SPEAK IN TONGUES ON THE CROSS?

Matthew 27:46 Eli, Eli, lama sabachthani, or Mark 15:34

Eloi, Eloi, lama sabachthani.

YES! By his own knowledge and utterance he spoke those words in Aramaic (Syro-Chaldaic), the common dialect of the people of Palestine in Christ's time, and the whole is a translation of the Hebrew(given in Matthew 27:46) of the first words of the 22nd Psalm.

Psalm 22:1 My God, my God, why hast thou forsaken me?

DURING JESUS'S life on earth did he ever speak in an unknown tongue?

NO! The words he spoke and the ones he wrote on the ground (John 8:8), were the words he had learned during his physical life on earth. (9) The words written on the ground were understood by the accusers otherwise they would not have walked away so soon).

DIDN'T HE SPEAK WITH TONGUES WHEN HE RECEIVED THE HOLY GHOST?

NO!

Matthew 3:16 And Jesus when he was baptized, went up straightway out of the water: and, lo, the heavens were opened unto him, and he saw the Spirit of God descending like a dove, and lighting upon him:

(17) And lo a voice from heaven, saying, THIS IS (as if speaking

with someone else) my beloved Son, in whom I am well pleased.

Mark 1:10 And straightway coming up out of the water, HE SAW the heavens opened, and the Spirit like a dove descending upon him; (11) And there came a voice from heaven saying, THOU ART (speaking directly with Jesus) my beloved Son, in whom I am well pleased.

Luke 3:22 And the ***Holy Ghost descended in a bodily shape like a dove upon him,*** and a voice came from heaven, which said, THOU ART my beloved Son; in thee I am well pleased.

Luke 4:1—and Jesus ***BEING FULL OF THE HOLY GHOST*** returned from Jordan, and was led by the Spirit into the wilderness.

JESUS ALONE HEARD THE VOICE INSIDE HIMSELF. Note: Luke 3:22 and Mark 1:11 states 'THOU ART', but Matthew 3:17 states 'THIS IS'. Here we have two witnesses for the words being said 'THOU ART', and only one witness that the words were 'THIS IS'.

DID JOHN HEAR THE VOICE?

NO! HE ONLY SAW THE VISION.

John 1:32 And John (the baptizer) bare record, saying, I SAW (in vision form) the spirit descending from heaven like a dove, and it abode upon him.

John 1:33 And ***I knew him not*** but he that sent me to baptize with water, the same said unto me, upon whom thou shalt see the Spirit (in vision form) descending, and remaining on him, the same is he which baptizeth with the Holy Ghost.

Note: Luke 1:36 The mothers, (Elisabeth and Mary),of John and Jesus were cousins. John did know Jesus, but up until then he did not know he was the one that was to be selected to make a way for the gift of the Holy Ghost to be given to the people.

TONGUES WERE NOT MENTIONED IN ANY OF THESE PRECEDING PASSAGES.

Jesus prayed to God and the Holy Ghost was given on the day of Pentecost. John 14:16 Acts 2:4 mentioned the tongues.

****

Tower of Babel.

Charlene asked this question.

Can the story of the Tower of Babel have a two fold meaning?

James gave this response.

Genesis 11 tells the story of the separation of people and the ultimate development of different languages. But it is also a good example of the confusion caused by the many names in religion.

Gen. 11:4 And (the people) said, Go to, let us build a city and a tower, whose top MAY REACH UNTO HEAVEN; and let us MAKE A NAME, lest we be scattered abroad upon the face of the whole earth.

Gen. 11:6 And the Lord said, Behold, the people is one, and they have all one language; and this they begin to do: and now NOTHING WILL BE restrained from them, which they have imagined to do.

Gen 11:7 Go to, let us go down, and there confound their language, that they may not understand one another's speech.

The many thousands of names in our religious societies are testimony that the people have made names for themselves.

They have imagined that through their particular name they have selected they may reach heaven. Because they have not accepted God's NAME ONLY he has taken their understanding away.

Acts 4:11 (Speaking of Jesus—the Name of God) This is the stone which was set at nought of you builders (religionists), which is become the head of the corner.

Acts 4:12 Neither is there salvation (saving of a person from sin or danger) in any other; for there is NONE OTHER NAME under heaven given among men, whereby we must be saved.

For those that become one in God's Name there will be nothing restrained from them.

Revelation 14:8 And there followed another angel, saying, Babylon (confusion) is fallen, is fallen, that great city—.

When the people become ONE in GOD'S NAME, they will understand that they should not follow the ideas of men, or Moses, or Elijah, ONLY JESUS, THE NAME OF GOD AND THE SON OF GOD.

Matthew 17:8 (After the vision, Peter, James and John) lifted up their eyes, and saw NO MAN, SAVE JESUS ONLY.

****

Tithing:

Edward asked this question.

What about tithing?

James gave this response.

The leaders of all Christian denominations are fully aware of all the passages in the Bible, including the various translations.

They are aware that the writings in the Bible were inspired by God to tell the truth whether good or bad. Those passages were recorded for instructions in doctrine, for reproof and correction, that the spiritual leaders may be perfect, thoroughly furnished unto all good works. 2 Tim. 3:16-17.

The spiritual leaders are aware of the fact that Jesus, nor any of the apostles advocated Tithing which was imposed first for the use of the government and the church led by Moses. The current churches, for the most part, do not perform the duties of the government, yet they claim they must continue receiving the ten percent to help the WORK OF GOD and to build his kingdom on the earth. The passage that states, 'This is the WORK OF GOD, that ye believe on him whom He hath sent, is completely overlooked. John 6:39.

The leaders may reason, 'How can we build and maintain all those great church buildings and pay the salaries of the ministers if we do not continue advocating the custom of tithing. But they are in luck. One passage stands out, and when used, the people will not question, and they will continue giving until it hurts.

The passage is this: Matthew 23:23—ye pay tithe of mint and anise and cummin, and have omitted the weightier matters of the law, judgment, mercy, and faith: THESE (tithe of mint and anise and cummin) OUGHT YE TO HAVE DONE, and not to leave the other undone. This passage represents only one witness and is not enough to establish every word. John 5:31, 8:13-18.

Spoken words are harder to erase than the words received from the written page. Instructions received from the orators to young ears are almost impossible to erase when adulthood arrives.

Even the clergy that sees and understands all the passages, find it futile to try to change the traditions of the well established churches. They are fully aware that new wine (doctrines) cannot be put into old bottles without catastrophic results. Matt. 9:17, Mark 2:22, Luke 5:37.

So there are two major hindrances to the establishment of unity in the Christian religion. The first is greed and the second is the established traditions that were also prevalent during the time Jesus taught in the Synagogues. Those traditions are still as strong in the earth today.

Of course there is an answer to the question of tithing.

2 Cor. 9:7 (Let) Every man according as he purposeth in his heart, so let him give; not grudgingly, or of necessity: for God loveth a cheerful giver.

(FREE WILL OFFERINGS IS THE ANSWER).

Jesus gave his all:

****

Traditions

Should we pray to angels or anyone that has passed on?

No!

Matthew 6:6—pray to thy Father—.

Matthew 6:9 After this manner therefore pray ye: Our Father which art in heaven. Luke 11:2

Should we ask Jesus or anyone else (that has passed on) to relay messages of prayer to God for us?

No! John 16:26 At that day ye shall ask in my Name: and I say not unto you, that I will pray the Father for you: (27) For the Father himself loveth you, because ye have loved me—.

Does God hear when we pray, or should we repeat our prayers over and over?

Matthew 6:7—When ye pray, use not vain repetitions, as the heathen do: for they think that they shall be heard for their much speaking. (8) Be not ye therefore like unto them: for your Father knoweth what things ye have need of, before ye ask him.

In the religious arena should we call any man 'Father.'

No! Matthew 23:9—Call NO MAN your father upon the earth: for one is your Father, which is in heaven.

These passages are all in the Bible. But because of the traditions established by the founders of the various churches it is next to impossible to change to what the Bible plainly states.

What is the answer? Call upon the Name of the Lord without ceasing and the Holy Ghost will come and guide you into all truth.

John 16:13—When he, the Spirit of Truth, is come, he will guide you into all truth—.

When the truth is established by the Holy Ghost, there will be no division. The Body of Christ will then become one.

****

Tree of Life: Name of God—

Ruth asked this question.

WHY IS THE NAME OF GOD SIGNIFICANT?

James gave this response.

People must have a 'peg' in life. They must have something to hang on to. The best object of faith is the 'handle of God' (His Name). As a person calls upon the Name of God, his faith increases and attracts the power of God (Christ) which is absorbed into his/her system. This anointing of God drives out the destructive thoughts caused by guilt and allows the mind to be free to do the perfect job of enhancing the immune system, allowing the body to live.

God knew people could fall by the force of the destructive elements of the earth, the actions of the other animals and the thoughts provoked by such actions, so he devised the formula of constantly CALLING UPON HIS NAME, so that men/women could withstand every conceivable pitfall that may surround them in their trek toward eternal life.

God constructed the body of man and woman as one unit, with the ability of all the cells to be renewed every seven years. With this process there would have been no reason for death. There was one catch: If the mind became depressed by too much guilt (the tree of Knowledge of evil) it would in turn disrupt the immune system and cause eventual death.

The main cause of man and woman's failure was centered around the fact that Adamah (man) and woman never, in their life time, called upon the Name of God. Adam's Grandson awakened the world of men and they began Calling upon the Name of God as they knew it (Gen. 4:26), Since Enos' Grandfather did not relay the 'SAVING NAME' of God to his Grandson, the men of that era could not perfectly reach God and the benefit of His Christ (Anointing). There were eight primary names attributed to God before his true SAVING NAME, JESUS, was revealed.

With these facts in mind, it becomes easier to understand why the man and the woman did not have strength to conform to the first necessary requirement God advised them of regarding the trees of the garden.

There were natural trees in the garden that the man and woman were to eat of for sustenance of their physical bodies. (Gen. 3:2)

The woman said,—***"We may eat of the fruit of the trees of the garden—."*** But for a spiritual understanding we must apply the 'fruit of the tree which is in the midst of the garden' to a symbolic meaning, Gen. 3:3 But of the fruit of the tree which is in the MIDST OF THE GARDEN, GOD HATH SAID, YE SHALL NOT EAT OF IT, NEITHER SHALL YE TOUCH IT, LEST YE DIE. (Man and woman was that tree).

The animals were designed to die, but God wanted to create physical beings that would live forever in a natural state somewhat like he and the other spiritual beings live in the spiritual realms.

In order for men and women to live forever, God must remain in control of the production of new life among the human inhabitants of the world. As God caused a deep sleep to fall upon Adam (Gen. 2:21) in the creation of the woman, so he planned to use that same process in the production of new life.

Well, didn't God say to the male and female (Gen.1:28) "Be fruitful, and multiply, and REPLENISH the earth? (replenish = stock or supply anew).

YES! HE SAID THIS TO THE SUBCONSCIOUS MIND!

****

Trip to the Holy Lands

RyansZion asked this question.

Hello,

My wife and I are considering a trip to the Holy Lands with a ministry and would like to know about your personal experiences and revelations if you've made the trip.

Please share your favorite places to see, what inspired you the most, etc, etc.

God Bless!

RyansZion

James gave this response.

My wife and I spent 14 days in Israel in 1985. Five days in Jerusalem and the rest of the time throughout Israel.

If you are taking a Video Camera please be informed in advance that their electric power is 48 cycles instead of our power produced at 60 cycles. You cannot charge your batteries unless you have a transformer. We spent 5 days in Jerusalem before we were released from the tour so that we could go and buy a transformer. As a result we lost all the taping in Jerusalem. We saw everything that was explained to you by previous answers. We even went on the Military tour at the West Bank. There was trouble even then in Israel. We were warned not to go to Old Jerusalem by ourselves at night, and even during the day, and with the guide, your money would not be safe. We were instructed to deposit our money in the Safe at the hotel, because the next day we were going to Old Jerusalem. Also when you go into the Dome of the Rock you must leave everything outside of the building, even your money and camera. Even your shoes must be taken off. One person was assigned to watch the stuff. In our case it was an elderly woman that was crippled.

The guide said that they have enemies all around them all the time, and that women as well as men are demanded to spend time in the service and they are on call at all times. If they, both the bus driver and guide, were called to the service at any time they would have to go instantly.

In our opinion they continually have enemies because they have not YET accepted the true Saving Name of God, which is Jesus.

God bless your understanding.

****

UNBELIEF AND REPETITION OF PRAYERS

Not to be revealed—asked this question.

When does repetition of a prayer turn into unbelief? Are we never to go back to the Father and ask Him again? And again? and again? Does this show we had no faith the first time, and that we are not walking in His rest?

James gave this response.

Jesus seldom prayed to the Father more than once. He did pray three times while in the garden of Gethsemane.

Matthew 26:36 Then cometh Jesus with them unto a place called Gethsemane, and saith unto the disciples, Sit ye here, while I go and pray yonder. He (Jesus) began to be sorrowful and very heavy. (38) Then saith he unto them, My soul is exceeding sorrowful, even unto death—.

(39) And he went a little farther, and fell on his face, and prayed, saying, O my Father, if it be possible, let this cup pass from me: nevertheless not as I will, but as thou wilt. (42) He went away again the second time, and prayed, saying O my Father, if this cup may not pass away from me, except I drink it, thy will be done. (44)—(He) prayed the third time, saying the same words.

Jesus was that Lamb slain from the foundation of the world. Rev. 13:8.

John 1:29. Behold the Lamb of God which taketh away the sin of the world.

Gen. 3:15 I will put enmity between thee and the woman, and between thy seed and her seed; it shall bruise thy head, AND THOU SHALT BRUISE HIS HEEL.

Isaiah 53:10 Yet it pleased the LORD to bruise him; he hath put him to grief: when thou shalt make his soul an offering for sin,—(11) He shall see of the travail of his soul, and shall be satisfied: by his knowledge shall my righteous servant justify many; for he shall bear their iniquities. (12) he hath poured out his soul unto death: and he was numbered with the transgressors; and he bare the sin of many, and made intercession for the transgressors.

Jesus was the last Adam—1 Cor. 15:45. He knew that he must do the will of His Father. It was determined at the time of the failure of the first man that God's second son must come to the earth to retrieve that which was lost, and to save them from the curse brought upon mankind by Adamah's (man's) failure. Of course it could have been different if men had reverenced HIS SON, but of course, knowing man's history, it was inevitable that they wouldn't. Matthew 21:37. Mark 12:6.

WHEN YE PRAY

Matthew 6:7 But when ye pray, use not vain repetitions, as the heathen do: for ***they think that they shall be heard for their much speaking.*** (8) Be not ye therefore like unto them: ***for your Father knoweth what things ye have need of, before ye ask him.***

THE FOLLOWING DOES NOT CONSTITUTE VAIN REPETITIONS.

Psalm 113:3 From the rising of the sun unto the going down of the same the LORD'S NAME is to be praised. (4) The LORD is high above all nations. Psalm 119:55 I have remembered thy NAME O LORD, in the night, and have kept thy law.

ONE STEP FURTHER

Psalm 80:18—quicken us, (give us life) and we will CALL UPON THY NAME.

Psalm 99:6 Moses and Aaron among his priests, and Samuel among them that ***CALL upon HIS NAME; they called upon the LORD, and he answered them***.

Psalm 116:13 I will take the cup of salvation (salvation—saving of a person from sin or danger), and CALL upon the NAME of the LORD.

Psalm 116:17 I will offer to thee the sacrifice of thanksgiving, and will **CALL upon the NAME of the LORD**.

Hebrews 13:15 By him therefore let us offer the sacrifice of praise ***to God CONTINUALLY***, that is, the fruit of our lips giving thanks to HIS NAME.

Isaiah 12:4 And in that day shall ye say, Praise the LORD, CALL upon HIS NAME—'

Jer. 10:25 Pour out thy fury upon the heathen that know thee not, and upon the families that CALL NOT ON THY NAME—.

Joel 2:32 And it shall come to pass, that WHOSOEVER shall CALL on the NAME OF THE LORD shall be delivered—.

Zeph. 3:9 For then will I turn to the people a pure language, that they may ALL CALL UPON THE NAME OF THE LORD—.

Zech. 13:9—they shall CALL on MY NAME, and I will hear them—.

Acts 2:21 And it shall come to pass, that WHOSOEVER shall CALL on the NAME of the Lord shall be saved.

THE EARLY CHURCH WAS CALLING UPON THE NAME OF JESUS.

Acts 9:14 And here he (Saul) hath authority from the chief priests to bind all THAT CALL ON THY NAME.

Romans 10:13 For WHOSOEVER shall CALL upon the NAME of the Lord shall be saved.

WHAT IS THE NAME OF THE MEDIATOR BETWEEN GOD AND MAN?

1 Cor. 1:2—all that in every place ***CALL upon the NAME of JESUS Christ our Lord,—.***

Luke 18:7 And shall not God avenge his own elect, which CRY DAY AND NIGHT unto him, though he bear long with them?

Calling upon God's Name was the formula for man from the beginning but was lost in Adamah. The fervent adherence of man and woman to the Name of God without ceasing was thought to be foolishness by their natural mind. The first man and woman never called upon the Name of the LORD. It was not until Adam's Grandson (Enos)came on the scene that men began to CALL UPON THE NAME OF THE LORD. Gen. 4:26. But this was short lived. When the way became rough, men have always forgotten. God has always tried to help men, but every time he turns his back, men have forgotten.

Peter became afraid; and beginning to sink, he cried, saying, Lord, save me. Matthew 14:30.

(31) And immediately Jesus stretched forth his hand, and caught him, and said unto him, O thou of little faith, wherefore didst thou doubt?

CALLING UPON THE NAME OF THE LORD INCREASES FAITH.

Mark 11:22 (Jesus said), have faith in God. (24) What things soever ye desire, when ye pray, believe that ye receive them, and ye shall have them. (According to God's will of course)

James 5:16 The effectual fervent prayer of a righteous man availeth much.

Generally, pray once through the NAME of the mediator, (Jesus) and let faith carry the prayer to God who LIVES WITHIN via the Holy Ghost.

****

Violence, Kingdom of Heaven.

Zenaide asked this question.

Why did the kingdom of heaven suffer violence?

James gave this response.

Jesus said, (Matt. 11:12) And from the days of John the Baptist until now (AD 31) the kingdom of heaven suffereth violence, and the violent take it by force.

WHY DID THE VIOLENT TAKE IT (THE KINGDOM OF HEAVEN) BY FORCE?

The night was coming. The evening shadows began to appear. Fear crept into the minds of the people because they neglected calling upon the Name of the Lord as fervently as they had been and should have continued.

As long as Jesus was in the world, LIGHT WAS ABUNDANT, but as soon as he went back to his Father in the third heaven, darkness began to overshadow the minds of the people. Little by little, the night crept in. It was the same night that Jesus spoke of. The night would not have affected the people if they had continued calling upon the Name of God. But Jesus knew by man's own history that they would also forget.

John 9:4 (A.D. 32) (Jesus said), I must work the works of him that sent me, while it is day: THE NIGHT COMETH, WHEN NO MAN CAN WORK. (5) AS LONG AS I AM IN THE WORLD, I AM THE LIGHT OF THE WORLD.

Jesus left the earth. He returned to his Father. While he was here he established the Name of God in the minds of men. After all this time men are beginning to understand what power resides in that NAME, and that all men should come together by faith in him.

Acts 17:26 And hath made of ONE BLOOD ALL NATIONS OF MEN for to dwell on all the face of the earth,—. (27) That they should seek the LORD, if haply they might feel after him, and find him, though he be NOT FAR FROM EVERY ONE OF US:

FOR IN HIM WE LIVE, AND MOVE, AND HAVE OUR BEING: as certain also of your own poets have said, FOR WE ARE ALSO HIS OFFSPRING.

ALL MEN can become the SONS OF GOD, NO MATTER WHAT RACE, CREED, COLOR, OR SINFUL BACKGROUND. All they need to do is CALL UPON THE NAME OF THE LORD, and GOD will cause them to be born again of their spirit.

Psalm 54:1 Save me, O GOD, by THY NAME—.

****

Televison Violence:

Zenaide asked this question.

HOW DO WE REMOVE VIOLENCE FROM TELEVISION?

James gave this response.

That is simple—***DON'T WATCH IT.*** When it becomes apparent products are not being sold on the strength of the television broadcasts, the sponsors will withdraw their support.

BUT THE PROBLEM IS MUCH DEEPER THAN THAT.

There were no televisions around when Cain killed Abel (Gen. 4:8), or when Moses THOUGHT HE WAS DOING GOD SERVICE when he gave the order to kill three thousand men, their companions and their neighbors. (Exo. 32:28).

There were no televisions around when Moses, Joshua, Saul the King and David, and many, many others killed tens of thousands of human beings. The majority of them thought they were helping God, as if he were not capable of running his own business, and recompensing by diseases, hunger, fear, etc., without the hands of men.

TELEVISION HAD NOT BEEN INVENTED WHEN THEY KILLED THE ONLY BEGOTTEN SON OF GOD.

With the exception of Abram and Cain the ***written commandment*** was in effect during the time of a large portion of those murders/ killlings—namely,

THOU SHALT NOT KILL.

(NOTE: The actions of Cain and Abram along with others was the beginning of the formation of the ten commandments.)

Along with this—***HOW DO YOU STOP DRUG TRAFFICKING AND DRUG USE?***

That is just as simple. DON'T USE DRUGS. If there is no demand, there is no need for the supply.

BUT, THEN WHAT WOULD THE PEOPLE DO IN ORDER TO FILL THE VOID?

It is that void that causes all men, women, boys and girls to turn to many things, including drugs and violence. It is the same void that men have felt since they first separated from God because they would not CALL UPON HIM BY HIS NAME.

IT IS FROM WITHIN EACH INDIVIDUAL THAT THE WORLD BEGINS TO CHANGE.

Outward physical conditions such as education and wealth have NO EFFECT upon the SPIRITUAL PART OF MAN.

MEN ARE ANIMALS. They have similar animalistic tendencies as other animals. It is this powerful force that always pulls man toward the destructive influences of the earth. It is this power that must be offset by the power of God. The power of God (Christ), is that light which lighteth every man that cometh into the world (John 1:9)but will not remain inside a human being unless it is maintained by their faith in God's Name and calling upon it.

SO, DO WE WANT PEACE WITHIN OURSELVES AND IN THE WORLD?

DO WE WANT A DRUG FREE SOCIETY?

DO WE WANT TO STOP VIOLENCE ONCE AND FOR ALL TIME?

LET US TURN TO GOD WITH OUR WHOLE HEART, SOUL AND MIND. Matthew 22:37

****

Violence

jdg asked this question.

What can be done about violence?

James gave this response.

Violence cannot be eliminated from the actions of men until their hearts are filled with the Holy Spirit of God; until they have been given the gift of the Holy Ghost; until their spirit has been killed, taken out, and a right spirit installed in its place; and until their nature has been changed from that of the animal.

(All this will be done by the direction of God through his spirit for those that will call upon God by His Saving Name without ceasing).

But in the meantime there is something the ministers and the parishioners can do to slow down the images of violence portrayed to the minds of their listeners.

WORDS ARE SPIRIT. They live on in the mind. Images of violence as received from television in make believe, or news reports as in reality, should never be reiterated by the ministers, or by the people of the churches.

Especially, the words of a preacher have a lasting impact upon the minds of the people. Those that are weak become weaker, as violence, illicit sex, drinking alcoholic beverages and the use of other drugs are portrayed to the minds by the formation of the words. Those pictures take over the mind as if they were real.

Raise the thoughts of the congregations by preaching Jesus, the Name of God, while disregarding the violence of the present and past whether that violence is in the newspapers or originated in the recordings of the Bible.

God wants peace on earth and good will toward men, all men (Luke 2:14). He wants people to move into paradise (the second heaven state), and divest themselves of the Adamic nature they have evolved into through observation and actions.

Look to the Name of God and the thoughts of tranquillity as portrayed to the eyes by observing God's creation. Place yourselves in the quiet place; the strong tower which is God's Name. Wait on God, until the turmoil of the world subsides. Proverbs 18:10 The NAME of the LORD is a strong tower—.

Psalms 61:2 From the end of the earth will I cry unto thee, when my heart is overwhelmed: lead me to the rock that is higher than I.

Psalms 61:3 For thou hast been a shelter for me, and a strong tower from the enemy.

LET THE PAST GO! It is not necessary to bring it to mind again. It does not help the weak to be told of weakness. Direct the minds to faith in God's Name, and calling upon it,—THAT'S ALL.

GOD CREATES EVIL FOR THOSE THAT WILL NOT CALL UPON HIS NAME.

Isaiah 45:5 I am the Lord, and there is none else, there is no God beside me: I girded thee, though thou hast not known me:(7) I form the light, and create darkness: I make peace, and CREATE EVIL:(for retribution against evil doers)I the Lord do all these things. (8) Drop down, ye heavens, from above, and let the skies pour down righteousness: let the earth open, and let them bring forth salvation, (saving of a person from sin or danger) and let righteousness spring up together; I the Lord have created it.

****

Violence: In the Bible.

Charlene asked this question.

Violence is throughout the Bible. Is this violence the will of God?

James gave this response.

Violence, even though recorded in the Bible, is not of God.

Well yes, the Bible is true. ***It is a recording, (inspired by God), (2 Tim. 3:16) of the thoughts and actions of men, versus the will of God.*** Violence comes from the minds of animals, both men and beasts. All recordings with instructions to do violence come from the minds of men portraying what God is thought by them to be.

Jesus came to the earth to show men 'who God is,' and to place within their minds, the ways of God, Jesus' Father. Even though the people had heard of the commandments, until Jesus began speaking, they had not considered such phrases as:

Matthew 5:21 Ye have heard that it was said by them of old time, 'Thou shalt not kill; and whosoever shall kill shall be in danger of the judgment. (38) Ye have heard—an eye for an eye, and a tooth for a tooth, (39) but I say—that ye resist not evil. (43) Ye have heard—Thou shalt love thy neighbor, and hate thine enemy, (44) but I say unto you, Love your enemies, bless them that curse you, do good to them that hate you, and pray for them which despitefully use you, and persecute you. Luke 3:14 And the ***soldiers***—demanded of him, saying, and what shall we do? And he said unto them, ***DO VIOLENCE to no man—.***

Matt. 26:52—Jesus said unto him (Peter—John 18:11), Put

up again thy sword into his place; for ALL they that take the sword shall perish with the sword.

John 1:17 ***The law came by Moses, but grace and TRUTH came by Jesus Christ***. (18) No man hath seen God at any time; the only begotten Son which is in the bosom of the Father, he hath declared him.

PETER, JAMES AND JOHN WITH JESUS ON THE MOUNTAIN

Matthew 17:4—Peter said to Jesus, "Lord, it is good for us to be here: if thou wilt, let us make here three tabernacles; one for thee, and one for Moses, and one for Elias."—(5) a voice said, "This is My beloved Son, in whom I am well please; HEAR YE HIM. (8) then they saw ***Jesus only . . . .***

2 Cor. 5:19—God was in Christ, reconciling the world unto himself, not imputing (blame on a person or cause) their trespasses unto them; and hath committed unto us the word of reconciliation.

It is time, way past time, for people to begin listening to Jesus and what he advocated, rather than to the penalties of the law as expressed by Moses. Rom. 12:19—avenge not yourselves, but rather give place unto wrath; for it is written, Vengeance is mine; I will repay.

Deut. 32:35 ***To me belongeth vengeance, and recompense; their foot shall slide in due time—.***

God is still in charge of retribution.

How does he accomplish revenge? Actions are recorded in the brain. Guilt arranges for the retribution if the person does not (Mark 12:30)—Love the Lord thy God with all thy heart, and with all thy soul, and with all thy mind, and with all thy strength; this is the first commandment.

Does God reject anyone?

EMPHATICALLY NO!

Acts 2:21—It shall come to pass, that WHOSOEVER SHALL CALL ON THE NAME OF THE LORD SHALL BE SAVED. (Also Rom. 10:13)

Here are the two witnesses that are required to establish every word—we need no other witnesses. Jesus said to the Pharisees (John 8:17) It is also written in your law, that the testimony of two men is true.

It shall come to pass *is the operative phrase here*. This is the time in the progression and development of man that God has looked forward to for the next step in the creation of the human race.

Look to God and He will give you the Holy Ghost. The Holy Ghost, in turn will guide you into ALL TRUTH.

John 16:13—when he, the Spirit of truth, is come, he will guide you into all truth—

****

WALK ON WATER.

Zenaide asked this question.

Did Peter walk on water?

James gave this response.

Job 9:8 ***(God)—ALONE spreadeth out the heavens and TREADETH UPON THE WAVES OF THE SEA.***

Physically, man cannot walk upon the water, but SPIRITUALLY HE CAN, IF HE HAS FAITH IN JESUS—THE NAME OF GOD.

Ps. 65:7 (God) Which stilleth the noise of the seas, the noise of their waves, and the tumult of the people.

Matt. 14:29 And he (Jesus) said, Come, and when Peter was come down out of the ship, he WALKED ON THE WATER, to go to Jesus.

John 5:31 If I (Jesus) bear witness of myself, my witness IS NOT TRUE.

John 8:17 It is written in your law, that the testimony of two men is true.

18 I am one that bear witness of myself, and the Father that sent me beareth witness of me.

NOTE that we do not have TWO WITNESSES to prove this statement, 'HE WALKED ON THE WATER'.

No one—not God, the Holy Ghost, Peter, or any other writer corroborated with Matthew in this statement.

IT IS THEN CONCLUDED that this passage should be viewed as a metaphor, if at all. (use of a word denoting one kind of idea in place of another to suggest a likeness between them.)

Matt. 14:30—when he (Peter) saw the wind boisterous, he was afraid; and beginning to sink, he cried saying, LORD SAVE ME.

31 And immediately Jesus stretched forth his hand, and caught him, and said unto him, O THOU OF LITTLE FAITH, WHEREFORE DIDST THOU DOUBT?

Ps. 105:4 Seek the Lord, and HIS STRENGTH: seek his face evermore.

PETER, KEEP YOUR EYES ON JESUS, NOT ON THE WAVES OF THE SEA.

****

Winds, rains and floods.

*j*dg asked this question.

Does God change the course of the winds, rains and floods for man, or does he save man from its destructive force?

James gave this response.

Tombstone

1961

Ruth and James were living in the better house on West Allen. The house across the street, next to the old shack James' father and mother were living in, had been torn down. Still bits of lumber, tin and roofing paper were strewn everywhere. The man that owned it would like to have it cleaned up. He lived in Tucson and didn't get out very often. There would be no pay involved, but it would make Pop's place look much better and James and his father needed the exercise.

Why was the wind so contrary to their good intentions? Steadily it hampered their progress. James looked in the direction of the wind. "God, stop this wind through the Name of Jesus." He waited. It did not stop. "Wind, I demand that you stop. I adjure you through the Name of God, JESUS." There was no let up. The wind continued even stronger than before.

""Pop, it's hard to work out here in the wind like this. I asked God to stop it but he didn't do it."

"You are not Jesus," he informed abruptly.

James was set back with nothing to say. He knew he wasn't Jesus. His name was James. He could have told anyone that. But Jesus was in him. Jesus said, John 14:20, 'At that day ye shall know that I am in my Father, and ye in me, and I in you. And, (14:16) I will pray the Father, and he shall give you another Comforter, that he may abide with you forever; (17) Even the Spirit of truth—, (18) I will not leave you comfortless; I WILL COME TO YOU. Also, John 16:13 Howbeit when he, the Spirit of truth, is come, he will guide you into ALL TRUTH: for he shall not speak of himself; but whatsoever he shall hear, that shall he speak:—(14) He shall receive of mine, and shall show it unto you.

James knew that Jesus could show him the truth of all matters through the Holy Ghost.

God is aware in advance of the winds and earth quakes as well as all other disturbances in the elements. Those things all have physical causes. Spirit does not change those causes for the convenience of man, no, not even for the convenience of God. He works in coordination with them.

THE NEW ENGLISH BIBLE

Gen. 6:17 (God said), I intend to bring the waters of the flood over the earth to destroy every human being under the heaven that has the spirit of life; everything on earth shall perish. Gen. 6:9 (But) Noah—walked with God—.

God designed the whole system of things. The heat and the cold meet together. Violent turbulence is formed. Those actions were in the original design for washing and cleansing the environment and they continue their actions with or without the presence of man or beast.

If there had been more men walking with God then many more boats would have been constructed for their safety.

Wake up world of men. Understand God and learn of his ways.

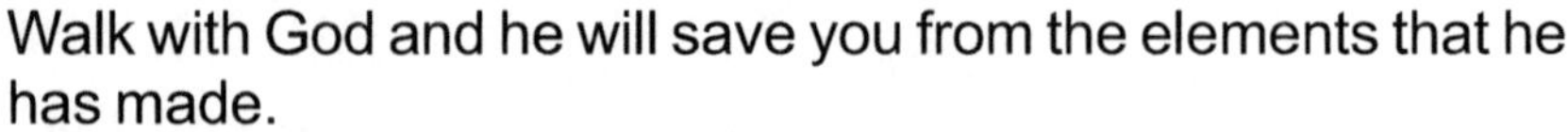

Walk with God and he will save you from the elements that he has made.

****

Wine

Anonymous asked this question.

Is It a sin to Drink Beer or wine. I Have looked for it but I just Can't Find it in the Bible, Many people have told me that it is, and quoted passages that speak of being drunk, but nothing about drinking. Did not Jesus turn water in to wine. any opinions

James gave this response.

When a person has an idea firmly planted in their mind, they may back up their preconceived thoughts by passages from the Bible. If the desire for alcoholic beverages is the force behind the motive, it is relatively easy to find many people to concur and use scripture to bolster the idea.

When the brain is deprived of oxygen it causes the cells to send out signals that resemble exhilaration, but in fact over a period of time has the potential of crippling the cells. It acts like a poison. These are the same feelings a person has when they are dying.

WINE, NOAH DRANK:

Genesis 9:24 Noah drank wine and it caused sin even though that sin was before the law had been reduced to its written form.

Romans 5:12 Sin entered into the world through the first man (Adam) and increased through Cain.

Romans 5:13 Sin was in the world but not imputed (blame on a person) when there is no law.

LOT DRANK WINE

Genesis 19:32-36 Lot drink wine and it caused a problem to develop between him and his family. His wife had already died.

WINE IS A MOCKER

Proverbs 20:1 Wine is a mocker, strong drink is raging: and WHOSOEVER IS DECEIVED THEREBY IS NOT WISE.

WINE BITETH LIKE A SERPENT

Proverbs 23:31 Look not thou upon the wine when it is red, when it giveth his color in the cup, when it moveth itself aright. (32) ***At the last it biteth like a serpent, and stingeth like an adder.***

It cannot be said that it is a sin to drink alcoholic beverages because it is evident that Jesus did drink alcoholic wine. However, when a person damages their body by the excessive use of anything, it is sinful. (Offense against God that is in the body).

1 Cor. 6:9 Know ye not that the unrighteous shall not inherit the kingdom of God? Be not deceived—***drunkards***—(10) shall not inherit the kingdom of God. (12) All things are lawful unto me—but I will not be brought under the power of any.

WINE? WHY DID JESUS DRINK

Jesus came to save his people from their sins. Matthew 1:21. He had a better chance of doing that if he lowered himself to their level. He was aware that it was not the drinking of wine that was sin. It was the effect of alcohol upon the brain cells that caused depression and allowed the acts of sin to be more easily accomplished.

Jesus knew he could not satisfy the scoffing world no matter which side of the fence he chose to be on. Jesus said (Matthew

11:18, Luke 7:33), John came neither eating nor drinking, and they say, He hath a devil, (19) The Son of man came eating and drinking, and they say, Behold a man gluttonous, and a wine bibber, a friend of publicans and sinners. But wisdom is justified of her children.

Jesus drank wine with his friends. But the drinking of natural wine should have been discontinued after the day of the feast of Pentecost, when they were filled with the Holy Ghost. Acts 2:4. That spirit of God filled their beings and eliminated craving for the natural stimulation of their minds.

Paul said (1 Tim 5:23), Drink no longer water, but use a little wine for they stomach's sake and thine often infirmities. 1 Cor. 13:12 In this statement Paul was seeing through a glass darkly. This confusion prevailed because they were not knowledgeable during that time in the process of purifying water through any other more proficient means.

We often hear that wine is good for the heart, but they do not go on to say that it destroys brain cells as a side affect. The fact is, grapes and grape juice, vinegar and many other products do the same thing without the alcohol content that cuts off the oxygen supply from the brain. Also, the liver is destroyed by the use of too much alcohol.

Paul also said (Ephesians 5:15), See thou that ye walk circumspectly, not as fools, but as wise. (17)—be not unwise, but understanding what the will of the Lord is. (18) And be not drunk with wine, wherein is excess, but be FILLED WITH THE SPIRIT.

NEW WINE

Yes, the new wine was intoxicating, otherwise the following statement would not have been written.

Acts 2:13 Others mocking said, "These men are full of

NEW WINE." Peter said in response (15) "These are not drunken, as ye suppose, seeing it is but the third hour of the day. (nine a.m., and the taverns were not yet open)—

If anyone is looking for a statement to be made that gives them more power to quit drinking alcoholic beverages, they cannot find access to that statement here. But alcohol and other drugs have caused, and have always caused major problems in the world. People must conscientiously direct their love emotion toward God through His Name instead of toward other destructive elements. They must turn to God with all their heart, and with all their soul, and with all their strength, and with all their mind—Luke 10:28—then God will give the spiritual gifts along with the gift of the Holy Ghost and the holy spirit. This will give them the strength to overcome the excessive use of alcohol or any other weakness they my have.

Acts 2:21—It shall come to pass that WHOSOEVER SHALL CALL ON THE NAME OF THE LORD SHALL BE SAVED.

SAVED FROM WHAT?

Saved from every conceivable destructive element in the world, including alcoholism and other drug addictions. When Jesus was walking on the earth there came a time when God, through his Son, healed all manner of sickness and disease among the people. Matthew 4:23.

This can happen again for those that will draw near God through His Name. Luke 18:7 And shall not God avenge his own elect, which cry day and night unto him? (8) I tell you that he will avenge them speedily. The Holy Ghost will guide into all truth. John 16:13 When he, the Spirit of truth, is come, he will guide you into all truth. James 4:8.

How do we reach God?

That is simple. God, along with his Christ (the power of God) is within you. (John 1:9) Christ was the light, which lighteth EVERY MAN that cometh into the world. This is the mediator between God and man. (1 Tim. 2:5) There is one God, and one mediator between God and men, the man Christ Jesus.

Jesus said (John 14:18) I will not leave you comfortless, I will come to you. (20) At that day ye shall know that I am in the Father, and ye in me, and I in you.

Acts 17:27—they should seek the Lord, if haply they might feel after him, and find him, though he be not far from every one of us. (28) For in him we live, and move, and have our being—.

It is sufficient to say, as previously stated, when the body deteriorates because of alcohol poisoning it is an offense again God. (Sin).

1 Cor. 3:16 Know ye not that ye are the temple of God, and that the Spirit of God dwelleth in you? (17) If any man defile the temple of God, him shall God destroy; for the temple of God is holy, which temple ye are.

WINE? MAKING OF

Ruth asked this question.

I know that Jesus drank wine from many reports, but did he actually make it?

James gave this response.

John 2:3 And when they wanted wine, the mother of Jesus saith unto him, They have no wine. (In other words

it had all been consumed because, as the story goes, they left the best to the last).

John 2:4 Jesus saith unto her, Woman, what have I to do with thee? Mine hour is not yet come. She was trying to stop Jesus from drinking any more, and he was displeased with her because of her attempted interference.

John 2:5 His mother (reluctantly) saith unto the servants, Whatsoever he saith unto you, do it.

John 2:6 And there were set there six water pots of stone, after the manner of the purifying of the Jews containing two or three firkins apiece.

John 2:7 Jesus saith unto them, Fill the water pots with water. And they filled them up to the brim.

John 2:8 And he saith unto them, Draw out now, and bear unto the governor of the feast. And they bare it.

John 2:9 When the ruler of the feast had tasted the water that was made wine, and knew not whence it was: (but the servants which drew the water knew); the governor of the feast called the bridegroom,

John 2:10 And saith unto him, Every man at the beginning doth set forth good wine; and when men have well drunk (indicating they had already 'drunk' all the other wine), then that which is worse: but thou hast kept the good wine until now.

John 2:11 This beginning of miracles did Jesus in Cana of Galilee, and manifested forth his glory; and HIS DISCIPLES BELIEVED ON HIM.

The new American Bible—Page 127 N.T. John 2:6 As prescribed for Jewish ceremonial washings, there were at hand six stone water jars, each one holding fifteen to twenty five gallons. 6 x 15=90 gallons—6x 25=150 gallons. Note: Fifteen to twenty-five gallons: literally, "two or three measures". The Measure in question was of eight or nine gallons.

Either way it is figured, a hundred and eight gallons to a hundred and sixty two gallons of wine has the potential of making many people intoxicated, especially since this 'good wine' was allegedly held to the last: yes, and even 'new wine' was intoxicating as implied by Acts 2:13.

If there is difficulty figuring out how this apparent miracle was performed: If after many experiments, using every logical means of mixing various concoctions without the usual time consuming fruit or vegetable fermentation, then consider this—.

TWO OR THREE WITNESSES ARE REQUIRED TO ESTABLISH EVERY WORD.

According to John, Jesus said (John 5:31) If I bear witness of myself, my witness is not true—.

According to John, Jesus also said, (John 8:17) It is also written in your law, that the testimony of TWO MEN IS TRUE.

John 8:18 I am one that bear witness of myself, and the Father that sent me beareth witness of me.

Jesus did not keep a journal or write an autobiography. He depended on God and others to witness for him.

In this case of making wine there was ONLY ONE WITNESS. If the other disciples believed on Jesus because of this apparent miracle (John 2:11), why didn't GOD INSPIRE A SECOND DISCIPLE TO RECORD IT?

Anonymous rated this answer:

Wow. That's in-depth.

WINE, continued use of

Ruby asked this question.

Jesus did drink wine, but did he intend for his followers to continue drinking natural wine after the Day of Pentecost?

James gave this response.

THE USAGE OF WINE MUST BE DISPLACED BY THE HOLY SPIRIT OF GOD.

Proverb 20:1 Wine is a mocker, strong drink is raging: and whosoever is deceived thereby is not wise.

Proverb 23:20 Be not among wine bibbers; among riotous eaters of flesh:

Proverb 23:21 For the drunkard and the glutton shall come to poverty: and drowsiness shall clothe a man with rags.

Proverb 23:29 Who hath woe? Who hath sorrow? Who hath contentions? Who hath babbling? Who hath wounds without cause? ***Who hath redness of eyes?***

Proverb 23:30 They that tarry long at the wine; they that go to seek mixed wine.

Proverb 23:31 Look not thou upon the wine when it is red, when it giveth his color in the cup, when it moveth itself aright.

Proverb 23:32 ***AT THE LAST IT BITETH LIKE A SERPENT, AND STINGETH LIKE AN ADDER.***

JESUS' PURPOSE

Jesus did not elevate himself above others. He lived among the people to raise them to a higher level. Jesus explained his intentions at the last passover.

Matthew 26:27 And he (Jesus) took the cup, and gave thanks, and gave it to them, saying, Drink ye all of it—.

Matthew 26:29 But I say unto you, I will not drink henceforth of this fruit of the vine, until that day (the day of Pentecost) when I drink it new with you in my Father's kingdom.

THE SPIRITUAL WINE CAME

Acts 2:13 Others mocking said, These men are full of new wine.

Acts 2:14 But Peter, standing up with the eleven, lifted up his voice, and said unto them, Ye men of Judaea, and all ye that dwell at Jerusalem, be this known unto you, and hearken to my words.

Acts 2:15 For these are not drunken, as ye suppose, seeing it is but the third hour of the day (Nine a.m.).

Acts 2:16 But this is that which was spoken by the prophet Joel. (Joel 2:29)

Acts 2:17 And it shall come to pass in the last days, saith God, I will pour out of my Spirit upon all flesh:

THE DRINKING OF NATURAL WINE SHOULD HAVE BEEN DISCONTINUED AT PENTECOST, AND REPLACED BY THE HOLY SPIRIT FROM GOD.

****

Wine, is it a sin?

Kathy asked this question.

So is it a sin to drink wine?

James gave this response.

It cannot be said that it is a sin to drink alcohol beverages because it is evident that Jesus did drink alcoholic wine. However, ***when a person damages their body by the excessive use of anything, it is sinful.*** (Offense against God).

1 Cor. 6:9 Know ye not that the unrighteous shall not inherit the kingdom of God? Be not deceived—***drunkards***—(10) shall not inherit the kingdom of God. (12) All things are lawful unto me—but I will not be brought under the power of any.

Romans 14:21 It is good neither to eat flesh, nor to drink wine, nor anything whereby thy brother stumbleth, or is offended, or is made weak. (22) Hast thou faith? Have it to thyself before God. ***Happy is he that condemneth not himself in that thing which he alloweth.***—(23) ***whatsoever is not of faith is sin.***

Not given to wine is mentioned by Paul in various places in the Bible, and Peter mentioned "***excess of wine***." 1 Peter 4:4. There are so many of these passages it is not feasible to list them all here.

It is sufficient to say, as previously stated, ***when the body deteriorates because of alcohol poisoning it is an offense again God. (Sin).***

If someone is looking for a statement to be made that gives them more power to quit drinking alcoholic beverages, they cannot get access to that statement here. ***They must conscientiously direct their love emotion toward God through His Name instead of toward other destructive elements***. They must turn to God with all their heart, and with all their soul, and with all their strength, and with all their mind—Luke 10:28—then God will give the spiritual gifts along with the gift of the Holy Ghost and the holy spirit. This will give them the strength to overcome the excessive use of alcohol or any other weakness they my have.

How do we reach God?

That is simple. God along with his Christ (the power of God) is within you. (John 1:9) Christ was the light, which lighteth EVERY MAN that cometh into the world. This is the mediator between God and man. (1 Tim. 2:5) There is one God, and one mediator between God and men, the man Christ Jesus.

Jesus said (John 14:18) I will not leave you comfortless, I will come to you. (20) At that day ye shall know that I am in the Father, and ye in me, and I in you. Acts 17:27—they should seek the Lord, if haply they might feel after him, and find him, though he be not far from every one of us. (28) For in him we live, and move, and have our being—.

****

Witnesses: Paul—Two or Three

Edward asked this question.

Did Paul fulfill the requirement that two or three witnesses were necessary to establish every word against persons that sinned?

James gave this response.

WHERE DID THIS REQUIREMENT START?

Deut. 17:6 At the mouth of two witnesses, shall he that is worthy of death be put to death; but at the mouth of one witness he shall not be put to death.

Deut. 19:15 One witness shall not rise up against a man for ***ANY INIQUITY (wickedness), or for ANY SIN***, in any sin that he sinneth: at the mouth of two witnesses, or at the mouth of three witnesses, shall the matter be established. Also see Matt. 18:16.

PAUL WROTE

2 Cor. 13:1 This is the ***third time*** I am coming to you. In the mouth of ***two or three*** witnesses shall every word be established.

2 Cor. 13:2 I told you before, and foretell you, as if I were present, the ***second time***; and being absent now I write to them which heretofore have sinned,—.

Paul tried to establish his own words on three occasions.

JESUS SAID, (John 5:31) ***If I witness of myself, my witness is not true.***

Jesus said, (John 8:17) It is also written in your law, that the testimony of TWO MEN is true. (Not one). (18) I am one that bear witness of myself, and the Father that sent me beareth witness of me.

God used at least two men to write about the things that was performed by God through Jesus.

One man could not speak or write the same thing on two or three occasions to fulfill the requirement of two men, or two or three witnesses to establish every word.

****

Wives, two

Anonymous asked this question.

Hello, does Christ prohibit men to have two or more wives?? Or are men still allowed to do so?

James gave this response.

Husband of one wife!

Genesis 2:18—The Lord God said, It is not good that a man should be alone; I will make him an help meet for him. (22)—The Lord God—made he a (not many) woman, and brought her unto the man.

Matthew 19:4 Jesus said to the Pharisees, Have ye not read, that he which made them at the beginning made them MALE and FEMALE. (ONE MALE AND ONE FEMALE). (5) And said, For this cause shall a man leave father and mother, and shall cleave to his wife: (one) and they (the male and the female) twain (2) shall be ONE FLESH?"

The first Adam was given one wife and the last Adam (1 Cor. 15:45), although he was not allowed to live on the earth long enough to be united with his (Eve), still advocated that a man should have only one counterpart.

The female is the positive side of the human unit and the male is the negative of that union. More than one positive or negative disrupts the power that flows between them, from the negative to the positive and from the positive to the negative again, causing continual life. More than one positive or negative in one unit causes a sin against the power of Christ which is light of life for that unit. (John 1:9) This constitutes a sin against God. (Gen. 39:9)

The masses of this world should read and ask God for understanding and not take the words of the many blind guides.

Their views are the product of thinking influenced by the fallen generations all the way back to the beginning when men patterned their actions after the other animals.

Anonymous asked this follow-up question. hello, the story of adam and eve does not support, in my opinion, a law that a man can only have one wife. the story was made to tell us about sin and how we turn away from God many times. so for the basis of the story, more women were not necessary.

now, for Gen 39:9

joseph is denied his “owner’s” wife because it is his owner’s wife, not his. she is already married to him, so joseph says he cannot marry the woman because she is already married. that doesnt mean one cannot have 2 or more wives, who are not married.

john 1:9 is talking about Jesus, it has nothing to do with having 2 wives.

is there a place where it says something like “ thou shall not have 2 wives”?

James gave this response.

Most of the time when a person asks a question they already know what they want the answer to be, and they will not accept anything less.

Words alone cannot change a man. It takes the rebirth of the person’s spirit (John 3:3) and the guidance of the Holy Ghost. (John 16:13)

(1 Cor. 2:14) But the natural man receiveth not the things of the Spirit of God: for they are foolishness unto him: neither can he know them, because they are spiritually discerned.

If you want two wives that is what you will have, one way or another, and there are plenty of passages in the Bible to back up that idea. (1 Kings 11:3) Solomon had seven hundred wives and 300 concubines (mistresses). That does not make it right.

Well, yes the Bible is true. But that does not mean that everything written therein is right. It is a recording of what men have said, thought, and done, versus the will of God. The actions of men were recorded for our learning. 2 Tim. 3:16 All scripture is given by inspiration of God, and is profitable for doctrine, for reproof, for correction, for instruction in righteousness: (17) That the man of God may be perfect, thoroughly furnished unto all good works.

How do you find power with God and his understanding? Start by calling upon the Name of the Mediator between God and man, that is Jesus. Joel 2:32, Rom. 10:13 and Acts 2:21—It shall come to pass, that WHOSOEVER shall call on the Name of the Lord shall be saved.

Saved from what?

Saved from every conceivable destructive element of the earth, including thoughts proceeding from the minds of natural men.

Anonymous asked this follow-up question. sorry to bother you one more time. I just need to clarify something for you.

you say that most people already have the answer they want when they ask a question. you probably mean me. i asked because i really have no idea, and i had a discussion with a muslim about multiple wives. he asked me about christianity, and i could not answer him becuase i simply dont know.

James gave this response.

'Most people' was stated and evidently you are not in that category. But it is very difficult, if not impossible, to change a person's ideas or views when they have been rooted and grounded for most of their lives in their brand of truth.

Jesus said, (Matthew 9:17) Neither do men put new wine (doctrine) into old bottles. This is one of the reasons why Jesus turned to fishermen, tax collectors and even prostitutes to impart the logical teachings of the kingdom of heaven.

One religion advocates that 'Give me a child until he is twelve years of age and when he is old he will not depart from the faith. This applies to all segments of religion.

The religious system did not accept Jesus or his teachings, nor do they now. Oh yes, they can change if they want to, but that is the problem, they do not want to.

Look around—the creation is enough to prove that God is a scientist. He is not concerned with their petty illogical religious views and rituals. God is only concerned that men live in peace with themselves and with those around them. God wants his creation of human life to prosper and be in health. The only way that can be accomplished is that they keep their minds focused upon one stabilized object. That is the handle of God, His Name. It is through faith in, and calling upon that Name, that all spiritual strength will come to them and they will be able to walk with confidence among all the devices of men without harm to themselves or those around them.

It is highly unlikely that they will accept the example as given in Genesis or the words of Jesus as expressed in my first response. eom (End of message) The logical truth may have to go to the young.

****

Women alone and violence.

Edward asked this question.

Would you please elaborate on women that believe they can do a spiritual work without the man, and men that are still following Moses and Elijah instead of Jesus only?

James gave this response.

The brisk air felt good to his face and nose. He was all dressed up in the blue suit, with hat and overcoat. The cold wind whistled around the corners of the brick buildings in the older part of north Saint Louis. The year was 1960.

The store front building arrived. Joyous melodies were heard from within. 'When the Roll is Called Up Yonder, I'll Be There.' It was sung by a group of very old and very young. Grandmothers and Grandfathers afraid of death, and trying to lead their Grandchildren in a different path than they themselves had walked. The teenagers and the middle aged were out sowing wild oats the same as many of the elders had done in years past.

James pondered the truth in such a scene. Yes, he knew their destiny. It would be the same pattern as always, unless they learn the truth about Jesus.

He moved closer to the window of the building in order to hear more clearly what was happening. He heard the words of an aged woman screaming out 'Hell fire and brimstone', in order to scare the devils out of the little children she had coerced into 'Her way to Heaven.'

WHEN WE ALL GET TO HEAVEN

Another song vibrated the large windows and echoed against the cold red bricks of the two story buildings nearby. The preacher was accompanied by one of her close lady friends on the piano. She played 'When we all get to Heaven, What a day of Rejoicing That Will Be.'

Yes, he thought, that is true. But how can anybody go to heaven as long as their minds are being filled with fear, hate, and violence from the pulpits? It was not really her fault, he supposed. She probably had had bad luck with her relationships with men, so decided to go to God on her own, in her OWN WAY. After all, the men did not know the way and she was tired of waiting for them. No doubt in her mind, she thought she could do it better. She did not NEED A MAN.

In that same manner, most of the leaders of the churches are guilty in varying degrees. James, at that point wanted to walk in all of those churches and say, “Preachers of violence—you should be ashamed. You claim to follow Jesus, yet he was a man that upheld all the commandments. You still look to men such as David, Samson and Moses, along with a host of others as good examples for the children in your Sunday schools.

Wake up! Wake up!—Men of the churches, Ask yourselves, ‘WHAT ARE WE DOING?’

John 10:8 Jesus said, “ALL THAT EVER CAME BEFORE ME ARE THIEVES AND ROBBERS.

John 10:10 The thief cometh not but for the STEAL and to KILL, and to DESTROY: I AM COME THAT THEY MIGHT HAVE LIFE,—.

All those men were murderers. They were killers. Arouse yourselves! You are men of the churches. You have almost waited too long. You cannot kill in the Name of God, no matter for what reason you do it. That is part of the reason we have violence overflowing in the world. It is that you have taught it in the Sunday schools.

David did come to Goliath in the Name of the Lord (1Sam. 17:45) and killed him. He disregarded that vengeance belonged to God and that God said, “Thou shalt not Kill. Yet, you say that David was right. Moses killed and you say that he was right. You claim this primarily because it is written in the Bible, without regard to the fact that it was not God’s will.

God said, “WELL, YES THE BIBLE IS TRUE.”—But that does

not make all of it RIGHT. It is a true recording of the actions of men as opposed to the 'Will of God.' If you will examine it carefully, you will plainly see where Jesus' life was not to be compared, in full, with any of them.

Peter wanted to build a tabernacle to Moses and Elijah, but God denounced both of them when He said, (Matt. 17:5) This is my beloved Son, in whom I am well pleased; HEAR YE HIM. And when the vision vanished, there was JESUS ONLY.

James could hear the crunching as he walked softly over the ice and snow. Those poor kids, he thought, tears streaming down their faces, ran to the altar for fear of the devil, or the images created by the preacher's mouth. They were pictures of a violent car wreck in full description, coupled with a threat that they may not live until tomorrow, if they did not come. Yes, they did go to the altar, but it was not for the love of God. It was because of fear and violence produced by preachers whose hearts and minds were filled with confusion.

It is in reverse to what they think. In trying to scare hell out of the minds of the people, the very mention kindles it and it remains a burning ember unless they receive help from God through faith in and calling upon his NAME JESUS

****

Women Healing.

Zenaide asked this question.

Does God sometimes work through women in matters of healing?

James gave this response.

DOES GOD SOMETIMES WORK THROUGH WOMEN IN MATTERS OF HEALING?

The morning came. James stood by the wash basin. His hands were filled with water. The hands were raised to his face. He twisted in the wrong way. A cartilage in his back slipped. Standing upright was made impossible.

Roland asked if James wanted to go with him to the store. He was still trying to keep him from thinking about things. "Yes, I will go," James said. He walked humped over to the car. Roland drove. He pulled up in front of the store. James' back was hurting as he sat in the car and waited.

The sign was there, just across the street. 'Chiropractor' was in large print. James could have gone. The trip had been made. He could ask Roland for the money, but he didn't want to incur the debt. Maybe God would heal him.

When they returned from the store, James left Roland at the side of the house. He was in worse pain. Soreness had spread throughout his back. He lay upon the bed. The throbbing pain would not let him rest nor could he get up. Ruth was in the living room.

"GO PRAY FOR HIS BACK"

Those were the words which came to Ruth's mind. Hesitantly she came to the door, moved slowly to the side of the bed, touched his back with both hands and said, "In the Name of Jesus make this pain go away. Immediately James felt power flow from her hands into his back. The pain and soreness instantly left.

James jumped from the bed. "We can go to church now," he said excitedly. He was still bent over. The disk was still out of place but the soreness was gone.

The church service was attended, but the disk was still not in proper alignment. Attempting to stand or sit straight too many times caused the pain and soreness to return even worse than before. James lay on the bed rolling turning. He could not be calm because of the throbbing pain.

It was impressed strongly upon Ruth's mind, almost as if it were a voice,

"HE DOES NOT NEED A CHIROPRACTOR. YOU CAN DO IT."

"I cannot do that," she replied, "I do not know how." She contemplated the words for a few moments, then said, "I will try if you will guide me"

She went to the bed room and stood along side the bed. With an audible voice she said, "through the Name of Jesus show me where to push in order to put this disk back into place. It seemed to her as if it were an intelligent being taking over her hands and guiding them down his spine. When the thumbs reached the proper place, they automatically pushed inward and the disk was put back in line with the vertebrae.

Ruth continued, "In the Name of Jesus, remove the pain and soreness." It all left and did not return. James stood up straight along side the bed.

Forty years later he has never gone to a Chiropractor.

(1960-2000)

John 5:19 (Jesus said) The Son can do nothing of himself, but what he seeth the Father do—. It is God working through the man or woman, preacher or laity.

God never works through inflated egos!

****

Word of God, Helping Jesus with the

Ronndonn asked this question.

This is a question for those who hold that the Bible is the Word of God.

Jesus said "if a man keeps my Word, he shall not see death." And as we know, the Word of God is a seed (this connection is made in the parable of the sower). And we also know that Jesus described Himself as the sower of seeds, so, I think we can safely assume that Jesus was giving out the Word of God.

Now, imagine if you will that Jesus asks you to assist Him in giving out the word of God to all his followers (of which it seems there were many, maybe hundreds or even more).

So my question is this, if the bible is the word of God and you were in charge of distributing it to all the disciples back in those days, HOW WOULD YOU GO ABOUT DOING IT?

Now, keep in mind, no printing presses back then, scriptures were painstakingly written out letter by letter by dipping a reed in ink and the ink was put on leaves or animal skins, AND if that wasn't enough, you have to consider that many could not read (illiteracy was high back then) and of those who read some were Greek, some were Jewish (hebrew) and some spoke aramaic.

So, how would you go about accomplishing the task that Jesus gave you? (as a point of reference, I was told that it takes over 3 months for one scribe to make a copy of a scripture).

How would you go about accomplishing the task that Jesus asked of you?

James gave this response.

HIS NAME IS CALLED THE WORD OF GOD. Rev. 19:13.

John 1:1 In the beginning was the WORD, and the WORD was with God, and the WORD was GOD.

(2) The same was in the beginning with God.

(4) In him was life; and the life was the light of men.

(9) That was the true light, which lighteth ***EVERY MAN*** that cometh into the world.

(14) And the ***WORD*** was made flesh, and dwelt among us.

Acts 2:21—It shall come to pass, that WHOSOEVER shall CALL ON THE ***NAME (WORD***) OF THE LORD SHALL BE ***SAVED***. Also Rom. 10:13, Joel 2:32. Gen. 4:26. And to Seth, to him also there was born a son; and he called his name Enos: THEN BEGAN MEN TO CALL UPON THE NAME OF THE LORD.

But when the sky becomes dark and the waves of the boisterous sea (world) become overwhelming, men become afraid and too much doubt causes them to grab hold of anything and everything, other than the Name of God.

Doubt is good and a necessary part of the human make-up, so that they will not become unbalanced, ***but too much doubt will cause them to sink into despair.*** (Lose of hope).

Consider the story of Peter:

Matthew 14:30—When he (NAB) perceived how strong the wind was, (KJV) he was afraid; and beginning to sink, he cried, saying ***LORD SAVE ME.*** (31) And immediately Jesus stretched forth his hand, and caught him, and said unto him, O thou of little faith, wherefore didst thou doubt?

Education is good and a must for the advancement of the human race as it pertains to knowledge, but ***God cannot be reached through the pages of books.***

Acts 4:12 Neither is there salvation in any other; for there is ***none other NAME*** under heaven given among men, whereby ***we MUST BE SAVED.***

Calling upon the Name of God is so simple it has been overlooked by the wise of the world. 1 Cor. 1:27 But God hath chosen the foolish things of the world to confound the wise—.

1 Cor. 2:14—The natural man receiveth not the things of the Spirit of God: for they are foolishness unto him, neither can he know them, because they are spiritually discerned.

When the mind drifts from the Name of God it becomes confused and produces complications. It concocts many avenues for 'THE WAY', and demands that others follow with the false hope of reaching God in heaven somewhere other than entering into the spiritual ***Paradise that God prepared for the human race to live in here on the earth.***

How do we spread the Word of God?

Tell people to Call upon it! It is God's Name. When we diligently seek him by calling upon His Name, the Holy Ghost guides into all truth and the Power of God, Christ, saves.

Ronndonn rated this answer:

God cannot be seen in the pages of a Book . . . I think you are right here. Interesting answer James.

****

Word of God? what is the

Question answered by James.

Ronndonn asked this question.

Someone just asked me the question "why aren't Paul's writings the word of God?" So it causes me to re-post a question that was posted a while ago . . . What is the Word of God? Jesus said that He is the sower of seeds and with reference to the parable of the sower, He said that the seed IS the "Word of God". So, my conclusion is that the word of God that Jesus is talking about here (the seed he was sowing) could not have had Paul's writings in it since Paul had not yet picked up a pen by then. Paul came later.

So again, whatever the Word of God is, I would think that Jesus Himself would know what it is and If he said he was giving it out before Paul came along, then I feel it is safe to say that Paul's writings were not in it.

And finally, I don't feel that Jesus would have been sowing seed that was infertile. I think the seed He was sowing was fertile and complete . . . and so the question becomes . . . What is it that Jesus Himself was sowing, for that is what I would say is the true "Word of God".

What do you think, do you think that the "Word of God" that Jesus is speaking of in the Parable of the Sower contained the writings of Paul or not?

James gave this response.

What is the Word of God?

I realize that Jesus spoke the words of God. John the Baptist said (John 3:31) He that cometh from above is above all: he that is of the earth is earthly, and speaketh of the earth: he that cometh from heaven is above all. (32) And what he hath seen and heard, that he testifieth; and no man receiveth his testimony. (33) He that hath received his testimony hath set to his seal that God is true. (34) For he whom God hath sent speaketh ***THE WORDS OF GOD: For God giveth not the Spirit by measure unto him.***

I am only trying to emphasize that God wants man to focus upon His Name instead of all the conglomerated sets of words encompassed in the whole bible.

Rev. 19:13 And he was clothed with a vesture dipped in blood: and ***HIS NAME IS CALLED THE WORD OF GOD***.

Proverbs 3:4—What is his (God's) name, and what is his son's name, if thou canst tell?

John 1:1 In the beginning was the Word, and the Word was with God, and the ***WORD WAS GOD.***

John 17:11.—Holy Father, keep through thine own NAME those whom thou hast given me,—(12) While I was with them in the world, ***I kept them in thy Name***—(14) I have given them thy ***WORD***—(17) Sanctify them through thy truth; ***thy word is truth.***

John 17:18 As thou hast sent me into the world, even so have I sent them into the world—

John 17:26 And I have declared unto them ***THY NAME***, and will declare it—.

John 17:20 (Jesus said) Neither pray I for these alone, but for them also which shall believe on me through their word—.

John 14:6 Jesus said,—I am the way, the truth, and the life, no man cometh unto the Father, but by me.

2 Tim. 2:16 All scripture is given by inspiration of God, and is profitable for doctrine, for reproof, for correction, for instruction in righteousness: (17) That the man of God may be perfect, thoroughly furnished unto all good works.

God inspired men to write about the thoughts and actions of men so that we can finally understand the difference between the ways of the world as opposed to the ways of God.

2 Cor. 5:19 God was in Christ, reconciling the world unto himself—, Therefore, the words that came from Jesus' mouth were the true words of God. Those words lived on in the minds of the apostles that had associated with Jesus throughout his ministry. Those same words of God were relayed to the then known world by those apostles from the time they received the Holy Ghost on the day of Pentecost.

But while Jesus was still with them, Peter, James and John were with Jesus on the mountain, (Matt. 17:40) Peter wanted to make three tabernacles, one for Jesus, one for Moses, and one for Elijah. God said—This is my beloved Son; HEAR YE HIM.

Although the Bible is true it is a recording of the thoughts and actions of men as opposed to the will of God. The commandments were good and right, but the penalties as established by Moses were not the will of, or the ways of God.

John 1:17—The law was given by Moses, but grace and TRUTH came by Jesus Christ.

People are still being taught the precepts as established by Moses and the teachings of Paul (Saul who was taught the ways of the straitest sect—the Pharisee—Acts 26:5—and who saw through a glass darkly 1 Cor. 13:12), rather than the ***WORD OF GOD as spoken by God through Jesus, his only begotten Son.***

Jesus is the way. There is no other. John 14:6 Jesus said,—no man cometh unto the father, but by me.

The words of God are the words spoken by God through

his Son. It is also HIS NAME. Call upon that name to be saved from the confusion that has always been prevalent in the minds of men ever since God confused their minds (language) at the tower of Babel because they wanted to make a name for themselves. Gen. 11:4.

There is a way out of all the confusion. Acts 2:21—It shall come to pass, that whosoever shall call on the NAME of the Lord shall be saved. (Also Rom. 10:13)

Oh yes, God was working with Paul through Jesus, but there are times when Paul reached back into his reservoir of knowledge received from his Pharisee education. 1 Cor. 7:25. Sort out the good from the not so good instructions.

Ronndonn rated this answer: thanks James.

****

WORK IN HEAVEN?

Anonymous asked this question.

Where does it say in the Bible there will be work in heaven?

James gave this response.

First of all—We are all living in the physical heavens. We are floating around in heaven. Jesus lived on the earth before men had the technology for going out into that natural heaven away from the earth.

Proverbs 30:4 Who hath ascended up into heaven, or descended? Who hath gathered the wind in his fists? Wh hath bound the waters in a garment? Who hath establishe the ends of the earth? WHAT IS HIS NAME AND WH HIS SON'S NAME, if thou canst tell?

Now we know God's name and the name of His Son. They are identical, for Jesus said (John 5:43), I am come in my Father's Name.

JESUS ANSWERED

Jesus said (John 3:13)—NO MAN HATH ASCENDED UP TO HEAVEN, BUT HE THAT CAME DOWN FROM HEAVEN, EVEN THE SON OF MAN WHICH IS IN HEAVEN.

Jesus was called the LAST ADAM (1 Cor. 15:45) He was in the same spiritual heaven where the FIRST ADAM had been placed—in the second heaven, Paradise. Rev. 2:7, 2 Cor. 12:4, Luke 23:43.

The FIRST ADAM was placed in heaven (a spiritual state) on the earth. He was not to be idle for physical and mental reasons. He was told to DRESS AND KEEP THE GARDEN.

Genesis 2:15 And the LORD GOD took the man, and put him into the garden of Eden to DRESS IT AND TO KEEP IT.

Is this not work?

Eccl. 1:9 The thing that hath been, it is that which shall be; and that which is done is that which shall be done: and there is no new thing under the sun.

The whole truth has been from the beginning. God created the spiritual state for men to live in on the earth eternally. It was man that created violence, hell, death and the grave by the power of his own confused mind.

There is no easy way to heaven. Men must come back to the reality of heaven on earth by their faith and calling upon the name of God. This will increase faith and attract and generate the power of Christ to and within themselves to effect a perfect understanding of spiritual and physical things alike.

Eph. 2:5 Even when we were dead in sins, (God) hath quickened us together with Christ, (by grace ye are saved;) (6) And hath raised us up together, and made us sit together in HEAVENLY PLACES in Christ Jesus: (In heavenly places ON THE EARTH). (7) That in the ages to come he might show the exceeding riches of his grace in his kindness toward us through Christ Jesus.

The last Adam (Jesus)was made a quickening (life giving) spirit. 1 Cor. 15:45. Without being 'quickened' by Christ (the power of God), it is impossible to understand spiritual things, for (1 Cor. 2:14)—The natural man receiveth not the things of the Spirit or God: for they are foolishness unto him: neither can he know them, because they are spiritually discerned.

Man was made a little lower than the angels. Psalms 8:5 For thou hast made him a little lower than the angels, and hast crowned him with glory and honor, (6) Thou madest him to have dominion over the works of thy hands; thou hast put all things under his feet: Psalms 8:7-8.

God has made a way for those that will walk with him in this world. Matthew 22:30 For in the resurrection they—are as the angels of God in heaven.

Do angels work? Yes!

Gen. 19:1,15: 28:12: 32:1, Psalms 68:17, 91:11, 103:20, 148:2, Matthew 4:6, 4:11, Reapers—Matt.13:39, Gatherers Matt. 24:31, 13:41,13:49, Dispensers of rewards 16:27, Matt.18:10, 26:53,Ministered Mark 1;13, Luke 2:15, John 1:51,John 20:12, Gal 3:19, Rev. 5:11, Etc., etc. There are more, but it is indeed foolish to list the concordance. These references can be checked by anyone.

****

WORLD, THE END OF

Anonymous asked this question.

I would like to find the predictions of the end of the world, the ones that have happened, what year, and the ones yet to come. Can you help me????

James gave this response.

THE END OF THE WORLDS

Adam and Eve's world ended and another beginning came into existence with Noah. During that time eight people were saved. (1 Pet. 3:20) Eight souls were saved by water.

Gen. 6:13 And God said unto Noah, The end of all flesh is come before me; for the earth is filled with violence through them—.

2 Pet 3:6 Whereby the ***world*** that then was, being overflowed with water ***perished.***

Another end was in the making. Matthew 24:1 through 34.

Matthew 24:3 And as he sat upon the mount of Olives, the disciples came unto him privately, saying, Tell us, when shall these things be? And what shall be the sign of thy coming, ***and of the end of the world?***

Matthew 24:34 Jesus said,—This GENERATION SHALL NOT PASS, tell ALL these things be fulfilled. (When Jesus spoke of 'THIS GENERATION', he was not speaking of two thousand [illegible] later). (35) Heaven and earth shall pass away, but ***my*** [illegible] ***not pass away***. (The Jewish earth or world [illegible] for the elect (22) in Anno Domini 70. Jesus' [illegible] recorded and placed in a book). (36) But of that day and hour knoweth no man, no, not the angels of heaven, but my Father only. God through Jesus came with judgment against Jerusalem in Anno Domini 70. In Mark 13:32 it was stated that even Jesus did not know when that end would be. But of that day and that hour knoweth no man, no, not the angels which are in heaven, ***neither the Son, but the father.*** (If Jesus were God, then he would have known.)

On a percentage basis the people of this earth are becoming better than they have ever been, but they still cannot control their own desires, and subdue their fallen Adamic nature without spiritual help which comes only through having faith in and calling upon the Name of God, Jesus.

If the people of this world will take hold of the Tree of Life (Jesus, the Name of God) with all their (1 Ths 5:23) spirit, soul, body and (Matt. 22:37) mind, they can withstand, and side-step all the destructive elements of this world as it approaches the END OF THIS AGE.

1 Cor. 15:24 Then cometh the end, when he shall have delivered up the kingdom to God, even the Father; when he shall have put down all rule and all authority and power. (25) For he must reign, till he hath put all enemies under his feet. (26) The last enemy that shall be destroyed is death.

Jesus said (John 17:15), I pray not that thou shouldest take them out of the world, but that thou shouldest keep them from the evil.

Eccl. 1:4 ***The earth abideth forever.***